SHACKLETON'S FORGOTTEN EXPEDITION

SHACKLETON'S FORGOTTEN EXPEDITION

The Voyage of the *Nimrod*

Beau Riffenburgh

BLOOMSBURY

Published by Bloomsbury Publishing, New York and London
Distributed to the trade by Holtzbrinck Publishers

All papers used by Bloomsbury Publishing are natural, recyclable products made from wood grown in well-managed forests. The manufacturing processes conform to the environmental regulations of the country of origin.

The Library of Congress has cataloged the hardcover edition as follows:

Riffenburgh, Beau, 1955–
Shackleton's forgotten expedition : the voyage of the Nimrod / by Beau Riffenburgh.
p. cm.
ISBN 1-58234-488-4 (hardcover)
1. Shackleton, Ernest Henry, Sir, 1874–1922—Travel—Antarctica. 2. British Antarctic Expedition (1907–1909). 3. Antarctica—Discovery and exploration—British. I. Title.

G8501907.S52 R54 2004
919.8'904—dc22
2004011999

First published in the United States by Bloomsbury Publishing in 2004
This paperback edition published in 2005

Paperback ISBN 1-58234-611-9
ISBN-13 978-1-58234-611-3

1 3 5 7 9 10 8 6 4 2

Typeset by Hewer Text Ltd, Edinburgh
Printed in the United States of America by Quebecor World Fairfield

Jacket images:

Top front cover photo: The first attainment of the South Magnetic Pole. From left: Alistair Mackay, Edgeworth David and Douglas Mawson. David is pulling the string to snap the picture. (Reproduced by permission of the Scott Polar Research Institute.)

Bottom front cover photo: *Nimrod* steaming away to a safe distance when the ice was breaking up around Cape Royds. (Reproduced by permission of the Scott Polar Research Institute.)

Back cover photo: At Cape Royds before the completion of the hut. From left; James Murray, George Marston, Frank Wild, Sir Philip Brocklehurst, Harry Dunlop and Ernest Joyce. (Reproduced by permission of Johnny Van Haeften, London.)

To my wife, Liz,
who has been an inspiration
for this book and so much else

CONTENTS

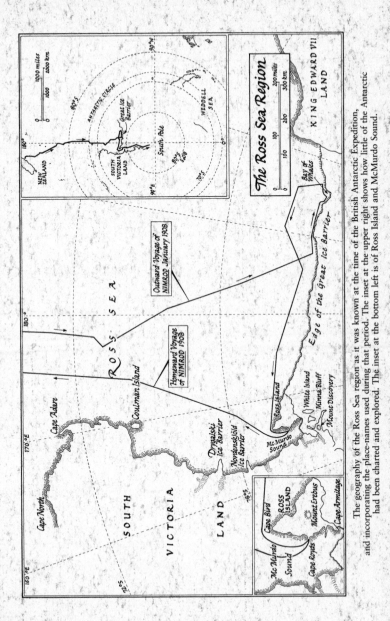

The geography of the Ross Sea region as it was known at the time of the British Antarctic Expedition, and incorporating the place-names used during that period. The inset at the upper right shows how little of the Antarctic had been charted and explored. The inset at the bottom left is of Ross Island and McMurdo Sound.

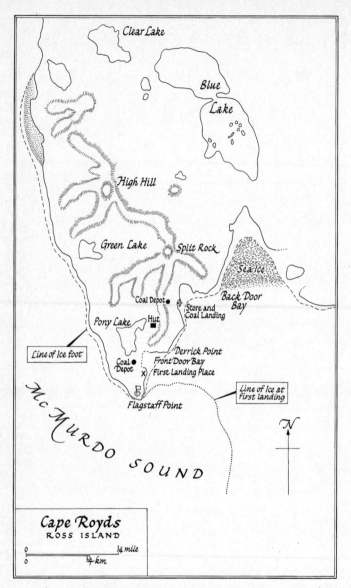

Cape Royds, and its prominent natural features.
Also indicated are locations established by Shackleton's party.

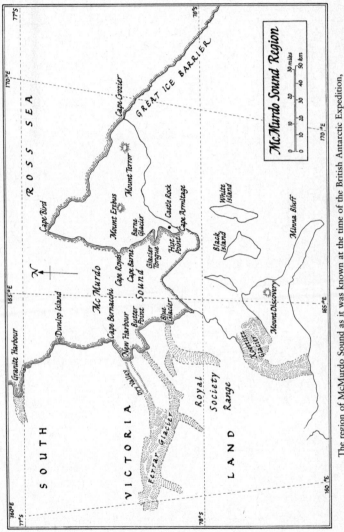

The region of McMurdo Sound as it was known at the time of the British Antarctic Expedition, and incorporating the place-names used during that period.

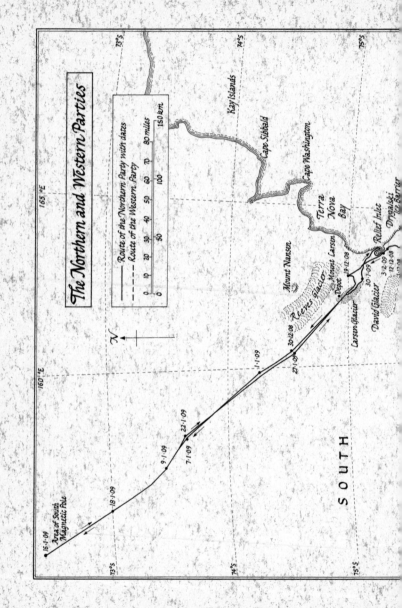

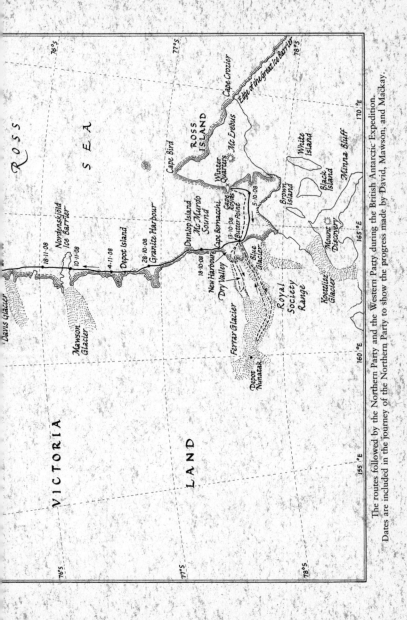

The routes followed by the Northern Party and the Western Party during the British Antarctic Expedition. Dates are included in the journey of the Northern Party to show the progress made by David, Mawson, and Mackay.

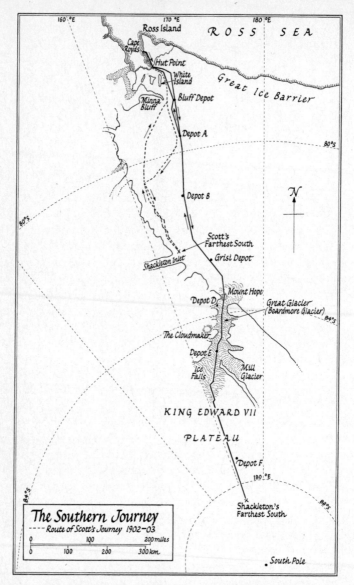

The route followed by Shackleton, Wild, Adams, and Marshall during the journey to the farthest south in 1908–09, including the depots set up by the Southern Party and by Joyce's party. The dashed line shows the route taken by Scott, Shackleton, and Wilson in 1902–03.

PREFACE

In recent years, the fame of Ernest Shackleton has spread beyond the relatively small community of polar scholars and enthusiasts, and he has captivated the imagination of a world-wide audience. Books, television documentaries and cinematic dramas have told the story of the Imperial Trans-Antarctic Expedition, and Shackleton's heroic exploits when his ship *Endurance* was caught in the ice of the Weddell Sea and crushed. Everyone now seems to know that he held his party together on the ice and brought his men safely to Elephant Island. And the tales of his open-boat journey to South Georgia, his crossing of that island's mountains, and the subsequent rescue of his party have been repeated until they are a firm part of the collective consciousness of the English-speaking world.

Yet, remarkably little has been recorded about what most polar historians agree were actually Shackleton's most significant geographical accomplishments, greatest deeds and most momentous decisions. These were all attained on the first expedition that he led, the grandly named British Antarctic Expedition of 1907–09. One should not be confused by Shackleton's title for the expedition, however. It was very much a private affair – under-funded, not backed by major geographical and scientific organisations, and sailing on a tiny former whaler called *Nimrod*. Never the less, its members not only achieved remarkable scientific results, but became the first to climb Mount Erebus, the first to attain the South Magnetic Pole, and the pioneers of the original route to the centre of the Antarctic continent, where a high plateau is home to the South Pole.

It was for the magnificent exploits of this expedition that Shackleton was knighted and received his greatest acclaim during his lifetime. But such glory was fleeting. Three decades after Shackleton's death, his daughter Cecily told the story of how:

> A short time ago the postman came here and said, 'I see the name Shackleton. Are you by any chance related to the cricketer?' I said, 'No, I'm afraid not.' He said, 'Oh, bad luck, I thought there was somebody connected with somebody interesting living here.'

Shackleton's return to celebrity status did not begin until the mid-1980s with the excellent biography by Roland Huntford. His standing with the public skyrocketed after Caroline Alexander's *The Endurance*, which accompanied an exhibition that opened in New York in 1999. Despite all the subsequent interest throughout the world, however, Shackleton's British Antarctic Expedition has remained surprisingly little known.

This is the first study of that expedition since Shackleton's account, *The Heart of the Antarctic*, was published in 1909. It is based on original sources, and, with so many documents having emerged in recent decades, it is the first time that all the known, extant diaries and correspondence of the members of the expedition have been consulted. These sources have allowed new understanding and interpretations, not just of Shackleton, but of the expedition in its entirety, for it is the whole expedition, not just one man, that is the subject of this book.

The use of original journals, letters and papers allows a historical authenticity not possible when dealing with secondary materials. Therefore, in quoting from these sources, the idiosyncrasies of punctuation and spelling have been retained. It is for similar reasons that throughout this book contemporary publication names and place-names have been used. References to and from any newspaper have used the paper's name at that time, rather than one to which it might later have been changed. This includes the use of *The* and the city of publication if they were officially part of the name. Likewise, what is now named the Ross Ice Shelf is called – as it was a century ago – the Great Ice Barrier, and the Beardmore Glacier is known, as it was by its discoverers, as the Great Glacier. In addition, Oslo appears under its former name of Christiania.

The original sources have also been used regarding units of measurement. Temperatures are recorded in Fahrenheit, as they were by the British Empire's explorers. The term 'degrees of frost', much used at that time, referred to the degrees below 32°F, the equivalent of 0°C (so that 'fifty degrees of frost' equals −18°F). Similarly, the altitudes on the journeys to the Polar Plateau appear in feet (one foot being equivalent to 0.3048 metres), which is doubly confusing to one looking at a modern topographic map because most of the measurements of the time were, in fact, inaccurate.

Generally during the British Antarctic Expedition, distances on land were measured in statute miles, rather than in nautical or geographical miles, as were commonly used at sea or by some other explorers, such as Robert Falcon Scott or Roald Amundsen, on land. Whereas the statute mile is 5,280 feet (1.61 kilometres), the geographical mile is 6,080 feet, which is 1½ statute miles or 1.85 kilometres. The geographical mile is based on one-sixtieth of a degree, or one minute of latitude, and for a brief period the members of Shackleton's party temporarily switched to keeping records in this system. As will be seen in this account, this changeover was made for the most transparent of reasons.

ACKNOWLEDGEMENTS

During the planning, research and writing of this book, I have been the recipient of the generosity and good graces of numerous individuals and organisations. My thanks are firstly due to my wife, Dr Elizabeth Cruwys, for her encouragement, enthusiasm and patience, as well as her insightful assessments and editorial recommendations.

This story would never have been written without the efforts of Sara Fisher of A.M. Heath, who had total faith in it, and who, with help from her colleague Bill Hamilton, found a home for *Nimrod* with Bloomsbury. There, Bill Swainson helped mould it into its final shape, and Sarah Marcus steered it through the numerous stages of the publishing process. To each of these, I am profoundly grateful.

The majority of the research was conducted at the Scott Polar Research Institute, University of Cambridge, where four individuals in particular made valuable contributions. Professor Julian Dowdeswell, the Director of the Institute, gave the project full support from the start, and helped overcome hurdles both real and theoretical. Caroline Gunn never failed to supply me immediately with archival materials, however inconvenient or troublesome the request, and presented me more than once with little-known gems of her own discovery. Robert Headland guided me through many unforeseen snares of research and publishing. And Lucy Martin made invaluable contributions to the book's photographic section. I sincerely thank each of them.

My great appreciation is also extended to my long-time friend and editorial adviser Ian Stone, who read and commented on the manuscript, showing there are many things I have still to learn from him.

Anyone who makes a serious study of Ernest Shackleton or his expeditions cannot help but be grateful to Margery and James Fisher. Almost half a century ago, while preparing their excellent biography, the Fishers compiled a remarkable set of typescripts of diaries, correspondence and interviews of Shackleton, his family, friends, fellow expedition members and many other individuals. These papers are held by the Scott Polar Research Institute, and form the most valuable collection of its kind in the world.

I also thank Roland Huntford, author of the definitive biography of Shackleton, for generously sharing with me his vast knowledge of Shackleton, the British Antarctic Expedition and polar history.

My warm thanks go to Johnny Van Haeften – one of the most enthusiastic and generous contributors to this book – who, with his wife Sarah and daughter Sophie, hosted and encouraged me at an early stage. Johnny not only shared with me the papers of his great-uncle Sir Philip Brocklehurst and a multitude of stories about the Brocklehurst clan, but contributed one of the most evocative photographs.

I much appreciate the kind help of the Hon. Alexandra Shackleton, and thank her for opening Shackleton family material and giving me permission to quote from it.

I also wish to express my gratitude to Dr David M. Wilson, who discussed his great-uncle Edward Wilson and valuable insights obtained in his own research; Professor G.E. Fogg, who shared his immense knowledge regarding the history of Antarctic science and the significance of the scientific results of the British Antarctic Expedition; and Douglas Wamsley, who guided my research into photography in the polar regions.

I am very grateful for the help that I received from the talented husband-and-wife writing team of Diana and Mike Preston, who were also an important factor in launching this project, although they did not realise it at the time. Bob and Phyllis Cruwys also gave constant support throughout the project, for which I am most grateful.

My vision of much of the historical background and context for this book owes an immense amount to the writings of Professor John M. MacKenzie, one of the world's foremost scholars in the study of the relationship between imperialism and popular culture.

I made extensive use of the Library at the Scott Polar Research Institute, and I would particularly like to thank Shirley Sawtell for all of her help, as well as her colleagues Sharon Banks, William Mills and Rebecca Stancombe. For additional friendly help and access to documents, I thank the Cambridge University Library; the Alexander Turnbull Library (Wellington, New Zealand); the British Library; the British

Newspaper Library, Colindale; the Caird Library of the National Maritime Museum Greenwich; the National Army Museum (London); the Public Record Office (London); and the Seeley Library of the Faculty of History, Cambridge.

My sincere appreciation is extended for generous assistance given by Jean Bray (Sudeley Castle); Dr Louise Crossley (Australian Antarctic Division); David Harrowfield; Janet Morris (Emmanuel College, Cambridge); Mark Pharaoh (Mawson Centre, Science Centre, South Australian Museum, Adelaide); Professor Patrick G. Quilty (School of Earth Sciences, University of Tasmania); Dr Steve and Anne Riffenburgh; Professor David W.H. Walton (British Antarctic Survey); Dr Frances Willmoth (Jesus College, Cambridge); and David Yelverton.

In addition, I thank Tracy Bentley (Copyright Office, The British Library); Lieutenant Colonel Roger J. Binks (The Royal Scots Dragoon Guards (Carabiniers & Greys)); Jennifer Broomhead (State Library of New South Wales); Andrew Davis and Daphne Knott (National Maritime Museum Greenwich); Victoria Hobbs and Tom Lloyd-Williams (A.M. Heath); Tim Lovell-Smith and Sean McMahon (Alexander Turnbull Library); Matthew March and Christine Whent (Royal Hospital School); Stephen Martin (Mitchell Library, State Library of New South Wales); Alastair Massie (National Army Museum); Leif Mills; Dr Geoff Parks (Jesus College, Cambridge); Jacqueline Pitcher (British Newspaper Library); Elize Rowan and Geoff Swinney (National Museums of Scotland); Jonathan Shackleton; Jo-Anne Smith (Canterbury Museum); Peter Speak; and Roland Symons (Monkton Combe Senior School). I also wish to recall the interest in the topic expressed by the late Cliff Wynne.

I am grateful to the following for permission to use copyright or privately held material: The Earl Attlee, for the writings of his grandfather Lord Clement Attlee; the Canterbury Museum (Christchurch, New Zealand), for the diary of J.G. Rutherford; Mrs G.E. Dowler, for the diary of her father Æneas Mackintosh; Sir Richard Eyre, for the diaries of his grandfather Admiral Sir Charles Royds; Mrs Anne M. Fright, for the memoirs of her uncle, Frank Wild; Alister Harbord, for the diary of his grandfather Commander A.E. Harbord; Roland Huntford, for quotations from his book *Shackleton*; the Mawson Centre, Science Centre, South Australian Museum, for the diaries of Douglas Mawson; the National Maritime Museum Greenwich, for the correspondence of Ernest Shackleton to Elspeth Beardmore (Lady

Invernairn); the National Museums of Scotland (Edinburgh), for a diary of Dr Alistair Mackay; Ms Jenya Osborne and Ms Ingrid Davis, for the writings of John King Davis; Sir Anthony Rawlinson, for the diaries and correspondence of Lord Rawlinson; the Royal Geographical Society (with the Institute of British Geographers), for two quotations from the diary of Dr Eric Marshall; the Scott Polar Research Institute, for the diaries and papers of Ernest Shackleton, Frank Wild, Raymond Priestley, Dr Edward Wilson, Captain Robert Falcon Scott, Sir Clements Markham, Margery and James Fisher, and numerous others, as well as the majority of photographs; the Hon. Alexandra Shackleton, for a variety of diaries and papers, including those of her grandfather Ernest Shackleton; Mr Neil Silverman, for the diary of Sir Philip Brocklehurst; the Mitchell Library, State Library of New South Wales, for the memoirs of Frank Wild and a diary of Ernest Shackleton; and Mr Johnny Van Haeften, for the correspondence of Sir Philip Brocklehurst and one of the photographs.

Acknowledgement of help does not imply endorsement of the views expressed in this book. These, together with any misinterpretations or errors, are my responsibility alone. If I have overlooked anybody, or failed to trace the correct copyright holders, I hope they will forgive me.

Finally, I would like to record my special thanks to my parents, Ralph and Angelyn Riffenburgh, who have encouraged me and given me unconditional support for much longer than simply the period of this book. My debt to them is incalculable.

MEMBERS OF THE BRITISH
ANTARCTIC EXPEDITION, 1907–09

Shore party

Name	Position	Date, place of birth
Ernest Henry Shackleton	commander	15 February 1874, Kilkea, Ireland (Died: 5 January 1922)
Jameson Boyd Adams	second-in-command, meteorologist	6 March 1880, Lincolnshire (Died: 30 April 1962)
Bertram Armytage	general helper, in charge of ponies	1869, Lara, Victoria, Australia (Died: 12 March 1910)
Sir Philip Lee Brocklehurst	assistant geologist	7 March 1887, Staffordshire (Died: 28 January 1975)
Tannatt William Edgeworth David	director of scientific staff	28 January 1858, St Fagans, Wales (Died: 28 August 1934)
Bernard C. Day	electrician, motor expert	18 August 1884, Oakham (Died: 1934)
Ernest Edward Mills Joyce	in charge of general stores, dogs, sledges, zoological collections	22 December 1875, Bognor, Sussex (Died: 2 May 1940)
Dr Alistair Forbes Mackay	assistant surgeon	22 February 1878, Carskey, Argyllshire (Died: February 1914)
Dr Eric Stewart Marshall	surgeon, cartographer	29 May 1879, Hampstead (Died: 26 February 1963)
George Edward Marston	artist	19 March 1882, Southsea (Died: 22 November 1940)
Douglas Mawson	physicist	5 May 1882, Shipley, Yorkshire (Died: 14 October 1958)
James Murray	biologist	21 July 1865, Glasgow (Died: February 1914)
Raymond Edward Priestley	geologist	20 July 1886, Tewkesbury (Died: 24 June 1974)
William C. Roberts	cook	1872, London
John Robert Francis Wild	in charge of provisions	10 April 1873, Skelton, Yorkshire (Died: 19 August 1939)

Nimrod officers

Name	Position	Date, place of birth
Rupert George A. England	master (1,2)	1878, Warthill, Yorkshire
Frederick Pryce Evans	master (3)	14 April 1874, Newtown, Wales
John King Davis	first officer (1,2,3) master (4)	19 February 1884, Kew
Æneas Lionel Acton Mackintosh	second officer (1,2) navigating officer (3)	1 July 1879, Tirhut, India

Name	Position	Date, place of birth
Arthur Edward Harbord	auxiliary second officer (2) second officer (2,3) first officer (4)	1883, Yorkshire
S. Richardson	second officer (4)	1881, London
Alfred Cheetham	third officer and boatswain (1,2,3,4)	1867, Liverpool
Harry J.L. Dunlop	chief engineer (1,2,3,4)	18 October 1876, Belfast, Ireland
Dr W.A. Rupert Michell	surgeon (1,2,3)	1883, Perth, Ontario, Canada

Nimrod crew

Frederick G. Abraham	AB (3)	1885, London
William Drummond Ansell	second steward (1,2,3,4)	1886, Wimbledon
Victor Berry	AB (1,2)	1883, London
Walter George Bilsby	carpenter (1,2,3,4)	1872, Hull
John Brolly	AB (4)	1886, Philadelphia, PA, USA
Alfred B. Bull	AB (3,4)	1887, London
Henry B. Bull	AB (1,2,3,4)	1884, Adelaide, Australia
Christian Craft	second engineer (1,2)	1871, Hull
D. Donovan	fireman (2)	1882, Kinsale, Cork, Ireland
Ernest W. Ellis	AB (1,2,3,4)	1878, Grimsby
J. Hancock	first steward (2)	1878, Lancashire
H. Holmes	fireman (1)	1874, Hull
Charles Hunt	assistant engineer (3,4)	1878, Jersey
G.R. Kemp	AB (1)	1863, Hamborough
Michael Thomas McGillion	trimmer (3)	1885, Dunedin, NZ
Hugh McGowan	third engineer (1,2) second engineer (in Lyttelton)	1875, Armagh, Ireland
John McMillan	AB (4)	1884, Glasgow
Robert McNeil	fireman (3)	1878, Dumbarton
Murdoch M. McRae	steward (1)	1867, Victoria, Australia
W.R. Meyrick	trimmer (3)	1880, Lyttelton, NZ
John Montague	cook (1,2,3,4)	1869, London
Edward Morrison	sailmaker (1,2)	1870, Dundee
David Nelson	assistant engineer (3,4)	1876, Fifeshire
R. Nodder	AB (3,4)	1878, Cornwall
James Paton	leading seaman (2,3,4)	1869, Glasgow
John Partridge	fireman (2)	1885, Lyttelton, NZ
E. Reynart	fireman (4)	1885, Kent
Sidney Riches	AB (1,2,3,4)	1880, London
Felix Rooney	fireman (1,2)	1885, Govan, Glasgow
G. Rooney	AB (3,4)	1883, Wellington, NZ
A. Schofield	fireman (1)	1875, Hull
W. Spice	AB (1)	1883, St Leonards
M. Vaughan	fireman (4)	1881, Lyttelton
W. Williams	AB (3,4)	1887, Tasmania

Supernumeraries

George Alexander McLean Buckley	visitor (2, returned on Koonya)	1866, Christchurch, NZ
Leo Arthur Cotton	geologist (2)	1883, Australia

The number following an individual's position aboard ship refers to the voyages of Nimrod on which he actually participated. 1 = London to Lyttelton, 1907; 2 = Lyttelton to the Antarctic and back, January–March 1908; 3 = Lyttelton to the Antarctic and back, December 1908–March 1909; 4 = Lyttelton to Sydney to London, 1909.

PROLOGUE

He saw nothing. Or virtually nothing – there, in the far distance, receding by the moment, was what several hours before had been recognisable as a ship, their ship, *Nimrod*. Now it was only a speck plying its way north, and he knew that to those aboard he would no longer be a solitary figure standing on a small rise silhouetted against the sky. Rather he was lost in a looming background of ice and rock; something left behind as they headed home to civilisation, safety and warmth; someone, for the time being, forgotten.

The sky was spectacular, a mixture of the indescribable pastels unique to the early morning hours of the polar regions. The lowering sun bathed the taller peaks before him in golden rays, from Horseshoe Mountain in the west, down through the Royal Society Range, to the high, remote ridges of Mount Discovery in the south. In the shadows, McMurdo Sound was a beautiful, deep blue, broken with slowly floating pieces of pure white ice, some the size of a piano, others vastly larger than the ship. Across the water, the western mountains stared down silently, rent by the tumbling, chaotic slopes of the Ferrar Glacier.

He turned around and looked at the godforsaken place below him, called Cape Royds. In a shallow dip, not far from where the shore rose sharply out of the water, was a small structure sitting near a freshwater lake. Around it, food supplies, coal, harnesses for the ponies, and a jumble of other materials were littered about randomly, like so much jetsam. Some were recognisable, most not, covered as they were by a thick rime of ice, which would take weeks to chip off. Behind the hollow were several ridges of rock, giving a modicum of protection to the tiny building sitting atop the volcanic rubble that covered the area. Beyond these, the land rose slowly, inexorably, over a distance of miles, some thirteen thousand feet up to the smoking summit of Mount Erebus.

His gaze wandered up the side of that dominating, unconquered mass, then jerked back to look down at the camp. He had thought he had heard footsteps behind him, but there was nothing there. It was not the first time he had felt that sensation, and Frank Wild, a veteran Antarctic hand, had told him about men getting panic-stricken and rushing back to base when left alone on the ice. He had already experienced the strange noises himself, and the footsteps that did not actually exist. Wild had said that when you went inland the noises stopped, but then you were even more oppressed by the intimidating silence.

An overwhelming sense of quiet would certainly not be a problem near the hut. Scattered about the rugged landscape, particularly to the west of the lake, was a rookery of hundreds of Adélie penguins. They moved to and fro constantly, squawking at each other and at the skuas, their natural enemies. They took no notice of the time or of whether their newly arrived neighbours from the north were trying to sleep. And worse than the noise was the overpowering stench.

Not that any of this seemed to bother the men at the moment. Despite the ship's departure just hours before, only a few remained awake after a day of humping five tons of coal to the shore. A pair stood just outside the strange apparition that was their new home, with voluminous overclothes, bizarre headwear set atop faces that had not been shaved in days, and a pipe in the mouth of each. The hut was inhabitable, but there was a huge amount of work still to do, both inside and out. And this on the heels of what had surely been one of the most uncomfortable fortnights and some of the hardest labour that any free men had ever experienced.

It had taken weeks of seemingly endless toil to haul all of their materials off the ship, sometimes slogging for more than eighteen consecutive hours. They had been fortunate at the beginning, when they had been able to dock next to ice thick enough to pull sledges across. But then, as the natural wharf broke up, the ship had retreated to a safe distance. They were compelled to launch boats and pull heavily at the oars for more than half a mile across the ice-dotted sound before reaching a wide belt of dense, floating ice. Thence followed the nightmare of trying to navigate through the ice floes: turning their oars into poles and nudging the craft forward, simultaneously trying to keep the heavy ice from crushing them. Once the shore was reached, the stores were either hauled up by a jerry-built derrick or, more frequently, by sheer grit, determination and human muscle. The result was total exhaustion: one night Douglas Mawson fell asleep on the ship, his long legs on top of an engine, the piston moving them with its rhythmic up-and-down stroke, but he was too tired to do anything but dream about the curious motion. The same night, Leo Cotton dropped off to sleep while ascending an iron ladder, nearly falling before he was shaken awake.

Then, four days before, with the suddenness so characteristic of the Antarctic, a tempest of Shakespearean proportion had crashed into their small world. The ship had disappeared, blown clear out of the sound by gusts approaching a hundred miles an hour, leaving the men ashore uncertain as to what had happened to her. Those aboard, meanwhile, had no time to consider their stranded comrades – the temperature dropped to $-16°$, and for three days the gale raged, frozen seas pounding the small vessel. The rudder-well became choked with ice, the top ropes froze into solid bars, and the deck became covered with more than a foot of freezing, sludgy water. Holes had to be broken into the bulwarks to allow the deluge to drain away.

When the storm finally blew out and *Nimrod* was able to return to Cape Royds, those coming ashore found the hut battered, shaken, and providing little warmth, but still standing. A second, temporary structure, constructed of bales of fodder and wooden planks and used as a cookhouse, had been blown down, killing one of the dogs. The stores – kept in containers weighing fifty to sixty pounds each – had been hurled around like paper balls, and were covered by several feet of ice, formed when the water from the sound was flung in sheets for a quarter of a mile inland.

A final day was spent unloading coal, increasing the amount on shore to eighteen tons, enough to get them through the winter – just. Against all odds – including weather, atrocious landing conditions, and human limitations – they had brought 180 tons of equipment ashore. It was an incredible amount, but, now the ship was gone, it looked as if there was almost nothing there. It certainly did not appear to be enough to keep fifteen men alive for a year.

As he left the rise and plodded down through the concrete-hard mixture of ice and scoria towards the hut, Raymond Priestley wondered what lay ahead. It was not unnatural to realise, now that their contact with the outside world had been cut, that what had seemed a great adventure was suddenly a frighteningly dangerous operation. After all, a dozen of them had never even been to the Antarctic before. It was only Wild and Ernest Joyce who had. And, of course, The Boss: the entire plan was his. There was going to be camaraderie, science, and geographical exploration. Personally, Priestley was most interested in the science, but he knew The Boss was planning on going home to fame and fortune. In the next year, he would bag the South Pole for the British Empire. Then everybody would know the name Ernest Shackleton.

A RACE FOR LIFE

One can only assume that most of the new inhabitants of Cape Royds had an unusual combination of ebullience and trepidation that night in February 1908. The only men on a mysterious continent larger than Europe or Australia, they had been abandoned by their ship farther south than anyone in history. Help would not be forthcoming until the next year. In fact, if *Nimrod* did not return safely to New Zealand, the rest of the world would not even know where they were. They were truly on their own, as isolated as if they were on the far side of the moon.

While most of the party undoubtedly concentrated on what was to come in the ensuing days and weeks, one of them must also have cast his mind back five years to the last time he had lived in the shadow of Mount Erebus. Then, Ernest Shackleton had been only a junior officer – and an outsider in many respects – on what was essentially a Royal Navy expedition. Now, he was in charge of his own mission, and determined to overcome the challenges that had defeated that earlier party.

In recent days, 'although a trifle worried . . . [with] good cause to be so', as Æneas Mackintosh had noted, Shackleton had 'managed in a wonderful way to disguise the fact for he was always to be seen with a cheery countenance: & some good joke to set us all laughing.'

Yet nagging in some corner of the leader's mind was the knowledge that the last time he had tested himself in the far south, he had been, in the Biblical phrase then popular, weighed in the balances and found wanting. His body had let down his drive, his determination, his will. Although he was motivated by a desire for fame and fortune – as were most explorers – and the need for a challenge, at a more basic level he had to prove himself, to gain redemption in his own eyes and those of the world.

It had been the final day of December 1902 when three men – Robert Falcon Scott, Edward Wilson, and Shackleton – faced north and started their long way back. Theirs had been a bitter journey, one that started in hope and high expectation, but that, after two months of nearly intolerable hardships and struggle, had come to grief, facing reality in the white wastes of the Great Ice Barrier.

The three forlorn figures, in the midst of an ice field the size of France, did not look to be in either the physical or mental condition to complete a gruelling journey. They were worn down from intense labour, and had not received the necessary food for such strenuous efforts for two months. More than a week before, two of them had been diagnosed as suffering from scurvy, a mysterious, wasting disease that no one truly understood (but that since has been proven to be caused by a deficiency of vitamin C). Yet they were lucky compared to their dogs, which had been systematically, if unintentionally, starved and worked to death.

The trek across the colossal desert of ice had been planned as the showpiece of the British National Antarctic Expedition, the first major, truly British expedition to the Antarctic in six decades. Although Scott – the leader of both the expedition and the party making the southern journey – had publicly avoided referring to specific geographic goals, it would be naïve not to think that the three men had hoped to make a vast indentation into the unknown and, with luck, to reach the South Pole. Certainly other expedition members engaged in wild speculation about attaining the Pole.

But a rapid start to the south soon slowed disappointingly to a crawl. From the beginning, Scott, the surgeon Wilson and Shackleton, who was the third officer of the expedition ship *Discovery*, suffered from inexperience in numerous aspects of polar travel. Chief among these was a lack of knowledge regarding the dogs they had brought to pull the sledges. There was no trained dog-handler on the expedition, so no one truly understood the nineteen animals' dietary needs, the best methods for harnessing them, the speed at which they naturally moved, or the optimum means of driving them. The men were also only painfully learning the relationship between skiing and hauling sledges. None of them had totally mastered the finer technical points of skiing, and they did not have ski-wax or ski-skins to help grip the snow on slopes. The lessons would slowly be learned, but, for the time being, it often seemed as profitable to carry the skis on the sledges as to use them.

Any hopes for a truly impressive southern record were laid to rest in the second half of November 1902, when the support party that had initially accompanied the men turned back. The overwhelming weight of the remaining equipment and supplies meant the dogs were being asked to pull twice the weight they should have been trying to move, and, when that proved impossible, forced the men to begin relaying. The loads were divided in half, the first part moved forward, and then they returned for the second portion, requiring them to travel three miles for every one actually gained southwards.

On 5 December a calculation indicated that they had been using too much fuel, so they cut back from three to two cooked meals a day. The problem was compounded the following day when Spud, one of the dogs, got into the seal meat and ate a full week's worth of their provisions. The daily food ration was consequently cut, and each man received a meagre midday meal of a small piece of seal meat, one and a half biscuits, and eight lumps of sugar. Even more significant, the loss of the ability to cook at midday meant they were no longer able to melt snow for water, and the men became increasingly dehydrated.

In mid-December they cached part of their load at what they called Depot B. They could now advance without relaying, but their progress was still maddeningly difficult, slowed by both deep snow and their dismal diet, which made them steadily weaker. With the dogs doing less and less work, the three men pulled their sledges mile after monotonous mile. Each day they thought constantly about food, and of trivial details such as the number of footsteps one made each minute, thereby trying to compute how many more would have to be taken before the next meal.

On 21 December, Wilson told Scott that Shackleton had 'decidedly angry-looking gums', one of the signs of scurvy. Three days later, he noted in his diary that Scott as well as Shackleton suffered from 'suspicious looking gums'. By Boxing Day, Wilson had problems of his own, his left eye so intensely painful that, despite his repeated use of drops of a cocaine solution to dull the throbbing, they had to stop at lunch and camp for the day. Wilson finally gave himself a dose of morphine in order to sleep, while Shackleton experienced the unpleasant duty of killing one of the dogs to provide food for the others. 'Got his heart first time,' he recorded with relief, although that wasn't the end of his miserable task, as 'soft snow so bad for cutting up'.

Several days later, after being confined to camp for much of two days due to fog and bad weather, Scott determined that it was time to head home. They were at 82°17′S, the farthest south ever reached by men, yet it was a disappointment. Compared with many journeys in the north, their wanderings had taken them an astonishingly short distance in two months. Moreover, their dogs were dying, their own health was precarious, their food was running out, and they still had to recross hundreds of miles.

But the misery and disappointment of all that had gone before was as nothing compared to the suffering of the journey north. On the second day of the trail home – the first of the new year – Spud fell in his trace, too weak to walk. He was placed on a sledge, but that evening, when the three men entered their tent, he was set upon and killed by the other dogs.

'What we have to consider is that we shall soon have no dogs at all and shall have to pull all our food and gear ourselves,' Wilson wrote, noting that, with food supplies dwindling, they *must* reach Depot B before 17 January. 'And we don't know anything about the snow surface of the Barrier during summer. It may be quite different to what it was on the way south. One must leave a margin for heavy surfaces, bad travelling, and weather, difficulty in picking up depots, and of course the possibility of one of us breaking down.' His cautious words were to prove all too prophetic.

Throughout the next week, the men were driven by the realisation that their chances for survival were slim. They were constantly hungry, a condition that made them feel the cold more intensely. Ironically, the dogs were fed better, as Scott decided that carrying extra dog food served no purpose and began distributing it freely to the seven remaining animals. This did little to prevent their decline, however, and on 7 January Shackleton recorded, 'Did march today without dogs at all . . . [one] dropped behind at lunch may come up in the night. We could not stop to drag him along. All the others walked either ahead or astern of their own sweet will.'

The three men now floundered through the snow, dropping into knee- or waist-deep powder while pulling more than 500 pounds. One day they advanced little more than a mile in three hours before camping. A warm snow in the night had changed the surface completely, so that each time they came to a standstill, they had to break the sledges away with sharp jerks. 'I suppose it is bound to come right, but we have less than a week's provisions and are at least fifty miles from the depot,' Scott wrote calmly, concluding with the great British understatement: 'Consequently the prospect of a daily rate of one mile and a quarter does not smile on us.'

Midday on 10 January a wind picked up from the south, and the party hoisted a sail made from the bottom lining of their tent. But a blinding blizzard soon developed, causing the sledges to go so fast and erratically that the men had to run to keep up and had difficulty steering, having at times to pull forward, at others backward, and yet others to the sides. 'Wilson and I are very much "done",' Scott wrote, 'but Shackleton is a good deal worse, I think.'

The next day a warm gale blew, and the men, wet through from melted snow, struggled over a sticky, slow surface. The snowstorm seemed particularly to affect Shackleton. His companions could hear him gasping and they feared his imminent demise, but he found an inner strength that seemed to derive at least in part from the poetry he so dearly loved. 'Tennyson's Ulysses keeps running through my head,' he wrote, perhaps thinking particularly of lines including those that would later be carved in memory of Scott:

> . . . that which we are, we are;
> One equal temper of heroic hearts,
> Made weak by time and fate, but strong in will
> To strive, to seek, to find, and not to yield.

But although personally and spiritually encouraging, poetry would not help them discover their depot, and, as they neared the area in which their food and supplies had been cached, they feared they might not find it. The depot was a snow-covered pile marked with a single flag that could only be seen for a couple of miles on a clear day. The ease with which they could miss it – not so apparent when they had built it – was only too obvious now. Equally anxiety-provoking was that their sledgemeter – a bicycle wheel hooked to the rear sledge that measured the distance travelled – had broken, which meant that they could only guess at their proximity to the depot. They could roughly determine their location by use of a theodolite, but this required a clear view of the sun. They expected that the end of the blizzard would allow them a good sun sighting, but their hopes receded when a heavy pall of cloud obliterated everything. 'The food-bag is a mere trifle to lift,' Scott wrote, 'we could finish all that remains in it at one sitting and still rise hungry; the depot cannot be far away, but where is it in this terrible expanse of grey?'

But they could not just wait helplessly in the tent, so on 13 January they moved into the thick, blank haze. With Shackleton navigating by watching the shadows of the others on the sastrugi (wind-blown ridges in the snow), they struggled forward. In three exhausting hours they gained two miles before stopping to lunch on short rations. Then, suddenly, the sun flashed into their tent, and Scott tumbled out of his sleeping bag to take a meridian altitude. Afterwards, he casually lowered the instrument, and there, in his sights, was Depot B two miles away. Within five minutes the party was on the move, and several hours later they reached their stores. They had made it – or had they?

The next morning was overcast, but they had a fine view of the road ahead. Northward rolled the Barrier, ever on and on, past countless unmarked crevasses and broken, irregular ice forced by pressure into rough mounds or hummocks. Finally it disappeared in a haze perhaps thirty miles away, perhaps fifty, perhaps more. They had long since realised it was impossible to tell distances on the high-latitude ice, but somewhere out there, more than a hundred miles away, was their next cache.

The arrival at Depot B would have left the explorers in much improved spirits had it not been for a medical examination carried out by Wilson. All three had signs of serious scurvy, with Scott noting problems with his right ankle and foot. But it was Shackleton who was the worst off. Ever since the start of the blizzard he had been short of breath and had had a persistent cough, occasionally spitting blood. He also seemed the most fatigued, had developed dark, swollen gums and loosened teeth, and usually coughed throughout the night. His condition was, Wilson noted, 'of no small consequence a hundred and sixty miles from the ship, and full loads to pull all the way.'

With their deteriorating health in mind, they spent the morning restocking their stores, rearranging their equipment, and discarding everything they did not absolutely need. Among the casualties of the overhaul were the skis and poles, except for one emergency set. After another day, they further lightened the load by discarding twenty-five pounds of dog food, an act made possible when the last two dogs,

Nigger and Jim, were killed by Wilson, who described them as 'utterly useless'.

In an effort to defeat the scurvy, the explorers changed their diet, eliminating the bacon that they feared might be contaminated, and doubling their allowance of seal meat. Although Scott and Wilson soon felt their symptoms slightly improving, that same night Shackleton had a desperate time, gasping for air and suffering violent coughing attacks. The next day he was forbidden to pull and walked along in his harness, while the others hauled the sledges.

For much of the following week the story was the same: the party making slow progress, while Shackleton trudged on his own during the day and struggled for breath at night. Unquestionably the weakest of the three, sheer will never the less drove him on. 'Am much better today & hope to be in full swing of work tomorrow,' he wrote optimistically on 17 January. His improvement was slow, however, and it was not until 20 January that he was allowed to cook while Scott and Wilson worked outside.

Although the three men did not know it at the time, the morning of 21 January was one of those junctures that, looking back, can be seen to have a profound influence on the future. After several days of relatively light breeze, a force four wind was blowing. Shackleton had improved enough to be back in harness, but soon the sail propelled the sledges so fast that the three could not keep up. In an attempt to slow the unwieldy train, Scott ordered Shackleton to sit on the aft sledge and break its pace with the ski pole. This proved less effective than hoped, however, and after an hour or two Scott adopted a new tactic: he controlled the port side of the front sledge to keep it running straight, while Wilson was tied to the starboard of the rear sledge to serve as a rudder. Both also served as brakes on what the wind insisted on making an express service. Shackleton, meanwhile, walked at his own pace. In the afternoon, he donned the skis, ending their period of inactivity. Although this switch certainly made travel easier – and an advance of twelve miles marked the day as one of their most successful – Shackleton still saw a dark lining in the silver cloud. 'Splendid day but for my trouble,' he wrote that night, 'which weighs on my mind for I would like to be doing more than just going along.' He was not the only one disquieted by his condition, and it would be an issue that would haunt him for years to come.

The next morning, a wind hammered in from the southwest, and

Shackleton spent the whole day on skis, while Scott and Wilson handled the sledges. For the three following days, according to Wilson, Shackleton went ahead to guide the party by use of a compass. Scott less charitably wrote that the younger man was 'having a cruel time', adding that the work he and Wilson were doing 'would finish Shackleton in no time'. Perhaps disturbed by what he interpreted as Scott's insensitive attitude, the doctor 'had it out with Scott' while Shackleton was out of hearing. It is not certain that Shackleton was the cause of the confrontation, but Wilson reportedly gave Scott a volley of 'home truths', resulting in a clearing of the air between them. In the following days, Scott and Wilson had a series of wide-ranging conversations that, although they did not ultimately bring any great understanding between Shackleton and Scott, forged a bond of friendship between Scott and Wilson that would last until their deaths a decade later.

Meanwhile, Shackleton continued to battle ahead, although Wilson forbade him to do any pulling, as 'the least exertion makes him breathless'. Then the clouds disappeared and the sun burst forth gloriously clear. The men's pleasure was short-lived, however, as they were soon seriously burned despite wearing wide-brimmed hats, while concurrently finding that 'the cold in the shade under [the hats] was such that our moustaches and whiskers all became frosted and covered with ice, making one's lips and nostrils sting and tingle very painfully.'

By 28 January, they had seen familiar, and comforting, landmarks, including the twin peaks of Ross Island – Mount Erebus and Mount Terror. That morning, with the sun burning down brightly and the prospect of reaching Depot A before the day was through, they had a large celebratory breakfast. As if in need of a final reminder of the true power of nature, however, when they came out of their tent they found that a bitterly cold gale had blown in from the south, obscuring what they had thought would be an unencumbered run to the depot.

Fortunately, the weather, which can turn remarkably quickly in the far south, did just that, and conditions improved by late morning. Shortly after lunch, Shackleton spotted the depot. They tore out the supplies with childish glee: letters indicating that all was well at the base at Hut Point, enough oil to allow them unrestrained use of it, and a vast quantity of food, including varieties that they had not seen for months. At last they seemed truly safe.

But that night they found that their trials were not yet over, and to Wilson, whose evangelical faith was unwavering, the continuing battles must have represented a Job-like series of calamities. They started on the less serious side after both Wilson and Scott had wolfed down large quantities of food, a dangerous action after long periods of privation. It was not long before each was in agony, which persisted late into the night and caused them to sleep fitfully. But worse was when they woke to find that a howling blizzard, perhaps the heaviest of the season, had blown in and that the air was 'chock a block with snow drift'.

The grimmest problem, however, was that Shackleton had suffered a serious setback. As before, he became worse in conditions of blizzard, and he again gasped desperately between his spells of heavy, persistent coughing. Previously, he had managed to struggle along, but now he could hardly move in his sleeping bag, and Scott and Wilson decided to remain there until the blizzard dropped. But Shackleton only seemed worse as the day continued.

That night he reached a crisis. 'His breathing has become more stertorous and laboured,' wrote Scott, 'his face looks pinched and worn, his strength is very much reduced, and for the first time he has lost his spirit and grown despondent.' As the blizzard roared outside and Shackleton lay panting, perhaps passing in and out of consciousness or delirium, he heard Wilson quietly tell Scott that he did not expect the sick man to last the night. Later in his life, Shackleton would say that that comment made him determined to pull through. And somehow he did.

Wilson had told Scott that although Shackleton was in no condition to be moved, his only chance was for them to struggle through the blizzard to the ship. Scott, in response, noted that he was uncertain if Shackleton's health would even allow him to be hauled on the sledge. But by morning, although weak and speechless, Shackleton was ready to travel. By good fortune the weather had cleared, and, although he became dizzy just kneeling to get out of the tent and took twenty minutes to struggle outside and on to his skis, he moved off, leading the way north.

Shackleton was constantly breathless during the next several days but, with the weather clear and the surface good for skiing, he kept up with his companions. Scott and Wilson had a much harder time. Moreover, despite an increase in food, scurvy now showed more strongly in Scott and Wilson, the latter attributing his lameness to the illness. Whether it was by comparison to his own deteriorating condition or an actual improvement in Shackleton is uncertain, but on

1 February, Scott noted that 'our invalid ... certainly has great recuperative powers'.

Meanwhile, local landmarks and tracks in the snow indicated that they were very near the ship, and on 3 February they were met by two members of the expedition, Reginald Skelton and Louis Bernacchi. 'They appeared to be very worn & tired & Shackleton seemed very ill indeed,' wrote Bernacchi, who effortlessly helped Skelton pull the sledge that had been so difficult for Scott and Wilson.

Upon their arrival, the entire crew came out to greet the weary threesome, but Shackleton did not attend the celebration. 'I turned in at once when I got on board, not being up to the mark,' he wrote, demonstrating either a mastery of understatement or a total lack of comprehension of his health, 'after having had a bath, – that is the first for ninety-four days. It is very nice to be back again; but it was a good time.'

Shackleton, Scott and Wilson were all back alive, if none of them healthy, and it would take them a lengthy period to complete their convalescence and return to their accustomed vigour. But before that, Shackleton was to receive another damaging blow, and it was to help set the course of his entire future.

2

A PRODUCT OF EMPIRE

The world into which Scott, Wilson and Shackleton were born and spent their formative years was very different from that in which they achieved lasting fame. It was a world that for more than half a century had been dominated by Britain – economically, technologically, morally and militarily. It was a time and place in which to be British meant belonging to a people destined to be paramount. The Briton demonstrated the qualities of faith, patriotism, superiority and duty, and in this time before two world wars, he had a mindset not pervaded by the doubts of future generations.

There are basic certainties – key assumptions and deeply held convictions – that are inculcated at an early age and by which most people are guided throughout their lives. As the three future explorers progressed through childhood, part of the underlying mentality that had a profound influence on each was the pre-eminence of the British people and their Empire. 'I contend that we are the finest race in the world,' that most unfailing of imperialists, Cecil Rhodes, once said, adding that Britons had the highest ideals of decency and justice, 'and the more of the world we inhabit, the better it is for the human race.'

No one will ever fully understand late Victorian Britain who does not appreciate the significance of that elitism and the Empire it helped drive, not just to Rhodes or other arch-imperialists, or even to successive governments, but through every level of society. From the working class to Queen Victoria herself, British pre-eminence was a source of unfettered pride, ultimately gaining the support of all classes and all major political parties. David Livingstone, then considered the greatest exemplar of self-help, spoke of the peoples of British stock as members of a 'superior race' with a divine mission 'to elevate the more degraded portions of the human family'. At the far end of the social spectrum was the patrician Prime Minister Lord Salisbury, whose Colonial Secretary, Joseph Chamberlain, crystallised the view of British transcendence: 'In the first place I believe in the British Empire, and in the second place I believe in the British race. I believe that the British race is the greatest of governing races that the world has ever seen.'

Victoria's Empire was certainly the largest, in both territory and population, that had ever existed. Her domain covered a fifth of the land surface of the Earth and included more than 400 million subjects. It is not surprising that possessing such a vast empire affected the mentality of the British populace. Yet, strangely, many historians have tended to ignore the obvious – that imperial ideas and enthusiasms penetrated deeply into the British consciousness. British society was, however, saturated with nationalist and imperialist concepts, the influence of which was highly pervasive not only in the political arena but in education and entertainment. Whereas the public might not have had a sophisticated concept of empire, or have been interested in specific imperial policies, individuals at every level believed without doubt in the superiority of their culture, race and Empire.

What is sometimes called the 'informal empire' – that based on a dominance of British trade and a system of influence rather than on actual rule – had long been an economic reality. But the triumph of imperialism as a social current underlying British culture and thought occurred later, at a time, coincidentally, concurrent with the births of the three men who struggled back to Hut Point in 1903.

If one were to select a specific time for the birth of the popular imperial spirit, it could well be a conjunction of events in the first half of 1868, the year in which Scott was born. The previous year had seen the Second Reform Bill extend the franchise in Britain by 89 per cent, in the process giving political leaders grave concerns about burgeoning social disorder. In February 1868 Benjamin Disraeli became Prime Minister and, according to many historians, immediately turned to foreign adventurism and imperial expansion in order to side-step potential internal social unrest. As the Liberal theorist and statesman John Morley wrote, 'the idea of a whole people, possessing a certain number of common convictions, susceptible of certain large common impulses, marching onwards for the execution of certain common national purposes' led Disraeli to emphasise foreign interventionism as a means of getting all of the classes of Britain to follow the same banner.

Disraeli was fortunate that a punitive mission against Emperor

Theodore of Abyssinia was already underway, and within two months of becoming Prime Minister, his strategy had proven successful, as had the Abyssinian campaign under Sir Robert Napier. The reports of the conflict not only catapulted the reporter Henry Morton Stanley to his first fame, but led to new heights of chauvinism in Britain and demonstrated that Disraeli had found the best way to bring into line the newly enfranchised working class. Despite shortly thereafter losing power, the Conservative Party had found imperialism could be a key platform.

Four years later, in June 1872 – a month before the birth of Edward Wilson – Disraeli embraced these principles even tighter with his masterful call at Crystal Palace for a future of greatness through imperial power. The English, he said, had a *right* to rule over the lesser peoples of the world, and it was time to determine whether they would do so. Would England remain small, comfortable, insular, and ordinary, or become 'a great country, an Imperial country, a country where your sons, when they rise, rise to paramount positions, and obtain not merely the esteem of their countrymen, but command the respect of the world'? It was a challenge to every Englishman to take up the cause of the Empire. But among the issues that it did not address was just what comprised that Empire.

Perhaps Britain's most problematic imperial burden in the late nineteenth century was the one closest to home – Ireland. The parliamentary integration brought about by the Act of Union of 1801 had not been accompanied by a carefully considered administrative or economic amalgamation, and as a result there were continuing and widely varying interpretations about Ireland's status. Was Ireland – like Scotland – an integral part of the United Kingdom? Was it a culturally separate entity that was little more than a backward province? Or was it a unique colony in the Empire? Those believing in continued political union, Home Rule, or full Irish independence had different answers to these questions.

What *is* certain is that the administration of Ireland remained distinctly colonial in both form and function. The compelling cultural necessity for Ireland to be considered subordinate to England regularly overrode the possibilities either of converting her into an integrated component of a unified Britain or of giving the Irish Home Rule. It also did not allow for the individual Irishman to be considered part of a greater British society. Many Britons, including politicians, administrators, absentee landlords, occupying soldiers, and sections of the general populace, viewed the Irish as an inferior, half-savage race imbued with inherent barbarism, not far removed from the peoples of Asia or Africa. Even the socialist reformers Sidney and Beatrice Webb found it difficult to extend their social consciousness to the Irish. While honeymooning in Dublin in 1892, the couple wrote that 'the people are charming but we detest them, as we should the Hottentots'.

From the opposite end of the political spectrum, Lord Salisbury showed equal disdain for the Irish, whose emigration, he wrote, was cause for 'unmixed congratulation' and 'the sooner they are gone the better'. However, despite a helping hand from the potato famine of the 1840s, which had been followed by the emigration of millions of Irish, Salisbury's hope that the Irishman would disappear and 'leave a place behind him to be filled up by a Scotchman or Englishman' had not been fulfilled.

That all attempts to Anglicise the Irish peasantry had failed only made the English despise them more. To the English way of thinking, they remained a strangely foreign people, whose literacy rate was no higher than that in Burma, and who continued to speak their alien tongue, worship their false Catholic god, and be, as Disraeli wrote, 'wild, reckless, indolent, uncertain and superstitious'.

Yet there was one sub-section of the population of Ireland to which the fullness of this caustic attitude was not extended. Spread among the primitive Celtic peasants, but separated from them by religion and caste, were the members of an imperial ruling class, who for centuries had been elevated above the common Irish by royal policy and social and economic privilege. These overlords were the members of the Protestant Ascendancy – the landowners of the country and the creators of Irish high society. Many were descendants of Englishmen and lowland Scots who had colonised the country on generous terms as part of the English government's effort to subdue local will and extinguish the Irish gentry. The preserve of these Anglo-Irish, The Pale as it came to be known, was in the green, fecund fields and hills of the territories surrounding Dublin. There, seven centuries earlier, the Anglo-Norman knights of Henry II had settled in fortified dwellings after invading and dominating the Irish, and there they established a broad, fertile enclave. Through the centuries, their heirs were joined by more members of the Ascendancy, whether English-born or English-descended.

To the west and southwest of Dublin, in the midst of The Pale, was County Kildare. A century and more ago, much of its economic and social existence revolved around an agrarian way of life. Here in 1872, on the banks of the River Griese, not far from the market town of Athy, Henry Shackleton moved with his new wife Henrietta into a large and commodious farmhouse, named Kilkea House. It was not a major move in a geographical sense – Henry's birthplace was less than five miles distant, and Henrietta's mother lived in nearby Carlow – but it was perhaps a surprising one in that Henry had seemed destined for more promising things. As a young man he had been sent to school in England, but illness had prevented him from obtaining a commission in the army. Instead he had attended Trinity College, Dublin, graduating with an Arts degree. When the Shackletons married, however, they decided on a life of farming, and they moved to Kilkea, some thirty miles from Dublin and due west of Wicklow.

Two years later, before sunrise on the morning of 15 February 1874, Ernest Henry Shackleton, the couple's second child and first son, was born in Kilkea House. Through the first year and a half of his life, the baby was, according to his mother, almost too good to live, never crying, and with blue eyes and golden hair that gave him an angelic beauty. That he was not a terror at an early age was as well for his parents, because, in the eight years they spent surrounded by the cultivated fields at Kilkea, they had six children, a brood that would eventually rise to ten.

Henry Shackleton's excursion into farming was made at the best of times and the worst of times. The year he initially leased the land from the Duke of Leinster, the plough reached its maximum extension over British soil. To be a farmer was hard, but in Britain it was more profitable than anywhere else in the world. However, in the mid-1870s Britain's leadership in farming crumbled, as an unprecedented agricultural depression descended on Europe. This was brought about principally by the flooding of European markets with American grain. This in turn was due to developments in farming machinery taking place at the same time as a massive extension of railroads across the United States. Suddenly the boundless American prairies could not only be as efficiently farmed as the more densely populated areas of Europe, but prodigious amounts of grain could be transported at a fraction of the previous price.

The governments in Paris and Berlin – sensing economic disaster –

quickly imposed heavy duties on cereals to protect their farmers, but the Tories in London failed to do so. When the plummet in the price of wheat and barley was combined with a series of wet summers in the middle of the decade, and major outbreaks of rinderpest, liver-rot, and foot-and-mouth, British agriculture suffered a collapse from which it never recovered.

There were additional problems for the Irish farmer. In 1879 a long-turbulent agrarian situation exploded into the Land War, a campaign of protest that was transformed into a struggle against landlordism. A multitude of groups and individuals engaged in broad spectrums of behaviour, ranging from parliamentary debate and legal mass meetings, to intimidation, outrages against farm animals, and murder. Facing both the acute agricultural depression and the political uncertainties of farming, Henry Shackleton decided to make a career change. In 1880, at the age of thirty-three, he packed up his family and returned to Trinity College to read medicine.

For the next four years, Ernest and his expanding number of siblings lived in Dublin, whence the first stories come of the lad's developing personality. It is told that he had a fascination with funerals, and that he would follow the local processions. When asked once what he wanted to be when he grew up, he replied, 'a gravedigger'.

Such sombre tales aside, it was also in Dublin that the mischievous twinkle in the eye and the impish delight in teasing and joking, which would later show themselves as regular parts of Shackleton's humour, first appeared. 'He loved playing practical jokes,' his younger sister Eleanor wrote. 'Once on April the first he got a number of his sisters out of bed at four a.m. to see the cat with four heads in the coal cellar.'

Shackleton also began to show a streak of independence that would mark his later life. His maternal grandmother played a great part in the family's home life, and she occasionally pasted together pages of the children's books. 'This was the censorship of ugliness,' Shackleton's sister Kathleen later said. 'Unpleasant sounding words, pictures that might frighten us were hidden from our impressionable little brains, and it was a point of honour with us not to try and look.' But young Ernest was more actively inquisitive than his siblings, and one day he and his sister Alice soaked some pages open. There they found the hidden word in all its horror – sow – and a picture of an exceptionally ugly porcine specimen. The next morning he triumphantly greeted his grandmother with the words, 'Good morning, Mrs Sow'.

More illustrative of the man whom the boy became – and of his developing charm, persuasiveness and planning – was a story linking him to hidden treasure. One day he convinced a maid that there was a fortune buried in the rear garden. He induced her to dig for it with him, and, lo!, they found a ruby ring. That it belonged to his mother and had been planted there by Shackleton did not seem to detract from his success in either the enlistment of aid or in the actual finding of the gem. In fact, his interest in such a bonanza would last throughout his life. 'He found real excitement in discussing buried treasure,' photographer Frank Hurley later wrote. 'He often spoke of pirate treasure – of King John's treasure being lost in the Wash – of Caligula's lost treasure.'

The aggregate of these traits has led biographers to make generalisations about Shackleton. Much has been written of the supposed Irishness of his charm, sense of humour, verbal eloquence and love of poetry, all, according to that argument, ensuing logically from his ten formative years in Ireland. Significance has also been attributed to his Anglo-Irish lineage – Henry Shackleton was of Yorkshire Quaker stock, although his family had lived in Ireland for four generations and he had been raised in the Church of England. That north-of-England heritage has been ascribed as the cause of Shackleton's courage and combativeness. In reality, ethnic generalisations do little to explain his development. Although a detailed history of his family can elucidate his background, it cannot give unambiguous clarity about the man.

'Lord Kitchener was not a real Irishman, only an accidental one,' Augustine Birrell wrote about another famous Anglo-Irishman who in later life showed little interest in the place of his birth. In many senses, Shackleton was not dissimilar. After his father graduated from Trinity with his medical degree and moved his family across the Irish Sea, Shackleton did not live on the Emerald Isle again, sojourn there at length or, except when convenient or beneficial, claim it as part of his mental or emotional world. His attitudes as an adult were much like those of another Anglo-Irishman, Garnet Wolseley, who adopted the mentality of the dominant culture, becoming psychologically more of an Englishman than what was deridingly called an 'Outer Briton'. Such a transformation was demonstrated in Wolseley's account of the Indian Mutiny, when he and his troops were forced to bivouac in the open after marching into Cawnpore. They camped a short distance from where British women and children had been massacred and thrown into a well. 'Upon entering those blood-stained rooms, the heart seemed to stop,' he recorded, his words showing his self-image, 'a more sickening, a more maddening sight no Englishman has ever looked upon.'

However, when Henry Shackleton moved his family to Croydon in December 1884 to open a medical practice, his eldest son was not yet English by any description. For one thing, Ernest's brogue, which his parents had worked on eliminating while in Dublin, led to his school-mates quickly giving him the nickname Mick, which in one variation or another he kept for the rest of his life – as indeed he did a hint of the accent. For another, his feistiness inclined him to use his fists when his Irish antecedents were mentioned negatively. But it was those very schools that helped shape Shackleton, leading him from becoming a 'professional Irishman' to being a wholehearted participant in 'the greatest club on Earth – the members of the British Empire'.

Pride in the Empire had been growing in the British populace throughout Shackleton's life. In the very month of his birth, three events took place that were not only of political or symbolic significance to the Empire, but in retrospect can be seen to have helped set the course of Shackleton's career. It was not that these occurrences augured specific developments that affected the explorer, but that they helped build the British imperial zeitgeist.

Most closely related to Shackleton's future was that, on the day after his birth, HMS *Challenger*, on a four-year circumnavigation that effectively founded the modern science of oceanography, became the first steam vessel to cross the Antarctic Circle. This cruise marked the first major study of Antarctic waters in decades and helped lead to the acceptance in scientific circles of the far south as a legitimate region for research.

Second, eleven days before Shackleton's birth, Wolseley, now Major-General Sir Garnet Wolseley, KCMG, CB – 'the very model of a modern major-general' according to W.S. Gilbert – had completed perhaps the most perfectly run campaign of all of the Victorian 'small wars'. In a lightning strike by the standards of the day, Wolseley's small army had stormed through the Gold Coast and sacked Kumasi, the capital of the kingdom of Ashanti, in order to stop the supposed aggression and rampant human sacrifice of the country's King Kofi Karikari. The total success of Wolseley's campaign set off bouts of popular excitement and dramatic displays of chauvinistic emotion.

Third, that same week, after more than five years in opposition,

Disraeli and his Tories were swept to power in the general elections. When he accepted the seals of his new office from Queen Victoria, a period was launched in which an imperial ideology dominated not only Britain's official international outlook but a much deeper intellectual and social current. Disraeli's emphasis on imperialism was to be followed so closely by later Conservative-led cabinets – under the influence of Lord Randolph Churchill and Joseph Chamberlain – that even William Ewart Gladstone's final two Liberal governments were unable to halt Britain's inexorable march through Africa.

Disraeli's timing was impeccable. In the period between his first fall from power and his second, several developments further instilled in the British people a sense of imperial destiny and purpose. The passage of the Forster Education Act in the summer of 1870 saw the initiation of the conversion of the British into a literate, school-taught society. This did not happen at once, but the extension of basic education meant a broad new range of society was able to read the popular newspapers that were a major factor in the distribution of imperial ideology. Through the organs of the press, foreign as well as domestic news became available, and the public became more knowledgeable – and more opinionated – about their country's international prestige and position.

The British public learned, for example, that a man named Bell had invented an instrument by which one could speak to someone in a different room. They knew that the opening of the Suez Canal was bringing India geographically closer to the mother country. And they read that, just as the Empire suffered occasional military setbacks, so the expansion of the United States was threatened by a military defeat at a place with the unlikely name of the Little Big Horn. All in all, they could find out what they wanted to know, and most of that was about *their* Empire.

Meanwhile, in the same period in which British agriculture suffered so dramatically, the British manufacturing industry also was challenged by foreign competition. Ever since the Industrial Revolution, Britain had dominated international markets. In the 1870s, however, the United States and Germany began manufacturing items they had previously obtained from the 'workshop of the world'. Soon these were being marketed worldwide, and foreign trade was presented to the British people as a Darwinian struggle for existence between manufacturing nations.

There were other factors involved in this new outward-looking vision. The same week that the Forster Education Act passed in Parliament, the Prussian war machine, which the previous decade had smashed Austria, began doing the same to France. Within a month of the beginning of the Franco-Prussian War, more than 100,000 French troops were killed, wounded or captured at the Battle of Sedan. The victory of what became the German Empire was utterly complete and transferred to that power military dominance over the European continent. Moreover, the prompt mobilisation of 475,000 men under arms – more than four times as many as Britain had for service abroad throughout the world – demonstrated Britain's inability to determine events on the continent.

In future years, the British government's military planning, political negotiations and economic decisions would take these changing realities into account. But to the public, foreign challenges had been issued, and throughout British society, support of the Empire turned surmise into fact, patriotism into jingoist bellicosity, and ethnic superiority into outright racism.

Ernest Shackleton's formative years in Ireland were during this period. They were embellished by a succession of brilliant imperial victories marred by shocking setbacks, all of which initiated passionate appeals for heroic self-sacrifice, following the call of duty, and upholding the cause of empire.

As the greatest imperial tragedy of all slowly unfolded, and Wolseley's army moved south across the deserts of Egypt and the Sudan, the Shackletons resettled in Croydon. What an impression must have been made on young Ernest as, in January 1885, only a month after their relocation, Khartoum was lost to the forces of the Mahdi. All of England went into mourning at the loss of her greatest Christian soldier, General Charles Gordon. The outrage about the government's dithering prior to sending relief did not cease until Gladstone fell from power in June. That same month, after failing to start a successful practice in Croydon, Henry Shackleton moved his family to Sydenham.

Ernest's educational career now entered a new phase. A governess had previously taught him at home, but once settled in Sydenham he began to attend Fir Lodge Preparatory School, not far from their new house on West Hill.

'Shackleton was a big strong, well-made youngster, & being a little older had little to do with us smaller fry, but he was always friendly & good natured,' wrote one of his fellow pupils seventy years later. 'His father . . . was our family doctor for some time, & I remember being sent to him to be overhauled. In spite of his alarming beard he was very kind & gentle. Mrs Shackleton I never saw. I believe she was an invalid.'

Indeed, it was around this period, or shortly after the birth of Gladys, the youngest of the ten children, that Henrietta Shackleton came down with a debilitating illness that sapped her energy. She soon withdrew from many aspects of life and kept herself confined to a sick room, where she remained, more or less, for forty years. The Shackleton children were thereafter raised primarily by their father, who also ran his medical practice and grew roses that were renowned in the local area. Not that Ernest suffered from lack of a woman's influence – he had eight sisters, all of whom, according to one of them, Eleanor, 'adored him, in fact they believed everything for gospel that he said'.

One of the most important contributions Henry Shackleton made to his children was to pass on his love of language, and particularly poetry. From an early age they engaged in linguistic contests around the dinner table, such as one in which Dr Shackleton quoted a verse and the children had to identify the author or continue the poem. This led to Ernest developing a fine vocabulary and to poetry coming sponta- neously to his mind later in life. 'I read poetry as a boy – and I've read poetry ever since,' he later stated. 'I am sure . . . that poetry is good for boys to read, and I think . . . teachers should be very careful not to spoil their taste for poetry by making it a task and an imposition.'

This telling comment indicates how Shackleton might have felt about his own teachers. He evidently found it difficult to maintain an interest in his studies, and, consequently, was rarely better than an average student. In 1887 he left Fir Lodge to be a day-boarder at Dulwich College, a solid Victorian public school that was within walking distance of his home. His behaviour changed little, however, according to the memory of one old friend, who later commented, 'from what I remember he did very little work, and if there was a scrap, he was usually in it.'

Although not on par with Eton or Harrow, Dulwich – founded in 1618 – was successful in its own goal of turning out imperial admin- istrators and businessmen. Thus, it was a key part of the English public school system that was of pivotal importance in producing the dominant culture. In Shackleton's time, this meant developing little British imperialists. This was not a phenomenon restricted to the public schools, but ran through the entire educational system, affecting the working classes as well.

However, the emphasis would have been considerably stronger at a public school like Dulwich. There, under the firm, forbidding headmaster A.H. Gilkes, a blend of patriotism, duty and reverence for the monarchy were promoted as cardinal elements of life. Students were exposed to the imperial cult and its building blocks of Christian militarism, public school athleticism and military virtues. Textbooks and literature for youth promoted a heroic national history, a quasi-religious approach to the obligations of international power, and an ideological justification for imperial conquest. It was a powerful mixture, as former Labour Prime Minister Clement Attlee indicated when he described the youthful thrill of imperialism. In December 1895, Attlee's father, a Gladstonian Liberal and a lawyer, was horrified by the actions culminating in the Jameson Raid, the attempt to lead the English-speaking 'uitlanders' in an armed rebellion against the Boer government of the Transvaal. However, to the young Attlee, born but nine years after Shackleton, 'Dr Jim [Jameson] was a hero . . . On the wall at school hung a great map with large portions of it coloured red. It was an intoxicating vision for a small boy . . . We believed in our great imperial mission.'

Shackleton's time at Dulwich would have helped build his interest in the Empire. The year he entered saw the celebration of Queen Victoria's golden jubilee. The country and Empire were swept with a wave of loyalty of a depth difficult to understand for those who have only experienced the lesser celebrations and memorials revolving around later royals. That same year, Stanley left on the most publicised of African journeys – the Emin Pasha Relief Expedition – with the stated goal of rescuing one of Gordon's lieutenants who was holding out against the forces of the Mahdi far up the Nile. Funded in part by a host of British newspapers, and promoted by financiers who saw a chance to establish a commercial empire along the upper Nile, the expedition received extensive and extremely patriotic propaganda.

Shackleton's horizons undoubtedly were expanded by such adventures in far-away places. He later claimed that, 'I was more or less acquainted from my earliest youth with all the problems of exploration, whether it was in Central Africa, Central Australia, Thibet, the North and South Poles, or New Guinea and Borneo.' It is said that one of his favourite books was the American Charles Francis Hall's *Life with the Esquimaux*, which told of travels in the high Arctic. And, like many boys his age, Shackleton was caught by the escapism, the release from daily humdrum, of such publications as the *Boy's Own Paper*. Launched in 1879 by the Religious Tract Society, the *BOP*, as it was known, had a goal of keeping Britain's new generation of readers away from the sensational 'penny dreadfuls'. It was a lively journal, containing quality juvenile literature, sports, travel and adventure stories, and guides to self-improvement. It attracted such renowned imperial fiction writers as R.M. Ballantyne and W.H.G. Kingston, and two of Shackleton's own favourites, G.A. Henty and Jules Verne. Shackleton so identified with the lonely, mysterious anti-hero of Verne's *Twenty Thousand Leagues Under the Sea* that he later adopted the name Nemo for himself, not only in letters to his future wife, but as a pseudonym for his writings.

How much Captain Nemo's way of life influenced Shackleton cannot be known, but what *is* certain is that the lad decided at an early age that he wanted to go to sea. 'He had no particular hobbies as a boy but anything to do with the sea was his special attraction,' one of his sisters later claimed. It is told how he and three schoolmates spent time they should have been in class in a local wood, smoking, dreaming of life under sail, and reading adventurous sea stories aloud. On one occasion, Shackleton and his chums are supposed to have gone to London Bridge, where they stood in a queue for jobs on a steamliner. The steward was having none of it from lads their age, and packed them back off home.

Shackleton's most intimate companion of the time was Nicetas Petrides, whose family lived on the same street as the Shackletons, and who used to walk to school with Ernest. When Shackleton was fifteen, the two of them and Petrides' younger brother spent a holiday together at St Leonards. When the tide was out, the trio walked far out on to the soft sand, Shackleton going beyond the others. 'He suddenly felt his feet gripped by quicksand and called for our help, as the waves were breaking over him and he could not extricate himself,' Petrides later recalled. 'We . . . formed a chain by holding hands and . . . gradually released him, the quicksand fortunately not being deep. For this we were duly rewarded by him by each being treated to an ice.'

Despite such an experience with reality, Shackleton's head remained firmly in the clouds – or the waves. As a result, he did not 'care tuppence about lessons' at Dulwich, although he did finish second out of eighteen in English History and Literature in 1889. His reports regularly pointed out that his low marks were due to a deficiency of interest rather than a lack of ability. 'I never learned much geography at school,' Shackleton later recalled in *The Captain*, a competitor to *Boy's Own Paper* founded by the press baron George Newnes. 'My first voyage taught me more geography than I should have learned had I remained at school to the age of eighty. School geography consisted in my time . . . in names of towns, lists of capes and bays and islands.'

Shackleton's father wanted his son to follow him into medicine. Ernest was equally determined to experience the romance – and hardships – of the sea. One of Dr Shackleton's happy attributes was his love and support for his children, and he eventually gave his blessing for a trial at sea. He couldn't afford to send his son to *Britannia*, the Royal Navy training ship, so instead they turned to the merchant marine. 'My father thought to cure me of my predilection for the sea by letting me go in the most primitive manner possible,' Shackleton recalled later, 'as a "boy" on board a sailing ship at a shilling a month!'

It might not sound an ideal situation to the modern mind, but in those heroic days of empire, there was both honour and excitement in such a venture, which could include visiting the empty, desolate regions of the world. There were many distant places where all but Britons feared to tread or sail, and Ernest Shackleton was going to seek them out.

3

LIFE AT SEA, LOVE ON LAND

Like many young lads in the late nineteenth century, Shackleton had probably acquired a romantic vision of life at sea. Once aboard ship, it did not take long for him to be disabused of any utopian conception.

In April 1890 Shackleton travelled to Liverpool to join the three-masted, full-rigged sailing ship *Hoghton Tower*. The appointment had been orchestrated by his father's cousin, the Reverend G.W. Woosnam, superintendent of the Mersey Mission to Seamen. Through contacts with the North Western Shipping Company, Woosnam arranged for Shackleton to make a voyage on which, although with the status of Boy, he would receive the uniform, accommodation and training of an Apprentice.

Shackleton had never been the ideal student at Dulwich, although in his final term his reports had greatly improved. However, when he joined *Hoghton Tower*, he quickly found himself considered an odd nut because of his superior education and his strange habits of reading and quoting poetry.

'When he wasn't on duty on the deck he was stowed away in his cabin, with books,' recalled a shipmate years later. 'And the other lads used to say "Old Shack's busy with his books" . . . he could quote poetry and read history. I think he was a bit of a lecturer. He certainly was well schooled.'

It was, of course, a matter of perspective. According to Shackleton, it was the sea that

> taught me things – and that is what Dulwich, with all its good points had not done . . . I learned more of literature in a year at sea than I did in half a dozen years at school. I seemed to get at the heart of it then, to see its meaning, to understand its message, and in some degree to catch its spirit.

The sea was a school in other ways as well, and, as the ship headed for Valparaiso on his first voyage, Shackleton had to learn the ropes – literally, as there were more than 200 in the rigging of *Hoghton Tower*, each with its own name and function, and to mistake one for another could be disastrous. He was exposed to the harshness and boredom of a life on the ocean: scrubbing decks, manning a watch, sleeping in the wet, and beginning to grasp the principles of sailing ships, a breed even then near the end of its day.

'I can tell you Nic that it is pretty hard work, and dirty work too,' he wrote to Petrides, continuing:

> It is a queer life and a risky one; you carry your life in your hand whenever you go aloft, in bad weather; how would you like to be 150 feet up in the air; hanging on with one hand to a rope while with the other you try and get the sail in frozen stiff with sleet and snow; and there is the ship rocking pitching and rolling about like a live creature.

Fortunately, Shackleton had a bit of time to adjust before the ship became so wild. But after a calm voyage to South America, they ran into a series of gales while trying to round Cape Horn in the depth of winter. 'It was one continuous blizzard all the way,' he recalled later, 'one wild whirl of stinging sleet and snow, and we were in constant peril of colliding with icebergs or even of foundering in the huge seas.' Members of the crew were injured, and the sails and spars were damaged. Even after they reached the Pacific, the gales continued, and it was more than two months before they finally anchored at Valparaiso. From there, they proceeded up the coast to Iquique (Chile), a miserable, stinking backwater where for six weeks they discharged a cargo of hay and brought aboard a load of nitrates. It was hard, unpleasant labour, as there were no quays, but Shackleton learned the valuable lesson of safely transporting cargo in boats between ship and shore.

By the time he returned to Liverpool in April 1891, Shackleton had been gone for almost a year. There were certainly aspects of life at sea for which he did not care, and the ship's captain felt the same about the young man, commenting to Reverend Woosnam, 'he is the most pigheaded, obstinate boy I have ever come across'. But the sea still had an undeniable appeal, and Shackleton now needed to make his decision as to whether to return to the security and love of his family or to commit to years of hard, arduous toil.

Had Shackleton been of a sedentary disposition, no doubt his life would have taken a different turn at this stage. However, there was something that constantly drove him to accept the greatest challenges and face the most difficult adventures. To Shackleton, the challenge was the thing, and one has the feeling that he lived in a state of continual conflict, always faithful to the endeavour and the fight, but never fully content with the result. In any case, he selected the difficult path, and he was formally indentured as an apprentice in the merchant marine.

Two months later he sailed again on *Hoghton Tower*, although under a captain who was a harsher disciplinarian than his predecessor. From Cardiff around Cape Horn to Iquique and back – it was the same trip, only worse. This time the ship's company included no one interested in literature or poetry. Moreover, there was only one sailor with whom he could discuss religion. On his first voyage, he had recorded that he was afraid he would be laughed at when he said his prayers, 'but the first night I took out my Bible to read they all stopped talking and laughing, and now everyone of them reads theirs excepting a Roman Catholic, and he reads his prayer-book.' On the second voyage, he could accomplish no such thing, as the captain gave no spiritual guidance, and the members of the crew were more inclined to drink and use foul language, 'making themselves', Shackleton noted, 'lower than the very beasts'.

At the age of only eighteen, Shackleton was being confronted with a change that would not only influence him, but would profoundly alter the character of British society. Like most members of staunch middle-class families, he had been raised to regularly attend church and habitually read the Bible. Traditional, fundamental Christian teachings had been seriously challenged throughout the nineteenth century by, first, the impact of geological and palaeontological discoveries and their influence on the understanding of the history of the Earth, and, second, the crisis in religious and scientific thought brought about by Darwinian theory. Never the less, until late in her reign, Queen Victoria's Britain remained one of the most religious societies in western civilisation. By the time Shackleton sailed on *Hoghton Tower* in 1890, this was beginning to change.

Some historians have suggested that to ignore the effect of Britain's particular type of Christianity on day-to-day Victorian life would be to render much of the period's history unintelligible. This is because,

ironically, much of the significance of Britain's brand of Christianity –
which, to use the term in the broad sense, could be called evangelicalism
– lay not so much in the spiritual kingdom as in the secular domain. The
evangelical belief structure laid a direct emphasis upon the conduct of
the individual, because, although it recognised grace and faith as
essential, it believed that salvation was a doctrine of works. There
were three key elements of this evangelicalism. First was its emphasis on
a literal reading of the Bible, which made the British a true 'people of the
book'. Second was its unquestioned certainty of an afterlife with
rewards and punishments for one's acts on Earth, and, therefore,
the acceptance that earthly existence was only important as a preparation for eternal life. And third – the logical progression from the second
– that in this life, pleasure, passion, and hedonism should be disre-
garded in favour of good works, charity, self-help, the enlightenment of
the heathen and the most Victorian of concepts: duty.

When considered in this broad manner, the term 'evangelical' did not
apply simply to individuals who were members of the Evangelical sect
nor to other supporters of low-church principles. Certainly such were
included, but perhaps the most remarkable aspect of evangelicalism in
the broader sense is how it broke down sectarian barriers and was
espoused by men of all creeds. It pervaded the beliefs, writings, and
actions of those considered high church, such as Gladstone; of the
convert Cardinal Newman; of the self-proclaimed agnostic T.H. Hux-
ley; and of the reborn Glaswegian Congregationalist David Livingstone. Even Disraeli, by birth as far removed from evangelicalism as any
major politician of the time, paid deference to it in his political and
administrative decisions.

Shackleton was never as stalwart in his evangelical religious beliefs as
two of his future colleagues, Edward Wilson and Eric Marshall. Thus,
aboard *Hoghton Tower* he began to lose some of the youthful fervour
that he had possessed when he belonged to the Band of Hope, a
children's temperance organisation. This transition was noted by his
family. 'I used to get very worried because Ernest didn't go to church,'
his sister Kathleen later recalled. 'I won't say it wasn't important, but he
didn't need certain parts of the church service . . . He did [go to church]
when he got back from sea . . . I remember him going to St Bartholomew Church . . . being very naughty, pretending to be very solemn,
and holding his prayer book upside down.'

Shackleton certainly did not make light of the secular evangelical

concept of duty, however. Through the decades this had been transformed from William Wilberforce's struggle against slavery or Lord
Shaftesbury's championing of the poorer classes to a means of moral
self-elevation for the entire Empire. By Shackleton's time, so certain
were Britons in the superiority of their faith and civilisation that they
believed it to be their duty, however difficult, to help the heathen and
bring new lands – populated or not – under British sway. 'In the Empire
we have found not merely the key to glory and wealth,' stated the
Viceroy of India, George Curzon, 'but the call to duty, and the means of
service to mankind.'

Thus, as Shackleton made his third voyage on *Hoghton Tower* –
which took more than two years – he felt a profound pride in playing a
role in the magnificent heritage of the Empire. Wherever he sailed, there
was a reminder of the courage of those who had won the Empire and
the indication of how the spread of British rule extended the benefits of
justice, trade, legitimate government, evangelicalism and good will.
From the Cape of Good Hope they went to Madras, where, amid weeks
of working cargo, Shackleton went rhinoceros hunting with the local
commissioner. Then, after falling seriously ill with fever while in
Mauritius, at their next stop he was nursed back to health by the
hospitable people of Newcastle, New South Wales.

That was almost Shackleton's final stop. Midway across the Pacific
they were struck by 'a whirlwind – a sudden gust, thunder and lightning, and before we could even shorten sail . . . we were on our beam
ends almost.' The fore-royal mast, top-gallant mast and top-mast came
crashing down, landing where Shackleton had been an instant before.
Within moments, the main-royal mast and the yard snapped and went
overboard, to be used by the sea as a battering ram against the ship. All
night the storm raged, threatening to capsize the ship or to knock a hole
in it. Finally, with the morning, the storm abated, revealing catastrophic
damage. For four days they cleared the wreckage and then, minus masts
and sails, they slowly made their way to Talcahuano, Chile, where they
learned that the ship sailing from Newcastle with them had disappeared. 'We were loaded with coal', one of Shackleton's shipmates
recalled years later. '*Woolton* [was a] four-masted ship, also partly
laden with coal . . . part cargo of tallow on board. She wasn't as deep in
the water as we were . . . . She turned over.'

Several months later, having been refitted, *Hoghton Tower* was again
demasted in a gale and had to limp back to Valparaiso. It was not until

July 1894 that Shackleton finally returned to Britain, his indenture complete. He soon started to attend a nautical school in London, and in October he passed the examination for second mate.

But even during such a time, when he was at home soaking up the adoration of his sisters and studying for his mate's exam, were the seeds actually being sown for his future in the far south? For who can tell the impact on a man not yet one and twenty years old when, immediately upon him reaching home, the newspapers were full of stories about an expedition departing for adventure and imperial glory, sailing for the frozen seas and unknown lands of the high Arctic.

On the surface, Alfred Harmsworth had many things in common with Shackleton. The eldest son of an English father and Irish mother, he was born near Dublin, but grew up in London after his parents, disquieted by Fenian violence, left Ireland in 1867. Although he was memorable for the lack of promise he showed in the schoolroom, his teachers still found him to be one of their brightest pupils. But whereas the sea caught Shackleton's fancy, Harmsworth had an early fascination with journalism.

As a young man Harmsworth contributed to *Tit-Bits*, George Newnes' pioneering weekly aimed at the lower end of the newly educated reading public and consisting of a melange of anecdotes, puzzles and articles featuring short paragraphs, short sentences and short words. In 1888, the twenty-two-year-old Harmsworth launched *Answers*, a halfpenny magazine that followed Newnes' formula, while adding to it an invitation to readers to ask their own questions. Whether truly from readers or not, questions such as 'Can Fish Speak?' 'Do Dogs Commit Murder?' and 'Why Don't Jews Ride Bicycles?' gave *Answers* an unlimited supply of material, and helped make it a huge success.

In 1894, as Shackleton rounded Cape Horn again and bobbed across the Atlantic, Harmsworth followed Newnes into the newspaper market, purchasing London's foundering halfpenny daily *The Evening News and Post*. He shortened the name to *The Evening News*, cut down on the amount of political coverage, and established a column for women. Within a year, the circulation had doubled. But Harmsworth went beyond changes in the presentation of the newspaper and followed the lead of James Gordon Bennett of *The New York Herald* in creating news himself, news that, like that of Bennett, related to the exploration of mysterious, new lands.

Believing that coverage of a British effort to reach the North Pole would boost sales, Harmsworth agreed to finance the Jackson–Harmsworth Expedition to explore the little-known archipelago of Franz Josef Land and find a route to the Pole. The other London newspapers also followed the expedition's preparations with something akin to idolatry, and one letter published in *The Times*, *The Daily Telegraph* and *The Evening News and Post* was bound to have caught Shackleton's eye. Written by the president of the Royal Geographical Society, Clements Markham, it stated: 'I cannot let you leave England without wishing you all possible success in the glorious, but most arduous enterprise . . . In your hands, for the time, is the Arctic fame. Your country and I feel sure that you will . . . worthily uphold British credit and renown.'

By the time Shackleton read this letter, the cult of heroism had experienced unrestrained growth in the Victorian mentality. The Queen had been transformed from a petulant, withdrawn widow to the symbol of a living Britannia. And amid a maturation of imperial myths, a veneration for heroic soldiers and explorers was being celebrated not only in the popular press, but via children's literature, songs and tableaux at music halls, imperial exhibitions, theatres and church sermons. As Jackson departed for the north, the polar regions were being brought very much to the forefront of British imperial thought.

Shackleton had his own future to think about, however, so, sporting his new second mate's certificate, he sought out Owen Burne, a friend from Dulwich who was a wine merchant, and who, therefore, Shackleton assumed would know the owners of ships. Burne took him to see Major Jenkins, the senior partner in the Welsh Shire Line, who offered him a position as fourth mate. It was only several days later, when he next saw Jenkins, that Burne heard the rest of the story. 'That's a rum fellow,' Jenkins said, indicating that Shackleton had been to see the ship and, as he did not like the fourth mate's quarters, had offered to go as third mate instead. But already Shackleton's outgoing, breezy personality was charming people of rank, so, Jenkins said, 'I rather liked the chap and gave it him.'

His new ship was *Monmouthshire*, a tramp steamer only slightly larger than *Hoghton Tower*, and in November Shackleton left London, bound for the Far East. One of the third mate's duties was to check and restow cargo at each port, and he now gained valuable experience for his later expeditions. After an eight-month journey, he returned home for a week in the summer of 1895, before rejoining *Monmouthshire* and sailing for China.

The year 1895 has been noted by historians as a watershed date, the events of which reflected significant changes in the British mentality. It was the year of the trial of Oscar Wilde, which triggered a public reaction against decadence. It marked the opening of the Kiel Canal, and its implicit statement of German naval power. It saw the retirement of the most long-lasting and dominant of British political figures, William Gladstone, and the defeat of his party in an election that emphasised the imperialism that had caught the fancy of the British public. And at year's end came the Jameson Raid, releasing a train of events that led inexorably to war in South Africa. But whether, as conflicting arguments have stated, this was a period of uncertainty or of hopeful anticipation, none of this would have had much impact on Shackleton, who was in Britain for only a week of the calendar year.

Even the significance of an event that would be closely related to his future was almost certainly overlooked as he crossed the ocean on *Monmouthshire*. On 24 January 1895 – the day that also marked the untimely death of one of the most magnificent spokesmen for empire, Lord Randolph Churchill – an event occurred that would help lead to British involvement in the Antarctic. Far to the south of New Zealand, a party from a whaling ship approached the shore at Cape Adare in Victoria Land, Antarctica. As the captain prepared to step ashore, one of his crew, Carsten Borchgrevink, leaped out and helped steady the boat. A Norwegian who had been living in Australia, Borchgrevink used this incident to claim to be the first man ever to land on the Antarctic continent. He had actually been beaten by some seventy-four years (the American sealer John Davis had landed on the Antarctic Peninsula in February 1821), but it was not to be the first time that a claim of dubious veracity would influence later events.

Coincidentally, it was during this same period that Shackleton, so he later stated, decided to become an explorer. The story is undoubtedly apocryphal, but he claimed that, between Gibraltar and New York:

> I dreamt that I was standing on the bridge in mid-Atlantic and looking northward . . . I seemed to vow to myself that some day I would go to the

region of ice and snow and go on and on till I came to one of the poles of the earth . . . I am sure my thoughts then turned to the North Pole, because it was more in men's minds . . . After that I never had any doubt that sooner or later I should go upon a polar expedition.

When Shackleton returned from his second trip on *Monmouthshire*, he spent two months at home, during which he passed his examination for first mate. He went back as the second mate aboard *Flintshire*, a much larger ship of the Welsh Shire Line, and fell into a pattern of spending three to four weeks with his family between cruises of four to seven months. He would arrive to find the family house bedecked in flags, cardboard messages and coloured greetings, all signs of his sisters' affection. He once asked them not to repeat the decorations, but he was not unhappy when they ignored his request.

'Ernest had one comprehensive name for the lot of us,' Kathleen later wrote. 'He used to call us his Harem. I suppose we spoilt him, at any rate we all loved him very much. Home from the sea on a hot summer's day he would fling himself on the sofa. "Come, my wives, you must entertain me. Zuleika, you may fan me, Fatima, stroke my ankles, and you must play to me" he used to say.'

It was during one of these brief, idyllic periods in Sydenham that Shackleton found the most intriguing challenge he had yet experienced. It came via a totally unexpected route – his sisters.

For the first twenty-three years of Shackleton's life, the only women who held a firm place in his affections were his sisters, mother and grandmother. That changed after July 1897, when, at the Shackleton family home, he met a woman who had become friendly with his sister Ethel – Emily Dorman. A tall, slim beauty with brilliant blue eyes and a smile at once alluring and quizzical, Emily had an ease about herself that was unusual for a woman in the reign of Victoria. She was one of six children of Charles Dorman, a successful solicitor, and his wife Janie, who had raised their three sons and three daughters in a comfortable and secure family environment, and had always encouraged Emily's interests in travel and the arts.

The week Shackleton returned to England – that of Queen Victoria's magnificent Diamond Jubilee – Emily was twenty-nine, six years older than the young seaman. She had a great deal of natural talent as an artist and a singer, and had been instructed in acting by Elsie Fogerty (who later founded the Central School of Speech Training and Dramatic Art, trained such actors as Laurence Olivier and John Gielgud, and became a pioneer of speech therapy). Sociable, intelligent and popular, Emily had, according to her daughter, received no fewer than sixteen proposals of marriage.

When they met, however, it seems that Emily was unhappy. One can assume she felt Shackleton was pleasant and interesting, a diversion from other thoughts. He had grown into an attractive man, his years of toil at sea having helped build great strength in his broad shoulders and barrel-chest, in spite of him being slim-hipped and having unusually small hands. He had a heavy-jawed but pleasing face, with intense eyes and long, curly eyelashes. Despite his physical appeal, an exuberant vitality and an indisputable personal magnetism, Shackleton, rarely a man of half measures, seems to have been smitten much more quickly than Emily. It is likely that, as he returned to *Flintshire* after too short a period in Emily's company, he had little interest in the humdrum tasks of the sea.

When he next returned home in February 1898, Shackleton wasted no time in pursuing Emily. In his two weeks of leave, they visited the National Gallery and the British Museum. They also spoke of their mutual love of poetry. Emily later recalled that Shackleton read a great deal of Swinburne and was particularly fond of Tennyson and Charles Kingsley, both of whom he could quote extensively from memory. However, he did not, he told her, particularly care for her favourite, Browning. She promptly gave him a pocket volume of Browning and he was soon converted. 'I greatly love and admire Browning,' he later said. 'I like his optimism, his note of "Never say die," the grand way in which he faces the future, his outlook upon the world. Yes, I think Browning is great.'

During his next cruise, Shackleton earned his master's certificate, which was awarded in Singapore. And during his leave, he spent as much time at Mr Dorman's summer home as in Sydenham. When he went back to sea, Shackleton was spurred on by a goal stronger than any he had yet encountered. So passionate was he that, despite the Victorian restrictions on sentiment, one night he expressed his feelings to a shipmate. At the time, there existed 'a marked standoffishness' between officers and engineers, but Shackleton spoke from his heart to the engineer of *Flintshire*, who later wrote:

'Well, Shacky,' I remarked one evening, 'and what do you think of this old tub? You'll be skipper of her one day.' 'You see, old man,' he said, 'as long as I remain with this company I'll never be more than a skipper. But I think I can do something better. In fact, really, I would like to make a name for myself' – he paused for a moment or two – 'and for her.' He was looking pensively over the sea at the moment, and I noticed his face light up at the mention of 'her.' In my bunk that night I felt convinced that the ambition of that man's life was to do something worthy – not only for himself, but 'for her.'

Despite Shackleton's desire for Emily, he was uncertain of her love, and a welter of contradictory letters did little to ease his tortured mind. For more than four months he virtually lived from letter to letter. There is little doubt that, in September 1898, the heartsick sailor was almost indifferent to one of the most sensational triumphs of Victoria's reign – Kitchener's annihilation of the Khalifa's forces at Omdurman.

By the time of Shackleton's homecoming in early December, the public's attention had turned to a confrontation with the French hundreds of miles up the Nile at an unknown post called Fashoda. Shackleton cared little, as he had thoughts only for Emily. He had hoped to spend Christmas near her – his first with his family since before he went to sea – but such was not the sailor's lot, and he sailed on Christmas Day for a voyage around Britain. It was to prove a short cruise, however, as on the night of Boxing Day *Flintshire* ran aground near Redcar.

After safety measures were taken, Shackleton was granted leave to go home for his father's birthday on New Year's Day. On the way, he stopped at the Firs, the home of the Dormans. 'We spent the evening in the billiard room,' Emily recalled years later.

He told me how he loved me – I was deeply moved – I remember so well – because he put his cigarette on a ledge in the big oak chimney piece – & it burnt a deep dent – which we tried to rub out – and we often looked at it in after days – but no one else noticed it! . . . I let him out through the conservatory about 10.30 I think and he kissed my hand – he went home then to wish his father 'many happy returns'.

Shackleton now believed that Emily would ultimately be his. The next step was to impress her father, and for that he needed better prospects. On 7 January 1899 he was discharged from *Flintshire* and shortly thereafter resigned from the Welsh Shire Line. He again turned for help to Owen Burne.

4

WAR OR AN UNKNOWN PLACE?

On Tuesday, 12 September 1899, Brevet Lieutenant-Colonel Sir Henry Rawlinson, second Baronet and son of the famed diplomat and Assyriologist, was asked if, on the next Saturday, he would accompany Lieutenant-General Sir George White on what was expected to be a brief excursion to South Africa. Rawlinson accepted with the same alacrity as if it had been an invitation to a social weekend with his fellow officers of the Coldstream Guards. 'Wednesday, Thursday, and Friday were spent in getting my things together though there was not very much to do in this way as all my Indian things were available,' he noted. 'I just had to replenish a few medicines and odds and ends of uniform; this together with the purchase of a Brochardt pistol really completed my preparation.' As a final measure, he 'arranged to sell my two horses at Tattersalls at the earliest opportunity'.

And thence it was away for what, Rawlinson no doubt imagined, would be another swift and successful campaign, such as the army had conducted against overmatched peoples around the world during the preceding fifty years. After a rapturous send-off at Waterloo Station, Rawlinson, Colonel Ian Hamilton and the other members of Sir George's staff joined their leader in a private salon that had been attached to the Bournemouth Express to take them to Southampton. And from there, on a still evening broken only by the flutter of flags and the cheers of friends and 'come find outs' on the quay, they passed down the Solent aboard the Castle Mail Packet Company ship *Tantallon Castle*.

The departure of Rawlinson and his fellow officers was a step in a remarkable series of political wranglings that for a century since has divided historians debating the origins of the war between the largest empire on Earth and two tiny nations: the South African Republic (or

Transvaal) and the Orange Free State. What can be stated with certainty is that the Secretary of State for the Colonies, Joseph Chamberlain, and the High Commissioner for South Africa, Sir Alfred Milner, had convinced Lord Salisbury's Cabinet that the best way 'to avoid war was to make preparations for it'. Since, as Chamberlain wrote, President Paul Kruger of the Transvaal would 'bluff up to the cannon's mouth' regarding concessions demanded by the British government, it was determined that the best way forward was to send 10,000 troops to Natal as a show of force. On the day before the first soldiers of the Queen left for Durban, White, a bitterly contested selection as commander of that force, sailed from Southampton.

The Castle Mail Packet Company was part of the elite of Britain's merchant service, and in 1876 it had been awarded a joint contract with its fierce competitor, the Union Steam Ship Company, to carry the mail between England and South Africa. The ships of both companies were large by the standard of the day, immaculately maintained, and, in the areas reserved for passengers, exceptionally plush. However, even the best ships struggle to overcome the capricious whims of nature, and the voyage of *Tantallon Castle* that September was no exception. Rawlinson and several of his colleagues were forced to remain in their cabins early in the voyage, although 'with the aid of a couple of liver pills and forcing a certain amount of food down, I got fairly well by the end of the 3rd day.'

It was only then that the man ultimately destined to command the British Fourth Army at the Somme was able to make a study of the other people aboard. They were, Rawlinson wrote in his peculiarly uncapitalised script, 'less interesting to me personally . . . a curious mixture of dutch, english, and semitic'. He thought the most intriguing passenger was the secretary to Francis Reitz, the former President of the Orange Free State. 'We were warned against this man when coming aboard as a "spy" so for the first few days we gave him a wide berth but later on when we got to know him he seemed quite a decent fellow.' The others, he evidently believed, were less absorbing. 'Mr & Mrs Savage are of Johannesburg,' he wrote, conscious of his national and racial superiority, 'she a jew – he an ass, but they have rather a nice child of about 21 years . . . Mr & Mrs Sinclair we thought were interesting people at first but they do not improve on acquaintance.'

With the promise of an exciting conflict on the horizon and few intriguing passengers about, Rawlinson was eager to reach Cape Town.

'The voyage is a very long and tedious job and one gets deadly sick of the confinement . . . The rest of the people aboard are a very uninteresting lot.'

That a figure with Rawlinson's social background and education – he had attended Eton and Sandhurst – should dismiss a lowly fourth officer was not in the least surprising in the class-conscious final years of Victoria's reign. But only a decade later that seemingly insignificant officer would be one of the most famous explorers in the Empire – Ernest Shackleton.

The previous January, shortly after resigning from the Welsh Shire Line, Shackleton had again landed on his feet with the help of Owen Burne. Indeed, a position with the Castle Mail Packet Company was a plum of which most merchant seamen could only dream, and his move from second mate to fourth officer was an impressive, and unlikely, promotion. But in late March, there was Shackleton, standing proudly in a smart blue uniform as *Tantallon Castle* departed on one of her regular trips from Southampton to Cape Town.

It took almost no time for him to make an impression. 'He at once went to the cabin allotted to him,' a shipmate later recalled about when Shackleton joined *Tantallon Castle*, adding:

> I remember he was not wearing an overcoat and had one or two books under his arm. When I went to his cabin to see how he was assimilating himself, I found him reading – but willing enough to talk. He put down a volume of poems – and said he had been looking at his friend Browning . . . My impression of him then was that he was distinctive and a departure from our usual type of young officer. Later on I found he was several types bound in one volume.

Shackleton's new position meant more prestige, better pay, and a regular schedule, allowing him to return home every two months. 'I saw a good deal of him . . . between his voyages,' Emily later wrote. 'We lived at Sydenham till 1901 – when we moved to London. My father liked him and was very kind to us both – but there were others who thought the friendship rather a foolish one and it had ups and downs – though he had such a serious feeling for me – and we had books – poetry and small literary aspirations in common.'

Even if others were dubious about the relationship, Shackleton had no doubts. The story is told that, just back from one of his voyages, he was travelling on the train to see Emily, and in the same carriage were several antique dealers also going to the Dorman house, where an auction was being conducted. The men began to discuss what they were hoping to purchase, one mentioning a grand piano and another Chippendale chairs. Finally, one turned to Shackleton and said, 'What are you going to get out of the old man?' Shackleton looked up solemnly. 'A daughter, I hope.'

Shortly before the sun rose high enough to cast its pale, golden light on the fissured flanks of Table Mountain, after some three weeks at sea, *Tantallon Castle* steamed into the harbour at Cape Town. White and his staff promptly disembarked and, after a day of frantic consultation with Sir Alfred Milner about the possibility of Boer commandos invading Natal, they hurriedly caught the evening mail train to East London, from where they would sail to Durban.

In the ensuing days, as Shackleton began the voyage back to England, White made a crucial blunder that would affect the entire opening stages of the war. General Sir Redvers Buller, commander of the First Army Corps and the officer selected to lead the full expeditionary force to South Africa, had advised White not to advance too far north, but to occupy a defensive position behind the Tugela River. Ignoring this, White proceeded into Natal's rugged northern triangle. It was a mistake of unmitigated proportion. As Rawlinson wrote:

> The Boers are thought to have some 15,000 to 20,000 men on the frontier all told. We have not more than 10,000 at present. Yet they are split up half at Glencoe and half at Ladysmith both of which are too far forward . . . only thing is to hold the line of the Tugela River and withdraw from Glencoe and Ladysmith. The situation . . . which we are going to take up is one which from a military point of view . . . courts disaster for . . . the Boers can . . . surround or annihilate either place in detail. If I were in Sir George White's place I would insist on withdrawing to the Tugela.

On 11 October, the Boers declared war, and within days they had besieged British forces at Kimberley and Mafeking. By the beginning of November, White had been trapped in Ladysmith.

Shackleton returned home shortly after to find the British public totally absorbed with the action in southern Africa. 'Our days are spent with reading our papers – ever clamouring for more,' one of Milner's female admirers wrote to the High Commissioner.

> In my lifetime, this state of tension is unique . . . it is no exaggeration to say we are all plunged in gloom . . . I shall never forget last Tuesday in London . . . Picture the newsboys at the corners . . . shouting 'Terrible reverse of British Troops – Loss of 2000.' Imagine the rush for papers . . . Carriages stopped at the corners for papers to be bought – bus conductors rushed with handfuls of pennies as deputation for their passengers . . . People walked along speaking in whispers and muttering . . . no one goes to the theatres – concert rooms are empty – new books fall flat – nothing is spoken of save the War.

Within a month, Shackleton was involved in the effort in a more direct way than his brief brush with Rawlinson. He was promoted to third officer and transferred to *Tintagel Castle*, which was assigned to transport troops to the Cape Colony. He sailed on 14 December, just as the Boers were administering three successive defeats – at Stormberg, Magersfontein and Colenso – which would jointly go down in British history as 'Black Week'.

Any young man of Shackleton's temperament would have been caught up in the patriotic fervour that swept Britain as the old century faded, the great outburst that banished differences between political parties and social classes, and welded the British people into a united front, ready to sacrifice for the Empire. Would he not have been as thrilled as the rest of the country when, only two days after his return home, Buller's forces relieved Ladysmith?

Soon Shackleton was again heading south, *Tintagel Castle* departing on another trooping voyage on the very day that the merger of the competing mail lines resulted in the registration of the Union-Castle Mail Steamship Company. Aboard were 1,200 men from the South Staffordshire Regiment, the Middlesex Regiment (Duke of Cambridge's Own), the Somerset Light Infantry, The Queen's, and a host of other units, including Lovat's Scouts, a volunteer corps of game-keepers, deer-stalkers and gillies. One of the senior officers was Captain Sir W.G. Barttelot, the brother of Edmund Barttelot of the Emin Pasha Relief Expedition. When Stanley divided his party far up the Congo River in the strange, unexplored Ituri Forest in the heart of Africa, he left Edmund Barttelot in charge of what became called the 'Rear Column'. But when Stanley returned, he discovered that Barttelot had gone mad and then been murdered. The brother aboard *Tintagel Castle* was also soon to be killed in action, but his presence on the ship might well have kept Shackleton thinking about an explorer's life.

Somewhere on the way south, Shackleton and the ship's surgeon, William McLean, decided to produce a small book commemorating the trip. It would turn out to be a wonderful little *memoire de voyage*, giving a detailed description of the ship, short biographies of various officers, menus from special dinners, a selection of poetry, and much more. In a brief article about the ceremony for crossing the equator, Shackleton showed an early talent for writing, as well as a typically British bias:

> An unexpected visitor now appeared in the person of Krüger, who had been discovered by a soldier concealed in a wash-house, the last place in which any one would have looked for him . . . He appeared ill at ease, for he feared that water, with which he was little acquainted, would soon be liberally applied to him.

The little book also gave the roll of every regiment aboard and provided information about the regular speed of the ship ($13\frac{1}{2}$ knots); the washhouses, which could accommodate thirty-six men at a time; and the regular rifle, revolver and Maxim gun practice on the back deck. It was ultimately published with the title *O.H.M.S. An Illustrated Record of the Voyage of S.S. 'Tintagel Castle'*.

While in South Africa, elated by his first literary effort, Shackleton tried to give it mass appeal. Also in Cape Town was an unrivalled advocate of the British Empire – Rudyard Kipling. An Indian-born journalist whose star had blazed forth while Shackleton was at Dulwich, Kipling had achieved, with both poetry and short stories, a rare combination of critical acclaim and popular support. Beneath Kipling's thinking and writing was a rock-ribbed evangelical belief. To him, imperialism was the incarnation of the missionary spirit, for the British race had the duty to rule the 'lesser breeds' or – as he coined a phrase in an address to the Americans, then involved in the Philippines – to take up 'the White Man's Burden'.

Knowing the drawing power of Kipling's name, Shackleton wrote to invite him to contribute a poem to the book. The next morning, to his surprise, he looked at his old ship on the other side of the wharf, and saw the instantly recognisable Kipling in his shabby grey suit and gold-rimmed glasses. Shackleton crossed to *Tantallon Castle* to speak to the author, who was awaiting the ship's departure but said that if Shackleton sent him the proof of the book, he would do his best.

The poem never appeared, but one can only wonder about the impression that the explosive energy and personal magnetism of the young officer had on Kipling, a man who could see deep into the imperial soul. Later that year Kipling completed his novel *Kim*, which he had been working on irregularly for seven years, and in it appeared passages that leapt out as being inspired by Shackleton.

When Shackleton arrived home at the end of May, he had missed by two weeks one of the most extravagant, hysterical, jingoistic outpourings of emotion in British history. 'It is good to be an Englishman,' wrote F.D. Baillie, the war correspondent for *The Morning Post*, who was actually at the relief of Mafeking, which set off the euphoric displays. 'These foreigners start too quick and finish quicker. They are good men but we are better, and have proved so for several hundred years.'

It was a note echoed around the country and the Empire. It was the sound of patriotism, an honest-to-God love of Britain, right or wrong. It may seem arrogant now, but one must remember how steady men's convictions were in the late years of Victoria's reign. It was not simply a case of toasting the Queen at dinner or humming *Rule Britannia* as the Earl of Rosebery, Prime Minister in 1894–95, did to fight off depression or ennui. Britons had an unquestioning love of country and monarch, and a willingness to sacrifice, to fight, even to die for them. At that moment, it made being a soldier a most noble profession.

There were factors other than patriotism that drew men to soldiering in late Victorian Britain, among them the call to adventure and the discovery of exotic, far-away places. Another was that it was a way to become a hero and to gain all that went with that status. Whether from noble background or baseborn, a soldier had a chance to attain the twin deities of fame and fortune.

Between the beginning of the nineteenth century and its end, the reputation of the military in Britain had been totally transformed. In the reign of George III, the army had consisted of those who had been impressed or had nowhere else to turn and had been willing to sign up for the minimum twenty-one-year enlistment. They had been flogged and maltreated by their officers, billeted upon the people, and used to quell civil unrest. Yet by the end of Victoria's reign, Lords Wolseley, Roberts and Kitchener were among the greatest heroes of the Empire, and the common solider, 'Tommy Atkins', had even surpassed Jack Tar in the hearts of the British public.

This change in public perception began in the Crimean War, when the gruesome conditions faced both on the battlefield and in the hospitals – and reported home for the first time – made the soldier an object of sympathy and concern. The Indian Mutiny saw a continued metamorphosis, as those in the ranks became heroic saviours of the besieged and the avengers of British honour. The Mutiny also helped generate the hero-worship so characteristic of late-nineteenth-century imperialism. Service to Empire, Christian militarism, chivalric nobility and Cromwellian fervour formed a potent elixir to the need for heroes, and Sir Henry Havelock in particular evolved in the public imagination into much more than a victorious general. The man whose statue still adorns Trafalgar Square became an evangelical knight, a defender of the faith as well as the Empire, and the scenes of his triumph and martyrdom, Cawnpore and Lucknow, were recorded in the collective imperial consciousness.

This form of Hero of Empire reached its apogee in one man believed to be fearless, incorruptible, and committed unto death: General Charles Gordon. A passionate Christian fundamentalist who shunned society because it interfered with his spiritual life, Gordon became a Victorian hero for his role in putting down the Tai-Ping rebellion, for suppressing the slave trade in the Sudan, and for what was seen as extending Christianity and western morality into the dark regions. His death at Khartoum elevated him from heroic to mythic status, the poet John Greenleaf Whittier writing that he was 'the nearest approach to that one Man, Jesus Christ, of any man that ever lived'.

After the death of Gordon – whom Wolseley called 'God's friend' – army recruiting increased dramatically whenever his name was used. However, despite the power of the Gordon myth and the broad appeal of the military, Shackleton never evinced a desire to become a soldier, even when his younger brother Frank went to southern Africa with the Royal Irish Fusiliers. It is likely that, at one level or another, he already had another imperial occupation in mind.

*   *   *

The concept of conquest is usually one closely related to military force. In 1890, however, former French Prime Minister Jules Ferry was thinking of something else when he stated, 'An irresistible movement is bearing the great nations of Europe towards the conquest of fresh territories. It is a huge steeplechase into the unknown . . . whole continents are being annexed.'

It was this 'forward policy' that had exponentially expanded the size of the British Empire in previous decades. To some, national prestige had become correlated with sheer dimensions in a perverse reversion to medieval thinking, when land had conferred prominence and power. To others, including Lord Salisbury, such simplistic ideas were crude, but there was no denying that when new regions were coloured pink on the map, there was a swelling of the chests of the British public.

As the 'New Imperialism' became closely intertwined with geographical expansion, explorers began to occupy a more significant place in the pantheon of empire – after all, what was exploration but the initial stage of the imperial process? By the beginning of the twentieth century, explorers were perceived by the public in much the same way as the military: brave heroes expanding or maintaining empire, bringing Christianity and civilisation to benighted peoples, and triumphing in the struggle against nature. The two professions were fused together in the public mind when, in his classic book *Small Wars*, Charles Callwell wrote that, 'it is perhaps the most distinguishing characteristic of small wars . . . that they are in the main campaigns against nature.'

The struggle against nature was a driving force in nineteenth-century Britain, brought about not only by the Victorians' constant striving for progress, but by a new perception of man's relation to, and dominion over, the world. A variety of causes – the technological successes of the Industrial Revolution, a resurgence of the Biblical notion of man as a force above nature, and the popularisation of Darwinian theory – led to the intellectual triumph of what was known as 'the conquest of the world'.

Man's role as conqueror of the world was a persistent theme in numerous facets of life, including technology, medicine, and science. But in geography, the desire for knowledge, combined with the attitude that not only *could* everything be known, but that it *should* be, made it a sufficient reason to go somewhere merely because no one had been there before. By late in the century, filling in the white spaces on the map, and thereby proving man's dominion over nature, had become a virtual obsession. As the American explorer Anthony Fiala summed up:

> Beyond the geographical and scientific value of the discovery of the North Pole, and the solving of questions of popular curiosity, another reason exists to explain the ceaseless effort to reach that mystic point: The Spirit of the Age will never be satisfied until the command given to Adam in the beginning – the command to subdue the earth – has been obeyed, and the ends of the earth have revealed their secrets.

Another essential Victorian belief was how exemplary lives could illustrate social and spiritual objectives and provide moral touchstones. The prime example of this was David Livingstone, considered a deliverer of Christian virtues to the heathen, an explorer who opened the way for trade and white expansion, and a saintly medical man who endowed his activities with such a striking righteousness that his moral force was reflected upon all who followed him.

Many later explorers proclaimed themselves inspired by Livingstone, and, as he did, combined religious zeal, desire for the conquest of the world and belief in the expansion of Empire. Explorers were also lured to unknown areas such as the polar regions and the centre of Africa by their beauty and perceived purity, their challenges to one's manhood or their capacity for allowing physical and spiritual freedom in areas so unlike the rapidly industrialising west. As Joseph Thomson, the explorer of Kenya, stated: 'I am doomed to be a wanderer. I am not an empire-builder. I am not a missionary. I am not truly a scientist. I merely want to return to Africa to continue my wanderings.'

However, many explorers were driven by the same reasons as those joining the army: the chance for fame and fortune. Explorers were looked upon as among the noblest of the land. Their names were known to all classes, their lectures were presented to standing-room-only crowds, and their books exerted an extraordinary power over people's minds. Not that the public truly wanted to know about the day-to-day difficulties and realities of exploration: the romance, adventure and thrills were why they went to lectures and bought books.

Exploration also provided opportunities attainable by anyone. The possibility of instant fame – such as that of John Hanning Speke or Henry Morton Stanley – or remarkable fortune was never far from the thoughts of an explorer. Nor, indeed, had it ever been, as Francis

Drake, Martin Frobisher or the other great Elizabethan freebooters would have admitted. Loot was such a basic part of exploration – and of imperialism – that the Liberal statesman John Morley once exclaimed, 'All this Empire-building! Why the whole thing is tainted with the spirit of the hunt for gold.'

Upon his return from his second voyage on *Tintagel Castle*, Shackleton was as interested in fame and fortune as the next man. He could not have believed that he was on the road to El Dorado, however, when for the next several months he was assigned to serve with the transport ships fitting out to take soldiers to southern Africa. He helped with the stowing of equipment and the embarkation of troops going off to honour and glory, but he must have felt he was doing little to gain those himself.

Through the summer, much of his spare time was spent overseeing the progress of *O.H.M.S.* He managed to obtain sufficient subscribers for it to be printed in July. To his great pleasure, a specially bound copy was presented to Queen Victoria. But even more important was the one given to Emily, inscribed 'E. to E. July 1900. The First Fruits'. There is little doubt that Shackleton saw this as the first instalment, albeit a small one, of what he could offer Emily and of the proof of his future prospects, which Mr Dorman demanded.

It is also clear that by this time Shackleton had not only given thought to the life of an explorer, but to participation on a specific expedition. He had recently become a Fellow of the Royal Geographical Society, and had shown considerable interest in an expedition to the Antarctic being jointly planned by the RGS and the Royal Society.

There have been varying opinions about exactly why Shackleton made a sudden change of career in applying for the British National Antarctic Expedition. There can be little doubt that his desire for fame and fortune played a major role. But there was more. One of his Union-Castle colleagues later stated:

'he was attracted by the opportunity of breaking away from the monotony of method and routine – from an existence which might eventually strangle his individuality. He saw himself so slowly progressing to the command of a liner that his spirit rebelled at the thought of his best years of his life and virility passing away in weary waiting.'

This is insightful, because Shackleton required a spiritual freedom greater than most. He was at heart a nomad, one of a group of nineteenth-century Britons for whom travel to the white spaces on the map – the jungles of Africa, the deserts of Arabia, or the frozen wastes of the polar regions – seemed the sole cure for an innate wanderlust, an uneasy hunger for change, an overmastering restlessness. He was forever on the surface wishing to be at home, yet never at peace until he was away.

But even more fundamental than appeasing his appetite for the unknown was the challenge from such an environment. Throughout his life Shackleton was driven by the need to test himself – which his position with Union-Castle no longer satisfied. To him, the struggle was an end of its own; he sought not just the fulfilment of challenge but the fight to accomplish it.

Ironically, as 1900 grew old, the greatest competition confronting Shackleton was not that of a faraway land but of winning Emily. Exploration could – and would – give direction to many aspects of his life, but he initially followed that course in order to gain her. Without a doubt, she was the catalyst for his entry into that world. As their daughter Cecily commented:

> he was going to lay the world at her feet, and be worthy of this very lovely . . . woman, with brilliant blue eyes and wonderful smile . . . He wanted to pour something out round her feet and say 'there you are you see, you've married a man who's making his own way in life and I've brought you back the goods'.

Believing it was the road to Emily, on 13 September Shackleton volunteered for the British National Antarctic Expedition. By the time he sailed to Cape Town in Union-Castle's *Gaika* in October he had not received an official answer to his application, but he was ever ready with a contingency plan. So before he left again for the Cape on *Carisbrook Castle* at the beginning of January 1901, he had decided he would use military tactics after all, and unveil his secret weapon.

5

THE MAKING OF THE BRITISH NATIONAL ANTARCTIC EXPEDITION

The twenty-first century is far removed from the era of Victoria. Today, science is so specialised it is difficult for the average person to understand; generals master news conferences rather than battlefield strategy, and 'explorers' are adventurers backed by sophisticated technology. However, a hundred and more years ago, men in such professions were larger-than-life figures, heroes with a level of fame rarely accorded now to those who are not athletes or pop musicians, and who received the respect of a range of admirers as diverse as members of the House of Lords and readers of the halfpenny press. As the nineteenth century gave way to the twentieth, Joseph Dalton Hooker, Lord Wolseley, Henry Morton Stanley and Francis Galton were still alive. As had been its preceding generations, late-Victorian society was populated by a race of giants.

One of the places where men such as these could mingle and discuss the unveiling of new lands and faraway events was a four-storey building on the corner of Saville Row and Vigo Street in Bloomsbury, which, since 1871, had been the home of the Royal Geographical Society. Founded in 1830 after a brief incarnation as a dining club, the RGS had become a focal point for exploration as well as for the scientific, ethnographic, and economic enquiry that accompanied it. Not only did the Society have the best travel library in the world, and the most impressive collections of maps and charts, it published records of new discoveries.

Even more important was the role the RGS played in encouraging and sponsoring exploration. During its first three-quarters of a century, there were three men who, through their positions within the Society, their outside prominence, and their single-mindedness, became the most significant individuals backing exploration in the nineteenth and early twentieth centuries.

The first was Sir John Barrow, the chairman of the Council of the Society, whose actual power base was his post as the Second Secretary of the Admiralty. For thirty years he was the force behind expeditions to areas as widely divergent as West Africa and the high Arctic. He also sent out a remarkable effort under Sir James Clark Ross from 1839 to 1843, on which Ross proved that the ice pack surrounding much of the Antarctic could be navigated, and that beyond it was a huge sea. Ross not only established a new record for the farthest south, 78°10′, but at the base of this sea discovered an island with two volcanoes that he named after his ships, Mount Erebus and Mount Terror. He then found one of the Earth's most amazing geographical features, the immense expanse of ice that came to be known as the Great Ice Barrier and that today is named the Ross Ice Shelf.

Barrow's legacy eventually passed on to Sir Roderick Murchison, one of the most renowned theoretical geologists in the world, who served a record sixteen years as president of the RGS. It was Murchison who transformed the Society into a key national institution, and he sponsored and helped fund expeditions in virtually all corners of the world.

But as someone able to set forces in motion, and to mobilise support or manipulate opinion, Barrow and Murchison were surpassed by the third of these men – one of the most formidable and dynamic personalities of exploration history, the cantankerous, devious, heavily be-whiskered Sir Clements Markham. Born (without the whiskers) in the year the RGS was founded, Markham joined the Royal Navy at fourteen, and six years later participated in a search for Sir John Franklin's missing expedition in the vast, unexplored Canadian archipelago. The search expedition failed in its primary goals, but Markham was greatly impressed by the spirit aboard ship and on the sledging parties, and by the winter programme of education and entertainment. Shortly thereafter, he resigned from the Royal Navy, but there is no doubt that his experiences had permanently shaped his beliefs regarding how a polar expedition ought to be conducted.

Markham later became a figure of consequence at the India Office, and in 1863 he was named honorary secretary at the RGS. Three decades on, he was appointed president of the Society after three other individuals had declined the offer. He immediately launched a campaign for the revival of British Antarctic exploration, which had lapsed after Ross' expedition.

Markham had previously been one of the key figures in a similar effort to revive British exploration in the Arctic. However, when that expedition had become a reality, it had been handicapped by a number of old, backward-looking Arctic veterans on the organising committees – Markham among them – who had ensured that it followed slavishly the use of outdated equipment and techniques from the Franklin search expeditions, helping lead to a disastrous conclusion. It was as if nothing had been learned in the previous decades; unfortunately, little more would be learned in the following ones.

Never the less, with the aid of John Murray, Britain's foremost academic authority on the polar regions, Markham now made increasingly persistent and urgent efforts to galvanise interest in an Antarctic expedition.

Two years later, on the evening after Shackleton returned from his first voyage on *Monmouthshire*, Markham presided over the opening of the Sixth International Geographical Congress in London. The proceedings included a day devoted to polar exploration and a paper by Carsten Borchgrevink, who put forward his claim to be the first man ever to set foot on the Antarctic continent. To Markham's delight, a resolution was passed stating that

> the exploration of the Antarctic Regions is the greatest piece of geographical exploration still to be undertaken. That, in view of the additions to knowledge in almost every branch of science which would result from such a scientific exploration, the Congress recommends that the scientific societies throughout the world should urge, in whatever way seems to them most effective, that this work should be undertaken before the close of the century.

After the Congress, Markham pressed even more actively for British involvement. His goal remained the same: that any expedition be under the auspices of the Royal Navy. In contacting the Royal Society, the Admiralty and the Prime Minister, Markham – caught hopelessly in a romantic past that had never actually existed – emphasised that naval officers would benefit enormously from such participation. Polar exploration would serve, he wrote, as 'a school for our future Nelsons, and as affording the best opportunities for distinction to young naval officers in times of peace'.

But Markham's appeals for recognition, funding and the loan of officers were time and again rebuffed, so in 1897 the RGS established its own independent expedition, committing £5,000 for such a purpose. Later that year the Royal Society joined in backing the undertaking, but financial progress remained slow, despite a contribution of £5,000 from Alfred Harmsworth, who had previously sent the Jackson–Harmsworth expedition to the Arctic.

In August 1897, a Belgian expedition left for the south, helping raise the profile of Markham's drive and generating considerable popular interest in the Antarctic. Any advantages, however, were soon offset by the dispatch of another expedition, this one emphasising its British origins. After a couple of years of ineffective efforts, the Anglo-Norwegian Borchgrevink had overnight raised enough money for an expedition. Aware of the economic benefits accrued by other newspaper owners who sponsored exploration, George Newnes had offered Borchgrevink £40,000. Newnes' largesse completely funded the expedition, including the purchase and outfitting of a ship that was renamed *Southern Cross*. Borchgrevink and his primarily Norwegian crew departed for the south in August 1898. Markham was incensed that money he felt should have been applied to *his* expedition should go to a 'foreigner' whom he considered 'unfit'. In a letter to the librarian of the RGS, Hugh Robert Mill, he described Borchgrevink as stupid but very cunning and unprincipled. For the rest of his life Markham made vitriolic attacks on the explorer whenever given the opportunity.

Meanwhile, Markham's efforts had made little progress. But in March 1899, prospects dramatically changed when Llewellyn Longstaff, a successful businessman and long-term Fellow of the RGS, offered £25,000 to launch the project. Other important prerequisites for the expedition quickly fell into place, and the RGS and Royal Society began developing plans for a purpose-built ship. In June a deputation from the societies made a plea to Arthur Balfour – Salisbury's nephew, the First Lord of the Treasury and effectively deputy Prime Minister – who responded positively. With his support, it was only three weeks later that the government extended an offer of £45,000 on the condition that it be matched by private subscriptions. The British National Antarctic Expedition had become a reality.

The financial security of Markham's expedition did not end the crossing of political swords, however. He and the RGS were now firmly in a partnership with the Royal Society, and it was not long before the two organisations found that their goals and plans for the expedition were decidedly different. A variety of joint committees were formed, the RGS representatives of which tended to believe that geographical discovery was the primary objective of the expedition, while those from the Royal Society felt its purpose was to engage in scientific research.

This difference did not become problematic until the first half of 1900, when two appointments set the scene for dissension over the issue of leadership. Markham still envisioned the expedition as primarily a Royal Navy enterprise, with a small civilian scientific party under the command of the ship's captain. However, on German and Swedish expeditions then being planned, scientists – Erich von Drygalski and Otto Nordenskjöld respectively – were to be in command. In February, this pattern seemed to be followed when the distinguished geologist John W. Gregory was appointed director of the scientific staff. Gregory was eminently well qualified, not only as a scientist but an explorer. In 1892 he had made a pioneering study of the Great Rift Valley and the glaciers of Mount Kenya, and several years later had joined Sir Martin Conway on the first crossing of Spitsbergen.

However, Markham had other ideas. These centred on the torpedo lieutenant of HMS *Majestic*, Robert Falcon Scott. Scott had first come to Markham's attention in 1887, when, as a midshipman, he had won a sailing race that Markham had been watching. A dozen years later, Scott applied to command the Antarctic expedition, and it is clear that Markham supported him as early as July 1899. In April 1900, after months of behind-the-scenes manoeuvring by Markham, the Admiralty announced that Scott and Lieutenant Charles Royds would be released from duty in August in order to become commander and executive officer. Howls of protest came from members of the Royal Society, but Scott's nomination was ultimately approved in May.

That same month, Albert Armitage was appointed second-in-command. A merchant marine officer then employed by the P&O Company, Armitage had been the deputy commander on the Jackson–Harmsworth Expedition, during which he had established excellent credentials as both an ice-navigator and a polar traveller. As a former recipient of the Murchison Medal from the RGS, he had already met Markham, and had also been warmly recommended by Harmsworth.

While construction of the ship *Discovery* proceeded in Dundee, Scott took charge of preparations for the expedition, although he initially had little active help, as neither Royds nor Armitage was immediately available. Even two shipmates coming from *Majestic* were unable to join him in London: Michael Barne, the second officer, would not return from the China station until the Boxer Rebellion was suppressed, and Reginald Skelton, the engineer, went to Dundee to oversee the installation of the ship's machinery.

But it was the *return* of an expedition member, rather than his absence, that set off a row that threatened the very existence of the venture. In December 1900, Gregory came back from Australia – he had been appointed professor of geology at the University of Melbourne – and expressed strong reservations about the draft instructions for the expedition, which placed the scientific staff under the command of Scott. The politely suppressed differences between the RGS and the Royal Society exploded as representatives of the latter made it clear they were appalled that science had been made subservient to a naval officer who 'has had no experience in either Arctic or Antarctic seas . . . has not as yet the slightest reputation as a naturalist, a geologist, or an investigator of glacial problems . . . and is without experience in the branches of science.'

Gregory also expressed fears about Scott's preparations, but Markham was intractable about the purpose of the expedition – and it was not scientific study. 'These mud larkers,' he had written derogatorily about the members of the Royal Society as early as the summer of 1899, 'coolly ask us to turn our expedition into a cruise for their purposes.'

The ensuing battles between the societies eventually began to prove too much for Markham, who was 'quite exhausted'. Late in the contest, however, he convinced Sir George Goldie, another inveterate intriguer who was a member of both the RGS and the Royal Society, to enter the fray on his side. Markham correctly assessed that Goldie, the power behind the Royal Niger Company, 'would turn the RS officials round his finger with perfect ease'. Within a brief period 'the Pilot', as Markham called him for his manoeuvring, led an offensive that resulted in Gregory's resignation.

Hugh Robert Mill later indicated that with Gregory's departure, the emphasis of the expedition shifted irretrievably from serious research to adventure. But it was not only to Markham that this was a most welcome development. Even as the struggle reached its climax, the fifth and final officer of *Discovery* was appointed – and Ernest Shackleton was more interested in adventure than science.

*   *   *

In the spring of 1900, while Markham pestered the Admiralty to confirm Scott as commander, Shackleton made his second voyage in *Tintagel Castle* and pulled together the snippets that would form *O.H.M.S.* Shackleton did not know it, but of those aboard, the man who would play the most significant role in his life, albeit indirectly, was a young lieutenant from the 2nd East Surrey Regiment by the name of Cedric Longstaff. It was a year before that Longstaff's father had made Markham's dream possible, when he had donated £25,000 to the RGS.

On the surface, Shackleton did not have overwhelming reasons to be considered officer material for the British National Antarctic Expedition. He had more experience of sail than the Royal Navy officers, which could be important, since, to save coal, it was intended that *Discovery* make ample use of the wind. He was also a Fellow of the RGS. But these likely would have counted for little had he not also had the patronage of someone to whom Markham felt deeply indebted.

Throughout his life, whenever Shackleton faced a challenge, he took it on with an energy that allowed him to overcome enormous odds. His goal of serving on *Discovery* was no different. While in England between voyages, he took time to visit Cedric Longstaff's father. Llewellyn Longstaff was no doubt delighted to speak to anyone who had spent time with his son. It can also be assumed that Shackleton was at his most charming – and few could withstand his spell. The result was that Longstaff willingly took up Shackleton's cause when the younger man told him he wished to participate in the expedition that owed so much to Longstaff's munificence.

By January 1901, Shackleton's fortunes were on the rise. Longstaff had spoken to Markham about his desire for Shackleton to be taken on, and Markham had passed this to Scott. According to Armitage: 'Scott said that he had no time to attend to it, so . . . would leave the matter entirely in my hands.' Armitage made enquiries and found that Shackleton was considered 'more intelligent than the average officer . . . a very good fellow, always quoting poetry and full of erratic ideas.' On 17 February, two days after his twenty-seventh birthday, Shackleton was appointed the expedition's junior officer.

The life to which Shackleton returned in March 1901 showed all the hallmarks of an entirely new era. After nearly sixty-four years on the throne, Queen Victoria died on 22 January, and with her passing an epoch had closed. Swept away seemingly overnight were many of the restrictive mores that had long repressed British society. Victoria's rakish son and heir, Edward VII, brought with him a worldliness gained as much through cards, cigars and scandal as by the perusal of ministerial reports. This change extended to other aspects of the new Britain as well. In October 1900, at the instigation of Joseph Chamberlain, an early election had been called to capitalise on the patriotic emotions of military victories in South Africa and China. The 'Khaki election' had returned the rapidly ageing Salisbury to power, but high-minded students of politics were appalled at the extirpation of 'fair play' in calling an election simply because the government was popular. Similar notions of 'not quite cricket' also blew in from South Africa, where a war that the British public had been assured by Lord Roberts was 'practically over' continued to drag on, with the Boers – and even their wives and children – engaging in a new, unchivalrous form of combat: guerrilla warfare. These new concepts all contributed to Edwardian society's teeming flurry of thought and action.

Shackleton, working at the expedition office at London University near the centre of the city, found himself in the midst of this seething exuberance, and he immediately melded perfectly with it. 'I thought him extremely boyish and almost extravagantly enthusiastic,' Armitage said about his understudy. 'He had certainly kissed the Blarney stone and would, I believe, have become a great Journalist if he had taken it up . . . He had a great flow of talk, never being at a loss for a word.'

The father of the expedition was equally impressed by the young man who had been forced upon him. 'Scott was fortunate in finding such an excellent and zealous officer,' Markham wrote. 'He is a steady, high principled young man full of zeal, strong and hard working and exceedingly good tempered. He is remarkably well informed considering the rough life he has led.'

Shackleton now became an important component in the preparations for the expedition. His virtually limitless energy saw him involved in a multitude of projects, and he was charged with compiling the library, obtaining materials needed for entertainment during the winter and, most importantly, using his merchant marine expertise to oversee the stowing of supplies. *Discovery* had been launched less than three weeks after Shackleton returned from his Union-Castle voyage. On 14 May her engines were tested in measured conditions off Arbroath, and she responded excellently. Shackleton must have been pleased with the new ship, particularly as, the week before, *Tantallon Castle* had run aground on Robben Island off Cape Town while trying to navigate through a fog. Although everyone aboard had been rescued, the ship had been a total loss.

In June *Discovery* was brought to the East India Dock in London, and, as more supplies arrived, Shackleton increased an already busy workload. Included was a trip to Aldershot, where he and four others were taught how to inflate and operate an observation balloon, a piece of equipment currently proving its usefulness in the Boer War.

The total cost of the balloon and the sixty gas cylinders needed to fuel it was prohibitive – £1,380. However, Shackleton's charm proved an important adjunct to the expedition. According to one of his sisters, when visitors were being shown around *Discovery* one day, Shackleton noticed two ladies on their own. He asked if he could guide them through the ship, and they were so impressed and flattered by his pleasing attentions that one asked if there was anything the expedition required. He said they still needed £1,000 for the balloon, and shortly thereafter she contributed that amount. Her name was Elizabeth Dawson-Lambton, and she would reappear to encourage Shackleton throughout his career.

There is little doubt that Shackleton threw himself into all these new challenges with vigour. And there is even less doubt that in his mind grew the certainty that the expedition would be his making – not only would it lead to fame and fortune, but those, in turn, would lead to Emily. Perhaps the most important consideration of this period was that for the first time he was near her for an extended duration: the Dormans had recently moved to South Kensington. Certainly the courting couple had ups and downs – another, longer-term, suitor was also present – but it was perhaps Shackleton's regular attentions at this time that swung the balance in his favour. By June, Markham recorded that 'Shackleton had his fiancée and her two sisters' visit the ship.

The great adventure began on 31 July, when *Discovery* sailed from the East India Dock. Waiting for their brother to pass were Shackleton's three youngest sisters. 'We were armed with semaphore flags (Ernest had taught us signalling),' Kathleen later recalled, 'and as he passed we saw Ernest bring out a white handkerchief, then turn to someone, borrow another, then he signalled three times "Goodbye Helen, goodbye Kathleen, goodbye Gladys" in strict old nursery order of precedence.'

From London, *Discovery* proceeded to Cowes, where, on 5 August, King Edward VII, Queen Alexandra, and a number of other dignitaries came aboard to inspect her. Shackleton could have had few prouder moments as he stood in his new naval uniform, Markham having obtained for him a commission as a sub-lieutenant in the Royal Naval Reserve.

He must also have been pleased that participating in a review by the King could only help his pursuit of Emily. Just two days before he had finally written a letter to Mr Dorman asking for his daughter's hand in marriage. In the same letter, he had also opened his heart about his plans and prospects. 'As for me my future is all to make but I intend making it quickly. I would have spoken to you myself before only Emily had not given me a full answer. Now I feel it is all right so am asking you not now but when I have made money or position and money to marry her.'

It would not be until the post from home caught up with the slow-moving *Discovery* that he would find Mr Dorman's response had been positive. Now all Shackleton needed was success in the frigid, mysterious south – which was soon to capture his spirit in a way he had never foreseen.

6

THE GREAT WHITE SOUTH

'We set all sail to a fair though light wind,' Shackleton wrote on 16 August 1901, after *Discovery* left Madeira, 'but found that the ship steered badly, there being too much sail aft, and not enough forward. I am afraid this is unsatisfactory, and will be a serious matter when we get down south.'

They had left England little more than a week before, but already Shackleton and his colleagues had found to their chagrin numerous 'serious matters' with regard to their new home. *Discovery* used far more coal than had been planned, and when under sail she was sluggish and difficult to manoeuvre. But the barque's most worrisome problem became a crisis after they departed Madeira. At that stage, she was found to be not only full of faults, but full of water. Charles Royds, the executive officer, had reported leaks numerous times while still in London, but he had been 'poo poohed' and 'told not to worry or cause trouble'.

On 23 August, however, Royds recorded, 'Shackleton went down into the main hold, and was nearly terrified out of his senses by seeing or hearing water, and ran straight to the Captain, who at once began to panic.' The water in the main hold was nearly head-high, and cases of food three-deep had been 'soaking and are now black and slimy and stinking'. Shackleton was put in charge of clearing the holds and restowing the stores, and his long experience stood him in good stead. Throughout the following days, as rain poured down outside, the entire crew, including the scientists, were pressed into service. It was a filthy and rancid job, particularly as the dockers in London had opened food tins and then discarded them partially eaten into the area where the bilge water gathered, creating a rank, fermenting stench.

Despite the unpleasant duties, Shackleton maintained his poetic temperament. 'I see wide fields of waving corn, long grasses and budding heads of clover,' he wrote in the midst of reorganising the stores. 'It is dawn and the mists are lying in the valley and on the hillside . . . I feel once more the warm stillness of high noon,' In his mental wanderings, Shackleton was possibly not only hearkening back to home but to the departure, only days before, of a new friend.

Hugh Robert Mill had been a late, if welcome, addition to the scientific staff of *Discovery*. The newly appointed director of the British Rainfall Organisation, Mill had been invited to accompany them as far as Madeira to train officers and scientific staff in measurement and data collection. Not only had he been a positive influence on the entire wardroom – the centre of activity for officers and scientists – but he had established a particularly close friendship with Shackleton.

Mill was a small, delicate man, who had suffered from tuberculosis as a child and was subject to intermittent illness throughout his life. But attached to this frail body with the large, drooping moustache were a shrewd mind, a dry humour and a generous disposition. He and Shackleton quickly discovered in each other a deep love of poetry, a romantic soul and a source of endless enjoyable conversation. And Mill found in the strong, outgoing third officer someone through whom he could vicariously enjoy those adventures for which his brave spirit yearned. They soon developed a friendship that would last the rest of Shackleton's life.

While aboard, Mill carefully took the measure of his new friend. When, two decades later, he wrote the first biography of Shackleton, he recalled that in learning to measure the density and salinity of sea water, the younger man 'found the minute accuracy required rather irksome, and was long in grasping the importance of writing down one reading of an instrument before making the next.' This impatience and desire for an easily understood result was a basic part of Shackleton's make-up. Mill also clearly comprehended why Shackleton was aboard *Discovery* in the first place: 'To Shackleton the National Antarctic Expedition was an opportunity and nothing more. He would have tried to join just as eagerly a ship bound to seek buried treasure on the Spanish Main, or to scour the Atlantic in search of the Island of St Brendan.'

Quite the antithesis of Shackleton was another shipmate with whom he established a close friendship. A Cambridge man, Edward Wilson had studied medicine at Gonville and Caius, but his real interests had tended toward being a naturalist, and his artistic skills in this direction were remarkable. Although Shackleton enjoyed the ordinary pleasures and dissipations of the normal young men of his time, such trifles were not for Wilson, whose life was dominated by the practice of a Ruskinian ascetic ideal and of evangelical Christianity. Wilson was quiet, thoughtful and modest, although not humourless, and he carefully considered both his goals and the correctness of his actions. By any measurement he met the Victorian notion of what a young man ought to be: steady, abstemious and respectable.

Despite being rejected by the Admiralty Medical Board, which viewed him as not fully recovered from tuberculosis, Wilson's zoological skills and personal attitude were such that, regardless, Scott and Markham offered him the position of assistant surgeon. Wilson jumped at the opportunity – his desire to go was emphasised by his sailing only three weeks after he was married – and once aboard, his suspect stamina turned out to be a phantom, as he demonstrated an unrelenting capacity for work.

Early on, Wilson noted that Shackleton 'has quite taken me in his charge and puts me up to endless tips and does no end of things for me.' The two also found a mutual passion for poetry, and Shackleton took to rousing Wilson when there was an especially beautiful sunrise. In his more reserved way, Scott also was impressed by Wilson, and he, like Shackleton, found that underneath the cool and rather formal exterior there was an appealing charm.

Scott and Shackleton do not seem to have had any such mutual bonhomie, although there are indications that Scott was favourably impressed with his junior officer early on. Certainly the two would have been divided both by the traditional competition between Royal Navy and merchant marine and by the differing mentalities and social status of the services. 'There was always that feeling amongst Merchant officers in those days that they were being looked down upon,' James Dell, a naval rating, later said, adding that Shackleton 'was looked upon by all these as just a cargo-shifter'.

Such a view was not surprising at a time when the Royal Navy was still the pride of the Empire. In the middle of the nineteenth century, it had been the most advanced and powerful force of war that the world had ever known. By the reign of Edward VII, it was still the largest navy on the seas, although it was no longer unquestionably supreme in technology, strategic training or equipment. But the loss of naval hegemony had not yet affected the self-satisfied smugness of the Senior Service and many of its officers, who were happily beleaguered by tradition and former glories. Innovation in line officers had been curtailed by convention and a rigid adherence to decades-old methods. Appearance seemed to count most of all: swords were worn at sea, brasswork was maintained in gleaming condition, and ammunition was occasionally thrown overboard to prevent having to practise with the cannon, as their blast could blister the paintwork. This was the mentality with which Scott, Royds and Barne had reached adulthood. 'There was the Navy, in those days, living on the tradition of Trafalgar and all that sort of game,' Dell recalled, 'and thought of nothing else but bright-work and paint-work . . . it was the same thing with that expedition . . . they were just about as unprepared for that sort of job as they were for the war.'

Shackleton was thus totally different from his fellow officers, such as Royds, who was described as 'absolutely Navy from top to toe'. Barne later referred to Shackleton as 'a grand shipmate and good company . . . a great raconteur'. But to those on the lower deck, 'he was rather an enigma . . . He was both fore and aft, if you understand, due to the fact that he didn't fall in with all the views of all the Naval officers. And he never did.' It was a distinction that would ultimately be strongly felt.

To many who have spent time in the Antarctic reaches south of New Zealand, there is no memory as wondrous as the first sight of the pack ice, the wide belt of floating, closely packed sea ice that encloses the Ross Sea and the areas near the coast. To the uninitiated, the pack ice marks a seeming desolation that can feel vaster and emptier than anything else imaginable. It is not, of course: it is teeming with life both in the water and the air. But nothing is more mesmerising than the ice itself, a white surface stretching on and on until it blends into the horizon and one cannot tell what is sky and what is not.

This was the scene as *Discovery* ploughed carefully forward in early January 1902, the creaking and snapping of the ice announcing her grudging progress. At other points, she moved slowly backwards, and then thrust ahead at full speed, a violent and sudden stop sending judders throughout, indicating that it would take more than one assault to burst through that part of the pack.

With all of this around him, it is somewhat surprising that Shackleton did not record his emotions in his usual descriptive terms. Perhaps his mind still dwelt in his homeland; it had only been in late November, upon arrival in New Zealand, that he had learned Mr Dorman had died and Emily was now totally free. Or perhaps it was because, as Louis Bernacchi – the expedition physicist who had previously wintered with Borchgrevink – stated: 'although Shackleton was always alert for any new interest, energetic, full of flashing new ideas (many of them impractical), an omnivorous reader, and earnest student of poetry, an amateur astronomer, chiefly of the stars in a poetic sense, Antarctica to him did not exist.'

This assessment is not so extraordinary as it might seem. As one studies diaries of polar explorers, one of the most remarkable aspects is how seldom they were touched by the beauty or grandeur of the landscape. To most, the remarkable colours of the ice, the unveiling of the mountains blue in the distance, the soft light of the early morning could not compare to the 'picturesque' aesthetic with which they had been raised. As one British explorer wrote, drawing on the picturesque aesthetic, no 'object was to be seen on which the eye could long rest with pleasure, unless directed to the spot where the ships lay, and where our little colony was planted.'

Not that many explorers had previously reached the area that *Discovery* now entered – or, indeed, even tried. Antarctica had been a theoretical concept since the time of the ancient Greeks, but through the centuries in which Asia, the Americas, Australia, and the interior of Africa were opened to Europeans, the frozen south remained an enigma. After James Cook was the first to cross the Antarctic Circle in 1773, several waves of exploration helped fix the location of the continent. The most successful expedition was led by James Clark Ross at the same time that French and American efforts mapped other parts of the coastline.

Little geographical progress was then made until Borchgrevink and his small party wintered at Cape Adare at the northern tip of Victoria Land in 1899. The following spring Borchgrevink made a short trip on the Barrier, during which he had established a farthest south of 78°58'S.

Now, some two years later, *Discovery* followed in Borchgrevink's wake. On 9 January the members of Scott's expedition landed at Cape Adare. It was the first time any of them other than Bernacchi had set foot on Antarctica, and the vast Adélie penguin rookery they found on the small shingle spit would not have encouraged those with delicate sensibilities. 'There were literally millions of them,' Wilson recorded. 'It simply stunk like hell, and the noise was deafening.'

The ship proceeded south, examining the coastline. Then for more than a week they sailed slowly along the seaward wall of the Great Ice Barrier, surpassing Ross' most easterly point before, on 30 January, they spied a previously undiscovered peninsula, which they named King Edward VII Land. Here, Shackleton was finally caught by the excitement of geographical discovery: 'It is a unique sort of feeling to look on lands that have never been seen by human eye before.' Shortly thereafter, concerned by ice that threatened to trap the ship, Scott turned back towards McMurdo Sound, where the entire company would winter with the ship.

On 3 February, along the Barrier, they 'docked' at a natural quay that sloped down to the water's edge, a place they called 'Balloon Bight'. Armitage and Bernacchi led a small party man-hauling to the south, while others made efforts to learn how to use skis. A month previously, many of them, including Shackleton, had donned the unfamiliar equipment for the first time. That endeavour had not been an overwhelming success, and, although Scott, Skelton and Shackleton now made an investigatory journey to the south, there was still room for much improvement, Scott noting, 'skiing did not prove such good sport as was expected'.

The next day they brought into use an even more unusual mode of transportation: the balloon, which had been named 'Eva'. Much of the morning was spent inflating Eva with nineteen cylinders of gas, after which Scott claimed the honour of being 'the first aeronaut to make an ascent in the Antarctic regions'. He rose to about 550 feet, and, after rather hurriedly and nervously descending, was replaced in the basket by Shackleton. The third officer then rose to 650 feet and took the first aerial photographs in the Antarctic. Upon Shackleton's return, others made ascents, although Wilson firmly refused to participate in what he described as 'perfect madness'.

Discovery now steamed down McMurdo Sound, at its southern end reaching a long cape near to where Ross Island abutted the Barrier. Just north of the tip of Cape Armitage, as they named it, was a protected embayment, where Scott decided the ship could winter. While a hut was built, the downhill ski training continued, although Scott noted that skis would 'be of little use for men dragging'. This expectation and a lack of practical experience in the cross-country technique explained why, when a short while later the first party was sent south on a reconnaissance, they were man-hauling.

On 19 February, Shackleton, Wilson and Hartley Ferrar, the geologist, left the base at Hut Point and headed south towards a small island that had been spied from Observation Hill, near where *Discovery* was moored. In the grand old tradition so beloved of Clements Markham, the sledge they hauled was decorated with each man's 'sledging flag'. That Shackleton was part of the effort was as much luck as anything: Scott had allowed Shackleton and Barne to toss a coin for the privilege, and the third officer had won. Wilson determined that their destination was no more than five or ten miles away, and that they would easily reach it during the day. It was only one of many errors that they and their colleagues would make while learning about this unknown environment.

All day long, with only a brief break for lunch, the threesome hauled a back-breaking load comprising the sledge, tent, camping and cooking materials, two weeks' food supply and a 'pram', a small lifeboat taken in case they should come to open water or the sea ice break up. For most of the afternoon they churned through heavy snow blown in their faces by the first Antarctic blizzard they had ever experienced. Despite facing whiteout conditions – which made it difficult to know where they were going – they continued to slog ahead at a mile and a half per hour until, shortly before midnight, 'simply done', they camped.

Only someone who has tried to put up a tent in a heavy wind – or, worse yet, in the midst of wind-blown snow – can appreciate what the three novices now went through, as they erected their primitive tent in the continuing gale. Once inside the tiny enclosure, they made dinner with the primus stove none of them had ever used before, and tried to warm their painfully cold toes, fingers and faces. Then came the least pleasant part of the experience: struggling into wolfskin sleeping suits that had been brought rather than sleeping bags. 'They dressed me first, as I was constantly getting cramp in my thighs,' Wilson recorded, 'and having dressed me, they put me on the floor and sat on me while they dressed each other . . . We lay on our jaeger blouses, but the cold of the ice floor crept through and the points of contact got pretty chilly.'

After a miserable, and short, night, they rose at 3.30 a.m. to find the sky clear but White Island – as it would soon be named – still a long way off. Four hours later, their progress was stopped by crevasses, but after a sleep they left their gear behind and proceeded. Virtually every step was exceedingly dangerous, and it took them seven hours to cross the two miles to the island and then ascend to the top. The resulting view was worth the pain, however. The 2,500-foot summit gave a grand and unexpected sight, about which Wilson wrote:

> As far south as the eye could see was a level ice plain, the true Great Barrier surface, and no Antarctic continent at all. On our west was the coast line running west in a series of promontories as far as we could make out, promontories formed by splendid ranges of ice and snow covered mountains.

This was the first extended vision of the Barrier and the initial one of the farther reaches of the magnificent Transantarctic Mountains. The door to the road south had been opened.

The following day, the three men explored the southwest end of the island. Helped by fine weather the day after that, they marched north for eleven hours, arriving at Hut Point in time for a late bath and a dinner of sardines and cocoa. Then, wrote Wilson, 'we slept the sleep of the just'.

Well, perhaps *he* did. Shackleton, on the other hand, was, according to Royds, 'full of talk as was expected'. Indeed, one can imagine the glee with which he returned, having achieved the first major geographical success of the expedition. As Skelton recorded, he 'immediately started in with tremendous accounts, – & hardly stopped talking until everybody had turned in'.

Although the inexperience of Shackleton, Wilson and Ferrar had been highlighted when they continued to travel in whiteout conditions, they had suffered no ill consequences. One of the members of another early sledging trip was not so lucky.

In early March two sledging parties, led by Royds and Skelton, headed toward Cape Crozier on the eastern corner of Ross Island. Several days later, due to bad weather, Royds and Skelton continued, but sent one party back to the ship under Barne. As the exhausted men neared base, recklessly trying to reach the ship in the midst of a gale, they were split up in a swirling snow and three disappeared, including Barne. A short while later, while trying to make a descent, seaman George Vince was unable to stop on the slick surface and shot over the edge of a cliff into the sea. As the officer-less group waited, uncertain what to do, a short, wiry seaman named Frank Wild quietly but firmly took charge. Wild carefully led his messmates back to *Discovery*, reported the events and then guided a rescue party under Armitage to where the tragedy had occurred, in the process finding Barne and his companions. Although Vince's body was never discovered, a total disaster had been averted due to the leadership, bravery and cool judgement of Wild.

The son of a clergyman, Wild had been born in North Yorkshire in April 1873, and like Shackleton was the second child and eldest son in a large family. Also like Shackleton, he was broad-shouldered, power-fully chested, and had gone to sea in the merchant navy at sixteen. In 1900, after almost a dozen years on merchant ships, he had joined the Royal Navy as an able seaman, and the next year he had applied for a position on the British National Antarctic Expedition. He had not expected to be selected because he was trim in figure and slightly less than five feet, five inches tall. 'There were over 3000 applications from the Navy alone,' he later wrote, 'and greatly to my surprise I was chosen when hundreds of fine six footers were left behind.' But Wild was no ordinary AB: he not only had remarkable physical strength and endurance, he was comparatively well-educated, was a serious thinker, and wanted to learn and improve himself. And that is where Shackleton came in.

As the winter drew on, day-to-day life was increasingly confined to a small area near *Discovery*, on which the ship's entire company lived throughout the expedition. The scientists and officers had regular duties relating to taking observations and making measurements. But the crew was not slack either, as Wild noted:

> Apart from keeping the ship clean, bringing in ice for water from a nearby glacier, fishing through holes made in the ice, killing and skinning occasional seals that managed to get on to the ice near us and taking regular meteorological observations etc. there was a lot of work to be done in altering our sledging equipment, which had proved unsatisfac-tory on our early journeys.

But Wild still found time to study navigation.

'It was certainly not at Scott's suggestion that any help was given to Wild,' Clarence Hare, the wardroom assistant, later recalled. 'Naval routine was rather strictly observed . . . there should be no fraternising between officers & men of the lower deck. Shackleton was RNR and did not abide by this unwritten law.' One result was that Shackleton was the most popular officer among the crew, and another that he developed a particularly good friendship with Wild, to whom he gave guidance in his navigational studies.

Shackleton also proved his worth in other ways through the autumn and winter. He was in charge of all stores, including food supplies, and it was his duty to arrange, weigh and pack all sledging rations for the coming season. He was also the editor of *The South Polar Times*, a monthly periodical that was to be, according to Armitage, 'something like a London magazine'. In reality, it was more a cross between *O.H.M.S.* and a public-school magazine, but that did not matter either to its audience or to the two key figures in its production, Shackleton and Wilson. Both were naturals, Wilson with his unlimited artistic ability and Shackleton with his 'aptitude for satire, for bantering his companions . . . always done without malice'.

Once selected editor, Shackleton threw himself into the project, writing articles and poetry, soliciting other pieces – humorous, scholarly and satirical – accepting and editing the hopeful submissions, and generally bestowing it with creativity, enthusiasm and vitality. He cleared out one of the stores in the hold and made it an office, where he and Wilson would spend hours working, Shackleton's wit and vision matched by Wilson's talent with pen and paints. The first issue came out on Wednesday 23 April, when 'the sun disappeared from our view for 121 days and the long Antarctic night has commenced'.

Throughout that interminable period of shadow fading into darkness, Shackleton and Wilson were as thick as thieves. Not only did they spend large amounts of time on *The South Polar Times* (four more came out that winter), but their diaries show regular trips to their own informal meteorological station. 'Went with Shackle to the top of Crater Hill' became a frequent refrain in Wilson's diary.

The junior doctor did not restrict himself to a friendship with Shackleton, however. He also had a great admiration for Scott, who, in turn, found in Wilson a man in whom he could confide and whose opinions he could trust and respect – a significant discovery for one placed in the lonely position of leadership. Although Shackleton 'is still my best friend,' Wilson wrote to his wife, 'The Captain and I understand one another better than anyone else on the ship, I think. He has adopted every one of my suggestions. It's a great help to have one's ideas appreciated by a man who is always trying new and knacky things on his own.'

So, in retrospect, it is not surprising that, on 12 June – in the midst of winter and, had they known it, only two weeks after the war in South Africa had finally ended – Scott asked Wilson if he would accompany him on the paramount journey of the expedition, the trek south the next summer. There were a good number of sledging trips planned, but Scott had decided to lead the southern one, taking either one or two men and all the dogs. Regardless of whether anyone else came, Scott wanted Wilson. The request caught Wilson off-guard, as he, like the rest of the ship's company, had been kept in the dark about Scott's plans. 'My surprise can be guessed,' he wrote. 'It was rather too good a thing to be true it seemed to me. Of course I reminded him that I hadn't got a clean bill of health and that if either of two broke down on a three months' sledge journey it would mean that neither would get back . . . I then argued for three men rather than two.'

The argument was sound, and Scott agreed that the party should consist of three men. He asked Wilson who the third should be, but the surgeon felt it wasn't his place to suggest anyone. Then, according to Wilson, Scott said that 'he need hardly have asked me because he knew who I would say, and added that as a matter of fact he was the man he would have chosen himself. So then I knew it was Shackleton, and I told him it was Shackleton's one ambition to go on the southern journey. So it was settled and we three are to go.'

Scott never publicly recorded his reasons for selecting Shackleton as the third member of the party, but certainly Wilson's friendship with him was one. Another would have been that the former merchant officer had shown himself to be resolute, energetic and resourceful. He also exuded overwhelming confidence and appeared to have all of the physical attributes necessary for the onerous task of man-hauling.

Strangely, the only doubter was Wilson. 'I feel more equal to it than I feel for Shackleton,' he wrote to his wife. 'For some reason I don't think he is fitted for the job. The Captain is strong and hard as a bull-dog, but Shackleton hasn't the legs that the job wants; he is so keen to go, however, that he will carry it through.'

Wilson kept his reservations to himself, because he would not interfere with his friend's selection. Besides they would need to focus on the goal, which, as Wilson recorded, 'is to get as far south in a straight line on the Barrier ice as we can, reach the Pole if possible, or find some new land'.

The Pole if possible! One can imagine Shackleton's elation the next day when Scott asked him, in confidence, to be the third member of the southern party. Undoubtedly the only negative was that he could not yet tell his comrades. But he would have time for that. In the meanwhile, he knew he was heading south: south to glory, south to his future, south to the Pole.

7

THE SOUTHERN JOURNEY

'A calm morning, but overcast,' Edward Wilson wrote on Friday 22 August 1902. 'At 12 went up harbour hill with Shackleton where we saw the sun, the whole sun, and nothing but the sun for a bit, for it was a great joy to see it again quite clear of the horizon and quite free of clouds.'

It was still too dark – and certainly too cold – for extensive travel, but the sun had announced the coming of spring in a glory only matched by the radiant relief of those who had not seen it for months. The occupants of the ship poured outdoors with a burst of energy meant to finalise all the little details of the sledging operations to come. Unfortunately, although efforts had been made throughout the winter to overcome problems that the autumn journeys had uncovered, certain difficulties now encountered were brought about because various *major* issues had not been properly resolved.

The previous month, as light began to extend across the sky for a portion of the day, Scott had put Shackleton in charge of the dogs for the southern journey. Although a necessary selection due to the limited size of the southern party, it was an unfortunate choice. Shackleton knew absolutely nothing about dog-driving and, although he approached the task with confidence, he lacked the basic patience required for any slow training process. He probably adhered to the adage that the British sailor could accomplish anything through improvisation, and it must have been frustrating when he found that dogs had minds of their own. In fact, nothing he tried – cajoling or crooning, blaspheming or beating – made them behave as he wished.

The truth is that Shackleton was no more unprepared than his colleagues, none of whom had any idea of how to drive dogs properly, an ability that takes years to develop. The underlying problem extended all the way back to London, and to the prejudices of Clements Markham against dogs and in favour of man-hauling, as had been done in the Arctic half a century before.

While preparing for the expedition, Scott had travelled to Christiania (now Oslo) to consult the Norwegian explorer and scientist Fridtjof Nansen. Nansen was the most accomplished and respected of polar explorers, as well as the most innovative and intellectual, and asking for his advice was part of the preliminary work for virtually all polar expeditions, north and south.

Nansen had given Scott recommendations about sledges, cookers, tents, clothing for sleeping and travelling, skis and dogs. Scott accepted most of Nansen's advice, but, unfortunately, Markham's wheedling about the dogs – in conjunction with Scott's sentimentality toward creatures he saw as pets rather than draught animals – had won out over Nansen's experience. That, and Markham's meddling, had meant that not only were too few dogs taken (twenty-four as opposed to three times that many by Borchgrevink) and that they were the wrong kind (western Siberian rather than the preferable eastern Siberian ones), but that they had not been considered a key part of the sledging plans.

This self-fulfilling prophecy was confirmed in April 1902 when Scott took the dogs on a short depot-laying exercise. With no experience in driving them, he was disappointed in their unwillingness to pull heavy loads, their unruly behaviour and their fighting among themselves. Scott and Shackleton were not the only members of the party with little comprehension of dogs. Petty Officer Edgar Evans, writing under the pseudonym Rhossilly, confessed to The South Polar Times that: 'I was under the impression from books . . . that a sledge journey was quite a sporting affair, and all one had to do was to walk alongside the sledges, and the dogs done the pulling part of the business, but I was quickly undeceived.'

Much of this ignorance and its associated problems could have been resolved by including an experienced dog-driver on the expedition, although Markham certainly would not have given that his blessing. Nevertheless, even without such an individual, spending more time learning the skills through the winter would have been beneficial. This, with the advantage of hindsight, Bernacchi noted years later:

competitions in making camp, including all the multifarious duties to be performed in a tiny tent before toggling down for the night, might advantageously have taken the place of moonlight football matches during the comparative idleness of the winter, and competitions in dog-driving would have taken the keen edge off our ignorance of that most important accomplishment.

Thus, on 2 September, when Scott led the first of a series of short sledging journeys designed as practice for the longer trips, Shackleton still had not gained any particular expertise. This was not only due to the unsuitability of his disposition for the assignment and the short time period, but because he had continued to carry out his usual scientific and editing duties, as well as attempting to be an inventor. Throughout July and August, with the assistance of Barne and the ship's carpenter, Shackleton secretly planned and constructed a new mode of Antarctic transport: his 'rum cart'. This was a sledge consisting of two rum barrels serving as large wheels under the front and back ends of a frame designed to carry a load. When he conducted his first public tests, the result provided great amusement for the ship's company, which 'scoffed unmercifully'.

Meanwhile, Shackleton's too-obvious pleasure at being selected for the southern journey was annoying his messmates, particularly Royds and Skelton. 'While they are preparing, the ward-room becomes a simple nursery,' Skelton wrote. 'Shackleton "gassing" & "eye-serving" the whole time, – ponderous jokes flying through the air . . . of course the Skipper's ideas are on the whole perfectly right . . . but . . . why he listens to Shackleton so much beats me, – the man is just an ordinary "gas-bag".'

Several weeks later Scott and Shackleton were out on their final depot-laying trip when Skelton's assessment was proven wrong – Shackleton and his merchant marine colleague Armitage clearly under-stood something that had escaped the Royal Navy officers and their surgeons. And that something was a matter of life and death.

Although the suffering it had caused went back much further in time, scurvy had become one of the most feared killers in the maritime world when Europeans first engaged in long-distance ocean voyages in the late fifteenth century. In the intervening 400 years, many people had discovered how to prevent or cure scurvy, but always it had reappeared, confusing the medical profession and making its practitioners incor-rectly reassess its cause. Thus, the history of exploration saw scurvy appear again and again.

It is known today that scurvy is a deficiency disease brought about by a lack of vitamin C (ascorbic acid). It is characterised by swollen and bleeding gums with loosened teeth, soreness and stiffness of the joints and lower extremities, bleeding under the skin and in deep tissues, slow wound healing and anaemia. However, a century ago vitamins were unknown and theories relating to the cause and prevention of scurvy were in a state of pandemonium.

There had long been anecdotal evidence – and even a limited amount of scientific data – linking the cure for scurvy to fresh vegetables or fruit, particularly oranges and lemons. Despite a continuing litany of theories about its cause, the most effective treatment in the early nineteenth century had been the issuing of lemon juice, which had virtually eliminated the scourge from the Royal Navy. However, in the 1840s the Admiralty replaced Mediterranean lemons with West Indian limes for the preparation of the juice. Unfortunately, the new fruit had only a fraction of the vitamin C of its predecessor, causing a mysterious reappearance of the disease. The question of scurvy in the polar regions was further confused because native peoples – and some explorers – managed to live scurvy-free on a diet with few fruits or vegetables but much fresh meat (which is a source of vitamin C).

In the years immediately before the departure of *Discovery*, a new theory was popularised, stating that if meat was not properly preserved, micro-organisms would contaminate it and would chemically change the albumen, fat and carbohydrates to ptomaines (alkaloid chemical products reported to be poisonous). Moreover, before the meat had gone so bad as to be repugnant to the senses, the bacteria could produce the ptomaines; thus it was slightly tainted meat, and not the meat that was obviously bad, that caused scurvy.

Although there was abundant evidence that scurvy could not simply be related to tainted meat, this theory received the support of Lord Lister, the president of the Royal Society, who had achieved fame for studies involving bacterial contamination during surgical operations. Following Lister's lead, Scott, Wilson and senior expedition surgeon Reginald Koettlitz accepted the ptomaine theory. Indeed, shortly before sailing, Koettlitz wrote: 'The benefit of the so-called anti-scorbutic is a delusion . . . That the cause of the outbreak of scurvy in so many polar expeditions has always been that something was radically wrong with the preserved meats, whether tinned or salted is practically certain. An animal food is scorbutic if bacteria have been able to produce ptomaines in it . . . otherwise it is not.' The safeguard on the expedition, therefore, was to examine every tin of meat before it was used.

Armitage, on the other hand, had noted on the Jackson–Harmsworth Expedition that the crew of the ship had suffered from scurvy, but the members of the land-party had not; the latter ate large amounts of fresh polar bear meat. Armitage made the assessment that fresh meat would ward off the disease, so he asked Scott to have fresh seal served regularly. Shackleton, too, although without Armitage's practical experience, believed in the value of fresh meat as a preventative and, as the officer in charge of stocks, attempted to have it provided for the men daily.

Unfortunately, Scott did not totally concur, and fresh seal meat was served only two or three times per week. Even that did not help as much as it might have, as Charles Brett, the dirty, foul-tempered cook, prepared it in such a way that virtually no one would eat it. When the lack of fresh meat was combined with tinned fruit and vegetables that had lost much of their vitamin content in the canning process – and more when cooked by Brett – the men's supply of vitamin C slowly ran down throughout the winter.

In late September, Armitage returned from a two-week excursion in the mountains of Victoria Land with, he feared, half his party suffering from scurvy. He proved correct: the problem that had its beginnings at Hut Point had been exacerbated because the sledging ration was based to a great extent on pemmican. This was an item originally prepared by Cree Indians, who pounded dried strips of meat into a paste, mixed it with fat and berries, and then pressed it into small cakes. Pemmican had been adopted as an easily transported food by French voyageurs and British traders in the North American sub-Arctic and, later, as the main sledging ration for the Royal Navy's polar expeditions. British-produced pemmican, however, had eliminated the fruit and had become a concentrated mixture of dried meat and fat or lard, and therefore was virtually devoid of vitamin C. It was a form of this that had been ordered for the *Discovery* Expedition.

The main meals of the sledging parties consisted of 'hoosh'. This was a thick, soup-like concoction made by melting the pemmican with water, and adding bits of hard biscuits fortified with gluten. For flavouring, the hoosh could also contain bacon, cheese, pea flour, sugar or oatmeal, and other sledging rations included chocolate, cocoa and tea.

When Armitage returned, Scott was still on a sledging trip, as was Koettlitz. But when Wilson confirmed that scurvy was showing in all six men, Armitage sprang into action. He ordered that fresh seal meat be served to all hands each dinner, that lime juice be placed on the mess tables, that porridge and meat be served at breakfast, and that extra bottled fruit, potatoes and vegetables be supplied. He also called in Brett and, with a combination of explanation, threat and bribery, encouraged him to serve food in a palatable manner in the future. The change in the cook was instantaneous, and Armitage's programme quickly improved the health of the men.

When Scott and Shackleton returned to Hut Point on 3 October 1902, the captain continued the procedures Armitage had initiated, as well as cancelling all use of tinned meat and ordering a massive disinfecting of the ship. Further, in order to improve the health of those comprising the sledging parties, he postponed the date of departure for the southern journey. Because of this, and also due to changes in Armitage's proposed journey, there would not be as many members in the southern support party, nor would they or the southern party itself stay out as long as originally planned. They would, it appeared, be unlikely to reach the Pole. Never the less, the southern journey remained the highlight of the expedition, and everyone waited anxiously for its start.

In later years, Armitage would recall the changes wrought in Shackleton during this period, and would express no reservation about what the driving force was for them. 'Several times during the winter in the South he would amuse us by pretending he had been to the Pole,' he wrote, 'and how he was received by all the crowned heads in Europe, and by all the principal Societies.' But those around him could see Shackleton becoming a different man. 'He was greatly influenced by the romance of his engagement and marriage,' Armitage continued. Emily 'was, no doubt, mainly responsible, together with the life of open spaces, in raising him from a rather dreamy, ambitious boy, with no settled ideas, to a man of strong character.'

And it was of Emily that Shackleton thought until the final moments before he left on the journey south. On 30 October, Barne led the support party toward the Barrier to the cheers and, for the first several miles, with the escort of a number of the ship's company, for whom the occasion had been declared a holiday. The next day was supposed to be the final one before the southern party departed, and Shackleton – perhaps facing his mortality, perhaps realising even more than usual her value – wrote a letter to Emily that was to be read only if he did not return.

> Beloved I hope you may never have to read this, but darling loved one if it comes to you, you will know that your lover left this world with all his heart yours my last thoughts will be of you my own dear Heart. Child I am carrying your little photo with me South and so your face will be with me to the last: Child remember that I am your true lover, that you and you alone have been in my heart and mind all this time. Beloved do not grieve for me for it has been a man's work and I have helped my little mite towards the increase of knowledge. Child there are millions in this world who have not had this chance. You will always remember me my own true woman and little girl. I cannot say more my heart is so full of love and longing for you and words will not avail. They are so poor in such a case. Child we may meet again in another world, and I believe in God, that is all I can say, but it covers all things: I have tried to do my best as a man the rest I leave to Him, and if there is another world and He wills it we shall find each other. I feel that there must be. This cannot be the end, but I do not know, I only believe from something in me. Yet again I cannot tell if there is, I hope. Child you will comfort those at home. Know once more that I love you truly and purely and as dearly as a woman can be loved. And now my true love goodnight.

This letter shows not only Shackleton's grammatically eccentric, stream-of-consciousness writing style, but a very typically Victorian dominance of the man, as demonstrated by his regular mode of address to Emily as 'Child' – despite she being six years older than he. This would last throughout their life together, although he would always remain equally dependent upon her emotionally. The letter also reflects his desire to comfort the woman he loved, as there is little doubt that by this time Shackleton had minimal belief in God and saw no practical use in organised religion. His assurances to Emily were designed to soothe and console rather than to express the kind of belief that was apparent in the writings of Wilson. In this, Shackleton was closer to Scott, about whom Wilson had commented, 'Only once have we got on religious subjects, but I soon found that his ideas are as settled in one direction as mine are in another, and our only agreement was that we differed.'

But any similarity of religious view between Scott and Shackleton was to prove an irrelevancy on the harsh journey on which they were about to depart. It was to be the differences that were more significant. Indeed, that Scott, a physically relentless, self-willed, impatient man with a remarkably inquiring mind beneath his Royal Navy rigidity, should have selected as his confrère someone so entirely contradictory to him as Shackleton is the epitome of irony. Not since Richard Burton had taken John Hanning Speke as his companion to Lake Tanganyika had such an ill-matched selection occurred. For, although subordinate to him, Shackleton was in no way servile to Scott. Indeed, he was the very reverse, and this in the end was the problem: instead of a follower, Scott found a rival.

The journey that ignited this rivalry finally got underway on 2 November 1902. Following photographs being taken of the 'three polar knights', they were off in a burst of speed, glory and excitement, sledging flags waving in the wind. The dogs made such light work of the loads for the first several miles that everyone seeing them off had to trot to keep up and, ultimately, men had to sit on the sledges to slow them down.

Late that afternoon the efficiency of dogs was demonstrated when the threesome caught up with Barne's man-hauling party. For the next several days the two parties, working on different schedules, passed and were passed by each other. But it was not until the third day that Scott and Wilson donned the skis they had brought, which Wilson found a great relief for his aching knees and hamstrings. At about the same time, Wilson complained of a nasty cold, which he evidently passed on to Shackleton, who began to suffer from a 'most persistent & annoying cough'.

On 10 November, after a day Scott, Wilson and Shackleton spent in the tent impatiently awaiting the end of a blizzard, they reached Depot A, the stockpile of food that had been cached at the southern extent of an earlier journey. Two days later, the entire party of fifteen camped at a more southerly latitude than anyone had previously reached – Borchgrevink's record had been broken. The next morning, half the support party turned back and, on 15 November, Barne began the return to the ship with the others.

The excitement of finally being on their own on the open way south did not last long for Scott and company. Scott had recorded the dogs were 'pretty done', and the poor creatures did not improve when Barne departed, the three men and their team making only three miles. The next morning the dogs could not even get the loads moving and, according to Scott, 'after a few yards of struggling seemed to lose all heart, and many looked round with the most pathetic expression as much as to say we were really expecting too much of them.' Faced with a problem they did not understand how to resolve, the men decided the only alternative was the back-breaking task of relaying.

Although Scott and his companions have been criticised for not comprehending why the efficiency of the dogs suddenly failed just when they lost the support party, the answer was actually due to a complex combination of reasons. Most importantly, no one understood dogs or dog-driving. The animals had not been efficiently used from the beginning, being harnessed in a single team to a long train of sledges rather than being divided up into several teams, each pulling fewer sledges with a more efficient system of traces. Then, with the sudden acquisition of the supplies that had been hauled by the support party, the men were asking the dogs to pull far more than people more conversant with their abilities would have done. In addition, there was now no one to break the way for the dogs, which pull much more willingly and efficiently if there is a path to follow. As Scott and his companions would realise in the days ahead, the dogs' diet – like their own – was not sufficiently nourishing to allow for optimum work. Scott also suspected that a change in the surface conditions had made the sledges harder to pull.

Thus, for the next thirty-one days the party had to relay: moving half of the supplies forward before returning for the rest, gaining only one mile for every three travelled. During this time the men joined the dogs in the traces, which exhausted them. Despite this, the dogs did not perk up, 'losing all their spirit', according to Scott, and making 'as much fuss over drawing the half load as a few days before they had done over the whole one'. Progress to the south diminished to only four to six miles daily, and the high hopes for a historic southern record began, as Scott noted, 'steadily melting away'.

There were also other problems. Scott, Wilson and Shackleton were still inexperienced with skis, and particularly with their use in hauling sledges, and subsequently did not use them to full advantage. It has been noted that at this same time Otto Sverdrup, high in the Canadian archipelago, was demonstrating the relationship between skiing and the use of dogs for sledging. Although Sverdrup made major advances on this front, his lessons had not yet reached the outside world, so it is unfair to damn Scott for lacking such knowledge. However, it *is* clear that, with some preparation, Scott and his companions could have been more efficient. In 1897 Sir Martin Conway – who the previous year had achieved the first crossing of Spitsbergen – had returned to the Arctic, where he learned to ski. 'The common idea in England is that the art of using ski is very difficult of acquisition,' Conway wrote in his expedition account, which was brought south on *Discovery*. 'This . . . is a mistake.' Despite never before having seen skis, Conway travelled through the glaciers and mountains of Spitsbergen on them, pulling a sledge. 'Without ski,' he wrote, 'progress in any direction would have involved intolerable discomfort and labour.'

Then again, just completing the day-to-day tasks of life on the Barrier – such as pitching camp – was excessively difficult and unpleasant. When the three men stopped in the evening, they first unfastened all of the gear from the sledge. One man crawled inside the unfixed tent and opened out the legs, while another pulled the corners out the correct distance and piled snow on them to anchor it down. With these secure, the inner man organised the floor cloth, which was not an integral part of the tent, while the outer man placed snow all around the foot. The third man, meanwhile, unpacked the sledge, filled the cooker with snow for melting and put fuel in the lamp.

Perhaps the most unpleasant ordeal, however, was changing into evening and sleeping clothes, which they had to do outside in order to avoid bringing snow in the tent. While on one of the early sledging journeys, Royds gave an extensive description of what it was like.

Having taken off your wind covering blouse and put your jaeger blouse on you start in with the foot gear. Your fingers are at once nearly frozen off in taking off the burberry leggings, which require bare fingers to undo and clear away the lacings, so you have to shove your hands into your mitts again to warm up, and the mitts in the meantime have become frozen and hard, and are no joy to get into . . . My night shift consisted of a pair of bed socks, which all day you have carried next your skin so as to be warm and dry to put on, a pair of human hair socks which you also carried next your body during the day, a pair of fur socks, with fur inside, and then your pimi's which are long fur boots, fur outside, reaching above the knee. Fur trousers came next, and then the big fur blouse. All these things are very nice to put on when they are soft and pliable, but after a short time in use, they become hard and stiff, and it's the devils own job to get into them. Round my neck I wore a comforter which had been inside and round my waist during the day, and on my head I had a balaclava helmet, which I never took off from the time I left the ship to the time I returned . . . After shifting [dressing] one was invariably puffing and blowing like a grampus, with fingers with no feeling left in them . . .

. . . the sides of the tent if touching your furs, send the cold right through furs and all. For a pillow I used to use my jaeger blouse, and over my feet I used to put my burberry wind blouse. The tent after a few days out gets coated with ice, and every time it shakes, down on your face comes a shower of ice and frost crystals. Not at all nice. At night I always wore a bib . . . as all your breath collects round the neck of the fur coat, and after a time this gets like a sheet of iron, and is beastly when it comes to putting it on at nights. Sledging is certainly not any joy.

Such an existence, combined with the tedious inching toward the south, must have disappointed all of them, particularly as both Scott and Shackleton tended toward impatience. Certainly there was a thrill of discovery, since everything they saw was new to the human eye. There was also an incredible majesty to the vast nothingness, leading Shackleton to write, 'What a little speck on the snowy wilderness is our camp, all around white save where the shadows fall on the snow mounds, and the sun shining down on it all.' But the overwhelming emotions must have been frustration and dissatisfaction, states of mind that could – particularly in conjunction with the pettiness and irritation that constant enforced proximity can cause – lead to disharmony.

There has never been any firm proof that there was a serious falling out between Shackleton and Scott on the journey south. The argument for it has been made with certainty and denied with equal confidence. The strongest case for it lies within a statement written two decades later, but which is clearly hearsay. But the acceptance of such discord does make later events and the interactions between the two men more understandable.

Shackleton and Scott had disparate – although equally strong – personalities. According to Hugh Robert Mill, Scott was 'at his best' when everything was as he planned, whereas he 'was at a loss to extemporize a new line of action when the well-laid plan went crookedly.' Shackleton, on the other hand, was, according to a number of those who knew him well, essentially a boy all his life. He had the enthusiasm of a boy, the romantic disposition of a boy and the fiery temper of a boy. On the *Discovery* Expedition, according to Bernacchi, 'he permitted no liberties . . . and could be brutally truculent if such occasion arose.' It may have been this combination of Scott's frustration at their lack of progress and Shackleton's direct and tempestuous approach that prompted a break between the two men that lasted through endless bitterness and tragedy to the attainment of the Pole.

The whole thing came about – according to Armitage, who wrote that he had been told of the incident by both Wilson and Shackleton – in a virtually haphazard fashion, which, as is so often the case, set off a totally unexpected chain of events. One morning during the southern journey, the story goes, Wilson and Shackleton were packing the sledges after breakfast, when they heard Scott shout, 'Come here you bloody fools.'

They went over to him, and Wilson quietly asked, 'Were you speaking to me?'

'No, Billy,' said Scott.

'Then it must have been me,' said Shackleton, who then awaited a response. When one was not coming, his temper got the better of him. 'Right,' he said, 'you are the worst bloody fool of the lot, and every time that you dare to speak to me like that you will get it back.'

Scott would not have put up with such a comment had he been anywhere but more than a hundred miles from the ship, and it could be expected that he would not have forgiven his subordinate for it, so this story would certainly provide an explanation for their future actions. It must, however, be noted that Armitage, who wrote about it to Mill after all three members of the southern journey had died, felt unfairly treated by Scott. He appears to have become more outspoken with the years, so the story could well be apocryphal.

On the other hand, even if the story did not unfold in this precise manner, the gist of it could well be true. Frank Debenham, a geologist on Scott's final expedition, later commented:

> I fancy there were divergences of view between them . . . I remember trying to get something out of Wilson about what happened and his 'cageyness' on the subject did more than anything to persuade me there

had been an incident . . . With [Shackleton's] volatile temperament and
Scott's comparative rigidity, it would be surprising if there were not
'words' once or twice when the party were in a parlous state.

Thus, it was probably not a very congenial party that marched steadily
southward, becoming the first men ever to pass the eightieth parallel on
25 November. Three weeks later they lightened their load by caching
supplies at Depot B, which allowed them to move ahead without
relaying. And on 30 December, they camped at what they figured to
be 82°17′S. As they faced north, they had before them a long, debilitating journey back to Hut Point, on which they would not only have to
struggle against time, progressive weakness, and a lack of food, but
scurvy and Shackleton's deteriorating condition.

'A beautiful day, but a sad one indeed for me,' Shackleton wrote on 1
March 1903, 'for today I left my home and all those who are chums . . .
I cannot write much about it, but it touched me more than I can say
when the men came up on deck and gave me 3 parting cheers.'
    The entry was one that Shackleton would not have foreseen writing,
because it described his leaving the Antarctic – and *Discovery* – on a
long, slow, lonely trip back to England, via New Zealand. His prospects
had certainly changed since that Tuesday less than four weeks before
when he, Scott and Wilson had returned to Hut Point, completing a
journey that had been difficult for each of them, but that was truly
touch-and-go for Shackleton. They had quickly learned not only of the
arrival of *Morning*, a relief ship sent by Markham, but of the news of
the outside world: the death of Cecil Rhodes, the end of the South
African war, and the elevation of Arthur Balfour to Prime Minister.
    But the most important thing they had learned was that, despite it
breaking out slowly, there were still miles of ice between *Discovery* and
open water. As February passed – and the three members of the
southern party recuperated – it became apparent that the ship would
have to winter again in the Antarctic. Scott – secretly pleased by the
development – wanted a trimmed down party, and he allowed anyone
to go home who wished to. All the merchant sailors chose to go.
    Shackleton was a different matter. In mid-February, Scott informed
him that, due to his medical condition, he would be invalided home.
Koettlitz had examined Shackleton, and had agreed with Wilson that his
breakdown had been due to scurvy. However, Koettlitz indicated that

Shackleton was practically recovered; in fact, he seemed much stronger than Wilson, having led a party bringing back stores from *Morning* on 16 February, well before the junior surgeon was healthy enough to be far afield. But Scott imposed health conditions on his officers that were more stringent than on the scientific staff, which meant that Shackleton would go home, while Wilson was allowed to stay.

Needless to say, Shackleton was extremely disappointed, as, according to Wilson, 'he was very keen indeed to stop & see the thing through. It is certainly wise for him to go home though.'

Armitage disagreed with Wilson's assessment. He became involved when Shackleton asked him for help. 'He was in great distress,' Armitage wrote.

> I consulted Koettlitz about S's health, and he informed me that Scott was in a worse condition than Shackleton. I then went to Scott, and . . . told him that there was no necessity from a health point of view, so after much beating about the bush, he said 'If he does not go back sick he will go in disgrace.'

There has been debate as to whether this statement referred to Shackleton's falling out with Scott on the southern journey or to Shackleton's breakdown, which Scott might have thought came in part because the third officer had concealed a weak constitution from the doctors in advance of the trip. Regardless of whether it was either, or if it was simply more bitterness expressed by Armitage years later, the second-in-command was unable to assist his fellow merchant marine officer.

Shackleton's last effort came when he consulted Reginald Ford, *Discovery*'s purser and his direct subordinate. 'Shackleton came to me . . . and asked me if I would volunteer to go Home if Captain Scott would allow him to take my place, my duties being less arduous than those of a deck officer,' Ford later recalled. 'This I declined to do as I was quite as anxious as Shackleton to remain.'

Thus, on 2 March *Morning* sailed north with the expedition's third officer aboard. 'Ah me it was a sad parting,' he wrote that night. 'Mount Discovery away down South from us was a splendid sight standing out in the clear blue of the Southern Sky . . . I turned in and read for a bit but thoughts would go back to those I left on the floe.'

One of those he had left behind was his closest friend from the mess deck, Frank Wild. The night before, there had been a party aboard

Morning, which, according to Shackleton, had been very pleasant 'and with songs and one thing and another it was 3 a.m. before we went to bed'. Perhaps in response to the loss of his comrade, Wild had so much to drink that, while returning to *Discovery*, he and another inebriated seaman had to be tied to the sledge in order to get them back safely.

It was a sad moment, but it would not be the last time that Shackleton and Wild would look together on the still, cold whiteness of the Antarctic. And together, they would reach places no man had ever seen before.

8

A SQUARE PEG AND A ROUND HOLE

Members of the public today – jaded by a plethora of gruesome news accounts, violent dramas in the cinema and unpleasant 'reality' shows – might shake their heads in disbelief and decide a tableau such as happened one day in June 1903 could never truly occur. It was, they would think, too gooey, too sickeningly sweet, to possibly be true. But sensibilities were different a century ago, and when Shackleton returned to England, having made his way via New Zealand and the United States, a scene that would have made the writers of *The Waltons* proud occurred in Sydenham.

'What a homecoming that was!' Shackleton's sister Kathleen recalled five decades later. 'Some of us went towards the station – the road was dotted with Shackleton sisters of all ages and sizes at various intervals. I could see his dear broad shoulders as he turned the first corner, his zigzag sailor's roll beside Daddy's springy walk . . . He kissed us all one by one.' When they reached the house, Mrs Shackleton was waiting in the hall, trembling, with tears in her eyes.

> The air was charged with emotion . . . Someone would have burst into tears only Ernest saved the situation. He spied a familiar brooch which Mother ever wore, a mosaic of the famous Canova doves around a bowl. Seizing Mother in his arms, he hugged her, said 'Well here I am, darling,' and putting her back, he looked at the brooch. 'What – those doves still drinking?'

It was a moment that was pure Shackleton. Ever was he able to take charge in an instant, whether it be a crisis on the ice, an unexpected question at a lecture or a personal emergency. He seemed to have the remarkable ability to draw forth at will reserves of physical strength, courage, cheerfulness, solicitude or the capacity to inspire. Little did he know it at the time, but in the next four years he would need these talents and more, because he would be faced with something new in his adulthood – an extended period on land.

The joy of Shackleton's homecoming must have been complete when he was reunited with Emily, patiently waiting for him and not only looking forward to marrying him but financially independent into the bargain. Her father's will had left her money in a trust that would produce a regular income, at that point some £700 a year, which would be enough to keep an average middle-class couple in comfort, including housing, food, clothing and a pair of servants.

But Emily was not all that was waiting for Shackleton. Posted before he even arrived back in the country was a letter from Sir Clements Markham, both gushing and insistent. 'I am quite unable to express to you my admiration,' he had written, continuing:

> It will be a great disappointment to you to have had to leave . . . but you will have the consolation of knowing that you will be as useful . . . here and I am sure as zealous, as you would be there . . . I am relying very much indeed on your knowledge and your advice about sending the things out that will be needed; and I want to see you to settle various things as soon as possible after your arrival.

Markham's references to Shackleton's assistance related to a second relief expedition, which had become imperative with *Discovery* still in the Antarctic. When Shackleton arrived home, *Morning* was already being fitted out in New Zealand for a return south. But the RGS and the Royal Society were far short of the funds needed, and had again asked the Treasury for support. Unfortunately, Markham's aggressive strategy to force the government's hand backfired. In a struggle between the president of the RGS and Prime Minister Balfour, the result was neither surprising nor what the conniving old man had hoped. The cost of government participation was that the Admiralty took over the entire relief operation, including, to Markham's chagrin, the ownership of *Morning*. It was then decided to send a second ship south, for which the Admiralty purchased a large Dundee whaler that would later become famous on Scott's second expedition: *Terra Nova*.

Shackleton now had three interactions with the Royal Navy in quick succession. With the blessing of Markham, he accepted a position under Vice-Admiral Pelham Aldrich, assisting with the general out-fitting and the provision of stores for *Terra Nova* in Dundee. He also applied to have his commission transferred from the Royal Naval Reserve to the Royal Navy proper, receiving a strong letter of support from Markham and William Huggins, the president of the Royal Society. This request was refused, however, and in the following year Shackleton resigned from the RNR. Strangely, despite the unwillingness to offer a regular appointment, the Admiralty asked Shackleton to sail as chief officer of *Terra Nova*. The opportunity to appear as Scott's rescuer – following his pronouncement by an Admiralty doctor as 'fit for service' – undoubtedly appealed to Shackleton, but he turned it down never the less, and began to search for a job that would allow him to focus on his approaching wedding and future life with Emily.

It must have been difficult, however, for Shackleton to avert his thoughts from the polar regions, news of which seemed to be on everyone's lips. In the very week of his return, a Norwegian who had participated in the *Belgica* expedition departed for the Canadian Arctic in a tiny ship; it would be three years before Roald Amundsen would reach civilisation, having attained the goal of centuries by completing the navigation of the Northwest Passage across the waters of Arctic Canada. A week later a highly publicised expedition under the command of Anthony Fiala left the United States for Franz Josef Land and an attempt on the North Pole. And soon thereafter Shackleton was consulted by Julían Irízar, an Argentine naval officer who was being sent to the Weddell Sea to try to rescue the missing members of Otto Nordenskjöld's Swedish Antarctic expedition.

Meanwhile, until Scott's return, Shackleton was an important voice for the British National Antarctic Expedition, and he made several public presentations. In addition, he quickly published two accounts in *The Illustrated London News*. It was perhaps this success, and his experiences with *The South Polar Times*, that led him briefly to pursue a career in journalism.

In the autumn of 1903 Shackleton was hired as a sub-editor for the *Royal Magazine*, one of the stable of publications owned by Sir Arthur Pearson, who had followed Newnes and Harmsworth in producing first popular periodicals (starting with *Pearson's Weekly* in 1890) and then daily newspapers (his most successful being the *Daily Express*, founded in 1900). But although Shackleton brought a cleverness with words, an infinite number of fresh, creative ideas and his usual effervescence, he soon proved unsuitable for office work.

'You may wonder why exactly I gave him this appointment,' F.W. Everett, the editor who hired Shackleton, later wrote.

> He had had no practical experience of journalism . . . and he was the first to admit, with that big laugh of his which one never forgets, that office work was out of his line altogether. But I am convinced that if he had gone to a stock-broker, a butcher, a carpenter, or a theatrical manager and asked for a job, he would have got it. There was something about him that compelled confidence . . . He was brimming over with original, unconventional, racy ideas, which, whether practical or not, were always stimulating . . . I remember well neglecting my work for the best part of a day, in company with two other Editors and several juniors, to sit in a circle round Shackleton while he related some particularly dangerous exploit. And no man told a story better.

It was this ability to tell stories, to captivate increasingly large crowds with his deep, clear voice so mesmerising in its resonant timbre, that soon launched Shackleton on to a new career path. In November, he intoxicated audiences in Dundee and Aberdeen while lecturing for the Royal Scottish Geographical Society. While in Scotland he learned that the secretary of the RSGS had recently retired, leaving available a paid post. The salary was roughly the same as the *Royal Magazine*, but the prestige was much greater and, he hoped, it might lead more quickly to the grand success it had become apparent would come only too gradually in Fleet Street.

With the support of Markham, Huggins and, most avidly, Hugh Robert Mill, in early December Shackleton began his single-minded pursuit of the position. There were, of course, other candidates, but Dr J.G. Bartholomew, a noted cartographer who was honorary secretary of the Society, strongly supported Shackleton, and in early January 1904 the twenty-nine-year-old former sailor was unanimously elected secretary and treasurer.

It was once noted by a great story-teller that the moments of life that are most enjoyable to spend do not normally make interesting tales, while incidents that are difficult, unpleasant or even gruesome become gripping stories. So it was now for Shackleton, who in the ensuing months experienced success and happiness on every front. He went through the conservative Society like a whirlwind, modernising its methods of functioning, increasing its membership and financing, and broadening its geographical horizons, which had traditionally emphasised Africa because Scottish missionaries, explorers and consuls had participated in its exploration. From his very first moments in Edinburgh he brought a breath of fresh air, shocking the formal, black-suited officers by wearing a light tweed suit his first day, when he entered with a cigarette and a joke.

But bringing him greater excitement and joy was furnishing the small house on the edge of the city, where he intended to settle with his new bride. Even Shackleton's energies and organising abilities must have been pushed to the limit by the constant stream of details that he oversaw there in addition to a job that was more than full-time and that included travel throughout the country.

Shackleton's letters to Emily during this period tell of his boundless stamina as well as his deep devotion to her and an ambition drawn in part from his wish to create a life worthy of her. 'My darling Sweeteyes' many of them begin, using a loving name that lasted throughout their lives together, before continuing to tell her both of his busy schedule and his anticipation of their life together: 'we shall soon have a meeting that will have no parting, dear one.' The letters show a tenderness and sensitivity that would perhaps not be expected from a man of action who had spent so much of his manhood in the rough company of others of his sex. Many are signed either 'Micky' – which she usually called him – or with a pet nickname, such as Mikeberry, Mikleham or, far the most frequent, 'Your boy, Emiky', a clever combination of 'Micky' and 'Emily'.

'I am missing you so much dearest one my whole heart and life is crying out for the loved one whom I shall see on Friday,' he wrote in a typical letter at the end of March 1904, continuing:

I am coming my own my sweet to you and all I can say to you is small and feeble to the great love that I feel which is welling up to overflowing dearest heart. The best of me is miserably poor to give you my Queen and yet my love is so strong that it will redeem the poverty of the rest of me. Money I have none but Child o'mine all my heart cries out for you. In the spring we are to be married and it will be spring always in our lives . . . for our love will be always spring and so we will go on and on till the

twilight . . . we have long long years before us of joy and love . . . and
you will ever feel my arm there to protect and keep to guide your feet and
smooth the path for you the fairest and dearest of women.

That Shackleton was becoming more emotionally charged was not
surprising, as he was due to be married ten days later. After seven years
of waiting, the day he had so longed for finally arrived on 9 April 1904,
when, at Christ Church, Westminster, he and Emily were married. Even
then – his daughter Cecily commented fifty years later – he remained
concerned that his financial status would not have pleased Emily's late
father. 'With all my worldly goods I thee endow', he whispered with
irony under his breath to Emily as the vicar pronounced them man and
wife.

There is no doubt that in the first months after his marriage
Shackleton was truly content. He threw himself into his work and
even delayed their honeymoon to continue with his programme at the
RSGS. But always Shackleton was driven by the need to test his
personal abilities and to emerge the victor in competition. Throughout
his career, he had gone from challenge to challenge, whether it be
earning his master's certificate, winning the heart of Emily, attaining a
farthest south, or being hired by the Geographical Society. It was not
long, therefore, before the restlessness that marked his life in between
such summons to action began to reappear. Certainly his job brought
moments of interest, as when in July he organised the welcome home of
the Scottish National Antarctic Expedition under William Spiers Bruce,
or in September he participated in the official return of *Discovery* to
London. But, in retrospect, it can be seen that his position in the Society
held little long-term challenge, and therefore that his relationship with it
had no serious future.

'With life before me, and strength and hope, all these things which time
will whittle down,' Shackleton wrote, 'I may achieve something before
the period at which life grows stale and strength wanes and hope flies,
or if it does not fly, assumes the dignified attitude of resignation.' It was
late November 1904 and Shackleton was attempting to justify himself
to Mill, who had been critical of the younger man's actions. More
importantly, Mills' views were not solely his own; they were shared by a
number of the members of the Council of the RSGS.

The cause for this dissatisfaction had originated the previous month.

On 15 October, while on a business trip to London, Shackleton had written in a letter to Emily, 'I went to the . . . Liberal Unionist Council and had a long talk with Boraston, he is going to wake them up in Dundee.' It was to herald a most unexpected divergence, for the sailor–explorer–administrator was suddenly considering standing for Parliament. There is no evidence that Shackleton had ever taken any particular interest in politics, but, as was so often the case in his life, he had seen a path that he thought had potential to lead to great success and had immediately taken it.

Not long after that trip, Shackleton travelled to Dundee to meet with the city's Liberal Unionist committee, and he was adopted as that party's candidate for the next general election, which, it was widely assumed, would shortly be called by the trouble-plagued Tory government. However, the committee then made a *faux pas* of considerable significance with the announcement that it had adopted a 'noted naval officer to contest seat'. This not only created problems with the party's General Committee, which had not approved Shackleton, but sprang the situation on the shocked members of the Council of the RSGS before he could raise it himself. Although the party soon approved his selection, certain members of the Society were less enchanted by his actions. Bartholomew, who approved of Shackleton's modernisation, argued that there was no conflict with standing for Parliament if he could also perform his duties to the Society, but others disagreed, believing that no officer of a learned society should take a political stance.

Unhappy with such an ambiguous situation, in January 1905 Shackleton tendered his resignation. It was not, however, immediately accepted, and during the following months the Council continued to avoid any concrete action, until in July his resignation was formally approved. In the meantime, Shackleton had more than just professional considerations: in February, his first son, Raymond, was born, the loving father instantly exclaiming, 'Good fists for fighting!'

In Dundee, meanwhile, Shackleton had propelled himself into a tougher fight than he undoubtedly imagined. Indeed, it could well be argued that in this case his ambition had overwhelmed his common sense. Most of those knowledgeable about politics realised that Dundee, a two-member constituency, was unlikely to replace either of its two Gladstonian Liberals unless an individual standing for the new

Labour Representation Committee – an organisation, but not a true party – could sneak in.

Shackleton did not represent either of these. The Liberal Unionists had come into being in 1886, following Prime Minister Gladstone's conversion to the concept of Home Rule, the establishment of an Irish parliament and executive in Dublin, which would have powers over Irish decisions. This was anathema not only to Tories but to a number of Liberals, who saw it as the first step towards independence and the break-up of the British Empire. In April 1886 Gladstone introduced his Home Rule Bill to the House of Commons, leading to the tearing asunder of the Liberal Party when the leaders of its opposite wings – Lord Hartington of the Whigs and Joseph Chamberlain of the Radicals – guided a revolt of their followers against it. The bill was defeated, Gladstone dissolved Parliament and, in the subsequent elections, the Liberals were thrown from power, with Salisbury's Tories gaining a decisive victory that would keep them in the ascendancy for sixteen of the next nineteen years. Within a decade, Chamberlain's Liberal Unionists had entered an official alliance with the Tories, and Chamberlain had joined Salisbury's Cabinet.

By 1904, when Shackleton joined the Liberal Unionist effort, Home Rule was still a significant political issue, but it no longer topped the agenda. It had been replaced by a debate over tariff reform. Once again the key figure in the dialectic was Chamberlain. Shortly after the close of the South African War, he became convinced that, in an effort to strengthen imperial unity, Britain should eliminate its long-standing economic policy of free trade and establish protective tariffs for its agricultural and manufacturing products. This, he argued, would draw the mother country together with her colonies in a powerful economic unit, would stimulate trade within the Empire, and would serve as fiscal retaliation for foreign tariffs. In September 1903 he resigned from the cabinet to take his argument directly to the people in a campaign throughout the country.

Chamberlain's move gave him a unique place in parliamentary history, for it helped him hopelessly split and ultimately wreck the dominant Unionist alliance, as previously he had done with the all-powerful Liberals; he had managed, from the inside in both cases, to blight both major political parties. Conservative unity began to disappear, as Chamberlain's call for protectionism was favoured by manufacturers and businessmen, but was rejected utterly by the majority of the people, who had grown up with a fundamental belief in the principles of laissez-faire and with deep-rooted fears of tariffs and a return to the hated Corn Laws. At the same time, Liberal Party differences were overcome in defence of free trade.

Tariff reform was not the only policy over which the government was struggling. The most emotive issue of the moment concerned the import of Chinese labourers into the Transvaal to work the mines, which, after the war, could not find enough African labour. In a remarkably short-sighted move, Sir Alfred Milner, the British High Commissioner for South Africa, allowed the mining companies to hire tens of thousands of Chinese. These came not as free men but as indentured workers required to toil in terrible conditions and to be confined, even during nonworking hours, in compounds where they were refused many basic liberties. This was a direct slap in the face of British labour. The Chinese labour scheme was approved ultimately by Balfour's Cabinet, a clear message that the government and small privileged class to which many of its leaders belonged regarded labour as a mere commodity rather than a human workforce. It turned out to be political suicide on a grand scale.

There were also other issues over which segments of the population had lost confidence in Balfour's ministry. But much of the public had simply tired, after most of two decades, of a government that reflected the aristocratic values of Salisbury, who believed in preserving the privileges of the propertied classes and who never attempted to conceal his disdain of the masses, 'not excluding the House of Commons'.

It was on to this politically disintegrating stage that Shackleton now trod, attempting to follow in the footsteps of fellow explorer Henry Morton Stanley, who had been elected MP for North Lambeth as a Liberal Unionist in 1895. But how frustrating it must have been for such a man to do nothing but wait, because the government did not, as was expected, call for an election. Rather it lumbered on like a drunkard, bumping into everything and accomplishing no serious forward movement. It was not until December 1905 that Balfour finally made his move, and even then he did the unexpected, refusing to dissolve Parliament but rather, following Gladstone's tactics in 1873 and 1885, resigning. He hoped that when put in power without a majority, the Liberals would be destroyed by in-fighting, allowing the Unionists to regain the momentum by the time of the election. Unfortunately for

Balfour, the new Prime Minister, Sir Henry Campbell-Bannerman, led a smooth political transition.

When finally held, the election was spread over a period of two weeks, the date in Dundee being 16 January 1906, which gave Shackleton only six weeks in which to campaign. Day after day he impressed the voters with his quick wit, straight talking, and enthusiasm. He spoke in shabby halls, the courthouse square, local foundries and seedy sections of the wharf, sometimes addressing thousands in a day at half a dozen different sites. His cause was not helped, however, when his party decided to have him share the platform at meetings with the Conservative candidate, a dull Dundee solicitor by the now all-too-familiar Tory surname of Duncan Smith.

Shackleton's campaign closely followed Chamberlain's programme of fiscal protection in the form of tariffs, opposition to Home Rule, the use of Chinese labour in South Africa, and a closer relationship between the peoples of the Empire. Whether he sincerely believed in everything the Liberal Unionists stood for is uncertain, but he eloquently argued their cause, even to the point of misrepresenting his own background, stating that he had come over from Ireland at the age of sixteen (when he was actually ten). He certainly gained support by being not just a typical politician, but a man able to take a situation in hand and deal with the unexpected. Four days before the election he and Duncan Smith were unable to gain access to the Jamaica Street Hall, where they were supposed to speak, because it was packed to capacity, and there were hundreds more waiting outside. Shackleton hired a carriage, drove it to the front of the hall, and from the top of it shouted, 'I'll tell you what it is, men; I'll address you from the cab.' His strong, full voice was heard all over the street, and people poured out of the hall to listen.

One would assume that Shackleton raised eyebrows by shamelessly emphasising his Irish background while speaking against Home Rule. 'As an Irishman myself, in sympathy with the Irish people,' he once claimed, 'I am convinced that my country has been gradually emerging from sad and bitter times to a more peaceful and brighter era; and that this has been accomplished by the wise measures, considerate administration and great pecuniary assistance due to the Unionist Government.'

But although, according to *The Courier and Argus*, 'the lieutenant's breezy personality and his attractive manner have gained him much popularity', and despite his convenient protestations of being a working man, it was hard reaping a field that had been sown for so long by the Liberals and was also being ploughed by the new labour movement, which, perhaps surprisingly by today's standards, was both truly new and truly labour. It was not yet a single party but consisted of a number of organisations, particularly the Labour Representation Committee, which represented the working man, and a variety of unions. 'Come on our side, boy,' an elderly working man supposedly shouted at one meeting, 'and we'll put you in at the top of the poll.' Had he listened, and followed the example of one sitting MP who, foreseeing the future, had ignored the jeers and crossed over from the Tories to the Liberals, he might well have been elected. It is intriguing to wonder if Shackleton would have been as successful as that other young man – Winston Churchill.

Early in the morning of 17 January 1906, Shackleton learned with certainty that his future would not be in politics. Of the five candidates, he finished a distant fourth, ahead of only Duncan Smith. 'I got all the applause,' he commented later, 'and the other fellows got all the votes.' Edmund Robertson, the incumbent Liberal candidate, and Alexander Wilkie, the labour representative, gained the places in Parliament. It was to be so throughout the country. In a staggering turnabout, the former ruling coalition, which had gone into the election with a majority of 161, saved a mere 157 seats, only 25 by Liberal Unionists. The Liberals obtained 377, while candidates from various labour organisations gained 53. Shackleton was at least in good company; even Arthur Balfour had been unseated.

Balfour, however, was soon back in Parliament as leader of the opposition. Shackleton had no such fall-back position. He now tried his hand at successive business ventures, each of which he hoped would make his fortune. None did. Late in 1904 he had formed a company named Tabard Cigarettes. It existed for a number of years, but at no point brought him significant financial success. In late 1905 he became involved in promoting Potentia, a news agency that would never leave the drawing board. And following the election he helped organise a plan to bring Russian soldiers back from Vladivostok, where they were stranded after their humiliating defeat in the Russo–Japanese War. Again, the scheme fell through.

What came to Shackleton's rescue was an offer that had been on the table for a year. While waiting for the RSGS to make a decision, he had engaged in discussions with William Beardmore, a former Dulwich boy who had amassed a fortune in armour plating for ships and then in shipbuilding on the Clyde before diversifying his financial interests at his massive Glasgow plant of Parkhead. Like so many others, Beardmore was quickly won over by Shackleton's charm, wit and drive. 'He tells me definitely that there are four separate things I can go into and showed me the lines on which I am to work if I go to Parkhead,' Shackleton wrote to Emily in April 1905. 'He tells me I can only begin at £300 but that the beginning is nothing if I do what he wishes and show that I can work then I am sure to get on.'

Almost a year later, his political fling over, Shackleton re-approached Beardmore and was given a position. It is obvious from Shackleton's letters that he thought the job might be the first step towards a company directorship and financial ease. It is equally apparent that Beardmore (who later became Lord Invernairn) realised that the likeable young man was not designed for life in an office or factory. Never the less, he was made the secretary of a committee examining the design of new gas engines. Aside from keeping the minutes of committee meetings, Shackleton was effectively given a roving commission that involved charming Beardmore's clients and entertaining his professional colleagues, both in London and at Parkhead.

In some senses, he was perfect for the new position, because of his remarkable personal magnetism. 'It's one of the things I remember so well,' Emily later told their daughter Cecily. 'He didn't have to lift a hand or a finger to get service in a restaurant. Poor old . . . clicking his fingers and getting half out of his chair, trying to get somebody to come and take his order . . . Your father never had to do that. He only had to raise his head for somebody to be standing beside him.'

Despite his natural flair for it, Shackleton must have realised that the position would not lead him to unqualified prosperity. 'A fine fellow,' A.B. Macduff, Beardmore's assistant, said years later, 'but it wasn't in any way a really important job in connection with the business.'

Regardless, his status in Beardmore's company was increasingly unimportant to him, because Shackleton had realised that neither this nor the other business opportunities were truly for him. His life's work, he now felt, was elsewhere. In a way seen again and again in the history of exploration, the wild, untamed, far-away regions had taken over the heart and mind of one who had dared journey to them. As with Burton in Africa or Nansen in the Arctic, in an indefinable way Antarctica had now become an essential part of Shackleton's psyche. It is only when this is realised that one can understand his relentless efforts through the rest of his life to return to the far south – the overwhelming drive that kept him making new plans and setting new goals when to many there appeared to be no point in his continuing.

Shackleton's preoccupation with the Antarctic likely received a boost late in 1906, when newspapers announced Robert E. Peary's claim to have attained a farthest *north*. But Shackleton's absorption with the Antarctic had actually been building since his premature return on *Morning*. At the beginning of October 1903 he had visited Markham, who gave little encouragement despite recording that the young man was 'full of plans for another expedition'. Throughout 1905 and into 1906 Shackleton had made efforts to interest potential sponsors in an Antarctic expedition, and some time either shortly before or after the election he had printed a four-page document entitled 'Plans for an Antarctic Expedition to proceed to the Ross Quadrant of the Antarctic with a view to reaching the Geographical South Pole and the South Magnetic Pole.'

Presumably produced in an effort to obtain sponsors, this shows many of Shackleton's earliest thoughts on an expedition. Although he indicated that there would be a modicum of scientific work, the clearly stated goal was the attainment of the Poles, both geographical and magnetic. This, Shackleton indicated, could be accomplished with the use of three modes of transport: some sixty dogs, several ponies and a specially designed automobile. As Shackleton had not mastered dog-driving, and as neither ponies nor automobiles had ever been tried in the Antarctic, the confidence of his statement, 'I am quite certain the South Pole could be reached' was remarkable.

Shackleton's unrealistic optimism showed through in other aspects of the document. He estimated that the entire expedition – including building a small, schooner-rigged vessel – would cost only £17,000. Fitted with a forty-horsepower engine, his ship would be able to make five knots under steam, and, although small, 'Ammundsen [*sic*] is attempting the North-West Passage with a specially built vessel only half this size'. Further, he indicated that he would need a party of only ten men, including five scientific observers and three with specific knowledge of working the engine (although whether that of the ship or the automobile, he did not say). 'By the time the vessel reaches New Zealand,' he wrote, his head firmly in the clouds, 'every one on board would be capable of managing the ship'. Yet how the ship was to be managed prior to reaching New Zealand seemed of no concern.

With such a plan, it is not surprising that Shackleton did not gain any significant backing. When his efforts went nowhere, he wrote to Mill that he had 'put a black mark' against the names of some seventy rich men who refused to help him.

But not all was discouraging. In the summer of 1905 or 1906 – depending on whose memory one wishes to trust – the Shackletons were staying in a bungalow near the Forth Bridge when HMS *Berwick* anchored nearby. Several days later, on a Sunday afternoon, one of the officers, Lieutenant Jameson Adams, was preparing to go ashore to play golf. 'No you aren't,' his commanding officer told him, 'you're going to call on Shackleton. He called on the ship last Thursday.'

So, according to Adams, he and several of his fellow officers 'went and called on Shackleton at tea-time, and we stayed there till ten o'clock at night, talking about his expedition and his ambitions and so on, and as we were going over the side, I said to Shackleton, "If you go again, will you take me with you?"' Shackleton immediately agreed, and it must have given him great pleasure to find someone who wished to be more than a willing listener.

But talk alone could not satisfy him, and throughout 1906 Shackleton became progressively more restless and uninterested in his job at Parkhead. 'I could see he was getting a bit unsettled,' Macduff recalled. 'I came to the conclusion he wanted to get away. And I had a talk with him, and he said "Yes, I want to go on a further expedition soon. This time I want to command it myself."'

9

A SOUL WHIPPED ON BY THE WANDERFIRE

One of the remarkable contradictions of the massive territorial expansion of the British Empire in the late nineteenth century was how little the government, and therefore the tax-payers of Britain, actually spent on exploring, conquering and expanding into the white spaces on the map. Clever, visionary, occasionally reckless entrepreneurs such as Cecil Rhodes and George Goldie had shown how private military force, economic bullying and subsequent royal charters would allow the take-over of huge sections of Africa.

Although there were numerous other such examples of British exploration and expansionism being driven by industrialists or rich amateurs, gaining this kind of backing in the polar regions had proven difficult. Few businessmen could be convinced that wealth could be gained from the Antarctic, although both Borchgrevink and Shackleton used this argument (unsuccessfully) at times. Funding for polar exploration had traditionally been based – in both Britain and the United States – on motives more nationalistic or personal than economic.

Therefore, it was somewhat surprising that when Shackleton finally did obtain a backer for his long-desired Antarctic expedition it was the stern, no-nonsense captain of industry by whom he was already employed – William Beardmore.

The Antarctic had never been far from Shackleton's mind, but as 1906 grew old, his plan began to actively occupy his thinking. On 26 December, only three days after his daughter Cecily was born, he wrote to Mill, 'I see nothing of the old *Discovery* people at all. We are all scattered, and the fickle public are tired of the polar work at present. What would I not give to be out there again doing the job, and this time really on the road to the Pole!'

It was not long after, pushed into action by rumours of French and

Belgian expeditions, that he approached Beardmore. Despite having become prosperous by being careful and hard working, Beardmore had a generous nature, as had been shown by his handsome treatment of Shackleton. Moreover, Shackleton had become close with Beardmore's wife Elspeth, who most probably lobbied on his behalf. Thus, despite Shackleton's previous assurances that he had given up the idea of leading an Antarctic expedition, the industrialist agreed to help.

Beardmore was not, however, so overwhelmed by Shackleton's charm that he was willing to donate a large sum, as Newnes had to Borchgrevink or Longstaff to Markham. His unwillingness was probably reinforced by Shackleton's casual way with money. Beardmore could not have helped but be aware that his employee had not even bothered to draw his salary regularly. 'He left the salary with us and forgot all about it for five months,' Macduff recalled later. 'Then it suddenly dawned upon him that he was due for some money.' Such tales of fiscal irresponsibility dot Shackleton's career, and they may be why Beardmore ultimately chose to guarantee a loan at Clydesdale Bank rather than to risk his own capital. Shackleton eventually signed a guarantee for £7,000, agreeing that:

> the first profits of the expedition shall be given to you up to an amount which will release the guarantee and also that you are to be cleared of this guarantee in three years from this date. Also that the vessel I propose purchasing for the expedition is to be your property but that you are to lend me the same for the period of the expedition, and that the vessel is to be entirely under my control during that period.

By the standards of what some earlier explorers had received, it was not a huge sum, but it was enough for Shackleton to sweep into action. With a previous promise of £1,000 from his old champion Elizabeth Dawson-Lambton and, he thought, support via an investment with Douglas Steuart of the City firm Poore, Pettit and Steuart, consulting mining engineers, he could now publicly announce his intentions – as soon as he broke the news to his wife.

Perhaps the most difficult part of launching the expedition was telling Emily. Through most of his planning, he had kept her in the dark in order not to worry her. Now, with a baby only weeks old, he had to tell her that he would be leaving for one to two years. That part of his reason was in order to prove his worth to her and to create a fortune on which she could live comfortably did not make the deed any easier, nor her any less distressed.

'You can imagine that it was with mingled feelings that I sent the wire to you that the Expedition was settled,' he wrote to her.

> Darling the main thought was sadness and I am afraid that when I got your wire so full of feeling and sweetness that I broke down. My own dear Heart you are a thousand times too good for me and I am feeling it very much now but it will only be one year and I shall come back with honour and with money and never never part from you again and we have nearly 10 months together now Sweeteyes; those words 'Best love' were the sweetest you have written to me ever; Darling I am full of distress mingled with great desire to do a great thing and you have risen like the real woman and real friend that you are and I am just longing to hold you and tell you that you will be a part of history, well can I dedicate my book to one who is the best of all.

Throughout their life together, Emily was always Shackleton's greatest support, and this time was no different. 'She wasn't feeble, she had tremendous character and strength,' Cecily stated years later. 'But then she subjected herself entirely to what she felt was my father's life of exploration. She was never the woman who wanted to raise a finger to make it difficult for him to go.'

So Emily agreed to remain behind and support his assault on the Pole, an effort that he guaranteed her would make them rich and happy, and that would be the last time he would ever leave. Certainly by now she understood his nature well enough to doubt such promises, but, she recalled later:

> I never wittingly hampered his ardent spirit, or tried to chain it to the domestic life which meant so much to me. He used to say he went on the *Discovery* 'to get out of the ruck' for me! – it was dear of him to say it because I cannot flatter myself that it was only for me – it was his own spirit 'a soul whipped on by the wanderfire.'

Monday 11 February 1907 was a very special evening for the Royal Geographical Society and those interested in polar exploration. The headline event of a busy agenda was the lecture by Roald Amundsen about his remarkable completion of the Northwest Passage. After three centuries of efforts to navigate through the Canadian archipelago, he had done so in a tiny ship with only six companions. The same evening, the Society's Kosmos Dining Club was the venue of the official announcement of the plans for not one, but two, *Antarctic* expeditions. One of them was Henryk Arçtowski's Belgian expedition that had helped set off Shackleton's recent burst of energy.

The second project was Shackleton's. The previous Friday evening, Beardmore had finally given his consent to guarantee the loan, and Shackleton was wasting no time in warning off any competition from his own destination. In an announcement reported in a variety of newspapers the next day, Shackleton indicated that his party would leave that very year and would winter at the old hut on Ross Island. His ship would return to New Zealand to avoid being frozen in, and would pick them up the next summer. In the meanwhile, efforts would be made to reach both the geographical South Pole and the South Magnetic Pole, the wandering location where the south-seeking end of a dip needle (a bar magnet suspended freely on a horizontal axis) points vertically downward towards the Earth's centre. 'It is held that the southern sledge party of the Discovery would have reached a much higher altitude [*sic*] if they had been more adequately equipped for sledge work,' the newspapers stated.

> In addition to dogs, Siberian ponies will be taken, as the surface of the land or ice . . . will be eminently suited for this mode of sledge travelling. But a new and novel feature is to be introduced . . . modern in method and, according to the opinion of many Polar explorers, absolutely feasible – the use of a motor-car.

Shackleton's speech set off a wave of publicity that must have pleased him immensely, but he none the less left London a touch mystified. Both J. Scott Keltie, the secretary of the RGS, and Sir George Goldie, who two years before had succeeded Markham as its president, had been lukewarm to his requests for support. This was not totally surprising from the unreadable Keltie, whose job it was to be positive to everyone without committing to anyone, but Shackleton must have thought his plans would appeal to Goldie, who had the heart of a buccaneer himself. Although now sixty years old, as a young man Goldie had matched his brilliant wit, logic, vision and powers of persuasion with equal parts of recklessness, debauchery and self-centred dissipation. Goldie – who had described himself as 'a human powder magazine' – had once aimlessly disappeared for three years into the mysterious reaches of the Sahara before executing a volte-face and, with insightful observation, precise planning and resolute action, single-mindedly establishing himself and his Royal Niger Company as the economic and political power in the vast region that would become Nigeria. Yet, despite the assistance he had given Markham in the intrigue leading to the British National Antarctic Expedition, Goldie did not evince an equal interest in the Antarctic, and he saw less of a kindred spirit in Shackleton than vice versa.

Puzzled as he no doubt was, Shackleton could not take the time to dwell on the lack of enthusiasm. He needed help to pull together an expedition if it were to leave within a matter of months, and he turned first to old colleagues from *Discovery*. Immediately upon his return to Edinburgh, he wrote to Wilson, then serving as a field observer for the Board of Agriculture's Commission on the Investigation of Grouse Disease, offering him second-in-command. Wilson reluctantly refused, stating that 'I am in honour bound to carry this grouse work through . . . it would be unfair to the Committee to make them find a new man, and waste all that they have spent on me and my work.' He expressed confidence in Shackleton's chances of success, and acknowledged that 'it is an intense disappointment to have to refuse . . . I would dearly love to have a hand in the work, and eventually with you in the book, but there you are.'

Shackleton, equally disappointed, followed with a series of telegrams and letters indicating that Wilson's decision should be 'the country before the grouse' and that he would gladly have his backers write to Lord Lovat of the Commission in an effort to get Wilson released. Wilson, however, was unmoveable. 'I must refuse entirely on my own, knowing what is the right thing to do . . . please take this as final – & don't waste more money in long telegrams.'

At the same time, Shackleton pursued other of his former colleagues, including asking Barne to command the Magnetic Pole party, which he envisioned wintering separately along the Victoria Land coast. Barne's negative, but enlightening, response was not returned promptly, however, due to Shackleton's letter being delayed. In the meantime, Armitage, Skelton and Hodgson all indicated they could not participate. Thus it was not until Shackleton heard back from George Mulock, the former officer of *Morning* who had replaced him when he had been invalided home, that the attitudes of Keltie, Goldie and the members of *Discovery* began to become clear.

'I wish you all good luck & would like to be coming with you,' Mulock wrote on 19 February 1907, 'but I have volunteered to go with Scott.' This spurred Shackleton to buttonhole Keltie, who said, 'Oh! Mulock has let the cat out of the bag.' Keltie then explained that Scott was considering again going south, but that it was a secret and that the RGS was uncertain either of the timing and if financial considerations would allow him to go at all.

It must have been trying for Shackleton, as, with the unveiling of Scott's intentions, he faced not just a vague possibility of competition but a distinct threat. 'I certainly should have been much annoyed if that fellow Arçtowski had gone poaching down in our preserves,' Markham wrote to him, 'but . . . Foreigners never get much beyond the Antarctic Circle.' At the same time as dismissing Arçtowski (who did not, in fact, ever acquire the needed funding), Markham had thus hit on the two major points now facing Shackleton: a serious competitor for the Pole and an issue of priority regarding domain.

These topics were further addressed in a pair of letters that Shackleton now received in quick order from Scott. The first was written in haste and more than a little anxiety, as Scott, now a captain and commanding HMS *Albemarle*, had been involved in 'a horrid accident the other day when we ran into HMS *Commonwealth* off the coast of Portugal.' He indicated not only that he had plans to return to the Antarctic, but that 'I feel I have a sort of right to my own field of work in the same way as Peary claimed Smith's Sound and many African travellers their particular locality.'

The second letter, written shortly thereafter, enlarged on Scott's hopes for going south, his need to remain in active naval service – 'I support my mother & family, it is therefore essential for me to have an assured income' – and the necessity of keeping his plans secret until the time was right for him to approach the Admiralty about further Antarctic leave. He also again claimed prescriptive rights to McMurdo Sound: 'I don't want to be selfish at anyone's expense and least of all at that of one of my own people but still I think anyone who has had to do with exploration will regard this region primarily as mine.'

Scott then appealed to what he saw as Shackleton's duty to his former commander. '[I]t must be clear to you now that you have placed yourself directly in the way of my life's work – a thing for which I have sacrificed much and worked with steady purpose . . . If you go to McMurdo Sound you go to winter quarters which are clearly mine . . . I do not like to remind you,' he wrote, doing just that, 'that it was I who took you to the South or of the loyalty with which we all stuck to one another or of incidents of our voyage or of my readiness to do you justice on our return.'

One can realise in hindsight that these were perhaps not the best arguments to use on Shackleton. He, too, had a family to support, and he did not have the security of falling back on half pay as did a naval officer. Moreover, to claim prescriptive rights for the exploration of an entire region was absurd, as even Scott's examples proved. Peary's claim to the rights of a region had never been taken seriously by most Arctic experts, particularly since he followed a course in which he had been preceded by expeditions under Charles Francis Hall, George Strong Nares and Adolphus W. Greely; Peary had even made use of Greely's hut. And dozens of expeditions towards the interior of Africa had begun in Zanzibar or Bagamoyo without anyone ever claiming rights to those as bases.

But it was undoubtedly Scott's insistence about his closeness with the members of his party that grated most with Shackleton. He remembered too clearly being sent home against his will. He recalled the embarrassment following Scott's lecture of November 1904 at the Albert Hall, when the impression passed on by the *Daily Mail* was that he had to be carried on the sledge for 150 miles on the return from the farthest south. That this was his inference had been denied by Scott, but that did not remove the stigma. And Shackleton certainly had felt humiliated in October 1905 when, in *The Voyage of the 'Discovery'*, Scott had placed on record that Shackleton had had to be carried on the sledge on 21 and 30 January 1903. This weakness had long mortified Shackleton, but what made it intolerable was what he would have seen as the faithlessness of the reporting. On the former date there was no reference to the fact, that, as Wilson recorded, 'Shackle at first was walking in harness, but we made him sit on the after sledge and break its pace with a ski pole, as the sledges were going too fast for us.' Similarly, on the latter date, Scott wrote in his book that 'Our invalid . . . was so exhausted that we thought it wiser he should sit on the sledges, where for the remainder of the forenoon, with the help of the sail, we carried him.' In contradiction, Wilson had recorded, 'He has been very weak and breathless all day, but has stuck to it well and kept up with us on ski.'

Such issues must have been in Shackleton's mind when he responded to Scott that he would give his letter 'very earnest consideration', but that Scott's wishes were not the only ones to be considered: 'I think my desires were as great if not greater than anybody else's to return seeing that I was cut off by a premature return to this country from further participating in the expedition.' Shackleton also had to take account of the expectations of those financing him: 'Naturally, I would like to fall in with your views as far as possible without creating a position that would be untenable to myself in view of the arrangements already made.'

With two such strong personalities in basic disagreement, here were the makings of a collision, as each wanted the other to withdraw, and neither seemed likely to do so. The situation also appears to have been exacerbated by the machinations of Markham. 'I am very glad to hear that you have succeeded in raising the funds for an expedition,' he wrote to Shackleton, adding, 'any advice or help I can give will be at your service.' But showing that retirement had not dulled his Machiavellian nature, he then wrote to Scott: 'I feel very indignant that he [Shackleton] should have treated you with such duplicity. He has behaved shamefully, and it grieves me more than I can say that an expedition which worked with such harmony throughout, should have had a black sheep . . .'

Markham's attitude could have done nothing but encourage Scott's initial beliefs that Shackleton was attempting to forestall him in a most unworthy manner. It also probably helped embolden Scott's arguments for his priority in the use of McMurdo Sound. Although these claims to the rights to an entire region might seem preposterous, he did honestly feel that he had a mission there. It is clear from his books that he wanted not only to establish geographical marks but to accomplish a symbolic act of conquest for the British Empire and, through overseeing careful scientific investigations, to resolve significant questions about the functioning of the world. Although a product of a Royal Navy system that could be stifling intellectually, Scott could at times transcend that background due to a simple, absorbing curiosity in things new and different.

Yet Shackleton could no more divorce himself from Antarctica than Scott. It was not simply that they had suffered there too much to put the frozen lands out of their lives. For Shackleton there were far more significant reasons: the Antarctic would not only provide the struggle that was such an important component of his being, it would also satisfy his fundamental restlessness. Neither of these, perhaps, was a conscious reason for his desire to go south, but there were other motives that clearly were, including proving that he was worthy of Emily, achieving fame and, he hoped, gaining a fortune. There was also the simple thrill of discovery, about which he said to his sister Kathleen, 'I don't want to race anyone, but you can't think what it's like to walk over places where no one has been before.'

Like Scott, Shackleton also wanted to achieve greatness for Britain, and he concluded a letter to Emily soon after announcing his expedition with the heart-felt postscript, 'I am representing 400 million British subjects.' A similar love of nation was felt by explorers throughout the world. In the midst of Africa, the French explorer Jean-Baptiste Marchand demonstrated an identical worship of his fatherland when he wrote:

> Don't go and think . . . that I'm exaggerating the role we're playing here . . . It is always respectable when it has for a motive the task of reminding this country of its true greatness, of its mission in the world, begun nearly 20 centuries ago, the mission which we all have the unavoidable obligation of continuing on pain of being guilty of national cowardice.

Shackleton could not have said it better. Finally, there was the simple but overwhelming desire to prove himself, to re-establish his manhood, to show that he should not have been sent back home. And to satisfy those goals, Shackleton was prepared to put up with anything, even the prospect of death itself.

A scene was thus set for a struggle of the wills that likely would have benefited neither explorer. But into the picture came a mediator, a man seemingly able to pour water on to Scott's raging fire and oil on to Shackleton's troubled waters at the same time. Not surprisingly, it was Edward Wilson.

Shackleton showed remarkable self-control in his response to Scott, not only in what he wrote, but in that he sent the letter to Wilson to read first, then pass on to Scott. Virtually immediately Shackleton had a response that must have shocked him. 'Now Shackles – I think your position is quite clear,' Wilson wrote on 28 February. 'I think you ought to retire from McMurdo Sound . . . it largely diminishes your prospects of a big or the biggest success. But I do wholly agree with the right lying with Scott to use that base before anyone else.' Ignoring that Scott's expedition did not have financial backing nor was even 'scheduled' for two years, Wilson continued: 'I think that if you go to McMurdo Sound & even reach the Pole – the gilt will be off the gingerbread because of the insinuation which will almost certainly appear in the minds of a good many, that you forestalled Scott who had a prior claim to the use of that base.'

This argument may not seem logical by today's standards, but Wilson had a strong emotional influence over his friend. Therefore, on 4 March Shackleton sent a cable to Scott stating, 'Will meet your wishes regarding base please keep absolutely private at present as certain supporters must be brought round to the new position.' And with this, a similar communication to Keltie, and an official announcement on 8 March stating that he would seek a base in King Edward VII Land, to the east of the Great Ice Barrier, Shackleton thought that one major issue had been resolved. He could not have been more wrong.

Within days he received a message from Wilson advising him not to make any new plans until he had heard from Scott 'what limits he puts on his rights. I have asked him to write to you as soon as possible to tell you his views as regards other possible bases.'

Shackleton was having no more of this chivalric tomfoolery, which was totally one-sided to boot. 'I do not agree with you, Billy, about holding up my plans until I hear what Scott considers his rights,' he dashed back.

> There is no doubt in my mind that his rights end at the base he asked for . . . I will not consider that he has any right to King Edward the Seventh's Land, and only regard it as a direct attempt to keep me out of the Ross quarter if he should even propose such a thing. I have given way to him in the greatest thing of all, and my limit has been reached . . . You know as well as I do that I have given up a certainty almost for a very uncertain base as regards the ultimate success of the Pole . . . I consider I have reached my limit, and I go no further.

Two weeks later, Shackleton continued to stand his ground, when he wrote firmly to Scott:

I have been ready, as you realise to meet you as regards McMurdo Base. I realise myself what I have given up in regard to this matter. Concerning the 170 Meridian West as a line of demarkation . . . I must tell you quite frankly that my agreement to this proposition might perhaps make a position untenable to me on my Southward journey and that I do not see my way, at the present moment, to accede to this. I also consider that the unknown land or the disputed land of Wilkes is free to anybody who wishes to explore that part . . . I do not desire to trouble you with further correspondence . . . in May we can finally discuss matters.

Those discussions finally happened in person when Scott returned from sea in May. But to Shackleton's chagrin, his former commander continued to push for the 170°W meridian – far to the east in the Ross Sea region – as a dividing point for the two expeditions. And now Scott had the unqualified backing of Wilson, who had, in late March, accepted an invitation to go south with him, on the understanding that he would not be available until the end of 1908. One might think that such an agreement would have cast Wilson out as a fair arbiter, but he never the less continued to play a 'mediating' role in the debate. It has been indicated that Wilson virtually dictated the final terms of the agreement between Scott and Shackleton, and whether that is accurate or not, such a declaration was signed by Shackleton on 17 May. It stated, in part:

I am leaving the McMurdo Sound base to you, and will land either at the place known as Barrier Inlet or at King Edward VII Land whichever is the most suitable, if I land at either of these places I will not work to the westward of 170 meridian W. and shall not make any sledge journey going W. of that meridian unless prevented when going to the South from keeping to the East of that meridian by the physical features of the country.

I shall not touch the coast of Victoria land at all.

If I find it impracticable to land at King Edward VII Land or at Barrier Inlet . . . I may possibly steam north, and then to the westward and try and land to the west of Kaiser Wilhelm II Land . . . This meridian is about 80 E.

I think this outlines my plan, which I shall rigidly adhere to, and I hope that this letter meets you on the points that you desire.

Scott must have viewed the document with enormous pleasure. After months of a wheedling campaign that would have made Markham proud, he had gained virtually exactly what he wanted, and Shackleton had forfeited, among other things, even an attempt at the South Magnetic Pole, one of the essential elements of his expedition. It is still an almost inconceivable episode in the history of Antarctic exploration: that Scott and Wilson had ultimately bullied Shackleton into accepting this extraordinary agreement. It was a promise that should never ethically have been demanded and one that should never have been given, impacting as it might on the safety of Shackleton's entire expedition. It was to the eternal discredit of each of them, although most of all to Scott and Wilson.

Never the less, the agreement had been made. In the short term it meant that Shackleton could return unmolested to his preparations. In the long run it would have far-reaching consequences for all of them.

10

NIMROD

Although negotiations with Scott had undoubtedly comprised the most soul-destroying of the tasks in which Shackleton was involved during the first half of 1907, they were not the only preparations he had to make. Previously the expedition had existed only in his head; now it had to spring to life in little more than half a year.

Shackleton needed an identifying name for his enterprise, and he quickly settled on the proud, promotional and over-generous 'British Antarctic Expedition, 1907'. He then opened an office at 9 Regent Street, at the edge of Waterloo Place, in London's 'Clubland'. He engaged a business manager named Alfred Reid, who had assisted previous polar ventures, and set to work compiling the thousands of items and sorting out the multitude of details for the expedition.

One of Shackleton's first steps – as it had been for Scott half a dozen years before – was to consult Fridtjof Nansen, the man acknowledged as the sage regarding all aspects of travel in the polar regions. Everything about Nansen – from his austere, forbidding demeanour to his formidable intellect to his unrivalled success on the ice of the far north – marked him as a giant. He had exploded on to the world scene almost two decades before when he had led the first crossing of the Greenland ice cap. On this, he had proved beyond doubt the value of skis to polar exploration, demonstrating that they would function at high altitude and on a wide variety of snow and ice. He also improved their design, as well as developing a sledge that became the prototype of those used since: lighter, more flexible and running on skis. Additionally, he made innovations in clothing, tents and cooking equipment, including the 'Nansen cooker', a saucepan that conserved heat and fuel.

In 1893 Nansen left on his greatest journey. He had hypothesised the existence of a current that could carry a ship across the Arctic basin. To test this, he needed a vessel that could not be crushed in the ice, so he engaged the shipbuilder Colin Archer to construct a small, rounded ship that he named *Fram* (Forward). Her sides were angled to prevent the ice from getting a firm hold on the hull; thus, when the ice closed in, rather than nipping her, it raised her out of the water. Nansen and his companions then disappeared into the mysterious regions north of Siberia. In February 1895 Nansen and Hjalmar Johansen left *Fram* drifting with the ice to dash for the North Pole. They reached 86°14′N, 170 miles farther north than had previously been attained, then made a dramatic retreat over the ice. Nansen's subsequent return to civilisation, the day after *Fram* reached Norway, made him the darling of the press world-wide, a man described as 'the most eminent explorer ever known'.

A decade later, when Shackleton visited Nansen, the older man was living in London, serving as the Minister to the Court of St James for the newly independent Norway. But his mind, like Shackleton's, was on the far south. His life's goal had never truly been the north; Nansen had always wanted to reach the South Pole.

That did not stop him doing his best by the British explorer who came seeking to steal his dream. How unlike Scott he was, Shackleton must have thought, as Nansen discussed clothing, food, cooking equipment and transport. He gave the younger man the benefit of his vast knowledge, which dictated, among other things, the use of dogs, skis and animal fur for clothing and sleeping bags.

Had Shackleton followed Nansen's recommendations, Amundsen–Scott Station at the South Pole might today be named for him rather than for the leaders of the first two parties to attain that destination. But on two crucial points Shackleton would veer from Nansen's recommendations, and that would make all the difference.

It was a fateful choice, one that, in retrospect, begs the question of how it could possibly have been reached. But the roots of the decision that Shackleton now made went back years earlier – to the time of the most remarkable meeting in polar history.

After retreating from their farthest north in 1895, Nansen and Johansen had been forced to winter in a dingy shelter they built under a driftwood log on a wretched island in Franz Josef Land. They did not actually know where they were, and in May 1896 they headed south-west through the archipelago in leaky kayaks, not realising that soon there would be nothing between them and Svalbard – hundreds of miles away. But while camped on Northbrook Island, Nansen heard dogs and then saw a man and approached him. 'I raised my hat; we extended a hand to one another,' Nansen wrote:

> On one side the civilised European in an English check suit and high rubber waterboots, well shaved, well groomed, bringing with him a perfume of scented soap . . . on the other side the wild man, clad in dirty rags, black with oil and soot, with long, uncombed hair and shaggy beard, black with smoke, with a face [with a] thick layer of fat and soot which a winter's endeavours with warm water, moss, rags, and at last a knife had sought in vain to remove.

They chatted for a few moments, and the other man said, 'Aren't you Nansen?' 'Yes, I am Nansen,' he replied. 'By Jove,' exclaimed Frederick Jackson, 'I am devilish glad to see you.'

Nansen remained with the leader of the Jackson–Harmsworth Expedition for more than a month before returning to Norway on Jackson's ship. In that time, Jackson proved himself to be a great British archetype of the time – the sportsman, a man who always took a massive armament with him in order to kill as many animals as possible. He revelled in the story of shooting hand-reared pheasants still in their covert, while he was only eight. And he took pride in that on his second day in Australia he killed numerous kangaroos, simply because they were the largest game available.

If there was anything in the world as important to Jackson as a gun, it was a horse. He dreamed as a youngster of soaring over five-bar gates when he was big enough to ride to hounds. He claimed to have introduced polo to Queensland. And he wrote that he had taken horses with him to Franz Josef Land to prove that they could be used effectively in the high Arctic. It was on a journey around the White Sea, Jackson wrote, that he 'fell in love with the hardy Russian ponies which did us such sovereign service . . . Ponies can be used to very great advantage in Arctic exploration.'

In fact, Jackson's horses suffered from numerous problems in Franz Josef Land. The pressure from their hooves broke holes in ice, hard-crusted snow, and, most dangerously, the snow bridges over glacier crevasses. They required massive amounts of fodder, but never the less regularly had digestive complaints. And grooming them away from camp was virtually impossible. Regardless, Jackson was 'thoroughly satisfied with my experiment . . . Horses . . . proved to be an unqualified success.'

The horses, many of which died, might not have agreed, but, remarkably, Shackleton did. He had discussed the advantages of horses with Armitage – Jackson's second-in-command – while in the Antarctic, and he held high hopes for their use. Now, after consulting Jackson, he was convinced.

Nansen must have been bewildered. Not only had *he* proven dogs successful, so had Sverdrup, Amundsen, Peary and the Italian Duke of the Abruzzi. They had not been as effective on *Discovery*, but was that not, he would have thought, blaming the dogs for the faults of their masters? Even Shackleton had once seemed to understand this, writing in *Pearson's Magazine* that 'I wish we had had about sixty or seventy [dogs], for then I think we could have reached the Pole.' Somehow, Jackson had swayed Shackleton, and, try as he might, Nansen could not convince him otherwise.

Equally as bizarre was Shackleton's reluctance to take skis, the very instruments that had brought him back alive from the farthest south. Inexplicably, Shackleton had already decided that if motor-car and horses should fail, he would follow the programme that Markham had passed down to Scott: man-hauling. This was, after all, a truly British method of operation, and Shackleton was no different from most of his contemporaries throughout the Empire, believing what was British was best.

One can only assume that in addition to this peculiarly British chauvinism, much of Shackleton's reluctance to follow Nansen's recommendations on these two fronts was due to his own lack of success with skiing and dog-driving. To attain a high level of efficiency in these required a patience that Shackleton simply did not have. But anybody, he most likely thought, can lead a horse. As a result, after his meeting with Nansen he contacted the London manager of the Hong Kong and Shanghai Bank, through whom he ordered fifteen Manchurian ponies; it was more than the number of pairs of skis that he took.

Shackleton could not, however, ignore Norwegian experience altogether. Norwegian companies were the world's premier producers of polar equipment, so in late April he and Reid travelled to Christiania to place orders. They were immediately confronted with the problem that certain items required months or even a year to produce, and it took all of Shackleton's charm – and no little part of his finance – to ensure that these could be delivered to London by June.

To his consternation, immediately upon arriving in Christiania Shackleton found that the man who had made the sledges for the *Discovery* Expedition was in the United States. At the recommendation of Sigurd Scott-Hansen, the former meteorologist on *Fram*, he turned instead to L.H. Hagen, one of the first mass producers of skis. Shackleton ordered thirty sledges of seasoned ash and American hickory: ten that were twelve feet long for use with the ponies, eighteen that were eleven feet long for man-hauling, and a pair of seven-footers for short trips.

Shackleton next visited W.C. Möller in Drammen, Norway, in order to obtain the necessary furs. The order was not large, as Shackleton had decided to use furs only for sleeping bags, gloves and footwear, but it was never the less critical. The company agreed to produce the items in a fraction of the time normally required, but this ultimately meant that it was unable to make all of the finnesko of the quality Shackleton wanted. These were an ancient Lapp item – soft boots made of reindeer fur, which were filled with sennegrass, a plant that absorbs moisture and provides insulation. The hardest wearing were made from the fur taken from the leg of the reindeer, but Shackleton was able to obtain only a dozen such pairs, and had to settle for another eighty pairs from other reindeer fur. He also ordered three three-man sleeping bags and a dozen one-man bags of reindeer fur. The final part of the order was sixty pairs of wolfskin and dogskin mittens, which were to be worn over wool gloves.

Shackleton's final major stop in Norway was at Sandefjord, where Adrien de Gerlache, the former commander of *Belgica*, had found a ship that he felt appropriate for the British Antarctic Expedition. Named *Björn* (Bear), she was a beauty: a three-year-old sealer built specifically for polar work. At some 700 tons she had berths for fifty men, vast storage space and powerful triple-expansion engines. She would easily be able to fight the ice near King Edward VII Land, and Shackleton wanted her immediately. The only problem was her cost: £11,000. He returned home to investigate the money that he had counted on from Douglas Steuart. It did not, in fact, exist.

* * *

During the past century and more, the popular press has, in many ways, not changed greatly. Items of significance seem only to be news if the media say so, and they frequently suffer in comparison to 'intriguing bits of nothing'. Such was now the case. As Shackleton ordered a specially designed hut and purchased clothing, travel equipment, and food he hoped would ward off scurvy, what appealed to the press was something that would not play a significant role in the expedition: the motor-car.

The motor-car was, ultimately, more a public relations exercise than anything else. Beardmore had recently taken over the only Scottish motor-car manufacturer, the Arrol-Johnston company of Paisley. In hopes of turning around a business that had faced bankruptcy, he ordered a specially designed automobile for Shackleton, accompanied by as much publicity as possible. 'Designed to withstand extreme cold', it included a chassis specially treated for low temperatures, an air-cooled engine capable of propelling it sixteen miles per hour, and an exhaust system utilised for warming purposes. It could be operated by a spirit designed to work in low temperatures, and it had two fuel tanks, one fed by gravity, the other by pressure. It also had three different sets of wheels for surfaces of varying hardness.

This was all very well, but Shackleton would much rather Beardmore had given him a ship. As it was, once he learned that he had less money than he had believed – and had made his supporters believe – he realised *Björn* was a dream. He looked instead for something he could afford. This turned out to be a grimy, mean little sealer sailing off of Newfoundland, which he could purchase for £5,000. Her name was *Nimrod*.

Built in Dundee in 1866 of oak, green heart and ironbark, by the firm A. Stephens & Son, *Nimrod* was a schooner of 334 gross tons and 136 feet. Her boiler and compound engines had been replaced in 1889, but she was under-powered and it was uncertain if she would be able to withstand the pounding fury and incessant storms of the Southern Ocean, not to mention the heavy ice in the Ross Sea. Never the less, Shackleton received a satisfactory inspection report, and bought her in early May.

Before he had even seen his new ship, Shackleton determined to rename her. 'Nimrod' had been appropriate for a seal hunter, coming as it did from the Book of Genesis, where Nimrod, the grandson of Ham and great-grandson of Noah, was 'the first on earth to be a mighty man.

He was a mighty hunter before the Lord.' However, Shackleton confided to Beardmore's wife Elspeth, 'I am going to change her name to "Endurance"'. This name was one Shackleton had long fancied, coming as it did from his family motto 'Fortitudine Vincimus,' or 'By endurance we conquer'. For reasons not known, Shackleton did not ultimately make the change, saving 'Endurance' for a later ship.

On 15 June *Nimrod* arrived in the Thames, and Shackleton was horrified. His new ship appeared even smaller than her measurements had made her sound, she was extremely dilapidated, her masts were rotten, and from top to bottom she was filthy and stank of the seal oil that had for decades filled her holds. Shackleton immediately turned her over to the shipyard of R. and H. Green in Blackwall, and work commenced to make her sea-worthy for some of the roughest conditions in the world. The hull was thoroughly caulked, the holds scraped and cleaned, and the masts and rigging were pulled down. In the ensuing weeks she was turned from a schooner to a barquentine, with square sails on the foremast and gaff-headed fore and aft sails on the main and mizzen. New quarters for the crew were constructed forward, temporary accommodation for the shore party was built in the aft hold, damage from former battles with ice was repaired, and new engines with sixty nominal horsepower were installed. By July, when the work was done, she could sail at eight-and-a-half knots and could make six knots under steam, using four tons of coal a day in smooth water.

The process of loading now had to begin. There were tons of stores at the expedition office, where equipment had officially been left on show, as Shackleton attempted to subsidise his enterprise by charging the public to view it. It was through this small commercial effort that he managed to meet John King Davis.

While on leave in London from his merchant ship, Davis, then only twenty-three, happened to meet a reporter friend who was on his way to interview Alfred Reid. With nothing better to do, Davis accompanied him to the expedition office, although, as he wrote, 'at that particular moment few places on the earth's surface were of less interest to me than the South Pole.' While looking over the exhibition of polar gear, Davis heard Reid indicate that the expedition was having a hard time finding a chief officer. With absolutely no forethought, Davis broke into the conversation, and within moments found himself ushered into Shackleton's office, where 'a young man dressed in a blue suit sat writing at a table. He had thick black hair carefully brushed down and

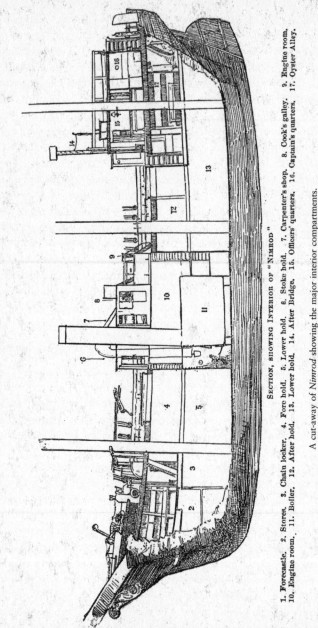

SECTION, SHOWING INTERIOR OF "NIMROD"

1. Forecastle. 2. Stores. 3. Chain locker. 4. Fore hold. 5. Lower hold. 6. Stoke hold. 7. Carpenter's shop. 8. Cook's galley. 9. Engine room.
10. Engine room. 11. Boiler. 12. After hold. 13. Lower hold. 14. After Bridge. 15. Officers' quarters. 16. Captain's quarters. 17. Oyster Alley.

A cut-away of *Nimrod* showing the major interior compartments.

From Shackleton, E.H. 1909, *The Heart of the Antarctic*. 2 vols. London: William Heinemann.

parted in the middle, heavy eyebrows, a piercing glance and a clean-shaven jaw of the variety known as "bulldog". There was about him the unmistakable look of a deep-water sailor.'

After a brief exchange, Shackleton sent Davis to *Nimrod* to speak to her master, Captain Rupert England. Davis's enthusiasm was knocked back a bit, however, when he saw the ship. 'My experience had been in deep-water sailing-ships which, though small by modern standards, seemed quite huge in comparison with this tiny vessel. Stripped for her refit and conversion, without masts, rigging or funnel, the little *Nimrod* looked little larger than a Thames barge.' England was not encouraging, and told Davis to come back a week later. When the congenial red-head showed up again, England gleefully told him that he had hired a man with 'transcendent qualifications' and wished him goodbye. Ten days later, on his way to his regular ship to sign on, Davis passed *Nimrod*. Coincidentally, England was at the gangway and asked him if he had another ship. When Davis answered in the negative, England told him the other man had not proved suitable after all and offered him the job. Davis immediately joined what would be the first of his seven major Antarctic voyages.

Just as Davis had not been immediately selected as first mate, England had not been Shackleton's top choice for captain. The man he originally had in mind was William Colbeck, who had been master of *Morning*, after having wintered at Cape Adare with Borchgrevink. Colbeck, however, had no interest, so he recommended England, his first mate on *Morning*, who was currently employed making a run along the coast of West Africa. The thirty-one-year-old England was to prove an unfortunate choice. Shackleton's selections for his shore party would – despite his seemingly random, helter-skelter methods of determining them – prove much better.

Shackleton's early attempts at gaining commitments from other members of Scott's expedition had all ended in failure. That did not finish his association with the former occupants of *Discovery*, however. Soon after he had opened the expedition office – if a story told years later is true – a most remarkable meeting occurred. One day he was looking out the window when an open-topped bus passed by. Sitting on the top deck was Ernest Joyce, a former AB on *Discovery* who had made several sledging trips with Shackleton and had later been promoted to petty officer. Shackleton immediately sent his secretary to find him, and, upon them returning, Joyce was offered the job of looking after the general stores, sledges and the few dogs they were to take. Shortly thereafter Joyce bought his release from the Royal Navy. In later years he would claim that Shackleton had promised to 'recompense me for so doing' but had not lived up to his word. However, there is no firm evidence of this.

Another *Discovery* rating who had made the step up to petty officer was Shackleton's old friend Frank Wild. In fact, Scott had recommended to the Admiralty that Wild be promoted to *chief* petty officer, but he had not been allowed to make such an uncommon jump. In the summer of 1907 Wild was serving on HMS *Wildfire* when Shackleton asked him if he would join the expedition. Wild immediately jumped at the opportunity and, like Joyce, attempted to purchase his release. He was refused, but in a surprising move the Admiralty agreed to assign him officially to HMS *President*, the London headquarters for the Royal Navy, and recorded that he was 'lent to British Antarctic Expedition 1907 and to be borne on books of HMS *President* for time only during period of service'. Shackleton put Wild in charge of provisions.

Wild and Joyce would spend much of their lives rootless and wandering. Both had found stability – but not happiness – in the Royal Navy, and now both were drawn back to Antarctica by a curious combination of affection and antipathy. They were never attracted by its natural splendours, and they did not record any particular excitement about being there, but they seemingly could not be actively happy elsewhere for long. They were both like addicts; once they had committed themselves to the hazards, difficulties and challenges of life in the far south, they felt impelled to return again and again.

But Wild and Joyce were the exception. It soon became apparent that none of the other men in the shore party would have previous Antarctic experience. This was subconsciously – or perhaps consciously – the way Shackleton wanted it. He had never been a leader before, and he could well have realised that the Antarctic was not the place for anything – whether comparable experience or force of personality – that could bring a challenge to his leadership. He therefore began to walk a fine line in his personnel decisions, attempting to find men with the skills and worldly experience that would make them successful in the south without giving them the status or ability to be independent. It was for such men that Shackleton now searched as he began to consider the more than 400 applications he had received after the announcement of the expedition had appeared in the press.

One of the easiest decisions was the appointment of the biologist. The former leader of the Scottish National Antarctic Expedition, William Speirs Bruce, introduced to him the forty-one-year-old James Murray, who also had a strong recommendation from Antarctic scholar Sir John Murray (to whom he was unrelated). It would have been a foolish man indeed who ignored such testimonials. The son of a grocer, Murray had a sporadic early education before leaving Glasgow's School of Art with a training in sculpture. However in the 1890s he became fascinated with natural history and particularly the study of microscopic creatures then just being discovered. Although virtually self-taught, Murray soon became an international expert, first studying tardigrades, of which he ultimately discovered more than sixty new varieties, and then turning his microscope to rotifers, describing more than one hundred new species or varieties. In 1902 he was engaged as assistant zoologist on Sir John's bathymetrical survey of the Scottish lochs. Unfortunately, this intensive programme contributed to a physical breakdown, causing Murray to note, 'I was just a little uneasy in my mind foisting upon Shackleton such a wreck of humanity.' Never the less, it was apparent from the start that he would make a strong scientific contribution.

The opposite in virtually every way from Murray – age, background, health and reasons for going south – was Sir Philip Brocklehurst, at twenty the expedition's youngest member. A baronet from Swythamley Park in Staffordshire, Brocklehurst was a tall, strapping Old Etonian currently at Trinity Hall, Cambridge, when he met Shackleton. He had received a Half Blue for boxing and spent a great deal of energy pursuing that pastime at the National Sporting Club in London. On one such trip to the City in March 1906 he was introduced to Shackleton over tea at the Brompton home of a friend. The young man was instantly impressed by the explorer, and wrote directly after their meeting, volunteering to go south.

The positive response was mutual, there being a spark that set off a life-long comradeship (Shackleton was Brocklehurst's best man in 1913). Sir Philip had good social connections, but more importantly – from a strictly mercenary standpoint – he had serious money, and he offered to contribute funds to the expedition. Shackleton wasted little time following up this financial avenue and visited Brocklehurst's mother, who, as her son was still a minor, controlled the purse strings.

He quickly charmed her and left promising to remember her son's interest in joining the expedition. With the money he hoped might be forthcoming, he was unlikely to forget.

In May 1907, feeling the pinch of the purchase and refitting of *Nimrod*, Shackleton followed through on his promise and accepted Brocklehurst, enclosing at the same time his instruction for the young man to guarantee £2,000 through his bank. Brocklehurst became the first subscribing member of an Antarctic expedition, a status followed three years later by Captain L.E.G. Oates and Apsley Cherry-Garrard on Scott's expedition.

Although Brocklehurst left Cambridge without taking a degree and was far more interested in his commission in the Derbyshire Yeomanry than in science, Shackleton hoped to get more than capital out of him. He sent instructions for the period prior to departure. 'Take up a course of practical surveying,' he directed. 'Learn to use the theodolite for usual angles and survey of a country. Learn to take your latitude and longitude with the theodolite. Learn to take bearings with the compass . . . Learn to take a survey with a plane table.' Then, perhaps remembering that he had named him assistant geologist, Shackleton added, 'Take up a course of field geology. Learn the particular formations of rocks . . . Learn to recognise the particular sedimentary, volcanic and igneous rocks.'

Brocklehurst turned to these tasks with a will, but it was for something far different that his usefulness was next proven, and it rescued Shackleton in a time of desperate need.

11

UNDERWAY AT LAST

At 3.00 p.m. on Sunday 4 August 1907 the little ship that for most of its career had been visited only by seals dead and dying received a collection of guests of a totally different calibre. It was Cowes Week, and those aboard *Nimrod* had become part of a spectacle that in memory seems to epitomise the proud, ostentatious, far-away days of Empire. Every year the Isle of Wight played host to this glorious gathering – part parade, part regatta, part obeisance to England's magnificent maritime history. It was one of the great occasions of the social season and the climax of the entire year for the yachting set, who turned out with their opulent cruisers and windjammers and J-class cutters showing acres of gleaming, snow-white canvas.

In 1907 Cowes Week was also a chance for the Royal Navy's grand review of its wares. Stretching for miles down the calm waters of the Solent was the Home Fleet, nearly 200 warships, the most powerful naval force in the world. Conspicuous as a giant among smaller siblings was the first of a new class of battleship that would alter all previous naval strategy – HMS *Dreadnought*, launched in 1906 and completed just months before. Floating regally at the head of this mighty armada and flying the Royal Standard was His Majesty's own *Victoria and Albert*; only a cable's length away from her, in the place of honour, was the former Newfoundland hunter.

The first to be piped aboard *Nimrod* from the Royal Yacht's pinnace was King Edward VII, decked out in fashionable yachting clothes. He was followed by Queen Alexandra, the Prince of Wales (later King George V), the Princess of Wales, the Duke of Connaught, Princess Victoria and Prince Edward (later King Edward VIII). The King asked Shackleton to introduce him to his officers and shore staff; he then asked many questions about the scientific instruments and the plans for the south.

Meanwhile, expedition members were detailed to entertain different guests. The second mate, Æneas Mackintosh, thought it particularly unfortunate that his lot fell to a taciturn fellow who evidently knew nothing about the polar regions and seemed to evince little interest in ships. Mackintosh, who had joined the expedition from the P&O Company, began to amuse himself by spinning tall tales of life at sea. Finally his soliloquy was interrupted by a grunt and a slap of his visitor's hand on the rail. 'I have my own ship,' he said, to let the mate know that *he* knew something of things maritime. The man nodded toward HMS *Dreadnought*. 'That's my ship. I built her.' With horror, Mackintosh realised he had been allotted Admiral Sir John Fisher, First Sea Lord and architect of Britain's new fleet.

As the royal visit ended, the King turned to Shackleton and, in front of the ship's company, pinned a medal on him. 'When Captain Scott left in the Discovery I conferred the Royal Victorian Order on him,' he announced. 'I now do the same to you as an incentive to scientific research and exploration.' That he had thus equalled Scott in his send-off must have pleased Shackleton immensely. But there was more. Queen Alexandra presented him with a flag, attached to which was a note that read, 'May this Union Jack, which I entrust to your keeping, lead you safely to the South Pole.' In modern history, such a gesture had not previously been made to a British explorer by a monarch: Shackleton had earned a unique status.

The King's visit to *Nimrod* was of enormous import in giving the British Antarctic Expedition a cachet with potential backers. This was significant because Shackleton was still trying to gain financing for his venture. Only two weeks before *Nimrod* had sailed from the East India Docks, he had found himself without the money to pay for the final work. He turned in desperation to a philanthropist he had never met, Edward Guinness (of the Irish brewers), the Earl of Iveagh. In an endeavour that showed Shackleton's charm and drive at their most effective, he convinced the Earl to guarantee £2,000 on the condition that the explorer came up with other guarantees taking the total to £8,000. Within a week and a half, with a strong helping hand from his enthusiastic new devotee Philip Brocklehurst – that is, from his mother – Shackleton had managed to do so.

The new loan did not mean Shackleton's financial troubles were over. Long before *Nimrod* departed, he knew that a number of expedition members would remain in England, continuing with preparations and raising funds. It was obvious that such efforts would be helped considerably by the public and press approval to be gained by the King's patronage, so in late July he had turned again to the Brocklehursts for assistance. In this case it was to the baronet's slick and well-placed cousin.

John Fielden Brocklehurst (later Baron Ranksborough) was ample proof of the success that could come in Victorian times if one were handsome, charming and socially skilled. Not graced by birthright to a mammoth inheritance, he entered the army after graduating from Trinity College, Cambridge. His contacts allowed him to gain a commission in the Royal Horse Guards, which, as part of the Queen's bodyguard, were based in Windsor. In 1882, Brocklehurst participated in the first foreign service for the Horse Guards since Waterloo, in Wolseley's victorious Egyptian campaign.

Two years later, promoted to brevet major, Brocklehurst served in the effort to relieve Khartoum. This was a very personal cause, as he was one of Gordon's dearest friends and the two had dined together at the 'Blues' Mess on the general's last night in Britain. In a letter smuggled out of Khartoum, Gordon told Wolseley that he prayed daily for two men: Wolseley and Brocklehurst. In 1894 Brocklehurst became commander of the Royal Horse Guards, a position he held for five years until sent to Natal as colonel in charge of the Third Cavalry Brigade at the beginning of the Boer War. There, unfortunately, he was caught in Ladysmith with General Sir George White, where he apparently fell afoul of the ever-present Colonel Henry Rawlinson. Throughout his career, few could help being charmed by Brocklehurst, but Rawlinson tersely noted that 'Pogglehurst' had neither 'the dash nor the brains' to command cavalry.

Brocklehurst had both aplenty for a position in court, however, and shortly before leaving for Natal, he was appointed Equerry to Queen Victoria, a role that after her death he followed with an analogous one for Queen Alexandra. This gave him the ear of the Queen and a certain input with the Royal Family (in fact, he later became Lord-in-Waiting to King George). It is highly likely that, although he was unable to obtain the King's patronage for the British Antarctic Expedition, he played a significant part in the command for *Nimrod* to proceed to

Cowes for Royal inspection. This order had reached Shackleton in the Thames estuary, the day after they had sailed. It is also not unlikely that Brocklehurst initiated the Queen's unprecedented gesture of giving a flag to the man who had invited her Equerry's cousin on the expedition. The Brocklehursts had clearly validated Shackleton's decision to take Sir Philip; it was not to be the last time.

Early on the morning after the King's inspection, *Nimrod* sailed quietly into the Channel. In the hours immediately following His Majesty's visit, numerous other men of distinction had been welcomed aboard and a message wishing success had been received from Sir Joseph Dalton Hooker, the famed botanist who was one of the last surviving members of James Clark Ross' expedition of two-thirds of a century before. A day and a half later, the ship arrived at Torquay, to be met by Emily, who had not been at Cowes. That night the Shackletons gave a farewell dinner for the officers and crew. 'Shackleton sat at his wife's right hand with the Queen's flag placed behind him and everyone felt proud, excited, and full of hope,' first mate John King Davis later wrote about the occasion. It was the last time for more than four months that all of the members of the expedition would be together, as Shackleton and most of the shore party disembarked for weeks of further preparations.

Nimrod finally departed England on 7 August 1907, sailing from Torquay across the rough waters of the Bay of Biscay to hot, dry São Vicente in the Portuguese sugar colony of the Cape Verde Islands. After re-coaling, they made the passage to Cape Town, where, seven years before, Davis had run away to sea. Then came *Nimrod*'s long haul across the Indian Ocean, driven by powerful westerlies that took them to Lyttelton, New Zealand. For sixteen long weeks they made agonisingly dull progress, the most excitement coming from the oceanic dredging operations lovingly carried out by two Scots who were the only members of the shore party still aboard, Murray and Dr Alistair Forbes Mackay.

One of two surgeons selected to winter in the Antarctic, the twenty-nine-year-old Mackay was a tough, muscular hothead who responded with action as quickly as words. The son of a colonel in the Gordon Highlanders, he studied medicine at Edinburgh University before enlisting in the City Imperial Volunteers after the disasters of Black Week. He then served as one of Robert Baden-Powell's police, and later returned to Edinburgh to complete his medical education. Mackay had been a naval surgeon for four years before resigning to join Shackleton's expedition.

In October, as *Nimrod* bobbed her way to New Zealand, eight more members of the shore party left Liverpool crammed into one small cabin on *Runic*, a single-class emigrant ship of the White Star line. Today, someone forcing his employees into such a restricted space would claim it was an exercise in 'team-building'; Shackleton made no pretence that it was anything but an effort to save money. In the next six weeks the men came to know each other better than they would ever have wished and, as Raymond Priestley, the youngest of them, later wrote: 'we formed a solid block with esprit-de-corps laid on with a trowel and . . . with deepest cleavages among ourselves which later developed to advantage when sharing out the work and picking out the sledge parties.' The eight men in the room demonstrated a wide variety of abilities, interests and personal habits, and long before they reached New Zealand, friendships and rivalries had been made that would only be terminated by death.

Although two of them – Wild and Joyce – had previous Antarctic experience, the man nominally in charge was Jameson Adams. He had been one of the first to volunteer to go south with Shackleton, when several officers from HMS *Berwick* had spent the evening chatting to the would-be explorer while their ship was anchored near his summer home. In 1907 Adams, then twenty-seven, was still a lieutenant in the Royal Naval Reserve after a dozen years of service, when suddenly the chance of a lifetime appeared. His commanding officer told him to prepare his best uniform because the next day he would be given 'a permanent commission in the Royal Navy with the requisite seniority, and your career is made'. This was a virtually unheard of opportunity, and Adams 'went down to the ward-room to celebrate this with the greatest joy in the world'.

It was a brief celebration. Within minutes, according to Adams, he received a message from Shackleton: 'Will you come as my second in command?' He immediately returned to the bridge and told his captain, 'Sir, I've changed my mind already: this is my offer and I'm going to take it. The Navy can go by.'

Adams worked with Shackleton at the office almost from the start, and he was present at the interviews of many applicants. He knew that although Shackleton had unusual selection methods, he had subtly sized up the character of those being interviewed and 'had great intuition as to whether the fellows concerned had the qualifications required'. But to many, Shackleton's appointments seemed impulsive. Certainly none came about in an odder set of circumstances than the hiring of Priestley, the geologist who was just finishing his second year at University College, Bristol.

Shackleton had neither great interest in nor knowledge about the scientific work that his party would carry out. When he had first spoken to Brocklehurst, he had explained the expedition as a dash to the Pole without any science at all. However, he was aware of the need for a scientific façade to obtain publicity and financial support. Unlike Scott, he did not want to spend time either selecting scientists or overseeing their work, so, early on, he sought the advice of noted scientists such as Sir John Murray and Arthur Schuster, the professor of physics at Manchester University.

As geologist, Murray recommended an individual at the Bristol Museum who had been on the *Challenger* Expedition and who re-luctantly agreed to be interviewed but then 'refused with some deci-sion'. Coincidentally, Priestley's older brother Bert, a botany lecturer, came into the interview room just at the end of the process, at which point he was asked in an off-hand way if Raymond would be interested. Shortly thereafter, as he passed through the library where his sibling was studying, Bert asked, 'How would you like to go to the Antarctic, Ray?' Priestley responded, 'I'd go anywhere to get out of this place'. He soon had a telegram from Shackleton asking him to come to London.

Although he spoke to Shackleton, Priestley assumed that he had no chance for the position, because 'I was not academically qualified, and I discovered later that at least a dozen Honours graduates had been after the job.' Moreover, Priestley thought the interview rather strange, as Shackleton did not ask many geological questions, the notable excep-tion being, 'Would you know gold if you saw it?' Priestley made no bones about that. Shackleton's other questions were about such things as whether he could play a musical instrument, to which he replied in the negative, although 'I was not bothered for I did not then understand the significance'. Priestley departed uncertain of whether he was being taken or not, but ten days later he received a telegram from Shackleton asking why he had not started collecting his equipment. The expedition had found its geologist.

An equally unusual story has been passed down for years about the hiring of the expedition artist, George Marston, a bulky twenty-five-year-old whom Priestley described as having 'the frame and face of a prize-fighter and the disposition of a fallen angel'. According to an article Shackleton later wrote for *Pearson's Magazine*, Marston was given the job because he was the only one of three final candidates to show up for a hastily scheduled interview, having interrupted a walking holiday in Cornwall to do so. It was a lovely story but, Marston's letters show, sadly not true. In fact, Marston, who trained in art at London's Regent Street Polytechnic, was part of a social circle of young artists and art students that also included Shackleton's sisters Helen and Kathleen, the latter of whom became a professional artist. While at a friend's studio, the sisters suggested that Marston apply for the job.

He did so but obviously tired of waiting for an answer, because on 4 August, the day the King inspected *Nimrod*, Helen Shackleton needed to encourage him not to give up:

> you simply *must* not chuck the idea of the Antarctic job, just because you haven't yet had Ernest's decision . . . I feel, and I believe (in his innermost heart) that Ernest feels that this expedition will reach the South Pole, & think how sick you would feel, if, before learning E's decision, you told them that you had changed your mind – and think if they reached the S. Pole! . . . I really feel that if you are passed you *ought* to go.

A week and a half later, their brother offered the position to 'Putty', as Marston quickly became known. Shackleton was progressively drawn to Marston, not only for his artistic skills but his physical strength and satirical, lampooning sense of humour. They both enjoyed donning unusual clothes and making their comrades laugh by impersonating other people. According to Shackleton's niece he once even fooled his family when they were on a picnic. 'They were all sitting around,' she recalled years later, 'and this awful old tramp came along, filthy, and said things like "Come on, dear, give me a kiss" and the children were all terrified, and suddenly someone recognised Uncle Ernest dressed up.' In Eastbourne, Shackleton was said to have borrowed one of Emily's dresses, a hat and false curls to successfully impersonate a beautiful and charming woman. Several times during the expedition, Marston put on women's clothes and makeup to bring light relief to his colleagues.

Similarly, it was a social contact that introduced Shackleton to the expedition's senior surgeon, Dr Eric Marshall, a powerful man with the physical ability to row for Emmanuel College, Cambridge, and then be a rugby forward for St Bartholomew's Hospital. In 1906 they had met at a party in London, and Marshall had been impressed by Shackleton's enthusiastic banter. He volunteered on the spot, and it is apparent that almost from the word go Shackleton intended him to be the surgeon and cartographer for the polar party. Although Marshall was to serve well in both capacities in addition to being one of the primary photographers, the selection was not in all respects one of Shackleton's better ones. Marshall had the inflexible, unforgiving manner that often marked the evangelical true believer; this he certainly was, having entered Emmanuel planning on taking Holy Orders, before leaving after a year to pursue medicine. A bitterly sardonic attitude, combined with an arrogant superiority, made it difficult for him to become close to other members of the expedition.

The final two men in that small cabin on *Runic* had been hired for very specific talents. Bernard Day had trained in motor engineering and had been employed by Beardmore's Arrol-Johnston Motor-Car Company. When Shackleton was given the motor-car, the twenty-three-year-old Day was more or less offered as part of the package as electrician and driver. The other specialist was William Roberts, selected as a result of the problems with the cook on *Discovery*. Roberts, at the age of thirty-five, had had extensive experience as a cook both on land and at sea, most recently serving as the pastry chef at the Naval and Military Club. He was obviously a man of different faces, as Priestley commented, 'not least from the point of view of entertainment value', whereas Brocklehurst thought Roberts 'was the only one who couldn't appeal to the ordinary man . . . he was a bit rough . . . he knew and felt it, and was very antagonistic for that reason. He never liked anybody.'

Brocklehurst himself was the last member of the party to leave Britain, departing on 7 November 1907. He crossed the Channel, caught an overnight train from Calais to Marseilles, and then sailed on *Omrah*, on which he had booked a first-class stateroom. His leisurely cruise included a stop at Pompeii, viewing the eruption of Stromboli, a passage through the Suez Canal, and a visit to Colombo in Ceylon before arriving in Australia. He then delayed his trip to New Zealand in order to see the Test Match in Sydney, before finally catching up with his shipmates in Christchurch.

Shackleton had taken much the same route – without the first-class ticket or relaxed pace – a week before Brocklehurst. During the previous months, much of his time had been spent on financial affairs, and in August he had optimistically written to Emily that:

> I have already made arrangements with Heinemann to publish the book on my return and it means £10,000 if we are successful: and that is quite apart from all newspaper news . . . the book can pay off guarantees if the people really want them but I am of the opinion that they will not ask for them if we are successful: I think it will be worth about £30,000 in the way of lectures alone.

This was typical of Shackleton's rose-coloured view of the future, but success was far from certain, and in the meantime he had many bills, but no money. He was temporarily rescued by a gift of £4,000 from his cousin William Bell, but when this proved not enough, the Brocklehurst connection again saved the day. The help came in the form of a donation by Campbell Mackellar, a close friend of Sir Philip and his mother. Mackellar was a verbose, and at times overwhelming, Scotsman and a strong supporter of the expedition, who wrote that upon meeting Shackleton, 'the opinion I formed then, and at once, of Shackleton as an ideal leader I never wavered in . . . and I was fully justified in my belief.'

Now, as always when he departed, Shackleton's mind focused not so much on what lay ahead as on what was waiting behind. 'Your dear brave face is before me now and I can see you just as you stand on the wharf and are smiling at me,' he wrote to Emily on the train across France, adding:

> My heart was too full to speak and I felt that I wanted just to come ashore and clasp you in my arms and love and care for you: Child honestly and truly it was the worst heart aching moment in my life: If I failed to get the Pole and was within 10 miles and had to turn back it would or will not mean so much sadness as was compressed into those few minutes.

On no account, he continued, would he 'run any risk for the sake of trying to get the "Pole" in the face of hard odds. I have not only myself but you and the children to consider and always remember that and . . .

if inclined to do anything rash I will think of my promise to you and not do it.'

During the next weeks, Shackleton thought constantly about Emily. 'It seems years already since I left and it really is only just over a fortnight,' he wrote as RMS *India* neared Colombo. 'Oh it is hard indeed to be away from it all and the only compensation that can be will be the doing of the work and then the homecoming *never* never again for us to be separated.' As usual at such times, Shackleton thus denied his nomadic nature. But he did acknowledge that, 'I want the glory of the Conquest for ourselves and for the country and I want to make this great in the golden world for you my Queen.'

But soon his mind was again turning away from Emily and back to his venture. He had written to her from Aden that he had lectured aboard ship and 'was glad to do it as there are some rich Australians on board who now seem interested in the Expedition'. As he reached Melbourne at the beginning of December, Shackleton was hoping that two public lectures he was scheduled to present there and in Sydney would assist his still struggling finances. In fact, they would help bring credibility and success to the entire expedition.

The stage was now set for the entrance of a man whose contributions to Antarctic scientific research cannot be overstated. Tannatt William Edge-worth David would not only be a key performer in a variety of roles on the British Antarctic Expedition, but would later influence Scott's final ex-pedition and, through his relationship with Douglas Mawson, have a profound impact on the development of Australian Antarctic research.

Born in St Fagan's, near Cardiff, in January 1858, David had early been educated at home by his father, the local rector, and then at Magdalen College School, Oxford. The award of a classical scholarship – after placing first out of more than seventy candidates from public schools – allowed David to enter New College, Oxford, where he intended to take Holy Orders. But it was at 'The Other Place' – as Cambridge men such as Brocklehurst and Marshall would have called it – that David discovered a subject that thrilled him like no other: geology. Despite a breakdown of his health, the treatment for which was a round-trip to Australia on the sailing ship *Yorkshire*, he grad-uated in 1880 and immediately began the study of the geology of St Fagan's and the local district.

David's independent work and subsequent papers quickly attracted attention, and in 1882 he was appointed to the position of assistant geological surveyor to the government of New South Wales. For the next eight years he carried out extensive fieldwork, made important discoveries of tin and coal deposits, and built an enormous scholarly reputation. In 1891 he was appointed professor of geology and physical geography at the University of Sydney, where his lucid, inspiring lectures soon drew students from all fields of study. 'As a lecturer he has rarely been surpassed,' wrote Griffith Taylor, one of his students who was a member of Scott's last expedition. David had a deep melodious voice that, Taylor wrote, 'would ring out like a clarion', combined with such a power of delivery that, according to Mawson, 'his students were at times held spell-bound'.

As early as 1895 David had shown a strong interest in the ice of the polar regions, and by 1907 he was one of the world's most respected glaciological experts. In September Shackleton, aware that David's immense academic reputation was equalled by his powerful political connections, invited him to accompany the expedition to King Edward VII Land to advise Priestley and Brocklehurst before returning to New Zealand with the ship. David immediately agreed and threw himself into preparations, including laying the groundwork for Shackleton's speaking engagements in Australia.

On 3 December, Shackleton gave his public lecture in Melbourne. Three days later, before a crowd of more than 4,000, he repeated it to a series of standing ovations. He desperately needed the money that he earned from these presentations, but he was so moved by the appreciative audiences that, in spontaneous gestures, he presented the fees to local charities. This on-the-spot generosity was one of the charming, if unpractical, aspects of Shackleton's personality. 'His heart was always bigger than his pockets,' James Dell, who had been on *Discovery* and would later join Shackleton for his final expedition, once said. 'He never worried about money, did he, not for one moment.'

The public response to Shackleton was overwhelming, and David seized the opportunity to write a letter to Alfred Deakin, the Prime Minister of Australia, asking for financial aid for the expedition. Shackleton had counted on an additional £4,500 coming from William Bell; due to bank failures in the United States, this had not materialised. In a lengthy letter, David spelled out the numerous gains to world knowledge, and more specifically the advantages to Australia, that would accrue from the expedition. 'In view of the fact Lieutenant Shackleton and his friends have contributed so liberally to a scientific expedition which so intimately concerns Australia,' he concluded, 'it would be a gracious act on the part of the Commonwealth Government to help this British Antarctic Expedition in its present need by granting a liberal contribution.'

Such was the regard in which David was held, that when the official proposal for a grant was made, the Leader of the Opposition was reported to say, 'If Professor David says he wants it, that ends it.' The Australian government awarded Shackleton a grant of £5,000, to which was soon added a grant of £1,000 from the government of New Zealand. These allowed not only an increase in expedition staff, but more stores and equipment to be purchased and last-minute alterations to be made on *Nimrod*.

Money was not all that David was to contribute, however. The day before arriving in Melbourne, *India* docked in Adelaide, and Shackleton was met by one of David's former students, Douglas Mawson, a lecturer in mineralogy and petrology at the University of Adelaide. Mawson asked if he, like David, could sail down and back with *Nimrod*. 'My idea,' he later wrote, 'was to see a continental ice-cap in being and become acquainted with glaciation and its geological repercussions.'

Shackleton said that he would consider it, but when he received the grant from the government, he promptly wired Mawson that he had been appointed physicist for the duration of the expedition. Although caught off guard because he was not a physicist, and by the length of the appointment, Mawson accepted.

Meanwhile, when Shackleton arrived in Sydney, David prepped him for his lectures. He also laid out a schedule for official calls to prominent individuals and organisations. David then raised the issue of other potential members of the expedition, starting with Leo Cotton, whom he wanted as his assistant because 'the possible usefulness of any work I might do would be more than doubled if I had Cotton's assistance'. David felt strongly enough about the intellectual but physically rugged Cotton that 'I am quite prepared to pay any reasonable personal expenses that may be charged to Cotton if taken.' It was a request that Shackleton could hardly turn down, and Cotton joined the growing number of scientists on the expedition.

Two other individuals mentioned by David did not go south,

including Lawrence Hargraves, who ran a kite laboratory that David was hoping would supply three kites for research purposes. The other was Peter Close, whom David referred to as a 'strongman'. The place he might have occupied was filled by another Australian, Bertram Armytage. Thirty-eight years of age, and therefore older than most of the expedition members, Armytage had been at Jesus College, Cambridge, as an undergraduate, rowing in the first boat at the Lent races of 1888 when Jesus finished head of the river. After leaving Cambridge, he moved back to Australia, and then served with distinction with the 6th Dragoon Guards (Carabiniers) in South Africa, winning the Queen's Medal and three clasps. An avid hunter, Armytage went deer-stalking in New Zealand before joining Shackleton's venture as a general helper, with special attention to the ponies.

Thus, as Shackleton hurried on to New Zealand in mid-December, it appeared that the final shape and size of the shore party had been determined. It had not.

Once in New Zealand, Shackleton made another addition, moving second officer Æneas Mackintosh to the shore party. Only a few days before *Nimrod* sailed south, Arthur Harbord joined her as auxiliary second officer. With a Square-rigged Extra Master's Certificate, Harbord held the highest qualification possible in sailing ships as well as those driven by steam. This emphasis on sail was unexpectedly very important, because in Lyttelton Shackleton had suddenly realised that *Nimrod* would have to be under sail a good deal of the time – she would not be able to hold enough coal to get to the Ross Ice Shelf and back. In fact, without good winds the expedition might never get to King Edward VII Land at all, or, worse yet, it might never come home.

12

A PROMISE BROKEN

Ballast. It was one of the most fundamental foundations of the maritime world, but it threatened to destroy the entire British Antarctic Expedition. As the date of departure from Lyttelton – New Year's Day 1908 – drew closer, and *Nimrod* was loaded heavier and packed tighter, Shackleton realised that it was simply impossible to cram everything aboard the tiny vessel. Most important was the coal, both the lack of it and, ironically, the inability to use what there was.

When Shackleton first appreciated that there would not be enough coal for a trip to and from the Great Ice Barrier, he turned to the wind as his saviour. However, it soon became apparent that this would not solve the problem of getting *Nimrod* back to New Zealand. Much of the coal might have to be used to force through the pack ice around the Ross Sea, both on the way south and then again north. Even a plan to allot just enough coal to get through the ice on the return, and sail the rest of the way was not feasible, because the coal was serving a dual purpose: as fuel and ballast. Were all of it consumed, there would be nothing to prevent the ship from capsizing in heavy seas, as no new source of ballast could be guaranteed.

This oversight – due a great extent to Shackleton's inexperience in command – must initially have been a devastating blow. However, he was always at his best in a crisis, and now he devised a creative new plan. He would have *Nimrod* towed to the Antarctic Circle, thereby preserving the coal and allowing her to return under steam with the excess providing the necessary ballast.

As he had with the Australians, Shackleton had been taken to the hearts of New Zealanders, who took great pride in bestowing official recognition and public support. He now turned this to his advantage and asked for help from the New Zealand government, which offered to pay half the cost of a tow to the edge of the ice. The other half came via the good graces of Sir James Mills, chairman of the Union Steam Ship Company, which also provided the towing ship. Mills appointed Captain Frederick Pryce Evans to be in charge, and Evans selected for the task *Koonya*, a steel-built steamer of 1,093 gross tons, which had been trading between Dunedin and Wellington.

That resolved, the stowing of *Nimrod* continued, although a variety of items had to be left behind. These included five of the fifteen ponies, which had made the trip from Tientsin to Hong Kong to Sydney to Quail Island, the New Zealand quarantine station. There, under the guidance of Mackay, they had been broken to handling and introduced to pulling sledges. The ten best were selected for the journey and put in narrow stalls on the deck. Nearby, packed carefully in a protective crate and strapped down tightly, was the motor-car. By the day of departure, the decks were heaving with supplies that had not found a place in the hold: sledges, tins of carbide fuel for lighting the hut, bales of maize for the ponies, excess coal and, virtually unnoticed, the nine dogs that Joyce had selected from the descendants of the Siberian huskies left on Stewart Island by Borchgrevink in 1900. To the shore party, the successful mustering of all these materials undoubtedly seemed a feat of which to be proud, but such would not have been the thoughts of *Nimrod*'s merchant sailors, uncomfortably treading the deck knowing that, beneath them, the Plimsoll line was two feet under water.

The first day of January broke warm and clear, and as morning changed to afternoon the people of Christchurch came to bid farewell to the small group of adventurers. In a remarkable outpouring of goodwill, 50,000 people descended on the small harbour town of Lyttelton, packing the wharf and making it almost impossible to approach the ship. With the time of departure drawing near, two men fought their way through the crowd, desperate to reach *Nimrod*. The first of them was a thin, unremarkable-looking man soon to be fifty years old, who, having finally reached the ship, was now confronted with his most serious challenge. 'In getting on board the Nimrod, with both my arms full of breakable packages,' Edgeworth David wrote of the incident to *The Daily Telegraph* of Sydney,

I was gently impelled backwards over the naked gang plank by the steady pressure of a stout lady moving resolutely in the opposite direction; she was for the shore, let who would be for the Pole. Fortunately for me, but unfortunately for some of my fellow-men, I fell on to their heads on the deck . . . I had hoped that my ignominious embarkation had escaped detection, but even before I had time to straighten myself up again, I was disillusioned by the mellow tones of Shackleton's voice from the bridge.

The second man was a last-moment addition. George McLean Buckley was a wealthy sheep-farmer who had donated £500 to the expedition. While saying his farewells, Buckley had suddenly asked if he could accompany the ship as far as the ice pack and return on *Koonya*. Shackleton consented, and Buckley was off, catching a train to his club in Christchurch, picking up a few toiletries, and dashing back to push through the seething crowd with just minutes to spare. He was now heading to the Antarctic with only a thin summer suit by way of polar gear.

At 4.00 p.m. *Nimrod* cast off and made her slow way through a flotilla of passenger ships and private yachts. Brass bands played 'Auld Lang Syne' and 'Heart of Oak', and Priestley noted that several excursion steamers had decidedly unsafe lists due to the passengers pushing to the side on which *Nimrod* passed. When they reached three ships of the Royal Navy's Australian fleet, hundreds of men rushed to the bows and rent the air with three cheers.

Having passed out of the harbour, they picked up the towline from *Koonya*: a four-inch-thick wire hawser made of steel. It was shackled to *Nimrod*'s chain cables, which were then let out thirty fathoms, hoping to ensure that the great weight on the cables – coming from riding far under the water – would give protection from sudden stresses. However, it was soon apparent that the tons of cable would force the small ship to attack every wave with her bow pulled down into the sea.

They had hoped for good weather, because the overloaded *Nimrod* had only three feet six inches of free board. It was not encouraging, therefore, when, within an hour of reaching the open sea, they were swamped by high waves, and water poured into the scupper holes. They were sailing into the angriest gale any of them had ever experienced. Worse yet, it would last for ten days, during which they would be doused, buffeted and battered in a manner previously unimaginable to even the career mariners. 'I have never seen such large seas in the whole of my seagoing career,' Arthur Harbord, the auxiliary second mate, wrote, 'one moment we can see the keel of "Koonya" and the next we cannot see the truck.'

Such violent movements led Captain Evans to signal for *Nimrod* to let out another thirty fathoms of cable. With her decades old windlass, this was no easy task. But the only thing worse than braving the conditions on deck was being inside. The majority of the shore party were crammed into the converted aft hold, to which they gave the mysterious name 'Oyster Alley'. It was a room that was only fifteen feet by eight and was, according to Priestley:

> a place that under ordinary circumstances I wouldn't put ten dogs in, much less 15 of the shore-party. It can be compared with no place on earth and is more like my idea of Hell than anything I have ever imagined . . . There are no portholes that will open, the ventilation is pre-historic, and on two successive nights we have had to have all doors shut owing to seas being continually taken fair over the weather side of the stern. Every blanket in the place is wet through with salt water and the smell is almost insufferable.

Crowding was faced throughout the ship. The captain's cabin was shared by England, Shackleton and Murray. David moved in with Dr Michell, the ship's surgeon, bringing along a quarter of a ton of instruments and books. And the tiny wardroom had to serve as the dining area for twenty-two men.

Conditions deteriorated further on the following days, leading Shackleton to institute a revolving watch over the ponies. Five stalls were located on the port side of the ship, and five to starboard, with the fore hatch between, an area that, with self-deprecating humour, became known as the Cavalry Club. It was here that Buckley earned undying respect, laughing throughout his two-hour watches and then joining the regular sessions at the hand-pumps, which were started after water began to fill the holds.

The scientific staff received the added bonus of making meteorological observations. These included hourly readings of the barometer, dry and wet bulb, and maximum and minimum thermometers, as well as measuring the temperature of the seawater. 'It is not pleasant to be waked up at four by having a notebook shoved into your hand and being informed that . . . a gale is blowing from the south west,' Priestley recorded. He added that one was

> immediately met by a wave in your face, another meets you as you are going up the ladder . . . [and] another lays hold of you . . . and does its

best to hurl you over the side while you are hauling up the canvas bucket
of sea water to take its temperature. Then you go into the wardroom and
sit down in your wet clothes until the next hour comes round.

On 5 January the barometer dropped still further and *Koonya* was
signalled with a request to pour oil over the rough water. Never the less,
Nimrod continued to roll uncontrollably, and that evening one of the
ponies, Doctor, was pitched on to his back. Despite continued efforts to
get him to stand, nothing worked, and the next morning Shackleton
ordered the dreadfully weakened creature shot. The next day Zulu also
fell, but after knocking away the partition between stalls they were able
to get him up again. The ponies – key to the entire operation – now
became the moment-to-moment concern of the shore party. 'They have
not slept since leaving Lyttelton, so one can imagine what game little
beasts they are, and it's no wonder we are all so interested for their
welfare,' wrote Mackintosh on 7 January, the second consecutive day
the storm had reached hurricane proportions. 'So, if there are any
prayers tonight, let a bit of them go towards our Siberian ponies, and
for finer weather.'

The prayers were not answered. The next morning gigantic seas were
running, and one particularly huge wave destroyed part of the starboard bulwarks and a small house on the upper deck. One of the dogs
was drowned on its chain. 'Always wet without any hope getting dry
again,' Marshall, the surgeon, recorded. 'Have not taken my clothes off
since I came aboard.'

On 9 January the storm reached its climax, 'blowing a living gale
with a sea like a mountain', according to AB Sidney Riches. It was no
better on *Koonya*, where J.G. Rutherford, the second engineer,
recorded that it 'was the worst day I have ever experienced, terrific
squalls and mountainous seas sweeping everything before them. The
Nimrod was continually swept with solid water from stem to stern,
all her crew had orders to keep off the deck as much as possible.' The
ship was in serious danger of capsizing, listing fifty degrees one way
and then jolting just as far the other. Priestley was almost lost when,
having gone to the round house at the stern, he 'was catapulted clean
out of it by a following wave', which Brocklehurst never the less
thought 'a wonderful sight, waves like great mountains, masses of
green water ever so much higher than the ship, & ever rushing
towards us.'

But it was the last great tempest of their passage. By noon the next day it was fair and clear, and the men began to dry out. On 14 January, icebergs were seen, and the following morning, in the distance, a band of ice. *Koonya* had towed *Nimrod* 1,400 nautical miles, all the way to the Antarctic Circle, and now, with no protection from ice for his steel ship, it was time for Evans to turn tail.

Despite a heavy swell, a boat carried England and Buckley, the latter returning home, to *Koonya*. It had been planned that a series of boat journeys would ferry fresh water to *Nimrod*, as well as eight tons of coal and the carcasses of twenty sheep that had been killed and skinned the previous day. The conditions of the sea made this impossible, so a line was passed between ships with ten sheep attached to it. After these had safely arrived, an effort was made to transfer over the second half, but as the wind and sea picked up, the line was carried away. All plans for the further conveyance of provisions were terminated, and England returned to *Nimrod*.

At 1.00 p.m., Evans cut the hawser connecting the ships, and, while *Koonya* steamed north, the crew of *Nimrod* commenced six hours of hard toil at the primitive windlass, hauling up what had increased to 140 fathoms of cable. 'Not more than one skipper in 100 would have hung on to us as Evans has done,' Marshall had written at the height of the gale. Evans had indeed performed magnificently, and his reward was a safe return home. With him went the post from the expedition. Among these letters were two that would convert Shackleton's helter-skelter scientific effort into a serious research programme.

'I felt in my bones somehow that he would not be content to put his nose into the place for a week or two and not stay,' David's brother commented when the professor's decision to remain in the Antarctic became public knowledge. 'Well, it is just like him.' It certainly was. If there was anything that David loved as much as his students, it was fieldwork, and he and his wife had spent much of their early life together living under canvas in remote areas. It could hardly have been an overwhelming surprise, therefore, when letters arrived for the Senate and Chancellor of the University of Sydney requesting a leave of absence due to 'the great scientific importance of the work to be done in Antarctica, and (if I can manage to do some of it well) the gain to the reputation of science at our University.' The request was approved, but it did not really matter, of course. The letters had been sent back with

Koonya while David, far out of touch with the world, proceeded with his *fait accompli*.

It has ever since been a matter of conjecture as to whether it was while aboard *Nimrod* or before he left Australia that David had decided to stay in the Antarctic. David claimed that Shackleton made him the offer several days before *Koonya* returned north, but he would have had to say that to keep up appearances. Whenever it was, and whether Shackleton convinced David to stay, or David persuaded Shackleton to let him, neither would have needed to work too hard at it. The man who could, according to Shackleton, 'charm a bird off a bough' would not only secure scientific and intellectual credibility for the expedition, he would have a grand time doing it. Both sides were winners.

Not that it seemed that way to everyone. On 11 January, the day after Shackleton first wrote to Emily that David was staying, Marshall bitterly recorded, 'Had a short talk with S., who means to keep Prof. David on ice & also useless swine Mawson. Great pity must make most of bad job. No doubt S. under David thumb who will take all the credit for scientific results.' Marshall – condescending, judgemental, and intransigent – had taken an immediate dislike to Mawson, who had been the most seasick man aboard ship. 'Mawson is useless & objectionable, lacking in guts & manners,' he had written several days earlier. 'Could leave him behind without a regret.' Seeing himself as the logical second-in-command – a position, in fact, he felt Shackleton had promised – Marshall resented the 'intrusion' of David, who had the credibility, respect and charm that he so patently lacked.

However, the esteem in which the rest of the expedition members held 'the Prof' or 'the Pro', as he was variously known, was underlined by Priestley, whose status was most affected. 'Prof. David is a trump, a brick and any other thing which means the same,' he wrote shortly before finding out David was to stay. 'He does more than his own share of work, he keeps a cheerful face under all circumstances and in fact in every way he is an example to all of us.' When Priestley found that part of his role was being usurped, it did not change his gracious attitude:

One rumour, or rather more than a rumour for Shackleton told me himself, that I have heard which has pleased me very much is that Prof. David is very likely going to be down with us the whole time. If so, though inevitably a great deal of credit will be lost to me, yet the geology done by the expedition will become vastly more valuable and I am sufficient of a scientist to be glad and very glad that he is likely to stay.

As *Nimrod* continued south, David proved to have aesthetic faculties as well as scientific. When they reached the line of ice in the distance, it proved not to be the pack at all, but a vast band of icebergs, unlike anything seen before. There were hundreds upon hundreds of them, up to 150 feet high and two miles long, forming a maze that *Nimrod* now had to penetrate. He wrote:

Mere words utterly fail to convey the beauty, grandeur and wonder of that scene . . . Imagine countless huge blocks . . . of pure alabaster or whitest Carrara marble above, shading into exquisite tints of turquoise and sapphire at the water's edge, and changing to a pale emerald green below the water . . . we seemed to have entered the great silent city of the Snow King, the Venice of the South; but never had Venice in her palmiest days . . . one-thousandth part the size of this oceanic ice city, which was 100 miles in width from north to south, and unknown hundreds of miles in length.

A day was spent dodging and weaving through the massive natural barricade before they suddenly burst into open water, to be confronted with a stiff breeze and thick snowfall. It was the Ross Sea, and, although they would face a second band of icebergs, they were in the process of making the quickest passage yet recorded through the protective barricade.

They were, however, to the forbidden side of the line of demarcation at 170°W agreed with Scott. *Nimrod* turned southeast, toward the reaches of the Barrier far from McMurdo Sound. It was there, at what he now called 'Barrier Inlet', that Shackleton had decided to winter. It was an innovative plan, but one fraught with danger. No one before had dared to camp on the ice shelf, and Shackleton was now suggesting it in the aftermath of having pushed through vast icebergs that all agreed must have calved from the Barrier.

Shackleton's destination was, in fact, Balloon Bight, where he had gone aloft during the *Discovery* Expedition. Attempting to erase its unpleasant associations, he called his hoped-for landing place by a new name. From there, he wrote to Emily, 'where we are going is only 660 [geographical] miles away and with the equipment we have it ought easily to be done across the "smooth Barrier" '. Had his memory been faithful, however, Shackleton would have remembered that the view he recalled from the balloon – what he now thought of as a 'straight road to the south and *no* crevasses' – was not a clear, unencumbered plain. Rather it was one that had given Scott, Skelton and him no end of trouble when they had made a short jaunt six years before.

On 23 January they spied the Barrier, and, as *Nimrod* cruised east, a mile or two from it, Shackleton's tentative plans were explained to the others. After setting up base, he, Adams, Joyce and Armytage would go due south to lay depots for the next spring's push on the Pole. Meanwhile, Marshall, David, Priestley, Marston, Wild and Mackintosh would take two ponies and journey east to King Edward VII Land. This decision was, as Priestley wrote in his diary,

> bad news as far as geology is concerned for it means a seventy-mile sledge journey before a chance of any rock is met with and also a journey of seventy miles back before the specimens are safe in the hut. That practically means little or no chance of getting specimens to work at during the winter.

As it turned out, Priestley need not have worried.

The key to Shackleton's plan was to find Barrier Inlet. This was not easy, because it was only a thin slice in the shelf and they could not go too close to the Barrier in case they were swamped by a calving colossus of ice. As the power of the midday sun changed to the pastels of evening and then the soft hues of a late-night glow, Shackleton and his companions stayed alert on deck. What looked to be a smooth wall of ice from a distance was much different when passed nearby, and simple dark spots became huge caverns. More problematically, the same thin lines could represent the edges of either shallow inlets or deep bays.

Around midnight, while seeking for 'Borchgrevink's Bight', where that party had landed in 1900 a short distance west of Barrier Inlet, *Nimrod* passed into a broad but sheltered bay. As they followed the indentation of the coast, to port were hundreds of whales, blowing, diving and floating undisturbed; the place was immediately named the Bay of Whales. Meanwhile, to starboard was a large sheet of fast ice, frozen sea ice still attached to the edge of the Barrier; a cursory examination showed it to be impenetrable by ship. Beyond, according to Priestley, the Barrier was 'undulating as convex slopes separated by long or fairly long flat stretches. This looks as if it were probably due either to the proximity of the land or to the fact that the ice has passed over land of a low lying character.'

What Priestley was describing was Roosevelt Island, an eighty-mile-long ice-covered piece of land that would officially be discovered on Richard E. Byrd's expedition in 1934. Only three miles from the Bay of Whales, Roosevelt Island affects two separate ice systems and helps maintain an instability in the natural ice harbour at the bay. Its influence in January 1908 was far different from what it would be three years later when Roald Amundsen was able to sail directly to the edge of the Barrier and use the site as his base for his dash to the Pole.

Meanwhile, Shackleton's party continued east, with a detour north around an area of pack ice. But by 7.30 a.m. on 24 January, they had not found anything resembling Barrier Inlet. They lay alongside an ice floe – a medium-sized, flat-topped piece of ice floating on the surface – and Shackleton conferred with England. A short while later observations were made to fix their position. Not only were they east of where Barrier Inlet ought to have been, they were at 78°20′S, in other words, *south* of where, six years previously, the Barrier had blocked their way. Bits of the ice shelf seemed to have broken off, taking Barrier Inlet with them.

Shackleton decided to continue east along an open waterway toward King Edward VII Land. Within the hour, however, *Nimrod* was threatened by a large pack of hummocky ice pressing closer to the Barrier from the north. The ship turned and fled the way it had come, shooting through a gap between the pack and the Barrier with only fifty yards of open water.

None of Shackleton's options seemed ideal, but, after a conversation with Adams and Marshall, he decided to trace the Barrier edge back to Borchgrevink's Bight, minus the northern detour. Six hours later, they reached the Bay of Whales. What had happened now became obvious: the alterations in the Barrier front were but a single dramatic change. When the Barrier had calved, a vast section, including the entire front from Borchgrevink's Bight to beyond Barrier Inlet, had simply floated away, creating the Bay of Whales.

Shackleton, appalled by the disaster that could have occurred had he set up on the ice and it broken away, determined immediately 'that under no circumstances would I winter on the Barrier, and that wherever we did land we would secure a solid rock foundation for our winter home.'

But having determined not to build his base on the Barrier, Shackleton now had to decide between two other possibilities: making another attempt on King Edward VII Land or going to McMurdo Sound. He soon was the centre of a small storm, as his men urged different solutions. England, concerned for an overloaded ship, felt the best plan was to go straight to McMurdo. David initially had encouraged Shackleton to push east, but soon began to emphasise the research opportunities in the McMurdo area. Joyce, too, lobbied strongly in favour of their old base.

Marshall, believing that 'the success of the Expedition depends on the new ground covered', pushed Shackleton the other way. He believed an all-out effort to the east might be successful, as 'up to present time ship has . . . certainly not rubbed an ounce of paint off her sides.' That evening, he grumpily opined that

> S. not going to make another attempt in K.E. Land but . . . says he will go to McMurdo Sound. If this is so he hasn't got the guts of a louse, in spite of what he may say to the world on his return. He has made no attempt to reach K.E. Land. In short he & England funk it. It is useless talking about it. Got very angry when I told him I was sorry he had not made an attempt on K.E. Land. Tried to make me believe that he had done as much as any human being could.

Perhaps due to Marshall's badgering, Shackleton decided to try once more to reach King Edward VII Land. On the night of 24 January, having spent several hours convincing England that the attempt was viable, Shackleton headed east. Less than twenty-four hours later, the immovable pack again stopped them. At 6.30 p.m. on 25 January, Nimrod altered course for McMurdo Sound.

In the aftermath of Shackleton's decision, virtually everybody aboard Nimrod agreed with Harbord, that it 'was dictated by common sense in the demanding difficulties of ice pressure, shortage of coal, pressing time and the lack of any sure base nearer than McMurdo Sound. There is no doubt in my mind, as a seaman, that the decision to seek winter quarters in McMurdo Sound was right.'

Even Marshall wrote grudgingly, 'at any rate, we have had a try for it.' The surgeon, however, never truly forgave the decision, or perhaps it was part of a long-term bitterness he felt for Shackleton – due to believing himself the better man, the one who should have been the leader. Regardless, some forty-five years later, the decision still preyed on his mind when he wrote about 'Shackleton's "double cross" in breaking his promise to Scott by using his old Base when other alternatives were available if he had had the guts to take a risk and land at the Bay of Whales.'

Alternatively, it has been speculated that the decision was not even Shackleton's, that, as master, England had the final say. The notion of England making such a decision unilaterally is unrealistic, however. Certainly he had been getting progressively more nervous and had urged Shackleton to turn west. But he would have sought Shackleton's blessing before altering course, and this he received. Shackleton acknowledged the soundness of England's judgement in a long, self-justifying letter that he wrote to Emily after the decision had been taken:

> . . . after a long talk with England who put the seriousness of my position frankly before me; by the attempt; the shortage of coal which even then was only sufficient to ensure the arrival of the ship at New Zealand: the strained condition of the vessel: the fact that even if we eventually arrived at King E VII Land I might not be able to find a safe place to discharge and would probably have to abandon it in view of the enormous masses of land ice and hummocked up pack that was breaking away which would make the ship's position untenable: my duty to the country and King since I was given the flag for the Pole and lastly but not least my duty to all who entrusted themselves to my keeping: I myself recognised the weight and truth of all he said.

Set on the scales against all of this was 'my private word of honour my promise given under pressure was the one thing that weighed in the balance against my going back.' There was, in terms not only of human life but of moral responsibility, only one decision to make, and there can be little cogent argument that Shackleton did not make the proper one. Never the less, a promise was a promise, and he had to live with breaking his word; in the following hours, 'I felt each mile that I went to the West was a horror to me.'

Like much of Victorian and Edwardian society, Shackleton was driven at a basic level by duty and honour. The one he had lived up to; the other he felt had been tarnished. 'My conscience is clear but my heart is sore,' he wrote to Emily,

> but I have one comfort that I did my best; if I had gone back without risking and trying all I did and if eventually I got the Pole from MacMurdo [*sic*] Sound Base it would have been ever tarnished and as ashes to me but now I have done my best and if the whole world were to cry out at me which I am sure they would not even then I would not worry myself for I know in my own heart that I am right.

Telling himself and Emily that, Shackleton watched the Barrier slowly pass as *Nimrod* made her way west through this weird, white world. An unexpected ordeal was over, he must have thought with a strange mixture of sadness and relief. But soon there would be another unanticipated challenge, and it would again threaten the existence of the expedition.

13

CAPE ROYDS

The first reference to a developing problem had appeared in Mackintosh's diary on 20 January, as *Nimrod* made her way toward the Great Ice Barrier. 'We are all very annoyed with the Skipper because he will not start the engines, although the sea has moderated and we could easily steam in to it,' the second mate had recorded, 'instead of which we are drifting helplessly about and rolling too. The poor horses are suffering terribly again.'

Although he did not sign off the Ship's Articles and on to a personal agreement with Shackleton until two days later, Mackintosh was already thinking like a member of the shore party. And, as were others with whom he was supposed to winter, he was developing ill will toward England, whose caution was viewed as a serious issue. This attitude had grown widespread with the captain's reluctance to attempt to reach King Edward VII Land. As *Nimrod* headed into McMurdo Sound, the problem was to increase manyfold.

On 28 January, Mount Terror and Mount Erebus were sighted in the distance. They were passed that evening during a party to celebrate David's fiftieth birthday. The next morning the little ship steamed through the terrain that Shackleton, Wild and Joyce recalled so well, before, sixteen miles north of Hut Point, they were stopped by an unbroken mass of ice. Efforts to ram through the decayed pack gained only a matter of yards as each effort left the ship stuck in the thick, sludgy ice without creating a crack. The operation was halted while Shackleton assessed the situation.

There was no doubt that reaching Hut Point was a high priority. It was the solid ground that Shackleton had decided was necessary. It was immediately adjacent to the Barrier. And it was the farthest southern point attainable on the only known road to the Pole.

The fundamental question, therefore, was when the ice might break up and allow them to disembark. Six years before, *Discovery* had sailed all the way to Hut Point in early February. The following year, when Shackleton was invalided home, *Morning* had not been able to reach it at all, getting only within five miles by March. Then, in January 1904, there was about twenty miles of ice blocking *Morning* and *Terra Nova*, but by the middle of February, this had broken away completely. So, they wondered, how much pack would the summer gales blow away this year, and how soon?

Shackleton had estimated that *Nimrod* could remain in the Antarctic until the beginning of March before being frozen in. If he could reach Hut Point, the ship could be unloaded in days. Under normal circumstances, this would have allowed him a month to see if the ice would start blowing out of the sound. These were not normal circumstances, however. Throughout the journey, England had proven far more nervous than Shackleton had expected. This had meant that several times Shackleton had been obliged to cajole England – his employee – into a specific course of action.

This strange situation was brought about by the circumstances regarding the command of a vessel. Shackleton was the expedition's leader; however, even when working directly for a superior, the captain of a ship is her master, with responsibility for her safety. When orders or directives endanger the ship, it is the captain's duty to think of safety first, regardless of the consequences to other plans. Some of the ship's company felt this had led England to be overly cautious, and, sitting at the edge of the ice, the issue arose again. England hoped to be away as quickly as possible, but Shackleton decided to wait several days to see if a good blustery storm or, better yet, a swell from the south could change the situation with the ice.

England was not Shackleton's only concern, however. He was desperate to get the ponies to land: they had been shipbound for a month, and the constant pounding had been hard on them. This was underlined on 30 January when the pony Nimrod was found to be in such bad shape that Shackleton ordered him put down. 'He was one mass of sores that he could scarcely walk,' seaman Sidney Riches wrote. 'The frost had taken effect on them, and our Doctor gave up hopes as they would never heal in this cold weather . . . so Nimrod was shot and his body consigned to the deep.' The number of the all-important ponies had dropped to eight.

While they waited for the ice to move, the stables were partially dismantled and the motor-car was unpacked, as Shackleton hoped to use both means of transport to haul supplies to Hut Point. 'Day is quite the most important man here at present and he has been all day getting the motor ready for action,' Priestly wrote. 'At present when we speak to him we take off our hats but someone suggested that in a few weeks if the motor-car did not come up to expectations our attitude towards him will be changed so much that when we wish to attract his attention we shall throw a brick at him.'

Such doubts proved prophetic. Several days later, after much intricate tinkering by Day, the motor-car was taken off the ship and dragged half a mile to where it could be tested on the ice. The company was cheered when the engine turned over, but, wrote Mackintosh,

> alas! It kept up the alleged peculiarities of its kind, went a few feet and stopped dead, pulsating violently, until Day, moved no doubt by a feeling of pity, soothed it by a series of hammerings and screwings. After a brief rest, the machinery was started again, and the after wheels in duty bound turned violently round in the snow, burying themselves to such an extent that the car moved not an inch.

Several hours later the disgraced machine was hauled back to the ship. Yet, that Mackintosh was even able to record these events was remarkable. On 31 January, while removing sledging gear through the aft hatch, a crate hook, released from a beer cask, swung across the deck and struck him in the eye. He was taken to England's cabin, where Marshall found 'what appeared to be portion of retina protruding through eye. Joyce tells me that when he fell he saw lens lying on his cheek.' That afternoon Marshall, with the assistance of Mackay and Michell, successfully excised Mackintosh's eye with instruments that included a retractor made from rigging wire. 'Mackay's Edinburgh method of giving anaesthetics with a towel added to the difficulties,' Marshall wrote. 'Mackintosh lay on the cabin floor, on which we knelt, and the only light was a single oil lamp.'

When he awoke after the surgery, Mackintosh was more distraught about having to go back to New Zealand than about the loss of his eye. Never the less, his mind immediately returned to his duty, his first question being, 'Who is going to take my watch?'

It was now that the expedition could have dissolved, with the disappointment of not reaching King Edward VII Land and the inability to attain Hut Point followed by the killing of Nimrod and Mackintosh's accident. But Shackleton, according to Harry Dunlop, the red-headed chief engineer, 'saw that he must not give way to disappointments and accidents. If he gave way to the blues, everybody else would, so he was around all the time with a smile and a cheery word for everyone. He is a marvellous man, and I would follow him anywhere.'

Within several days, Shackleton had determined to where Dunlop and the others would follow him. On 1 February he had sent Adams, Wild and Joyce to man-haul to Hut Point to check the condition of the hut. They returned from the gruelling journey on the morning of 3 February, and reported it still in excellent condition and virtually clear of snow. In the meantime, Shackleton and England had tentatively skied over a broad expanse of ice, looking for cracks to assist Nimrod in making her way south. When none appeared, Shackleton decided to find a different site for the base without delay.

In the afternoon of 3 February, Shackleton began his search, and Nimrod headed up the coast of Ross Island toward Cape Barne and the small hook north of it: Cape Royds, a rocky promontory where Scott and Wilson had camped in 1904 while awaiting the relief ships. The small bay extending south from the tip of Cape Royds was almost entirely covered with fast ice, but very near that tip – later named Flagstaff Point – was a natural dock, formed by a portion of the ice having broken away.

Shackleton, Adams and Wild took a boat out to sound the uncharted waters near the shoreline. The approaches proved to be of sufficient depth for the ship to enter the little dock and discharge its stores directly on to the ice foot – the fringing line of ice that remained attached to the coastline after the fast ice had broken out. The three scrambled up a smooth, snow slope about fifteen yards wide to reach a large area of bare rock. Some 200 yards inland was a dip protected from the slopes of Mount Erebus by several rocky ridges. Nearby lay a freshwater lake around which were hundreds of Adélie penguins, forming, although Shackleton's party did not know it, the southernmost breeding site in the world for the species. Shackleton immediately decided he had found his wintering site.

Within an hour Nimrod docked at the ice foot, and the party hastened to get as much ashore as possible, while Marshall brought out the cinematograph and started the first filming ever in the Antarctic. The motor-car was followed by a lifeboat, the dogs – which were tethered to rocks – foundations for the hut, and a large supply of pony fodder. For five hours they engaged in some of the heaviest lifting and pulling any of them had ever done, breaking off at 3.00 a.m. for a rest. Before they could return to work, however, the wind picked up and the ship began dragging anchor. Fearing for her safety, they 'cut and run', as Harbord wrote, eventually returning to where they had been the past several days.

Now began a fortnight that combined sustained and difficult labour with periods of sheer frustration. The cause of that frustration was the continuous string of interruptions that dangerously slowed the unloading; the source of it was England's excessive caution.

All day on 4 February *Nimrod* was buffeted by heavy winds at the ice edge, before returning briefly to Cape Royds the next day. 'It got on my nerves witnessing the extreme precautions which were taken nearing our base,' Dunlop wrote.

> He convinced our leader that it was not safe to take our ship alongside, so we steamed back to the bay ice again; needless to say, I was disgusted . . . Here we were burning coal and doing nothing, and we had a ship which was considered able to stand a few bumps. I firmly believe we would have been quite safe to go alongside and get on with discharging.

Never the less, it was not until the evening of 5 February that England was willing to come near the landing site, following, as Marshall wrote, a 'terrible waste of time & bad seamanship'. And even then, according to Mackintosh, 'the Captain did all sorts of extraordinary manoeuvres with the ship & eventually took to a place which meant a mile to drag the stores – instead of 100 yards, which we could easily have done.'

For the next eighteen hours the shore party worked like slaves, hauling ashore large quantities of stores via the first landing site, which became known as Front Door Bay. Meanwhile, Dunlop supervised laying the foundations for the hut. Most urgently, the ponies were finally brought to land. One by one they were put in a box, which was lowered over the side of the ship, and taken up the slope to where they were picketed fifty yards from the hut. 'We thought that this would be a good place,' Shackleton later wrote, 'but the selection was to cost us dearly.'

As a precaution, Adams, Brocklehurst, Marston, Mackay, Joyce and Wild were assigned to stay ashore to look after the ponies, and they immediately moved into two tents close to the foundations of the hut. The dogs were more able to take care of themselves, and one night Scamp and Queenie got loose and ravaged more than a hundred penguins. Queenie was so frenzied that she disappeared over a cliff into the sea, never to be seen again.

By the afternoon of 6 February, the foundation piles for the hut had been finished, but when the wind suddenly freshened from the south-east, Dunlop was called to the ship. 'All hands were ordered on board . . . and off we steamed once more to the bay ice,' he wrote. 'We all gave vent to our feelings again, as the water was quite smooth. We did not let Shackleton hear us though.'

This was because Shackleton had already reprimanded Marshall for complaining about England – calling the captain a 'rotter' – and had threatened to send home anyone who did so again. The problem was that many of the members of both the wintering party and the ship's crew agreed with Marshall. England had, according to Wild, 'entirely lost his nerve, & is, in fact off his rocker.'

It was almost forty-eight hours later that Shackleton was finally able to coax England back, but when the ship did eventually approach the ice, it was even farther away than before. 'Being at this distance off meant hard work dragging the sledges and unnecessary long distances, when it could have been done with much less labour,' Mackintosh wrote in disgust. 'This disheartened the whole party & everyone felt while they were doing there [sic] utmost & willing to do more they were being made to do what was ridiculously unnecessary.'

In addition, those who had stayed ashore were boiling over by the time Shackleton reached them. He was horrified to hear not only that the members of the shore party believed England was unfit to command, but that, as Shackleton had given in so regularly to him, they were beginning to lose confidence in him as well. But before Shackleton had a chance to placate the men, Nimrod again bore off into open water. He was forced to signal for a boat and to go as quickly as possible after the ship.

The incident that may have followed was to cause enormous controversy in the future, and yet it is impossible to determine if it actually occurred right then, or at a point a week or so later, around 16 or 17

February. The ship's log does not mention an altercation, and the diaries and letters of the ship's officers and the members of the shore party are not consistent in reporting a specific date when a possible confrontation occurred between Shackleton and England. Neither of the participants wrote about any conflict, except to members of their families. Never the less, there are enough references to it to be able to reconstruct what happened.

Shackleton raced to the bridge to persuade England to bring the ship back into what the others viewed as calm water. England refused, saying that the risk was too great. Exasperated, Shackleton put his hand on the telegraph to the engine-room to signal 'full speed ahead'. England put his hand over Shackleton's and altered the order to 'full speed astern'. Facing a stand-off, the two men left the bridge to settle their differences.

The situation was, however, unresolvable. Normally Shackleton was able by force of personality to convince or overwhelm those with whom he disagreed. But he could not persuade England, nor could he remove him until they reached a port of call. Therefore, he asked England to stand down from command on the grounds that he was ill.

England refused. In a letter to his fiancée, he acknowledged the strain and confided that his anxiety was increasing. And well it should have: the ship was proving difficult to handle as, due to being hurriedly unloaded, it was becoming progressively more unbalanced. England clearly found the burden of commanding the unwieldy vessel home an onerous one, particularly as, should he not arrive safely, no one would know where the expedition had landed. Never the less, *Nimrod* was his command, and he felt that he was successfully carrying out his duties. The test of wills would continue.

For the time being, however, some understanding must have been reached, because the work of discharging the ship continued. In fact, *Nimrod* now spent three days within reach of the shore, despite having to be moved from one landing point to another due to the ice breaking up. To speed up the operation, the ponies were brought on to the ice to haul the loads, and the ship's crew joined the efforts of the land party. As Alf Cheetham, the third officer and bosun, wrote of the work:

> all hands called at 5.30 a.m. and starting sledging the store while part of the men were putting it on the ice we had to rush the work along on account of the ice breaking up and there was very Large Cracks

dangerous for the ponies the ship had to keep shifting as she was
sometime in Great Danger of being crushed with Large ice Berg we
worked on till 10.30 p.m. and landed 30 ton of store by hand beside
sledging it a great Distance.

At midday on 10 February the moving ice forced England to take
Nimrod farther into the small bay south of the winter quarters. Some
350 yards along the shore were cliffs towering fifty feet over a narrow
snow slope. This became a new landing area, the stores being slowly
hauled up by a boom and tackle at the top of what was named Derrick
Point. This site was not suitable for hauling up the coal needed for
heating and cooking, however, so it was taken still farther along the
coast to a cove with a gentle slope, called Back Door Bay. Here several
tons of coal were left on the ice near the shore.

The ponies had expedited the off-loading of the ship, but continuing
to use them on the ice almost proved disastrous the next day. Cheetham
recorded that:

At 8 a.m. the Ponies was brought to the ship and the sledges loaded with
Coal the first two sledges . . . were waiting for there Load when the
Whole of the ice Between the ship and the shore parted and left Large
Gaps so that neither the Ponies or ourself Could get ashore here we were
in a strange predicament . . . But on turning back Chinaman refused to
cross over a Crack and began Bucking & rearing till he Became
unmanageable and got into the water Between the ice floes and was
in great Danger of being Crushed to Death here a great struggle began
between man and beast which ended in 4 men actually Lifting the Horse
Bodily out of the water the next then was to get them on shore, so the
ship Head was put up against the ice her Engine started Full speed and
the ice pushed in the Bay again and after two hours pushing the Ponies
got safely on shore Chinaman none the worse a Bottle of Brandy was
poured down his throat to prevent him from catching Cold.

This movement of the sea ice forced England to take the ship to a safer
location and ended three days of furious discharging. It did not end the
work, however. A widening crack threatened the safety of the stores
that had been unloaded and left on the fast ice near Derrick Point and
Back Door Bay, so Shackleton signalled that all hands who could
possibly be spared should immediately be sent ashore. The men work-

ing on the hut were also transferred to the ice, and virtually the entire ship's complement laboured until after midnight moving the stores to safety. 'Every man jack worked like a bally nigger,' Harbord wrote through his exhaustion early the next morning, 'but he got more than a nigger's praise from Shackleton, who was delighted to see everybody come right up to scratch in such an emergency.'

It was just as well that Shackleton had formed his emergency party. That night most of the remaining sea ice broke out. The next day heavy winds prevented *Nimrod* from coming close to shore, although the work went on as, according to Davis, 'with twenty-four hours of daylight to each day, men worked until they were completely exhausted . . . this period of our lives became one continuous working day, a veritable day without end, and thirty-six hours at a stretch was almost a normal shift.'

When the winds continued on 13 February, Shackleton requested England to land supplies at Glacier Tongue, a long, floating spit of ice extending far into McMurdo Sound approximately half way between Cape Royds and Cape Armitage. Such a depot could be of assistance to the sledging parties at a later point. By the time *Nimrod* returned a day later than expected, however, the shore party was once again fed up, and it took intervention by David to prevent a quarrel.

A debate now occurred between the captain and Shackleton over the remaining coal. They finally agreed that England would keep ninety-two tons, and that the rest would be landed for the shore party, although this would be far less than what Shackleton had counted on. But although the sea ice had broken away from the shore, it had not left the vicinity altogether, and England became more cautious than ever. Refusing to go within a mile of the landing area, he condemned the men transporting the coal to agonisingly difficult labour. A party consisting of David, Mawson, Cotton, Armytage and Michell rowed and poled back and forth for more than twelve hours straight.

'First about 20 strong canvas bags, with eyes or loops of ropes at the top corners, would be let down into the boat (about 24 bags go to the ton),' David wrote.

we would pull for about half a mile across a nearly ice free sea; then we would reach the belt of dense floe ice . . . The heaving of the sea scrunched the floe-ice together every now and then, so that Davis had to choose, and choose quickly, from moment to moment down which opening to force our boat . . . the little lanes, or rather paths, of water were so narrow that they were barely wide enough for the boat itself; indeed, we frequently had to force the floes apart in order to make room for the boat, so that the blades of the oars had nothing on which to catch but the soft snow or an occasional lump of ice frozen down on to the top of the ice floe . . . After much meandering and skilful steering, but not without a few slight scrunches, Davis piloted us at last safely to the landing place.

This was the other point at which a confrontation between Shackleton and England might have involved the telegraph to the engine room. Something certainly seems to have occurred. 'Shacks had a bit of a dust up with England, so its said,' Brocklehurst wrote. 'The ship came nearer into the bay but turned out again. She keeps a long way out, four loads were humped in four hours.'

Despite Shackleton's exhortations to bring the ship closer in, the following days were mind-numbingly difficult, as the party worked beyond exhaustion rowing the coal to the shore and lugging it up the slopes. When their human limitations forced them temporarily to stop, David observed that: 'Byron's description of the host of Sennacherib after the Angel of Death had breathed in the face of the Assyrian foe, as he passed, about fitted them . . . They had all fallen asleep, dead to the world, in all sorts of grotesque attitudes.'

This labour, more closely resembling that of a Stalinist Gulag than of free men, was interrupted on 18 February when a howling southeaster blew in at a hundred miles an hour. England stood out, but this was no ordinary storm: for the next two days *Nimrod* steamed full ahead into it, yet was steadily blown in the opposite direction, finally reaching a point fifty miles north of Cape Royds. Worse than the frighteningly heavy seas and the intense winds was the drop in temperature, from $17°$ to $-16°$.

Hour after hour the gale shrieked at those both on land and aboard ship, and members of each party wondered if they would ever see the others again. The base was covered with water that immediately froze into rock-hard ice, and the decks of the ship were swamped. Davis and Harbord were held over the rails so that they could chop away planks of the bulwarks with axes in order to free the ship of the freezing water collecting aboard. Meanwhile, the cliffs far behind the camp were coloured white with frozen spray, and the men supposedly safe in the new hut were aghast to find that three feet from the stove the temperature registered thirteen degrees of frost.

After four days the blizzard finally blew itself out, and on 22 February Shackleton and the other members of the shore party who had been caught aboard ship returned to find the hut still standing but tons of supplies covered under feet of ice. Now the most urgent requirement was landing the remainder of the coal, and again they worked all day, increasing the shore party's load to eighteen tons, enough, with economies, to make it through the winter. They had, according to Dunlop,

> lost about eight days and burned a lot of coal unnecessarily. However, poor England is not to blame, as his health went bung, but its pretty hard luck that four of the best years of our leader's life should be messed up by the lack of nerve, and I think cussedness, of an individual who should have been his right-hand man.

Shackleton agreed with all Dunlop wrote, except that England was not to blame. He now wanted to be free of the man who had become his nemesis, so, as the shore party had enough coal – just – he ignored the sledges and other supplies still aboard *Nimrod* and told Davis that the ship could head north. Ironically, the weather was perfect, the water was almost calm, and the filthy, coal-dust-covered rowers reached their destination in what seemed a flash. England did not need to be told twice by Davis, and within minutes the normally cautious captain had the ship steaming north as the lowering sun bathed the mountains and the sound in golden rays.

'Amidst cheers from ship and shore we sailed towards the known world and civilization,' wrote Mackintosh, still wishing he were remaining with those cut off from all other humanity. 'The last we saw of the shore-party was one solitary figure silhouetted against the sky, gazing after the ship with thoughts mingled with pain, no doubt.'

Young Ernest Shackleton and his siblings. This picture was taken around 1894, when Ernest was about 20. Standing, *from left*: Clara (1881–1958), Ernest (1874–1922), and Eleanor (1879–1960). Seated, *from left*: Kathleen (1884–1961), Ethel (1878–1935), Frank (1876–1941), Amy (1875–1953), Alice (1872–1938), Gladys (1887–1962), and Helen (1882–1962).

Emily Dorman a number of years before she married Shackleton. Emily proved a tower of strength for Shackleton and supported him emotionally throughout all his adventures.

Shackleton prior to the British Antarctic Expedition. His good looks combined with his breezy, naturally easy manner would make him a favourite with audiences around the world.

The 'three polar knights' at the start of the southern journey on Scott's first expedition, 2 November 1902. Shackleton (*left*) and Robert Falcon Scott (*centre*) had high hopes of attaining the South Pole, but Edward Wilson (*right*) was much less confident about attaining that level of success.

Sir Clements Markham was the 'father' of the British National Antarctic Expedition on *Discovery*, and the man who selected Scott to lead that expedition. Markham was one of the most irascible, headstrong men of his time, and was a master of manipulation and political wrangling.

On their way to New Zealand at the beginning of the British Antarctic Expedition, eight members of the shore party were crushed into one cabin on *Runic*, a single-class emigrant ship of the White Star Line. Here they developed a camaraderie only possible amongst those obliged to live in close proximity to others. Seven of them posed for this picture aboard ship; standing, *from left*: Raymond Priestley, Eric Marshall, Bernard Day, and George Marston. Seated, *from left*: Frank Wild, Ernest Joyce, and William Roberts. Missing from the picture was Jameson Adams.

Once the Manchurian ponies arrived at Quail Island, the quarantine station off Port Lyttelton, they had to be broken in to handling and hauling sledges. This procedure was carried out under the guidance of Alistair Mackay, one of the two members of the shore party to sail all the way to New Zealand on *Nimrod*.

When *Nimrod* departed from New Zealand, more than fifty thousand well-wishers descended on Lyttelton Harbour to say farewell. So many crowded on the local excursion steamers — and then rushed to one side as *Nimrod* sailed past — that the boats listed dangerously far over into the water.

In the heavy seas and stormy conditions that plagued the expedition after the departure from New Zealand, all that the men on *Nimrod* could see was the funnel and tops of the masts of *Koonya*, which was towing them south. The wave shown about to break over *Nimrod* did considerable damage to the little ship.

Sir Philip Brocklehurst, the youngest member of the British Antarctic Expedition. By contributing to expedition funds in order to be selected as a member of the shore party, he set a precedent later followed by Captain L.E.G. Oates and Apsley Cherry-Garrard on Scott's last expedition.

Three key members of the expedition aboard *Nimrod*. *From left*: second officer Æneas Mackintosh, expedition second-in-command and meteorologist Jameson Adams, and Bertram Armytage, who was in charge of the ponies. Armytage committed suicide a year after the expedition returned to civilisation; Mackintosh died while participating in Shackleton's next expedition.

Members of the expedition taking soundings near a grounded iceberg to see if it was safe for *Nimrod* to anchor in that area. Shackleton himself carried out the task of sounding when examining the approaches to Cape Royds.

Nimrod held up in the ice. When the ice was heavy, neither steam nor wind power allowed the tiny ship to force her way through. But Shackleton's party tended to be relatively lucky with the ice in the McMurdo Sound region — something that would prove not to be the case in the Weddell Sea on his next expedition.

The shore party unloading stores from a boat at the first landing place after the ice-foot had broken away. Each container — some 2,500 of them made of Venesta board — had to be hauled up individually.

At Cape Royds before the completion of the hut. *From left*: James Murray, George Marston, Frank Wild, Sir Philip Brocklehurst, Harry Dunlop, and Ernest Joyce.

Nimrod had to steam away to a safe distance when the ice began to break up around Cape Royds. The large pieces of ice led to Captain England keeping the ship much farther from shore than some of the shore party or crew considered necessary.

'The Boss' at Cape Royds. Several of his colleagues later said that Shackleton's pose in this photo — with hands (or fists) on hips — was the most characteristic of the expedition leader.

The conquest of Mount Erebus was the first major triumph for the members of the British Antarctic Expedition. Shown at the summit of the higher, active crater are Alistair Mackay, Eric Marshall, Jameson Adams and T.W. Edgeworth David. Steam can be seen rising on the left.

Improving equipment and clothing was one of the most important tasks during the long winter at Cape Royds. Here Frank Wild works on the runners of a sledge, while other members of the shore party look on.

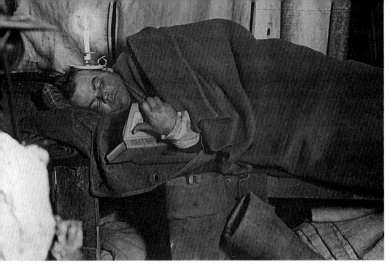

George 'Putty' Marston, the expedition artist and unofficial clown. Marston shared his cubicle in the hut — known as 'the Gables' — with Bernard Day. He was one of Shackleton's personal favourites, and later accompanied 'the Boss' on *Endurance* during the Imperial Trans-Antarctic Expedition.

The hut at Cape Royds. Some of the supplies were scattered around the vicinity of the hut as insurance against fire. Others were never released from the ice that gripped them after the terrible storm that began on 18 February 1908.

Few aspects of the British Antarctic Expedition generated more interest in advance than the use of the Arrol-Johnston motor-car, which had been donated by William Beardmore. Bernard Day came along as the electrician and motor expert, but none of his hammerings and tunings were able to make the motor-car run efficiently on a snow-covered surface. Although it was useful for travelling on smooth sea ice, it was of no value on the snowy, uneven terrain of the Great Ice Barrier.

The start of the southern journey at the ice edge south of Hut Point. The four ponies — *from left*, Socks, Grisi, Quan, and Chinaman — each pulled a sledge, and the support party man-hauled the other.

The Christmas camp in the middle of the Plateau, where the men had a special dinner and then decided to further reduce their rations in order to be able to reach the South Pole. *From left*: Adams, Marshall, and Wild.

The farthest south, at 88°23'S, 162°E on 9 January 1909. Marshall took the picture of (*from left*) Adams, Wild, and Shackleton.

The Lower Glacier Depot, which marked the end of the longest, hardest march the members of the Southern Party had to make. On 27 January, Marshall left his exhausted companions and went ahead to collect food that he could bring back to them. The stores had been buried in the snow near the rock in the foreground, and Marshall had to dig them out.

'There burst upon our vision,' wrote Shackleton after ascending Mount Hope, 'an open road to the South.' It was breathtaking in its vastness and magnificence, and what they would call the Great Glacier would lead the Southern Party to the Plateau. Here is what Shackleton saw, as he looked south from Mount Hope, with the Glacier running off to the left of the photograph. To the right of the centre, under the rock casting the long shadow, is where they would establish the Lower Glacier Depot.

No one had ever seen this panorama before Shackleton, Wild, Adams, and Marshall attained the southern reaches of the Great Ice Barrier. At the left of the photograph is Mount Hope and near the centre is The Gateway through which the Southern Party was able to reach the Great Glacier. The main body of the glacier joins the Barrier farther to the left, outside this photograph.

Raymond Priestley sitting contentedly beside an erratic granite boulder, which lies on kenyte at Cape Royds. Priestley later joined Scott's last expedition and became one of the founders of the Scott Polar Research Institute at Cambridge.

Expedition biologist James Murray holding an Adélie penguin chick.

While the attempts were being made on the South Pole and the South Magnetic Pole, and the Western Party examined the geology of the mountains across McMurdo Sound, five men remained at Cape Royds during the summer of 1908–09. Here Ernest Joyce works on the sewing machine, while sitting next to him is Bernard Day. Standing behind are, *from left*: William Roberts, James Murray and George Marston.

On 16 January 1909, the three-man party of (*from left*) Alistair Mackay, T.W. Edgeworth David, and Douglas Mawson reached the vicinity of the South Magnetic Pole, at 72°15'S, 155°16'E, and a measured height of 7,260 feet. Mackay and David hoisted the Union Jack while Mawson set up the camera so that it could be triggered by a string, which can be seen in David's hand.

The rescue of the Northern Party by *Nimrod*, which 'docked' next to the edge of the ice in Relief Inlet, on the northern coast of the Drygalski Ice Barrier. Several crewmen help the members of the Northern Party move their sledge down toward the ship.

As *Nimrod* approaches Hut Point, Shackleton and Wild wait to be picked up at the end of the southern journey. The men aboard ship were ecstatic to find the pair waiting for them, when Captain Evans' gloomy predictions had indicated they were about to start a search to 'find the bodies'.

On 4 March 1909 all members of the Southern Party were finally safely aboard *Nimrod*, looking a little the worse for wear. *From left*: Wild, Shackleton, Marshall, and Adams.

14

NEW WORLDS TO CONQUER

Worse than being cut off from the world to the north was the elimination of the road south. Cape Royds is an extension of Mount Erebus as it tumbles down to the sea – cones and ridges of lava with snow valleys in between. Although it was possible to reach Cape Barne overland, immediately to the south of that was the Barne Glacier, which terminated in an ice cliff into the sound. Beyond the crevasses of the glacier were the ice falls around Turks Head Ridge, which extended several miles and some 4,000 vertical feet up the slopes of Erebus. With the climbing technology available at the time, these were essentially impassable.

Therefore the only way to reach Hut Point, and from there the Great Ice Barrier, was over the sea ice. By the time *Nimrod* steamed north, the ice that had halted the initial efforts to gain the old *Discovery* quarters had blown out to sea. South of Cape Royds was now open water – and until it froze over again they were trapped. There would be no autumn sledging on the Barrier, no depots established to help the polar party. Not only had the attempt on the Pole been hindered before it even began, but the lack of potentially useful work could prove soul-destroying for the men.

Morale could also have been a problem for those heading back to New Zealand, but Shackleton had kept most of them in the dark about certain unpleasant issues that would surface when they reached civilisation. Thus, it was not until the ship reached Port Chalmers, New Zealand, that the conflicts plaguing the expedition in the south returned to haunt England.

Shackleton had decided that he could no longer work with the captain. As early as 15 February he had written to Emily: 'I cannot have England down again he is ill and has lost his nerve and it has given

me an awful time of it. I have asked Mackintosh to tell you everything.'
Remarkably, although Mackintosh and Dunlop knew of their leader's
plan, Shackleton had not told England, who carried with him directions
for the relief of the expedition the next spring.

Dunlop, in fact, held a letter of instruction from Shackleton to
Joseph Kinsey, the English-born, Christchurch-based shipping mag-
nate who was serving as the expedition's New Zealand agent.
Enclosed with this letter was another for Kinsey to forward to
England. Both letters would supersede the orders that Shackleton
had given his captain and would indicate that England was to resign
due to illness and retire on full pay until the expedition returned. The
following summer *Nimrod* was to be taken south by Mackintosh,
unless his injured eye prevented him from so doing, in which case
Kinsey was to appoint Evans of *Koonya*, William Colbeck (formerly
captain of *Morning*) or another appropriate seafarer as captain.

When *Nimrod* reached Port Chalmers, the documents were passed to
Kinsey by Mackintosh, who then headed to Sydney 'to consult an
oculist and have a glass eye fixed in'. Dunlop, meanwhile, felt it
incumbent upon him to help prepare England for the approaching
shock, so he informed him of the existence of the despatches. England
was devastated.

There is little doubt that Shackleton truly believed England was ill.
'He has not been well and has delayed things greatly by loss of nerve,'
he had written to Emily only hours before *Nimrod* departed. 'I am very
sorry for him but must consider the safety of the Expedition.' This view
was backed by not only the shore party but Mackintosh and Dunlop,
the latter writing:

He is the most careful Navigator ever I have seen or heard of, but in my
opinion, he was totally unfitted to occupy the position as Master of the
NIMROD, because of the nervous state in which he was in, and his
absolute loss of self-control, nor was he able to bring to bear clear
judgment of the manner in which the ship should be best navigated . . . I
place on record my firm belief that it was nothing but the splendid
qualities and firm determination of Commander Shackleton . . . which
saved the Expedition from total disaster . . . [England's] faults and
mistakes were not by any means imaginary but were, I regret to state,
only too real.

England begged to differ, believing he had done his job satisfactorily. The entire issue of illness, he wrote to Kinsey, was fabrication: 'since the question of my health in mind and body has been quoted as the reason for my resignation, I beg to inform you that I am perfectly sound both in body and mind, and that my resignation has been forced upon me.' However, he was much too dignified to debate any failings of the expedition in public, so he did resign. But 'my resignation was not of my own choosing: it was Mr Shackleton's request and command,' he wrote to Emily. 'It was his own statement that I resigned through illness and I have merely consented to that without comment.'

Although England had been caught unawares, his termination was common knowledge among the wintering party. Shackleton had realised that to uphold his authority with the men staying in the south, he needed to show he had taken decisive action. The members of the shore party clearly approved, none more than Marshall, who wrote after the ship departed: 'England got his congé . . . Ship to clear off suddenly, leaving 4 sledges . . . glad to see last of her & England. Davis nervous towards end. Unnecessary rush . . . whole thing damned disgrace to name of country!'

If the members of the shore party thought that the departure of the ship would somehow improve their lot, they were sadly wrong. The first week on their own showed that the next year would consist of arduous labour, unpleasant tasks, rotten weather and rising personal antagonism increased by isolation and close proximity. Immediately upon waking on 23 February they had to set to work with picks, axes and crowbars to break through the thick envelope of concrete-like ice that covered hundreds of packing boxes, which had been picked up by the gale and distributed over a wide area.

This was bad enough, but in addition, on that day Marshall recorded 'Looks as if another blizzard is coming up' and 'another slaughter of penguins (104) a sickening performance some running round shot & covered with blood . . . winter store now amounts to 129 penguins must get a number of seals.' Marshall also registered his growing disenchantment with Shackleton, who had, he felt, betrayed him by announcing that Adams was second-in-command. 'Shacks and I are polite but distant,' he wrote, 'never will be confidence between us. Having not an iota of respect for him it is only course & I am content . . . took photo at which Shacks appeared & worked hard for 5 min then left.'

This was only the beginning of a litany of complaints by the surgeon. 'What a different show this is to what I anticipated when I first joined exped,' he wrote several days later, having found that the realities of an Antarctic expedition did not meet the romantic popular image. 'I thought I should be under a man. Soon disillusioned, but always hoping he would be all right on ice. Vacillating, erratic, & a liar, easily scared, moody & surly, a boaster.'

Shackleton had, in turn, expressed concerns about Marshall when writing to Emily in late January: 'Keen on his work; a bit young in mind was inclined to resent discipline; did not like the increased staff; had not quite settled down.' His comparative assessment of Adams – 'a splendid chap, keen on his work no change in any way to what he was in London just lives for the Expedition and for me: I have the greatest possible confidence in him' – made it clear why, if he actually had considered Marshall as second-in-command, he had ultimately selected the former naval officer.

For a week, life consisted of little more than finishing the hut, building the stables, and chipping stores out of their icy tombs. Even this had its lighter moments:

> Brocklehurst took great interest in the recovery of the chocolate, and during this work took charge of one particular case which had been covered by the ice . . . He carried it himself up to the hut so as to be sure of its safety, and he was greeted with joy by the Professor, who recognised some of his scientific instruments which were playing the part of the cuckoo in an old chocolate box . . . Brocklehurst's joy was not as heartfelt as the Professor's.

Shackleton knew that such amusements would not last long. Deprived of the opportunity to work towards the true purpose of the expedition – the journey south – he cast around for other endeavours to keep his men occupied and avert frustration. It has been suggested that the solution came from David. This is possible, but it might just as easily have come from looking up at nature's smoking chimney high above their camp. They would conquer Erebus.

Sixty-seven years previously, the active volcano had first been seen by James Clark Ross, who had named it – and its extinct sister to the east – after his ships, *Erebus* and *Terror*. In Greek mythology Erebus was the part of the underworld through which the dead passed before reaching Hades. Although several expeditions had visited the region dominated by Mount Erebus, no one had ever climbed it, and the only men ever to ascend its foothills were Wild, Joyce and Arthur Pilbeam, who had reached about 3,000 feet above sea level in January 1904. This was only a small part of a peak measuring 12,448 feet.

On the night of 2 March, Shackleton, David, Adams and Marshall first discussed an ascent. Two days later, in typical hasty fashion, Shackleton announced that the climb would commence the following morning. David, Mawson and Mackay would form a summit party, to be supported in the early stages by Adams, Marshall and Brocklehurst. None had significant mountaineering experience, but Shackleton saw the effort as an opportunity for the six to demonstrate their energy and resourcefulness, while engaging in both a scientific excursion and an adventure that would unite the entire company.

The base exploded into frenetic preparations, and it was hardly noticed that the previous day the pony Zulu had died, his stomach destroyed somehow by corrosive poison. The summit party was provisioned for eleven days and the support party for six. An effort was made to overcome a lack of mountaineering equipment by improvising: crampons were produced by poking nails through pieces of leather that were then attached to the bottom of finnesko. The last bits of equipment were not completed until after midnight, and, all in all, it was not the best-prepared party that departed on the morning of 5 March.

At Blue Lake, half a mile from the camp, the well-wishers turned back and the six men continued up a snow slope, pulling a sledge weighing some 600 pounds. About a mile on, they had to carry it over a glacial moraine, just the beginning of a brutal day pushing and dragging it up steep grades of blue ice, their progress impeded by a series of sastrugi. By 6.00 p.m., when they stopped, they had reached approximately 2,750 feet above sea level, some seven miles from base.

The next day, Adams' birthday, was more of the same, except that the gradient became steeper and the sastrugi increased. These caused the sledge occasionally to flip over, requiring that it be pulled back on to its skis and the supplies restowed. By evening, when they reached a campsite near the base of the main cone, they had travelled only three miles, although ascending another 2,800 feet.

The following morning Adams announced that the support party would continue with the others. Although he had Shackleton's blessing for this, the decision revealed weaknesses in the original plan. The steep slope required that the sledge and part of the provisions be depoted, but there were no rucksacks to carry necessary items onward, and not enough safety equipment for a party of six. 'Mac Mawson & David each took a single man bag & food each for four days. also a tent & poles,' recorded Brocklehurst after noting that it was his twenty-first birthday. He continued:

> Marshall started with the three man bag, Adams with the primus cooker & tent, & I had the food & spare kit in a brown canvas bag, Marshall & I used the sledge straps to fix our loads & Adams had cod line & rope. This make shift way of fixing our loads made it much more awkward to carry and we must have had 40 lbs each at least. Getting to the actual foot of the Mt we found it was quite impossible to carry the tent poles, so Adams went back with them and we went on climbing slowly, very slow and all of us suffered badly from thirst. Adams & I had ski boots and no nails, the others had finskoe & crampons.

By evening they had reached a rocky arête (a sharp, ascending mountain ridge or spur) some 8,750 feet above sea level. The combination of altitude and a temperature that dropped to $-34°$ meant that the cooker was exceedingly slow and all they could do was stay in their sleeping bags while waiting for dinner. The view, Marshall thought, was worth the struggle. 'Never forget sunset,' he wrote. 'Sound freezing over with wonderful opal tints on open sea. W. mountains topped with gold & base of Erebus with glaciers a sea of gold & purple. Sun dipped, whole scene changed to cold purple. Temp falls rapidly.'

As the temperature crashed, the wind picked up, and by the middle of the night a blizzard was screaming over the party. The snow was so thick and the roar of the wind so loud that the groups could not see or hear each other, despite being only ten yards apart. The lack of poles meant that the tents had not been set up and had simply been doubled over the sleeping bags to protect their toggled ends from the snow. The drifting powder was so fine, however, that it worked its way inside the bags.

When the blizzard finally subsided around 4.00 a.m. on 9 March, they had been confined to their sleeping bags for thirty-two hours, having had nothing to drink and only a biscuit and a piece of chocolate to eat. Brocklehurst's feet had been very cold ever since he had temporarily left the sleeping bag to answer a call of nature. Never the less, David determined to climb on, so the entire party slogged toward the summit of the lower, main crater. The angle of the ascent was steeper than ever, and more than once someone slid downhill before arresting his fall wtih his ice axe. Then, suddenly, Mackay left the group and started cutting steps up a long and very steep slope of névé, a granular snow with a chalky consistency, which is in the process of being transformed to ice. Ignoring their calls, he finally reached the rocky summit just before fainting.

While David, Mawson and Adams established a camp at the summit of the main crater and cooked a meal, Marshall examined Brockle-hurst's feet. Sir Philip had refused to change from ski boots to finnesko and the crease across the boots, which were too large, had cut off his circulation, resulting in six toes being severely frostbitten, particularly the two big ones. That afternoon he remained in the sleeping bag while the others examined the way to the upper, active crater.

When the party arose at 5.00 the next morning, they were greeted with a stunningly beautiful sight. 'All the land below the base of the main cone, and for forty miles to the west of it, across McMurdo Sound, was a rolling sea of dense cumulus cloud,' David wrote.

> Projected obliquely on this, as on a vast magic lantern screen, was the huge bulk of the giant volcano . . . Every detail of the profile of Erebus, as outlined on the clouds, could be readily recognized. There to the right was the great black fang . . . far above and beyond that was to be seen the rim of the main crater, near our camp; then further to the left, and still higher, rose the active crater with its canopy of steam faithfully portrayed on the cloud screen . . . All within the shadow of Erebus was a soft bluish grey; all without was warm, bright, and golden.

Leaving Brocklehurst, the others roped themselves together and headed towards the summit of the active crater. The cold and altitude made breathing difficult and progress painfully slow, but after four hours they reached the edge of the steam-filled crater, a massive abyss half a mile across according to Mawson, and 900 feet deep. 'After a continuous loud hissing sound, lasting for some minutes,' wrote David, 'there would come from below a big dull boom, and im-mediately afterwards a great globular mass of steam would rush upwards to swell the volume of the snow-white cloud which ever sways over the crater.'

The scene was magnificent even though the view of the Barrier was obscured by clouds. But they had little time to enjoy it. The effects of the high altitude were exacerbated by high latitude – where the air is thinner – and they needed to conduct their tests and depart. Marshall attempted to find out the correct elevation by means of a hypsometer, an instrument that measures the temperature at which distilled water boils. Since the temperature of boiling drops as height above sea level increases, it allows a determination of altitude. The figure they arrived at was 13,500 feet, which was eventually shown to be about 1,000 feet too high.

Mawson took some photographs and the party began its descent. On the way, they made a traverse of the main crater, took levels for constructing a geological section, and collected specimens. Reaching their camp, they had a hurried lunch before continuing their retreat, Brocklehurst struggling due to his damaged toes. When they reached an ice slope, they hurled their loads down before them, sat and slid down. 'We all reached the bottom of the slope safely', David wrote, 'and fired with the success of our first glissade, and finding an almost endless succession of snow slopes below us, we let ourselves go again and again, in a series of wild rushes towards the foot of the main cone.'

Their progress was rapid, but not without difficulties. Each time they threw provisions ahead of them, they had to stop their slides part way down and cut across a steep ice face to fetch them. 'Very steep & tiring,' wrote Marshall. 'Arrived safely pretty done . . . Pushing bag, glissading, following up, recovering it, dragging, shoving, soaked through.' Never the less, that night they reached the depot. Rising at 3.00 a.m., they made good time to their first camp, where, fearing a building southeasterly would turn into a blizzard, they stowed the sledge and headed on with all speed. 'Fell 100ds of times,' Marshall wrote. 'Bruised all over dead tired lost bearings. Arrived hut 11 am nearly dead.'

Marshall might have felt almost dead, but he quickly recovered. A number of the ponies were not able to recuperate so well, and when they appeared nearly dead, they soon expired. While both surgeons were on Erebus, Sandy died. Joyce and Day cut open the poor creature's stomach, which turned out to contain twelve to fourteen pounds of volcanic sand. Without salt in their diets, the ponies had been eating the sand, which had been covered with salt water during the three-day blizzard in February. The others were quickly moved to a new shelter, but the delay had been fatal. On 13 March Billy died, again due to the sand. 'If we lose many more ponies our chances of getting to the Pole will become chimerical,' wrote Priestley. Yet four days later another was gone, as Mac was in such distress that he was shot. Shackleton had projected that he needed a minimum of six ponies for the southern journey – there were only four remaining.

Things were not going well for the expedition in the outside world, either. On 8 March *Nimrod* reached Lyttelton, where England was informed of his 'resignation'. Although he did not dispute Shackleton's orders publicly, someone else related a very different tale.

On 11 March, under the headline 'Explorers Fight', the *Daily Mail* – the paper to which Shackleton had contracted to send reports – gave provocative details of serious dissension between the leader and his captain. 'Shackleton, when the ship was in a dangerous position,' the article stated, 'tried to take charge of the vessel . . . a personal struggle ensued . . . one of the combatants being knocked down.' The tale had evidently come from one of the ship's crew, upset by the forced resignation. Although England and Kinsey both denied the story, it received increasingly dramatic attention in Britain and New Zealand for more than a fortnight, and the next month it was taken up again when Henry Bull, who had been at the wheel at the time of the incident, gave *The Sydney Morning Herald* an expanded version.

This bad publicity was followed by more when *Nimrod* proved to be unfit to carry out magnetic and oceanographic surveys that Shackleton had promised in the aftermath of the Australian and New Zealand governments' generosity. A flurry of righteous indignation came from the New Zealand press, and, although it was acknowledged that neither government had based its grant on the survey work, the public was left with a certain unease about the explorer's handling of money and the differences between his statements and actions.

Shackleton's reputation was taking a similar beating in Britain. For one thing, his finances were unravelling, as there were still numerous debts. Most important was the loss of any further backing from Beardmore. Shortly before leaving Britain, Shackleton had borrowed £1,000 from the Scottish industrialist on a short-term basis. When the

money had not been repaid, Beardmore refused to have anything more
to do with him.

There were also those who were indignant about Shackleton occupying McMurdo Sound. Scott was far more than indignant. 'I have been
getting some copies made of Shackleton's letter to me,' he heatedly
informed his mother. 'His breach of faith is so emphatic that I propose
to let certain persons see the letter.'

Undoubtedly these 'certain persons' included the hierarchy of the
Royal Geographical Society, but they, like everyone else north of Cape
Royds, were incapable of doing anything. Despite Scott wailing that
Shackleton was a 'liar', Keltie remained outwardly removed, as was
Keltie's way in a controversial situation. 'It is certainly very painful to
read of the dilemma in which your husband was placed,' he wrote
smoothly to Emily, 'between what he regarded as the safety and success
of the expedition, and his loyalty to his agreement with Capt Scott.
Under the circumstances as described by him it was difficult to see what
he could have done otherwise.'

Keltie was more straightforward with Markham. 'Personally I am all
with Scott,' he wrote, 'but don't you think it places the Society in an
awkward position, supposing Shackleton should return successful, that
is . . . having reached the Pole or somewhere near it.'

Despite his own preference for Scott, the political animal in Markham forced him to agree. While evidently encouraging Scott's agitation,
he wrote to Emily of his efforts to hush up the entire business.

I strongly advised Dr. Keltie not to put anything in the RGS journal
about the reasons for giving up King Edward VII Land, and he has taken
my advice. The reason is that an excuse would be implied; when the
public are not aware that any excuse is needed. It is a pity that Ernest
worded his promise so strongly, and now the best thing is that nothing
more should be heard of it.

Holding Shackleton at arm's length the RGS might have been, but there
was one old friend true to the last. 'It is in a way unfortunate that King
Edward Land could not be reached,' Hugh Robert Mill wrote to Emily,

but I for one never saw the reasonableness of looking upon the
McMurdo Sound route as reserved for a possible future expedition
which had not even been planned. It seems to me . . . that region is

absolutely open and free to any one who has the courage, perseverance and good luck to reach it, and whether my friend Shackleton brings back the South Pole or not I am quite sure that he will bring back a splendid record.

It was on 22 June that Mill wrote to Emily. On another continent, in another hemisphere, on what could have been another planet, it was midwinter. Time was passing slowly in the darkness of the south, but soon the light would return in the sky, a bit of warmth to the waste-lands, and with them a glorious challenge would open to the men clinging to the vestiges of land at the edge of the unknown.

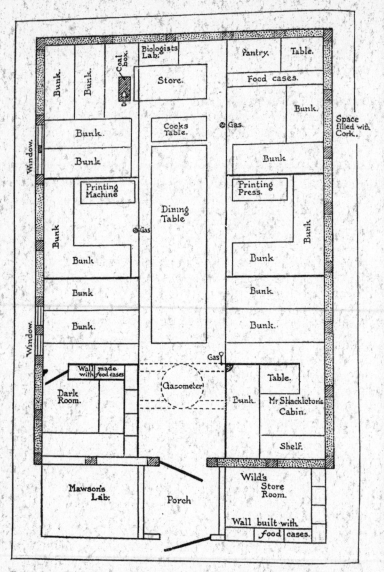

Plan of the hut at Cape Royds. The cubicle closest to Shackleton's was occupied by Adams and Marshall. That with the printing press housed Marston and Day, and next to them were Brocklehurst and Armytage. On the opposite side, next to the coal box, were Mackay and Roberts, and immediately adjacent to them Priestley and Murray. Wild and Joyce shared a space with the printing machine, and David and Mawson were closest to the dark room. From Shackleton, E.H. 1909, *The Heart of the Antarctic.* 2 vols. London: William Heinemann.

15

WAITING OUT THE WINTER

There were numerous rooms at Swythamley Park, near Leek in north Staffordshire – where Philip Brocklehurst had been raised – that were considerably larger than the hut at Cape Royds in which fifteen men planned to spend the next seven months. Even Sir Philip's rooms at Trinity Hall, Cambridge, would have put to shame the living conditions he and his companions were about to experience. Yet they quickly adapted to the new environment; so much so that five months and six days after they sailed from Lyttelton, Brocklehurst recorded with no embarrassment, 'Washed my head first time since leaving New Zealand; Day & Wild also had washes & looked quite different.'

Considering that Shackleton had no experience living in a hut in the far south – the men of *Discovery* had wintered aboard ship – the new quarters at Cape Royds showed remarkable foresight and planning. The hut had been placed so as to face northwest; across Pony Lake, which lay directly in front of it, was an impressive view of McMurdo Sound and the western mountains. Next to Pony Lake was a flat sheet of ice that soon became snow covered, and thereby allowed the men to exercise the ponies daily throughout the winter, as well as to play football and hockey. This quickly became known as Green Park.

The hut itself was rectangular, thirty-three feet by nineteen, with eight feet to the eaves. It had been built of sections of fir timber and lined with match-boarding. The external walls and roof were covered with heavy roofing felt, a one-inch layer of tongue-and-groove boards, and then another layer of felt. In order to provide further insulation against the cold, the four-inch space between the match-boarding and the inner felt was filled with granulated cork. For added protection, a wall six to seven feet in height was built of provision cases around the back of the hut, which faced the prevailing southerly winds. Next to the leeward side were the stables, one wall made of a double row of maize cases, the other of bales of fodder, and a ceiling of canvas tarpaulin.

The entrance to the hut consisted of a small porch between double doors. To the right of this, constructed of biscuit cases, was a storeroom. On the other side was a room intended to be Mawson's laboratory. However, it lacked significant insulation, so it was invariably the same temperature as the outside. The invasion of warmer, moist air from the hut therefore caused everything inside to become covered with ice crystals, making it unusable as a laboratory and leading to it becoming a second storage room.

The inside of the hut was divided between a communal area and the cubicles that provided a bit of privacy to the occupants. In order to save space and weight on the ship, Shackleton had brought virtually no furniture, assuming it could be built out of packing crates. One of the first items to be constructed was a long dining table built by Murray from the lids of the cases and set in the centre of the hut. When not in use, the table could be hauled above head level by ropes, creating a work area. Beyond this were a small cook's table and the four-foot-wide stove. The stove burned anthracite coal constantly, not only allowing Roberts to produce three hot meals and fresh bread daily, but to melt ice for drinking water for the men and ponies. Although the stove had not kept the hut warm during the blizzard in mid-February, it was discovered that several important parts had not been properly installed. When they were, it maintained the temperature sixty to seventy degrees above that outside.

On a platform above the area immediately inside the porch was an acetylene gas plant that Day installed and daily recharged with carbide. Flexible steel tubes connected to the tank allowed the use of four portable lamps, which helped make up for a lack of inside light due to the hut only having two windows – which were partially blocked by the stables.

To the right of the entrance door was a small separate room complete with interior roof, which served as Shackleton's quarters, as well as housing the library. Shackleton felt it important that he not be lodged in the main room, so that the men would not feel constrained by his presence. Like various others, he made his bed from fruit boxes facing the outside, so that, when emptied, they could serve as storage lockers.

Ranged around the interior of the main part of the hut were cubicles six feet wide by seven feet, each housing two members of the shore party. These were separated from one another by walls of packing boxes, or sacking hung from wires, and from the central area by blankets. Each cubicle had distinctive features, reflecting the work and personalities of its inhabitants. Closest to Shackleton's room was that occupied by Adams and Marshall, which was so tidy and ordered that it was known as 'No. 1 Park Lane'. Adams' shelves housed a complete set of Dickens as well as books about the French Revolution and Napoleon, whereas Marshall's were dominated by medical supplies, as the small area also served as the local surgery. On the dividing curtain, Marston had drawn life-size portraits of Napoleon and Joan of Arc.

The next cubicle, 'The Gables', was shared by Marston and Day. The boxes forming the shelves were made of Venesta board – a forerunner to plywood made of triple layers of chestnut or oak glued together – that had been stained brown with permanganate of potash. Marston had painted the curtains to include a vase of flowers on a mantelpiece and a fire burning in a grate. The cubicle also included a lithographic press that was to be used to produce pictures for a book Shackleton intended to print during the winter. Next along was 'The Shruggery' of Brocklehurst and Armytage, which was minimally furnished, and beyond that a small pantry.

On the opposite side was the cubicle of Mackay and Roberts, both of whom unsuccessfully tried to make beds out of bamboo. Adjacent to this, and not divided by the usual curtain, Priestley and Murray lived in the 'Taproom', a name that was a 'somewhat indelicate reference' to the diarrhoea from which Murray suffered much of the winter. Priestley complained that his area was encroached upon by both Mackay and Murray, but he in turn filled much of the cubicle with rocks, geological hammers, chisels and other tools of his trade.

The next compartment, occupied by Joyce and Wild, was known as 'Rogues' Retreat' for a sign that Marston had painted above its entrance. The elaborate picture showed two rough customers drinking beer out of pint mugs. The two veterans of *Discovery* were joined in their room by a printing press and type case. The final cubicle, known variously as the 'Pawn Shop' or 'The Old Curiosity Shop', was occupied by Mawson and David and was full of a confusing collection of scientific instruments and specimens. The Professor, according to Shackleton, 'made a pile of glittering tins and coloured wrappers at one end of his bunk, and the heap looked like the nest of the Australian bower bird.'

In the corner nearest Mawson's bunk and opposite Shackleton's room, was a photographic dark room constructed of fruit cases and lined on the inside with roofing felt. Mawson carefully fitted out the room with all the necessary equipment for developing and printing both glass-plate negatives and film. Although photographs had been taken by Borchgrevink's and Scott's parties, the emphasis was much greater on the British Antarctic Expedition.

Shackleton had purchased nine still cameras of varying types – including a stereoscopic model and one with a 'telephotographic apparatus' – as well as a cinematographic camera. A number of the men also brought their own cameras, and at least nine of them took photographs using no fewer than fifteen cameras. Marshall, who was in charge of the cinematograph, later estimated that 4,000 feet of film were shot. Despite the introduction of roll-film cameras, a high proportion of serious photographers still used bulky, dry-plate cameras, and there were several of these on the expedition. There were also smaller, portable, roll-film cameras.

Regardless of which camera was used, photography was not an easy process in Antarctica's freezing temperatures and long periods of darkness. Marshall found that when the temperature dropped to thirty degrees below freezing, cameras stopped functioning because the oil had frozen. He therefore made a point of removing the oil from all of them. The temperature similarly affected other stages of the process. Most of the developing and printing was carried out by Brocklehurst or Mawson, both of whom found glass plates easier to work with because film became brittle in extreme cold. One of the best places to develop photographs had been aboard ship, because sea water proved better as a stop for the developer than fresh water. This brought its own risks, however. Shortly after developing photographs of the Ferrar Glacier, Brocklehurst noted, 'put them in a bucket & lowered them into salt water till after lunch and then washed them in fresh water . . . but when I was away for a short time a piece of floe ice drifted against the bucket & crushed it so I lost all those plates.'

Taking photographs in the winter was also difficult due to the long exposures required, something affecting more than just the photographers. A famous photo of Murray and Priestley in a trench at Green Lake was taken in June 1908 by the light of hurricane lamps. 'The temperature was −22°F and we sat for ten minutes,' Priestley wrote, 'such agonies will ordinary mortals undergo for the pleasure of having their faces perpetuated.'

Throughout a seemingly endless winter, the fifteen men experienced agonies far worse than having a picture taken at $-22\,°F$. Their diaries record how the cold, wind and darkness interfered with every aspect of life, from taking scientific measurements to exercising the ponies to preparing meals. When combined with a forced proximity on a day-to-day basis, this at times created an atmosphere of tension and hostility.

In fact, even some of the 'good times' brought stress. In March, most were greatly amused when, coming back from various jobs, they were greeted by Marston, 'dressed up as a woman,' Priestley wrote, 'and behaving very affectionately to the whole expedition. He was so pressing in his attentions in fact that Mackay had to tell him that he would spit at him unless he took himself off.' As his colleagues were finding out, Mackay was quick-tempered and not a man to tease; Marston's efforts at light relief might have ended in violence without Shackleton's presence.

'This amalgamation of (it must be admitted) somewhat strangely assorted men was made possible by Shackleton's particular form of control, based on his almost supernatural intuition for selecting men who believed in him implicitly,' Adams later wrote, continuing:

> The Antarctic winter, with its four months of complete darkness and its month of twilight at both ends was indeed a testing time. There were days on end during blizzards when no-one left the hut save for a natural purpose or to feed the ponies or take meteorological observations, but I never heard an angry word spoken during the whole of that period . . . Shackleton did not insist on excessive formality towards himself; he was accepted as, and addressed as, The Boss . . . His exceptional powers of leadership were just as much in evidence during the sometimes tiresome and intimate life in the hut as they were on the sledging journey to the Pole.

'Shackleton was very tactful and very genial,' Brocklehurst added. 'He had a faculty for treating each member of the expedition as though he were valuable to it. He made us feel more important than we could have been.'

This ability to communicate with each man helped keep the party relatively happy and focused. One of Shackleton's strengths was his gift for delegation, perhaps nowhere better shown than in a project in which he was trying to go one better than Scott. Shackleton had edited *The South Polar Times*, but, he decided, the members of *his* expedition would publish an entire book.

The printers Joseph Causton & Sons were intrigued by Shackleton's idea, and they lent him a printing press, a small lithographic press for etching, ink, type and high-quality paper. They also gave instruction in typesetting and printing to Joyce and Wild and taught Marston the basics of print etching and lithography. Although Shackleton styled himself editor-in-chief of what was first called *Antarctic Ice-Flowers*, the project was primarily carried out by Joyce, Wild, Marston and Day. The final publication, named *Aurora Australis*, featured ten written contributions – including two by Shackleton – and was dedicated to Elizabeth Dawson-Lambton and her sister.

As Murray and Marston later described, the production of the books was a nightmare:

Dust from the stove fills the air and settles on the paper as it is being printed . . . If anything falls on the floor it is done for; if somebody jogs the compositor's elbow as he is setting up matter, and upsets the type into the mire, I can only leave the reader to imagine the result.

The temperature varies; it is too cold to keep the printer's ink fluid; it gets sticky and freezes. To cope with this a candle was set burning underneath the plate on which the ink was. This was alright but it made the ink too fluid, and the temperature had to be regulated by moving the candle about. Once the printers were called away while the candle was burning . . . When they returned they found that the plate had over-heated and had melted the inking roller . . . it was the only one on the Continent and had to be recast . . . So much for the ordinary printing. The lithography was still worse.

When the entire book had been printed, Day took over. He carefully sanded down Venesta boards for covers, joined them with a leather spine and then attached the pages to the hinges with silk cord. Between ninety and a hundred copies were produced.

Shackleton also used other tactics to keep up spirits throughout the winter. He encouraged birthday or other parties, initiated debate and discussion at dinner, actively carried out his full share of the work and showed himself to be appreciative. In helping avoid friction and antagonism, he was aided immensely by David, who, although not nominally second-in-command, was psychologically so. The Prof was the great peacemaker, taking charge to help side-step damaging incidents. He also kept the men positive by his very nature and daily actions.

'To read a few thermometers in a screen a few yards away from the hut, in a blizzard, was quite an undertaking,' Day wrote, adding:

> Returning from one of these journeys, in a blizzard outfit including fur mitts (for the fear of frost-bite was ever with the ordinary man), I was nearing the hut, head down, when I almost collided with the Professor who had been on duty in the stables. He had no mitts on, and with his bare hands opened the door, and held it for me to pass in first, saying 'After you, Day.'

It might seem a little thing, but it was not. Nor was a weeks-long effort David made after returning from Erebus. Wanting those who had not made the trek up the volcano not to miss out, he laboriously sorted, catalogued and labelled numerous rocks collected from the summit so that each member of the expedition might have his own set.

Even in the least popular job of all, David shone. Once every two weeks, on a rotating basis, each of the party served as messman. This consisted of bringing in bags of coal and strips of blubber for the fire; providing enough ice for cooking, washing, drinking and the ponies; keeping the common part of the hut clean; pulling the table down and laying it for three meals a day; assisting Roberts to pass out the food; and washing up after each meal. As always, David was slow but thorough. 'Volunteers have been known to assist in getting grease off the plates and in drying them,' Priestley wrote. 'It was a sight for the gods to see a well-known FRS, drying a wet plate with a wetter cloth, and looking ruefully at the islands of grease remaining, after he has spent five minutes hard work on it.'

Clearly the entire expedition benefited from David's presence. The Boss, in turn, rewarded the Professor by giving him unlimited control of the scientific programme. Of course, Shackleton had little interest in science, but he knew success on that front would bring additional kudos. Plus he had assembled a powerful scientific team almost despite himself. In fact, the scientific success of Shackleton's party has long been overlooked due to the adventurous image of its leader. However, the reality is that the expedition compiled a vast supply of significant scientific data, starting with that brought back from the heights of Mount Erebus.

To Shackleton, an even more important aspect of the conquest of Erebus was the successful combination of David, Mawson and Mackay. It likely soon set him to thinking that the three would form the party attempting to reach the South Magnetic Pole. Although the attainment of that site was a major geographical goal, much of the work would be of a scientific nature, so David and Mawson seemed natural. Mackay also had biological training, and would give the party medical support in case of emergency.

The composition of the party for the southern journey was much less certain, in part due to problems that had arisen on Erebus. From the beginning, Shackleton had promised Brocklehurst that he would be a member of the six-man Southern Party. But the baronet's toes did not improve. In April, after one of the large ones showed signs of gangrene, Marshall amputated it, preserving it in a small vial.

In the aftermath of the surgery, Shackleton gave his room to Brocklehurst, and moved into the cubicle with Armytage. His goals were not only to allow Brocklehurst to recover comfortably, but to take the chance to influence the depressed Armytage. Early on, Shackleton had written to Emily that he was a 'splendid man obedient reliable ready for any work . . . Gets on with all extremely popular because he is a man of the world and knows the ways of younger men. He was the 1st to make the English section reconsider their attitude to Australians.' But since then, Armytage had shown little ability to be part of the team, and his despondency had not been viewed positively. 'Shackleton had a good talk with "What what",' Marshall wrote, applying the unpleasant nickname he had given to the older man due to his habit of frequently using that expression. 'Told him that it must be his own fault that he cannot get on with the men as the remaining 14 can.' A week later Marshall continued, 'Armytage still in extraordinary sulky mood. Everyone else getting on A1.' But Shackleton seems to have had some temporary success, as Marshall later noted that the Australian 'has certainly improved and taken over sole charge of the ponies.'

Shackleton's attempts to raise Armytage's spirits exhibited two parts of his own basic temperament. First, he cared deeply for and took great interest in his men. Not long after the beginning of winter, Murray's health required him to be confined to the hut, so Priestley was given charge of the dredging. Priestley later recalled that the work required he go out all day, with a packed lunch, and only return home for the evening meal. Shackleton, he found, would often visit him. 'He used to come along and dig and yarn and sing and after a couple of hours he'd go away,' remembered Priestley. 'He was the only chap who came down and helped normally, was Shackleton.'

Second, Shackleton was a natural optimist who felt he could achieve anything. His letters to Emily telling her they would reach the Pole were an indication of his confident, positive personality. He also had the ability to inspire in most his presumption of success, which meant that when he asked them to take on tasks they might normally have thought impossible, they felt capable of doing so. Optimism, inspiration and honest regard for them gave him a strong hold over his men. Or at least most of them.

There was still one man that Shackleton could not win over, although it was not outwardly obvious. Marshall remained as negative as ever. 'By Gd he has not played the game & is not capable of doing so & a consummate liar & a practised hypocrite,' he wailed in his diary after returning from Erebus. 'By God I have been a damned fool to trust him. He is incapable of a decent action or thought.' The next day Marshall was still unforgiving: 'Shall get my own back before I have finished.'

It was not only Shackleton with whom Marshall was unhappy. Perhaps under his cold, unreadable exterior the doctor was not adjusting well to the strange combination of isolation and stifling immediacy. Perhaps it was the difference he had found between his romantic image of exploration and its reality. Or perhaps he was simply a misery guts. Regardless, his diary is a litany of negatives. Brocklehurst, he unfeelingly wrote in mid-April when the foot was not healing well, was 'very down, seems to have no guts'. A month later, it was, 'Just seen Pro's account of Erebus. Parts quite misleading. Especially of our party.' And following the midwinter party he seethed that Wild 'showed signs of being drunk . . . Was seriously thinking of getting him outside to give me a hand with the ponies & then giving him a damn good hammering, as he was becoming very talkative and objectionable.'

Most of Marshall's venom, however, was reserved for Shackleton, whose crimes included kicking the dogs and not holding regular church services. 'Sunday but no service,' Marshall wrote on 14 June. 'It being fine weather Sh thinks it unnecessary to beseech the help of the Almighty.'

It is one of those strange twists of fate that at the very time Marshall became increasingly recalcitrant, his significance as an adviser to Shackleton increased dramatically. His input was twofold: the food supplies for the southern journey, and who would be hauling them.

Before he left Britain, Marshall had investigated the current knowledge of scurvy, but had found there was little agreement as to its cause. The ptomaine theory was still widely accepted, but a new theory also held sway. Supported by Sir Almroth Wright, this indicated the disease was a condition of acid intoxication due to an increased acidity in the blood. Marshall believed in neither of these views, but accepted the 'fresh food' theory. This was not a casual decision, but one made after extensive study, which a paper in *The British Medical Journal* by Edward Wilson supported. Wilson – who had initially held to the ptomaine theory – noted that scurvy had disappeared after the party began to eat fresh seal meat 'for breakfast, as well as dinner, six days in every week'.

Marshall's view was also strongly upheld by what has been called 'the most important single paper in the whole history of this subject'. Published by Axel Holst, the professor of hygiene and bacteriology at the University of Christiania, in Norway, and Theodore Frölich, a Norwegian paediatrician, it showed scurvy to be a deficiency disease that 'could be produced by diet and . . . cured by diet. Of the three theories of scurvy then existing, infection, toxication, and faulty diet, only the last was supported by their findings.' However, as this paper appeared in the *Journal of Hygiene* only in October 1907, the month that Marshall left England on *Runic*, it is uncertain whether he saw it before the expedition.

Like his surgeon, Shackleton placed great importance on the expedition's food, not just to serve as a preventative for scurvy, but for psychological reasons. Later explorers who used the supplies left behind were amazed at their lavishness. The stores included large amounts of bottled or tinned fruit and jams and preservatives – much of which was purchased in New Zealand – as well as other products that provided high levels of nutrition and vitamin C. These included Glaxo dried milk and milk powder; plasmon biscuits, made with fortified milk protein; and New Zealand butter, cheese and vegetables. These all helped in the fight against scurvy, as did Marshall's plan to 'prime' the sledge parties, the members of which would receive extra fresh meat – lightly cooked penguin or seal – every day for a month before departing.

The only question left was who would be going on those sledge journeys. For the Magnetic Pole, the choice remained David, Mawson and Mackay. However, due to the loss of all but four ponies, the Southern Party would be cut to four men. By the middle of winter it was obvious that Brocklehurst's foot would not allow him to participate on the long journey, and at the end of July Shackleton informed him he would not be coming. Instead, Brocklehurst would join Armytage and Priestley on a geology field trip to the western mountains.

The other casualty from the original plan would eventually be Joyce, whom Marshall failed medically for a variety of reasons. Joyce showed, he noted, a liver problem and the beginning of heart disease, 'a myocarditis in a very early stage'. Marshall also felt that Joyce would be dangerous to take because he considered him mentally limited, resentful and incompatible with the others; for two of these, one might wonder if the doctor had been looking into a mirror. Regardless, Marshall stuck by his decision, and more than forty years later wrote that he had 'ploughed him for the "Southern Journey" and if I had not done so we should have had the same experience as Scott had with P.O. Evans on the glacier.'

Marshall was not positive about Adams either – 'I saw much on Erebus to make me doubt his nerve and judgement,' he wrote mysteriously in late June. Never the less, he passed him physically. With Wild there was never any question, as Marshall regarded him as the fittest in the party. Finally, there was Shackleton. 'Pulm[onary] Systolic murmur still present', Marshall noted in his diary about Shackleton five weeks after he first examined him. What did it mean? Was it what had caused Shackleton's 'asthma' – the term The Boss used for the condition he had experienced on his return from the farthest south with Scott? Was it something that had been exacerbated by the scurvy? Would it prove problematic this time? Neither doctor nor patient knew for certain, and neither was comfortable with the fact. Marshall passed his chief for the southern journey, but realised he would have to be constantly on the lookout for problems. Shackleton, too, may have inwardly doubted his powerful physique, but he had no questions about his strength of will.

*   *   *

By the beginning of August, everyone was ready for action. In Mackay's case, too ready. Early in the morning on the third, Roberts, with whom he shared a cubicle, put his feet on Mackay's locker to lace up his boots. Mackay's tightly wound disposition unravelled. 'Aroused by expostulations of Bobs whom Mac had gripped by the throat in a more than friendly manner,' Marshall recorded. The situation might have become more disagreeable had not Mawson intervened with Mackay: 'choked him off and turned him back to bed.'

As Priestley pointed out, it was fortunate that it was the end of winter rather than the beginning. The men had been indoors too long, and they all needed to focus their attention on the real work of the expedition. So, despite the sun having not yet returned, Shackleton decided it was time they 'received a good baptism of frost'.

Shackleton did not intend for the Southern Party to leave until the end of October. But McMurdo Sound was frozen over, so that gave him two months to lay the depots that should have been put out the previous autumn. Since it was too cold to use the ponies, he had plenty of time to break his men into the true horrors of man-hauling.

On 12 August Shackleton left with David and Armytage for Hut Point. The pony Quan pulled the sledge until they neared Cape Barne, but then returned with a support party, while the three men donned their harnesses. On the morning of 14 August they reached the hut. The next morning they pushed a dozen miles out on the Barrier, finding many patches of soft snow, which confirmed, to their disappointment, that the motor-car would be ineffective there. By 6.00 p.m. the temperature had crashed to $-56°$ and was still dropping. An appallingly miserable night was followed in the morning by the threat of a blizzard, so they headed north, reaching Hut Point only shortly before the gale did. For the next five days they cleaned and ordered the hut, while waiting for the terrible weather to break. On 22 August, when the sun finally appeared above the horizon, they marched all the way back to Cape Royds.

Shackleton now began a programme whereby each week different parties hauled supplies to Hut Point. Not only did this turn the hut into an advance base, it blooded all the polar newcomers to the realities of the season ahead. It also woke some of them up to aspects of life with which they had been blissfully unfamiliar. 'A curious reflection of my "Victorian" upbringing as a non-swearing, teetotaller Wesleyan Methodist is the absence of any mention of one of the circumstances which etched this sledge journey deeply in my memory,' Priestley wrote fifty years later, having reread his diary's account of his second depot trip, on which he travelled with Adams and Mackay. 'For three days we marched to a monotonous repetition of blasphemy every few steps from Adams, his favourite being "Jesus f . . . g God Almighty!" '

Each party came back with stories to tell of cold, adventure, misery and more cold. Never the less, by late September, having had tenuous help from the motor-car, they had stocked the *Discovery* hut with provisions and food for the ninety-one days Shackleton planned for the Southern Party to be in the field. There was also a supply of ten pounds per day per pony of a combination of maize, Maujee ration and compressed fodder.

The last great preparatory trip began on 22 September, when Shackleton, Adams, Marshall, Wild, Joyce and Marston left Cape Royds to establish the one depot out on the Barrier. On the first stage of the actual southern journey, Shackleton planned to steer much farther to the east than Scott had done, thereby avoiding the broken, crevassed ice they had encountered six years before. This meant that in the barren expanse of the snow-covered Barrier, there would be no particular landmarks to guide them to the depot, which Shackleton decided would be one hundred geographic miles south of Hut Point. The potential difficulty in finding the depot meant they did not want to leave there any provisions necessary for their own existence. So, as they left for the south, with a load of 170 pounds per man, they were actually pulling not their own supplies, but pony rations.

On 6 October they established Depot A at 79° 36'S, approximately 120 miles from Cape Royds, having experienced temperatures as low as −59°. There they piled up 167 pounds of maize, added a gallon tin of oil, and marked it with an upturned sledge and a black flag. Remarkably, the conditions for the return journey were even worse, and they arrived at Hut Point having run out of food. The next day they started for Cape Royds and had the good fortune of meeting Day with the motor-car a mile and a half south of Cape Barne. They returned the rest of the way in style.

Shackleton and the depot party reached their base on the evening of 13 October. There they relaxed, had a cup of cocoa and ate a meal. But the hut seemed emptier than normal, and, as they looked around, they realised that three of their friends had disappeared.

16

ACROSS THE GREAT ICE BARRIER

That evening, as Shackleton and his five companions relaxed in the hut at Cape Royds, David, Mawson and Mackay – the members of the Northern Party – were spending a much less pleasant time at Butter Point, a low-lying ice cliff on the west side of McMurdo Sound. They had left the winter quarters eight days before with a task every bit as daunting as that facing those heading south.

David had received Shackleton's written instructions before The Boss left on the depot trip. The key objective was, '(1) To take magnetic observations at every suitable point with a view to determining the dip and the position of the Magnetic Pole. If time permits . . . you will try and reach the Magnetic Pole.' The instructions also told them: '(2) To make a general geological survey of the coast of Victoria Land . . . [and] (3) I particularly wish . . . Mawson to spend at least one fortnight at Dry Valley to prospect for minerals of economic value on your return . . . I consider that the *thorough* investigation of Dry Valley is of supreme importance.' In the last, Shackleton had mentioned what was actually important to *him*. It was his long-term fascination with treasure.

Shackleton had hoped that David's party would depart on 1 October, but thick weather and an injury to Day meant that they could not leave until four days later, after, with the help of the motor-car, they had left two depots ten and fifteen miles from base. Uncertain ice conditions forced them to start south toward Glacier Tongue before turning west and crossing to Butter Point, which had been named by Scott's party for a tin of butter that had been left there. The plan was for them to head north along the coast of Victoria Land, hoping to find a passage up to the high Polar Plateau, which Albert Armitage had been the first to reach six years before, while Scott, Shackleton and Wilson had been on their southern adventure.

The first day – having been given a ride part way by Day – they reached the ten-mile depot. It was there that the reality of their task hit them. Not able to pull both sledges, which totalled 710 pounds, they immediately had to settle into relay work. They would haul one sledge – nicknamed the 'Christmas Tree' sledge because so many things remembered at the last moment had been tied on to it willy-nilly – for anywhere up to a mile, then return for the 'Plum Duff' sledge on which most of the provisions were kept. In this way, they progressed about four miles per day.

The partially thawed sea ice made a slow, sticky surface for the sledge runners, and the work was cruelly difficult. The strain quickly led Mawson to tire of the eccentricities of his mentor. 'Prof finds it necessary to change his socks in morning before breakfast, also has to wear 2 per day,' he grumbled on the fourth day out. 'And comes in late for [three-man sleeping] bag and sits on everybody. God only knows what he does . . . He is so covered with clothes that he can hardly walk and hardly get into bag – that is to say, hardly leaves any room for us as he very nicely made us take side places.'

After a day lost to blizzard conditions, on 13 October the party finally reached Butter Point. They realised that at their present speed they would not be able to attain the Magnetic Pole, estimated at 500 miles from Cape Royds, and return in time for the relief ship. So they depoted seventy pounds, 40 per cent of which was biscuits, and left a note warning they would likely not return until 12 January. Then they moved off north across New Harbour, the wide, ice-covered entrance to the Ferrar Glacier and Dry Valley (known today as Taylor Valley). On the morning of 17 October, they reached the northern edge of the harbour at Cape Bernacchi, a low, rocky promontory dominated by a pure white crystalline marble. Here, following Shackleton's instructions, and with a flag that Day had laboriously made out of a red handkerchief with white spots, some blue fabric, and the light duck material for the cubicle dividers, they took possession of Victoria Land for the British Empire.

While David and his party worked north, Shackleton finalised his preparations for his journey the other direction. He wrote a series of letters, clarifying the goals and movements for each party, and setting out contingencies if rescue were required (although these were vague). He also outlined a new financial arrangement with each man.

Most important was the responsibility he delegated to Murray. If Shackleton were not to return, Adams would assume command, but if neither did, Murray was to take charge, over the heads of David and Marshall. That this burden was not passed to David would be surprising except that Shackleton had no way of knowing when, or if, David would return to Cape Royds. If the ice were to break out early, his party could be trapped on the western shore, and Shackleton needed someone he could trust, including dealing with the master of *Nimrod*, whoever that might be. Murray fit the bill. 'You have never for one moment caused me the slightest anxiety in any way: I am most deeply indebted to you for the good quick influence you have had on the Expedition; also for the good sound advice you have given me,' Shackleton wrote. 'I am not a good hand at saying things in praise but I hope you will know that your high character has been an incentive to me keeping up my heart in downward times.'

Outlined in the three letters that Shackleton wrote to Murray were the plans for the rest of the expedition. When the support party returned, Priestley was to be allowed to investigate the geology of the north slope of Erebus. Then, at the beginning of December, Priestley, Brocklehurst and Armytage – the Western Party – were to leave for a survey of the western mountains. The Northern Party, upon its return, was to meet these three at Butter Point. Mawson, Priestley and Brocklehurst were to investigate the 'economic side of the geology' of the area, while David, Mackay and Armytage were to proceed to Cape Royds to confirm their safe return. David could then take stores back to Butter Point and continue his geological work. Although Shackleton's orders included directions of where to leave messages and how to signal across open water if it prevented them reaching base, the difficulty in planning for all contingencies was shown by a lack of precise instructions should the Northern Party not be able to return south at all.

Shackleton also ordered Day and Marston to move supplies to Hut Point in late December. From there, in the middle of January, the two of them and Joyce were to make a depot on the Barrier eight miles off Minna Bluff – a narrow peninsula running east from Mount Discovery – with enough food to allow the Southern Party to return to the *Discovery* hut.

Murray was put in charge of making certain that all the collections and scientific gear were loaded on to *Nimrod* when she arrived around

15 January. He was additionally assigned to give Shackleton's letter of instructions to the ship's master. These took into account conditions of the ice as well as variables relating to the two parties on the western shore, and directed the captain to pick up the men and gather the scientific material. Included was the order that if the Southern Party had not returned by 25 February, Murray was to land sufficient coal and provisions at Cape Royds to support seven men for a year. He would then select three volunteers to stay behind (or appoint three if no one volunteered), who would proceed at once in search of the Southern Party and would continue the search, if necessary, the next summer. Shackleton's solicitors would arrange for the relief of the party the following year.

As a final point, Shackleton noted that Murray

> suggested that it might be as well if latitude were given you and the acting master of Nimrod to consult as to a further detention of the ship beyond the 1st of March 1909. I therefore give you permission to do so: but the ship must on the first of March steam to the entrance of MacMurdo Sound to see the ice conditions and if there is no heavy pack . . . she can return to Cape Royds again: but I think the utmost limit you should remain here is the 10th of March.

After dealing with his men, Shackleton turned his attention to Emily. 'My own darling Sweeteyes and Wife,' he wrote in a letter that was supposed to be read only in case of his death.

> I want to tell you beloved that whatever I may have been all the time I have loved you truly and you have been an angel of light and an arm of strength to me . . . Child o' mine think kindly of me and remember that if I did wrong in going away from you and our children that it was not just selfishness . . . your husband will have died in one of the few great things left to be done . . . I have written to you my life with a trembling hand for it is too hard to think that it means that if you get this it will be years before we meet in another life.

The letter was not unlike that he wrote before the southern journey with Scott and Wilson, attempting to comfort Emily by convincing her of his faith in God and their everlasting unity. He did not believe it, of course. As with a number of other supposed tenets in his life, such as his

ACROSS THE GREAT ICE BARRIER 199

Irishness or his 'firm' political stance, Shackleton professed to religious devotion when it was convenient or helpful – in this case helpful to Emily. His true beliefs were somewhat different. 'He used to say to me that he didn't believe in calling on the Almighty when you were in a hole,' Leonard Hussey, a colleague from a later expedition said. 'If he didn't believe in the Lord when things were going well, he wasn't going to call on His protection when they weren't going well.' And one can see in Shackleton's diary that his true belief was in 'providence', in good fortune, in luck. And, as he recorded, the sign of his good luck came to him the night before the journey south finally began:

> Last night as we sat at dinner the evening sun entered through the ventilator and the circle of light shone full on the portrait of HM . . . Slowly it moved across and found the portrait of Her Majesty: it seemed an omen of good luck for only on this day and at that particular time could this have happened and today we started to strive & plant her flag on the last spot of the world that counts as worth striving for.

It was thus with boundless enthusiasm that on 29 October 1908 began what Wild called 'the Great Southern Journey'. At 9.00 a.m. the motor-car left with two sledges and the five members of the support party: Joyce, Marston, Armytage, Brocklehurst and Priestley. 'We had tremendous faith in Shackleton's ability, but like him we had no idea what he had to meet with,' Brocklehurst recalled almost half a century later. 'If we'd known what a high altitude they'd have to get to, I think we'd have had much more doubt as to whether they'd reach the Pole or not. But Shackleton was so enthusiastic and so confident in his own ability that he didn't leave very much for us to think other than success.'

Shackleton, for the moment, was ecstatic. 'A glorious day for our start,' he wrote, 'brilliant sunshine and a cloudless sky. A fair wind from the north in fact everything that could conduce to an auspicious beginning.' At 10.00 a.m. the polar party said their farewells to Murray and Roberts – the only men left at base – and turned south, each guiding a pony harnessed to a sledge: Wild with Socks, Adams with Chinaman, Marshall with Grisi, and Shackleton with Quan. 'At last we are out on the long trail after 4 years thought and work,' Shackleton wrote. 'I pray that we may be successful for my Heart has been so much in this.'

Even from the beginning, however, there were problems. Within an hour Socks went lame, and it became obvious that they would have to give him a few days' rest. Then, when they stopped for lunch, Grisi suddenly kicked out, catching Adams three inches below the knee and exposing the bone. 'He was in great pain but pluckily said little about it,' Shackleton wrote. 'It is a mercy that Adams is better tonight. I cannot imagine what he would have done if he had been knocked out for the Southern Journey.'

That night was spent at Glacier Tongue with the support party, and the following morning the four members of the Southern Party pro- ceeded to Hut Point, while the others ground the quarter ton of maize that had been depoted there by *Nimrod* into pony food. The next few days most of the men remained at Hut Point, weighing and stowing provisions while Socks improved. Shackleton made a trip back to Cape Royds, returning with edible luxuries for the men, salt for the ponies, and wire rope, as the ponies had been eating through their leather halters. It was not all that the ponies ate. On the night of 1 November a heavy snow fell, and the next morning the men found that Quan had bitten through his tether and headed directly for the food. 'The sledges with maize, pony rations, and fodder on looked as if they had been attacked by a herd of elephants who had been without food for a century or more,' Priestley recorded. Quan then led them a merry chase before being caught.

It was the ponies' last great escape. The next morning the real start towards the Pole began, as they headed out on to the Barrier, 'Quan pulling 660, Grisi 615, Socks 600, Chinaman 600. 5 men hauling 660: 153 being pony food.' At the edge of the Barrier, Brocklehurst photo- graphed the group, complete with sledging flags and the Queen's Union Jack. Then they plunged ahead, on to a surface that was exceptionally soft, 'the ponies at times sinking in up to their bellies and always over their hocks'. It was just as hard for the men of the support party, who rotated with the others pulling the sledge. Never the less they could not keep the pace of the ponies, and Shackleton decided he could not afford to be slowed down by them.

On the morning of 4 November they depoted 100 pounds of paraffin and provisions, and as a result the support party managed to pull all day at a marvellous rate, totalling sixteen miles. The next day they again started well, but a driving snow after lunch made it difficult to navigate and they found themselves too far west. They had stumbled into an area where the Barrier becomes heavily crevassed due to its proximity to White Island – Shackleton's destination on his first jaunt in 1902 – and Minna Bluff. Shortly after Grisi and Marshall almost disappeared down a crevasse, the party halted to await better weather. It did not come soon. The following day a blizzard kept them in their tents, and Shackleton reduced their lunch ration to two biscuits to make up for the lost time. 'We must retrench at every setback if we are going to have enough food to carry us through,' he noted. 'We started with 91 days food but with careful management we can make it spin out to 110 days.'

Shackleton's decision had been based on elementary arithmetic. He had calculated that the Pole was 859 statute miles from Cape Royds, which meant that his party needed to travel almost nineteen miles a day to reach it and return on the allotted food. With the delays due to Socks and the weather, they had so far averaged only seven miles. His cutting of the daily allowance meant that they would need to cover only fifteen miles. It was still a large distance, but it gave him hope, which the early problems had begun to take away.

On 7 November conditions were still not ideal, but the four men said farewell to the support party and moved south to the ringing of three cheers. The light proved extremely poor, however, and they pushed into 'a dead white wall with nothing even in the shape of a cloud to guide our steering'. Within minutes of starting, Marshall put his left leg through a hole into a crevasse, Grisi just missing the same. 'Examined hole, could see no bottom,' Marshall wrote laconically, 'most uninviting.'

They were still too far west, but marching east was courting disaster, as the light was such that they could not identify crevasses until they were on top of them. Within the next hour each member of the party stepped into a hole that could have meant the end of him and his pony. The group was forced again to camp, and they remained there for almost forty-eight hours, between two large crevasses. To conserve oil and protect their valuable four-hoofed partners they forfeited a hot lunch, instead boiling up a 'maujee hoosh' for the ponies.

The wait again demonstrated Shackleton's understanding of psychology. The four men were in two tents, and in order not to break into two cliques, he decided that each week they would rotate tent-mates, as well as cooking duties. Unfortunately, neither he nor the others showed such comprehension of the equine species. The ponies had constantly broken through the crust of snow that dogs would have lightly run across; this was also true of the men, whose weight would have been advantageously distributed on skis. But unlike the men, who could retire to tents, the ponies were forced to bivouac outside, exposed to the bitter cold and wind. Whereas this would not have troubled dogs, the ponies were not designed for it, as they sweated throughout their bodies, and had hides that helped dissipate heat rather than retain it. Each evening the men were forced to build snow walls to protect them from the wind, to rub them down and to cover them with blankets. Then in the morning they had to scrape the snow off their hooves.

Through all of this the ponies suffered miserably, and the men showed a remarkable lack of understanding as to why. 'Poor little Gresi & Socks who are the most intelligent & domesticated of 4 ponies seem very unhappy at being left out in blizzard without companionship & are off their feeds,' Marshall wrote, echoing what Wild had written about the two most 'sensitive' ponies.

Finally, on 9 November, the weather cleared. They initially moved ahead at a snail's pace because they found themselves in the centre of a maze of crevasses. 'There was nothing for it but to trust to Providence,' wrote Shackleton. 'We had to cross somewhere.' They made their way across or around many crevasses before, right in front of Shackleton, Chinaman went down a crack some two feet wide. They managed to get him on to firm ice only just in time, as the crack suddenly broke out into a great, fathomless chasm. 'But when things seem the worst they turn to the best,' wrote Shackleton, paraphrasing Browning's poem 'Prospice', which had long been the secret greeting between him and Emily. 'For that was the last crevasse we encountered.'

They now made excellent time, completing fourteen and a half miles that day. For a while they mistakenly started heading back toward the crevasses, until, Wild noted, 'I spoke about it when Shacks altered it, he always listens to me now.' This had been written in a cipher that Wild used in his diary for some of his more contentious comments. Shackleton, too, was cautious: regardless of what he might truly think, he assiduously avoided passing judgement in writing. It was only Marshall who unreservedly recorded his innermost thoughts.

For the next week they continued unhindered, and, other than Shackleton's snow blindness, only Wild was troubled. 'I have been leading all day, so have been able to keep a decent course,' he wrote in pointed dissatisfaction with his comrades. 'I pray daily that A. may be struck dumb, his incessant idiotic chatter would make a saint curse. His pony is getting like him and don't pull.' It was an astute observation: Chinaman was the oldest and weakest of the ponies.

On 15 November, Wild spied Depot A, which they had laid in the spring. They picked up fodder and deposited three days' worth of food, enough, with no delays, to reach the depot Joyce was due to lay for their return. They were so pleased with their achievement that they put a cupful of the ponies' Maujee ration in their own pemmican and 'enjoyed it immensely'.

They continued to make good progress, although their views were frequently cut off by overcast weather. 'Surely there is no more desolate or barren spot in the world,' wrote Marshall, 'well suited to what one would imagine the end of the world to be like.' Shackleton, conversely, wrote, 'It has been a wonderful and successful week so different to this time 6 years ago when I was toiling along 5 miles a day over the same ground.'

The difference, clearly, was the ponies, but their longevity would soon become an issue, as Shackleton noted:

> We seem to have arrived at a latitude where there is no wind and the snow remains where it falls . . . for we were sinking in well over our ankles and the poor ponies are having a most trying time. They break through the crust on the surface and flounder up to their hocks; and each step they have to pull their feet out through the brittle crust: It is telling more on Chinaman than on the others and he is going slowly the chafe of the snow crust on his fetlocks has galled him so we will have to shoot him at the next depot.

That came three days later, on the evening of 21 November, when, having passed 81°S, they stopped for the night, built a snow wall, and took the poor thing behind it, where he was shot. Marshall then cut the pony's throat to bleed him, and he and Wild cut off most of the meat, leaving sixty pounds at Depot B and taking another eighty, not only varying their diet but giving them added protection from scurvy. The men were only too glad of the meat, because they had not received enough since Marshall's carefully planned food allowances had been cut.

The depot, with a single black flag flying on a piece of bamboo lashed to the now discarded sledge, was left behind the next morning. In order to expedite their return journey and help them reach the stash of food, they began constructing a snow cairn each night, the series marking their way home. They now virtually flew along, making more than seventeen miles on four consecutive days, despite Wild, as well as Quan and Grisi, feeling ill. Wild slowly came around, in part due to the horse meat, which was served both cooked and not. 'Lunched on raw frozen horse flesh dipped in fat,' Marshall recorded exuberantly one evening. 'This saves oil & ordinary lunch ration. Not v. filling or pleasant, but when hungry it does not come amiss.'

Meanwhile, Marshall's primary medical effort had been an attempt to pull an aching tooth from Adams. Not having any forceps, however, he broke it. It was not until twenty-four hours later that a second attempt, like the first without any anaesthetic, was successful.

But all of this faded into insignificance on 26 November when they camped to the east of what Scott had called the Shackleton Inlet. 'A day to remember,' wrote the man for whom it was named, 'for we have passed the Furthest South yet reached by man. Tonight we are in Latitude 82.18½ S 168°E.' The men celebrated with 'a nice little tot of curaçoa [sic], which made us all feel quite happy.'

For Shackleton, the torment of years – the stigma of being invalided home and the embarrassment of Scott's descriptions of him being pulled on a sledge – had been overcome. But not forgotten. 'This we have been able to do,' he crowed, 'in much less time than we did on the last long march . . . with Captain Scott.' Indeed, they had achieved it in a full month less than Scott – twenty-nine days compared to fifty-nine – and that boded well for their assault on the Pole. Even Wild, not normally an optimist, thought the prize within their grasp. 'I am beginning to think we shall get to the Pole all right,' he wrote, 'but am doubtful about getting back again.'

It was now all totally new – sights never before seen by human eyes, paths never before trodden. As huge new mountains appeared in the clear air – with sheer granite cliffs towering thousands of feet over the plain – the men marvelled at a place 'so strange and unlike anything else in the world'. They were also mystified by what Wild described as 'quite a brilliant gleam of light in the sky above the southern horizon which we cannot account for'. But two days later they were brought back to Earth with a large dose of reality.

'Noble little Grisi was shot tonight,' recorded Marshall. 'He had worked faithfully & pluckily without refusing & was never touched with a whip.' They again made a depot and left behind enough pony flesh and other provisions for their return. But they were down to two ponies and the increase in weight on each sledge meant that the men had to go into harness and share the pulling. This in turn meant an increase in the calories they burned and, therefore, in their hunger.

Equally as worrisome, the mountains that had long been to their right curved to the east so as to cut straight in front of their path. Shackleton had hoped to find the Pole located on the Barrier; climbing mountains was not on his agenda. Yet another problem was developing: the Barrier itself seemed to be changing. They started going over a series of long undulations that Wild described as being like 'a long and quiet deep sea swell with crests about half a mile apart'. In the hollow of these the snow was so deep and soft that the ponies could hardly advance, and within several days Quan was exhausted.

All along Quan had not only drawn the heaviest load, but had been the comedian and mischief-maker. In one brief period he had consumed 'the great part of the inside of a horse cloth, about a fathom of rope, several pieces of leather and other odds and ends such as nosebag buckle . . . he would rather eat a yard of creosoted rope than his maize and maujee indeed, he often in sheer wantonness throws it all over the snow.' Now he was worn out. On 1 December he broke down and they had to take him out of the harness. As soon as they camped, Wild shot him. 'Got only enough meat for about 5 days off him,' Marshall noted disappointedly; there would be no provisions at 'Quan Depot'. Marshall was not the only one unhappy. 'Last night,' Wild recorded, 'poor little Socks kept us all awake for a long time neighing and whinnying for his lost companions.'

The party had now come to a decision point. They had been moving south-southeast, but ahead appeared a jumble of pressure ridges and exceptionally difficult ice. 'It seems as though the Barrier end had come and there is going to be a change in some gigantic way in keeping with the vastness of the whole place,' Shackleton wrote the evening Quan was killed. 'We fervently trust it will not delay us in our march South.' The unknown geography and the lack of ponies were two obvious reasons for his concerns. Another was food. 'At one moment our thoughts are in the grandeur of the scene,' he wrote, 'the next on what we would have to eat if only we were let loose in a good restaurant, for we are very hungry these days and we know that we are likely to be for another three months.'

Their minds were made up for them by lunchtime the next day. 'We had got close enough to the disturbance ahead of us to see that it consisted of enormous pressure ridges heavily crevassed running a long way East and not the slightest chance of our being able to get Southing that way any longer on the Barrier,' Shackleton wrote. However, directly south of them appeared to be a large glacier leading south rather than southeast, in front of which stood a small red-coloured mountain. During their meal, according to Marshall, 'it was unan-imously agreed to change course going S. to what appears to be the Golden Gateway to the S.'

Marshall's ethereal description was of a low, snow-filled pass be-tween the red mountain and a bare rock point three miles southwest of it. Beyond this, Wild thought, 'a glacier opens up leading through the mountains in an almost due south direction.' With anticipation matched only by uncertainty, they gingerly made their way south until they reached a field of hard sastrugi seven miles from the mountain. There they camped and prepared for the morrow by attaching spikes to the bottom of their ski boots and fitting themselves out with anything that could resemble climbing gear.

The next morning, bad light delayed their departure until 9.00, when they headed out, 'leaving Socks in charge of camp'. Soon they found themselves in a sea of crevasses and roped together. 'These got larger and more frequent,' wrote Wild, until 'our way was barred by an immense chasm about 60 to 80 feet deep, and about 60 wide, with overhanging sides.' Several hundred yards to the west, however, the chasm closed and they were able to continue. After a passage over dozens more crevasses and an area of smooth blue ice, they reached the mountain and clambered up a rock face followed by a snow slope and then more rock. At 3.00 p.m., after six hours on the move, they attained the summit and saw a scene of almost indescribable grandeur.

'There burst upon our vision an open road to the South,' wrote Shackleton, 'for there stretched a great glacier running almost South and North between the great mountain ranges.' It extended, according to Marshall:

as far as the eye could reach, flanked on either side by rugged ice-covered mountains, until lost sight of 60 miles distant where the mountains on the East flank and . . . the West formed a 'narrow' or waist, which forecast great ice disturbances as the glacier flowed from the distant plateau, which we now realised guarded the secrets of the Pole itself.

The glacier, wrote Wild:

> must be the largest in the world; it is at least 30 miles wide and we could see over 100 miles of its length, beyond that must be the Great Plateau. Our Gateway is only a very small side entrance . . . the main flow runs out E & has made a fearful mess of the Barrier for many miles in that direction.

They had thus in one fell swoop answered all of their questions of recent days. To the south of the red mountain, which they named Mount Hope, the colossal glacier smashed into the Barrier, causing the disturbances they had seen. What this meant was that Marshall's Golden Gateway – 'The Gateway' as it is now named – was not only the beginning of the path through the mountains, but the only one they would have been able to cross on to the glacier. And the glow in the southern horizon for which Wild could not account was the glacier's ice blink – a bright white light in the sky reflected up from the vast areas of ice beyond the viewer's sight.

They had also answered beyond doubt where their trail would lead. From their pinnacle they could see the mountain chain running far to the southeast, and they realised that continuing on the Barrier would mean finding their way blocked by impassable heights. Indeed, although they did not know it, they had found one of the few paths available to convey them through the Transantarctic Mountains. They all agreed upon following it.

'Tomorrow we hope to enter this Southern gateway,' wrote Marshall, who took several photographs after carrying the heavy plate camera all the way to the top of Mount Hope. 'Shall never forget the 1st sight of this promised land. The Almighty has indeed been good to us.'

Their good fortune continued the next day, with weather so warm that they stripped to their shirts. Shackleton, Adams and Marshall pulled one sledge, followed by Wild leading Socks. They found 'that taking two loaded sledges and a pony across crevasses is a much more difficult business than getting over them unencumbered, but with care and caution we got through without any serious mishap.' The three men would break through any snow bridges over the crevasses with ice axes, so that Wild and Socks could see them, 'and then I took him over with a rush, and the good little fellow cleared them all splendidly.' After ascending a long slope through The Gateway, they camped near the edge of the glacier.

On 5 December they began struggling up what they called 'The Great Glacier', experiencing again the drawbacks of being accompanied by a pony. Being unshod, Socks could not pull over the bare, glassy blue ice they had to cross most of the day, so he was unharnessed and led by Wild as the others relayed. 'He behaved remarkably well under the circumstances,' Wild wrote, 'several times he got his hind quarters into crevasses, but he did not get much scared. It was an awful job though . . . on several occasions I thought both he and I were going straight to Hell.'

They camped that night under a vast granite cliff rising sheer 2,000 feet, a site so recognisable that Shackleton decided to establish another depot so that they need not haul as much up the glacier. Never the less, the next day they advanced little more than three miles, relaying three loads over a steep jumble of ice. 'Two of us pulled the sledge in front and two went alongside to steady it,' Wild wrote. 'I would rather walk 40 miles than do it again.' Shackleton suffered terribly from snowblindness, but most trying of all was moving Socks. They could not take him over most sections, so Wild guided him close to the cliffs and they walked over huge piles of rocks and rubble. When he did have to cross the ice, they cut a road for him with their ice axes.

One might assume that prior to falling asleep that night Wild looked into a crystal ball, for he wrote: 'Just before camping tonight we passed close to two huge crevasses on our right and as we stopped we could see others looming up ahead, so possibly we are in for another exciting day tomorrow.' The next morning the party moved closer to the centre of the glacier, away from the frightening and brutally difficult edges, where secondary glaciers debouched into it from the mountains. It was a fateful choice.

Not long after lunch, Wild suddenly stepped into space, felt a violent blow on his shoulder, and experienced a fearful rush of something past him as he dropped into a horrible chasm. The others, ten yards ahead, heard a muffled cry and looked behind them. In the instant that they turned their heads, they saw nothing – Wild and Socks had vanished.

17

THE WESTERN PARTY

When the support party turned north on 7 November, its members were relieved. Danger, they believed, would no longer be accompanying them, but had followed the four men who had continued south. Their assumption was totally wrong. Perhaps it was the aura of the motor-car, but they were to find that many problems occur within a short distance of home.

Joyce, who was in charge of the support party, wanted to get the men off the Barrier as quickly as possible. To do so, he ordered a forced march, and they made excellent progress despite a poor surface. With stops only for lunch and dinner, they ploughed ahead from 7.00 a.m. until reaching the *Discovery* hut at 1.30 the next morning. Several days later, after recovering, they continued towards Cape Royds. Near Glacier Tongue they met Murray, Day and Roberts, who had brought out 1,800 pounds of provisions and gear that Shackleton wanted depoted in case later parties were cut off by open water. The entire group had an easy return that night thanks to the motor-car.

For the next several weeks the men engaged in their own duties. Murray concentrated on freshwater biology. Priestley went to the lower slopes of Mount Erebus to examine a series of cones composed of kenyte (a feldspar first noted by J.W. Gregory on Mount Kenya). Joyce skinned and preserved nine Weddell seals and continued work on *Aurora Australis*. And Marston attempted to capture the wondrous natural colours of the Antarctic in his oil paintings.

Throughout this time, Priestley patiently waited for the threat of bad weather to disappear so that an investigation of several parasitic cones on the northern slopes of Mount Erebus could be launched. The skies did not clear totally, but the scheduled departure date for the Western Party drew closer, so the Erebus trip had to start regardless of weather. On 23 November Murray, Priestley, Joyce, Marston and Brocklehurst left the base. In order to travel lightly and quickly, they took a week's supply of food but only one three-man tent, the plan being for two men to sleep outside each night.

The weather was bright when they left, but that afternoon a strong southerly wind arose. They camped 2,000 feet above sea level about five miles from base, near a steep nunatak – a rocky outcrop exposed through the ice. 'When we camped the drift had ceased,' Priestley later wrote,

> and we were thus unable to notice as we should have done that the nunatak simply caused the wind to deflect its course from across the mountain to straight down the slopes we were perched on. Another mistake we were betrayed into was that of camping on a glacier instead of on a snowdrift, and this was due to the fact that the glacier was covered with several inches of recent snow.

Priestley had volunteered to sleep outside that night, while the other four crammed uncomfortably into the small tent. He moved to a nook in some rocks near the top of a small hill. 'A few hours later I woke up to find . . . a blizzard and that the drift was sweeping in a steady cloud over my head.' Fighting a fierce wind, Priestley crawled to the sledge, where he wrapped the tent cloth around his sleeping bag. He remembered:

> It was in this position that I spent the next seventy-two hours . . . getting gradually at every change in the direction of the wind shifted down a yard or two at a time and pushed along the wind-swept surface of the glacier until I was some twenty or thirty yards from the tent and in danger of getting swept . . . either on to some rocks a quarter of a mile below or else straight down the glacier and over a hundred foot drop into Horseshoe Bay.

Meanwhile one of the tent poles gave way and it was impossible to keep any snow on the skirting of the tent, so the men inside lay terrified at the 'constant expectation of seeing the tent leave them in the lurch'. For the time being they were warm enough, and, although they could not cook anything, according to Murray, 'we ate the dry biscuit and pemmican. The little snow under the floor-cloth was squeezed in the hand till it became ice, and we sucked this for drink. We were anxious about Priestley and occasionally opened the doorflap and hailed him, when he always replied that he was all right.'

Three times in the ensuing days the men in the tent passed biscuits and raw pemmican to Priestley, and one time Marston brought him chocolate, but for nearly eighty hours he drank nothing 'but such fragments of ice as I could prize up with the point of a small safety pin'. Once when Joyce came to see him, the drift was so thick that he had to find his way back by shouting and listening for the return calls. He was frostbitten so badly that the others felt it unsafe to attempt to reach Priestley again.

'To an experienced floe and barrier sledger it may sound a lie that we could not reach the sledge which was four yards or less from the tent,' Priestley wrote. 'But it must be remembered that we were lying on the slopes of a clean swept glacier which finnesko could get no hold on; our spiked ski-boots were on the icepicks round the sledge where they had been hung to dry.'

After three days there came a brief respite from the blizzard, and Marston carefully crawled down to Priestley. The two of them pains-takingly dragged the sleeping bag up to the tent. 'Four men in a three-man tent is a big squeeze,' Priestley wrote, 'but five was fearful, and it was some time before I managed to get even sitting room.' After checking his feet for frostbite, Priestley lay down on top of Murray and Marston and 'by a system of wriggling we managed to get fairly settled.'

At about 5.30 the next morning, the wind began to die away. They had a quick breakfast, although it was not pleasant because the paraffin had spilled in the food. Then, after a delay to revive Priestley's frostbitten feet, they headed back for the base as quickly as their stiff, starving bodies would go, their scientific objectives abandoned. 'We left all the provisions there,' Priestley noted, 'and unanimously named the nunatak "Misery Nunatak", and we were all about as glad to leave the place as a soul would be to leave Purgatory.'

As the party reached the hut, Mount Erebus 'was noticed to be in eruption . . . Huge diverging columns of steam were rising from the

crater, and behind could be seen curious clouds of feathery cirrus.' The
mountain, seemingly, wanted to remind them who was more powerful.

None of the frostbite received on Mount Erebus proved significant, and
on 1 December Armytage, Priestley and Brocklehurst left to stock the
depot at Butter Point for the return of the Northern Party. They were
then to return, pick up supplies for themselves, and proceed back to the
west coast and up the Ferrar Glacier to Depot Nunatak in search of
fossils in the sandstone soil of the surrounding mountain range. For
sixteen miles they and 1,200 pounds of equipment and provisions were
carried by the motor-car. The sea ice was very unstable, however, and
Day and Marston were almost trapped on their return by fresh cracks in
the ice. It was the last journey for the motor-car, which was taken up to
the hut and retired.

Four days later, the three men reached Butter Point. 'The going was
very heavy and the sun very hot,' Brocklehurst wrote. 'We took off all
our clothes except drawers & vest. I took photos of the sledge with our
friend the Skua [but] Armytage got behind the sledge as he did not fancy
being in his drawers & vest in a photo.'

After establishing the depot, they returned to Cape Royds only to
turn about face and start all over again on 9 December. With their
departure, Murray, Joyce, Day, Marston and Roberts continued the
routine scientific observations, made a variety of zoological studies and
slowly prepared the base for the return of *Nimrod*.

The journey back to Butter Point was a misery. 'It was bad going on
the ice & we broke through & let us into water in place so we got our
feet very wet,' Brocklehurst wrote about the day of their arrival at
Butter Point. 'The sun beat down on us splitting our faces & lips, one
could feel one's skin crack, the last mile to Butter Point seemed to be
endless.'

On 15 December the party started to ascend the Ferrar Glacier,
Priestley carefully looking for fossils. He was to be disappointed, in
more ways than one. 'I have seldom seen a sedimentary rock that looks
more unfossiliferous,' he wrote on 21 December. 'Many of the boulders
are coated with a hard crust of white opaque salt and if there was any
lime in the sandstone it has probably been dissolved out long ago.' He
was also frustrated because Armytage informed him that they would
not be able to go all the way to Depot Nunatak due to having to be back
at Butter Point by 1 January. On that date they were scheduled to meet

the Northern Party, with Mawson, Priestley and Brocklehurst looking
for precious metals and David, Mackay and Armytage returning to
base.

Even more, however, Priestley was chagrined by having been let
down by the maps and reports from Scott's expedition. 'There are
evidently serious defects in the map near this point,' he wrote. 'The
whole of the bluff opposite is marked as Beacon Sandstone, and from
the face of the cliff here it is easily seen for at least 3000 feet to be
granite, the very grain in the stones can be seen.' Later still he found a
'grave error' in the map of the mass of rocks that Scott's party had
named 'Solitary Rocks'. The previous expedition had indicated that
they formed an island with the glacier flowing down on either side.
However, Priestley wrote,

> Armytage and myself have taken advantage of the settled fine weather to
> . . . walk down to the north end of the Solitary Rocks. We have followed
> the bulge of the glacier round and have definitely proved the Solitary
> Rocks to be a peninsula joined to the main north wall of the glacier by an
> isthmus of granite at least 1000 feet high.

In the ensuing period, they further contributed to the knowledge of the
area. 'One good comprehensive, although rough, survey of the northern
lobe of the glacier has thus been made in the last 3 or 4 days,' Priestley
wrote with pride.

> As far as the idea of geographical and geological exploration being the
> main object I have already gathered more information and made more
> corrections to the map than I could have hoped to do in the whole time.
> As far as finding fossils is concerned, however, we are as far from that as
> ever, as owing to our being misled . . . by the map.

Shortly after Christmas the party retreated towards Butter Point,
arriving as scheduled on New Year's Day. The Northern Party was
nowhere to be seen. For most of the next three weeks, Shackleton's
orders forced them to remain there, frustrated by the lack of scientific
study the location offered, and able to concentrate only on little things,
pleasant and not. 'One of the worst things I know is to wake up with a
mouth full of little white hairs, and for every hair one pulls out six seem
to take its place,' Brocklehurst wrote crossly one day. 'Everything is

covered with these little hairs about an inch and a half long out of our Reindeer sleeping bags. Last night I turned the bag inside out and shook it, but it is every bit as bad if not worse.'

To relieve their ennui and their growing concern for the Northern Party, on 6 January they went to the Strand Moraines, a day's hike to the south, to gather geological specimens. Then on 12 January they made a short trip to Dry Valley, where Priestley discovered a raised beach about sixty feet above sea level and Brocklehurst climbed a nearby mountain. By 15 January they were back at Butter Point. 'Today the ship is due,' Brocklehurst wrote, '& we wonder whether she will come and hope she will, are looking forward to getting our mails.'

But the ship did *not* come, nor did the Northern Party. One can only wonder if, during that long wait, the three men were sobered by a vision one night when Brocklehurst dreamed

> that the ponies died early and Shackleton was unsuccessful, while Mackay sat on Butter Point when we arrived back explaining how he had quarrelled with the Professor and Mawson and the rope had broken while the Professor and Mawson were on some very thin ice. About as ill-omened a dream as I have ever heard.

While the Western Party waited, ill at ease, across McMurdo Sound an effort was made to alleviate any problems for Shackleton and his companions. On 15 January a party left Cape Royds under Joyce to establish the depot near Minna Bluff, approximately seventy miles on to the Barrier. With them was a strange sight – eight dogs pulling a sledge. Throughout his time at the base, Joyce had been the only one interested in working with the dogs. The others had enjoyed them as pets, but had made no effort to drive them.

Joyce, however, persisted, and on the morning of 19 January the dogs were to be found pulling a sledge so quickly over the Barrier that he had to put two men on it to reduce the speed, so they could keep up. Four days later they came to a heavily crevassed area, where once the four centre dogs all fell through a snow bridge to the length of their traces. A dog, however – even a standard sledge dog weighing 100 pounds, which Marshall indicated these did not – can be hauled up by a single man, and they were soon on their way.

Late at night on 25 January they reached the target site, upon which Shackleton and Joyce had agreed during the spring depot journey. It lay on a line drawn through a specific peak on the Bluff and the top of Mount Discovery, with, according to Shackleton, 'a cross bearing secured by getting the centre peak of White Island in line with a peak of Mount Erebus'. The party erected a mound of snow ten feet high, on top of which they put two eleven-foot bamboo poles, tied together and flying three black flags. It could be seen, they estimated, for eight miles.

After leaving supplies at the depot, they headed north on 27 January, stopping later that day when they sighted a pole projecting from the snow. It turned out to be a depot that had been laid for Scott's southern party in spring 1902. A southerly wind led the men to hoist a sail on the sledge, which raced along behind the dogs at a zippy four miles an hour. When they reached the region of the crevasses, Joyce counted them, reporting that they passed 127, ranging from two to thirty feet in width. After a day lost to a blizzard, they arrived at Hut Point on 30 January.

Not yet satisfied, Joyce procured a second load of stores and on 2 February started out again. In order to avoid the crevasses, they headed almost due east, towards Cape Crozier, for two days. They then turned south and, after being held in their tents by a blizzard for two days, reached the depot without having seen a single crevasse.

'We expected to find the Southern Party camped there,' Joyce wrote, 'and to surprise them with the luxuries we had brought out for them, but they were not there. As our orders were to return on the 10th if the Southern Party did not turn up, we began to feel rather uneasy.'

They lay a series of flags towards the Bluff, so that Shackleton's group would not be able to miss the depot. They then headed south looking for their comrades. But it was to no avail. They reached the depot again at noon on 16 February, made certain that everything was secure, and began their return to the coast, full of gloomy thoughts. The dogs, on the other hand, were ecstatic about their chance to run: on the day of their return to Hut Point, they covered forty-five miles. Nothing, seemingly, would stop their love of the road, as Joyce recorded:

One day I released Tripp, because he had a chafed leg . . . for the whole day he ran in his place in the team, as if he had been harnessed up. He slept about half a mile from camp that night, and when I tried to coax him over in the morning he would not come, but as soon as we got under way he came running up to his old place.

It was a lesson finally learned, but it was too late to help Shackleton. The main question for Joyce and the others was could *anything* help Shackleton? Would the Southern Party come back at all?

Shortly before Joyce arrived at the Minna Bluff depot for the first time, Armytage, Priestley and Brocklehurst camped on the sea ice at the foot of Butter Point. Neither the ship nor the Northern Party had arrived, and they planned to start home after breakfast. Brocklehurst remained in his sleeping bag early that morning when Priestley left the tent. 'We heard him run towards the depot, then stop and hurry back, it was obvious that something had happened,' wrote Brocklehurst. Priestley burst into the tent to tell them that the ice they were on had broken away, and they were drifting north towards the open sea on a floe.

In an instant all three were outside. Priestley was only too correct – there were already two miles of open water between their floe and the shore. They quickly struck camp, loaded up the sledge, and headed north to see if they could get off the floe towards Cape Bernacchi. Their movement was checked by another lane of water, however, and after some discussion they returned to their original camp. Regular assessments throughout the day gave them little encouragement as, although they seemed to have stopped heading north, they could no long even see the Butter Point depot. Their anxiety was increased by the knowledge that they had food for only four days, but worse was the fact that unless the wind blew them back to shore they would be doomed to die anyway when their floe became battered by the open sea and disintegrated beneath them.

That night at around 11.30, as they lay in their sleeping bags to keep warm, they suddenly heard heavy bumps and the sounds of ice splitting. 'We began to realise the inevitable fate for us if we remained on the floe,' Priestley wrote matter-of-factly.

> It is a well known fact that the killer whale lives round about the pack and breaks it up by bumping it in order to get the animals off it for food, and outside our tent there was a large school of them playing and one of them bumped directly beneath our tent cracking the ice in all directions.

Brocklehurst was considerably less analytical. 'No joke to be eaten by one of those & we have seen them come right up on the ice to break it down to get seals off it,' he wrote nervously. 'Actually some of our ship's crew had been nearly caught last year.' It was not, he thought, what he had expected when he signed on. The ice floe, meanwhile, continued to be chipped away both by the waves and the killer whales.

18

NEAREST THE POLE

'The first few falls are decidedly upsetting to the nerves & heart,' Wild wrote with great understatement about dropping into a crevasse. 'To find oneself suddenly standing on nothing, then to be brought up with a painful jerk & looking down into a pitch black nothing is distinctly disturbing, & there is the additional fear that the rope may break. After a few dozen falls (I have had hundreds) the nervous shock lessens until the majority of men look upon the experience as lightly as an ordinary stumble.'

It was no ordinary stumble on 7 December on the Great Glacier, however. 'Saw the pony sledge with the forward end down a crevasse & Wild reaching out from the side of the gulf,' Shackleton wrote about the moments when the three men pulling the forward sledge raced back to help their comrade. 'No sign of the Pony.' Nor was there to be any. Socks had escaped the bullet that was his appointed fate, but only because his hooves had broken through a snow bridge that the men had safely passed over. He had disappeared into 'a black bottomless pit'.

'Wild had a most marvellous escape, as he had the leading rope twisted round his hand at the time & only saved himself by one arm,' Marshall wrote, also noting, 'on arrival he had climbed out & was deadly pale.' While Wild composed himself, the others looked in vain down the crevasse, but 'noble little Socks had found a resting place at last. He died in harness like a true soldier. Not a sign of him down this terrible abyss & not a sound to be heard. One only hopes he broke his neck.'

Things could have been worse. 'Fortunately for us and Wild, Socks swingletree snapped and so the sledge was saved,' Shackleton wrote. The swingletree was a horizontal crossbar to which the pony's harness traces were attached, and which in turn was attached to the sledge by a pivot at the centre, allowing for freedom in the movements of the pony, while still controlling the sledge. It had broken across the middle, saving Wild and the sledge. It was a near thing in more ways than one. 'After shooting my pony I had suggested the replacement of Socks swingletree with mine which was copperbound and reinforced,' Marshall wrote. 'Had this been done it would not have broken and we should have lost Wild, pony & sledge!'

As it was, they now had approximately half a ton to haul, a damaged sledge, and no store of fresh meat. All they could do was hitch themselves to both sledges and move ahead. It was not fun. 'Crossing crevasses all rest of afternoon,' wrote Marshall, 'a terribly treacherous surface, as there is nothing to indicate their presence . . . Sh. and I both went through just before camping. This has upset Sh. & he is not in good form. A whole line of nasty stuff ahead of us for tomorrow.'

As careful as they were, to a certain extent whether they went the way of Socks seemed out of their hands. All they could do, according to Marshall, was trust in Providence:

> 'Provy' became a personality and a dominant force in a world of our own, more than 2000 miles from civilisation, which no other human eye had ever seen. 'Luck' – there was no such thing, for luck comes to man whose foresight and planning can ensure perfection to the highest degree possible, and after that, what cannot be planned or foreseen is in the hands of 'Provy.' This was Shackleton's creed.

Providence or not, the following day proved better than expected, as they reached hard blue glacier ice, allowing them to gain more than twelve miles. The day after that more than atoned for their good fortune, however. A stiff incline that took them up to just shy of 3,000 feet forced them to relay the sledges, slowing them considerably.

It became no easier. Due to their crawling advance, they had to cut back on food to have any hope of reaching the Pole. Within several days they had consumed most of the maujee ration that had been meant for the ponies. The maize proved more difficult to eat, because they did not have enough paraffin to boil it, so on 10 December, while Shackleton looked for geological specimens, the others used flat rocks to grind up the grain. They managed only one pannikin of badly prepared flour, however, and stopped. The irony was that they now hauled rocks that weighed more than the pestle and mortar they had earlier discarded, and that would have allowed them to grind the maize efficiently.

The weather continued to be exceptionally fine, but that was not necessarily a benefit, as once they had to strip to pyjama trousers, singlets and shirts due to the heat, and their heavy perspiration caused a fluid loss that was difficult to replace due to limited oil for melting water. 'Hope there won't be more than a day or two of this killing heavy work,' Marshall wrote. But there was – and worse. On 12 December their progress dropped to three miles, a distance that, according to Shackleton, 'expresses more readily than I can write it the nature of the day's work . . . the worst surface possible sharp edged blue ice filled with chasm and crevasses, rising into hills and descending in gullies: in fact a surface that cannot be equal in any polar work for difficulty in travelling.'

Frustration began to show – at least in their diaries – as each blamed another for slowing the pace. 'Following Sh. to Pole is like following an old woman,' Marshall wrote. 'Always pausing.' The surgeon was not free from criticism himself. 'We were all dead tired tonight, except perhaps M. who does not pull the weight of his food, the big hulking lazy hog,' Wild wrote without bothering to use his cipher.

Yet remarkably, at a point when tempers were fraying and anger being easily expressed, a close relationship was being formed. Wild had always appreciated Shackleton as a helpful colleague and a determined leader, but now he began to see him as much more. 'Had a long yarn with S. today,' he wrote, 'find he is not such a – – as I thought.' A week later, he noted, 'Am waiting for another yarn with S.' Within days Wild was confiding to him and cheering him on in his diary. 'S. pulls like the devil,' he wrote. 'I would tell M. and A. what I thought of them only for the sake of poor old S.'

Throughout the expedition Shackleton had been developing more techniques for dealing with others. His early method had been to dominate or override lesser men by sheer force of will. Now, in the midst of the greatest dangers they had faced, his innate traits of leadership came to the fore. He showed an energy that went beyond his physical strength: a calm, measured decision-making ability; a continuing cheerfulness; and, most importantly, the talent to inspire. Adams, for one, became a firm believer in The Boss. 'He was the greatest leader,' Adams later recalled, 'that ever came on God's earth bar none, there's no doubt of that.' At the same time, Wild and

Shackleton were also totally won over – by each other. As they marched up the glacier, Wild found in Shackleton the leader he had sought, and Shackleton found in Wild his greatest disciple.

In the ensuing days, they began to take the full measure of the Great Glacier – and vice versa. Neither was willing to give in to the other: the men persevering relentlessly, ever recording their hopes that the morrow would bring the beginning of a level plateau, but the glacier continually rising higher before them. They ascended for more than a week but nothing changed: the slick, rippled ice that made walking in finnesko a menace each moment and the threat of slipping constant; the huge, cracked pressure ridges splitting out in all directions; the occasional rotten moraine; and ice falls they had to climb and then haul the sledges up with a rope hand over hand.

At lunch on 15 December their hopes rose anew, as stretching out in front of them was a long, wide plain. Through the afternoon they crossed a hard névé. 'Plateau practically in sight then for the rush,' Marshall wrote. He was thinking along the same lines as Wild, who recorded:

> We hope to make a depot tomorrow of food and oil and all the gear we
> can spare . . . By the look of things we should be on the plateau the day
> after tomorrow, and then 20 days of good going ought to put us at the
> pole. We are now very hopeful of doing the job and of getting back in
> time to catch the ship. S. is in the best of spirits, and I must say has been
> so all along.

But the next day came and went and, despite fourteen miles to the good, they found themselves still far from an ice fall that they hoped would be at the head of the glacier. On 17 December, near 85°S, they pulled hard for a nunatak they thought to be four miles away, but by late in the day when they reached it, they had travelled more than eleven. There, at what they measured as more than 6,000 feet above sea level, they named the last rocky outcrop they expected to see on the way south Mount Buckley. Near this obvious landmark they established Depot E, leaving behind what they thought they could spare, including all their clothes except what they had on. 'We have burnt our boats behind us now,' Shackleton wrote, intending to make an unimpeded dash for the Pole. Marshall agreed: 'Hope to gain plateau tomorrow. Then for it.'

It was not to be. Two days later, at an altitude of 7,888 feet, Wild recorded:

> Another disappointment, and also another hard days work. We are not clear of pressure and crevasses yet; all day long we have been slogging away uphill, mostly soft snow. The first part was too steep for two sledges, so we had to relay. We have crossed hundreds of crevasses . . . most of them snow bridged . . . while the rest of us were tearing our hearts out up the steep slopes, M. was walking along with a slack trace, once it was so slack that S. fell over it . . . I really believe A. does his best, but it is a very poor best. Poor S. works away like ten devils.

That same evening, Marshall viewed Shackleton a different way, recording laconically, 'Sh. rather done'. He also noted that, for a group of individuals obsessed with food and constantly hungry, they were making a dismal move: 'Tomorrow we cut short another biscuit at breakfast, leaving 1 only.' The food allowance they were living on had become dangerously inadequate. Worse, for the past several weeks they had not actually been eating as much as the small amount rationed, because the cook of the week would put aside bits for their special Christmas feeding. Their breakfast had been reduced to a pannikin of hoosh and one biscuit. For lunch they had four biscuits, a bit of chocolate and some tea with plasmon. And dinner consisted of only a small pot of hoosh, three biscuits and a pannikin of cocoa. It was no more than 2,500 calories per day, and men doing equivalent physical labour should have been receiving at least 6,000.

But that was not the worst of it. After weeks of brilliant weather, it began to turn nasty. A hard, cutting wind picked up from the south, and day after day it blew directly into their faces. Now Shackleton's decision to purchase furs only for sleeping bags, feet and hands came back to haunt him. The ill-chosen Burberry jackets and separate hats did not protect their faces and necks as fur anoraks would have done. They were also not as efficient protection from the falling temperatures. 'I can easily imagine that I am on a spring sledging journey,' Shackleton wrote on 22 December,

> for the temp is −5 and a chill SE wind blowing and finds its way through our tent which is getting worn: All day long . . . we have been hauling

our sledges in relays up the pressure mounds . . . Behind us lies a broken
sea of pressure ice. Please God ahead is a clear way to the Pole.

But there was no celestial response, only a reprise of past days at an
ever-increasing elevation now measured at more than 8,800 feet. There
was also a continuation of unspoken bitterness among them. 'I sincerely
wish he would fall down a crevasse about a thousand feet deep,' Wild
wrote of Marshall. 'He certainly does not pull the weight of the extra
tent and his kit, and that leaves the weight of his food for us to pull.'

Wild was more charitable on Christmas Day. 'May none but my
worst enemies ever spend their Xmas in such a dreary God forsaken
spot as this,' he wrote. 'Here we are 9500 ft above sea level, farther
away from civilisation than any human being has ever been . . . with
half a gale blowing, and drift snow flying, and a temperature of 52° of
frost, and yet we are not miserable.' This was because, despite plough-
ing ahead more than ten miles, they had had their best feed since Cape
Royds. Both breakfast and lunch had included extra. Then for dinner
they had a double allowance of pemmican thickened with biscuit and
the last of the Maujee ration and flavoured with Oxo, a plum pudding
boiled in cocoa water and flavoured with a drop of medical brandy,
cocoa, a spoonful of crème de menthe and a cigar. 'For the first time for
many days I feel replete,' Wild continued, 'and therefore I will not make
any nasty remarks about anyone, although I should very much like to.'

In this mood approaching generosity, the four sat in one tent after
Christmas dinner and assessed the situation. They were just short of the
eighty-sixth parallel, some 280 statute miles from the Pole. They did not
have the food to attain their target and return. So they arrived at a
simple solution: they once again would cut their intake. 'We are going
to make each weeks food last 10 days and have 1 biscuit in morning, 3
midday & 2 at night,' Shackleton wrote. 'It is the only thing to do for
we must get the Pole come what may.' He also noted another worrying
fact: 'Marshall took our temperatures tonight. we are all 2° subnormal.'

On the morning of Boxing Day they ditched everything they possibly
could, including the runners that they had taken off the second sledge
when they abandoned it two days previously, and items they had felt
indispensable at Mount Buckley. With their limited food supply, they
now needed to average fourteen miles per day, which still left no margin
for safety. But for the moment, the lightened load seemed to help:
despite the continuing uphill march, they slogged fourteen and a half

miles. And finally they seemed to have left the glacier. 'As we have not crossed any pressure or crevasses all day,' Wild wrote on 27 December after again attaining their target distance, 'I think it is safe to assume this is the Plateau.'

Yet they continued to make a slow ascent – passing 10,000 feet according to the hypsometer. Shackleton and Adams both suffered from the height, enduring prolonged headaches and giddiness. In addition, they were confronted by virtually every problem imaginable: a strong head wind, more than forty degrees of frost, a horrible surface and a sledge becoming progressively more deformed and difficult to pull. Then, on the evening of 29 December, Marshall found all of their temperatures to be between three and four degrees below normal. 'Reverting to regular hoosh,' he wrote, having determined that they simply were not eating enough to maintain their basic core temperatures. 'Shall depot all return food & make a rush for last degree.'

But there was no rush. The four weakened men turned out on 30 December only to be chased back into their tent after four miles by the first real blizzard since they had passed White Island. 'I cannot express my feelings,' Shackleton wrote. 'We lie here and think of how to make things better but we cannot reduce food now . . . We will and are doing all humanly possible. It lies with Providence to help us more.'

It was too much to ask. Even Providence could not help these four scarecrows, freezing, starving and stumbling through soft, foot-deep snow against a bitter head wind. Their tents were wearing out, their poorly designed clothing needed regular repair, and their rime-filled sleeping bags were damp, cold and insufficient to protect them against temperatures dropping to $-15°$ despite it being the height of summer. Their food did not give them even the strength they had possessed coming up the glacier, and at this extreme altitude they were suffering from dehydration, as decreasing fuel limited the ability to melt snow. 'We are so tired after each hour's pulling we throw ourselves on our backs for 3 minutes spell,' Shackleton recorded. Meanwhile the mental strains and rifts became worse than ever. 'Neither A. nor M. have been pulling worth a damn, and consequently S. and I have to suffer,' wrote Wild on the final night of the year. 'I am beginning to be doubtful of success, as I don't think we can make our food supply last long enough. If we had only had Joyce and Marston here instead of those two grubscoffing useless beggars we would have done it easily.'

Never the less, on the first day of 1909 it was not the grubscoffing beggars but Shackleton himself who was the weak link. His headache was so debilitating that even Marshall felt for him and called a stop at 5.30 p.m. They were only a mile short of the record for the highest latitude ever reached on the planet, Robert E. Peary having claimed a farthest north at 87° 06′ in 1906. It was a sign of their fixation with that record and their latitude in general that each of them simultaneously started recording their advance in geographic rather than statute miles and that their current location began to appear more frequently in their diaries.

The following morning Peary's record was beaten, as on a day in which 'every inch an effort' they plodded ahead for ten and a half geographic miles (twelve statute miles). But it was still short of the average they needed. 'God knows we are doing all we can but the outlook is serious if this surface continues and the rise,' Shackleton wrote, adding:

> For we are not travelling fast enough to make our food spin out and get back to our depot in time: I cannot think of failure yet I must look at the matter sensibly and the lives of those who are with me. I feel that if we go on too far it will be impossible to get back over this surface and then all the results will be lost to the world. We can now definitely locate the South Pole on the highest plateau in the world and our geological work and meteorology will be of great use to science: But all this is not the Pole and man can only do his best and we have arrayed against us the strongest forces of Nature.

It was the first note of defeat sounded by Shackleton, the first time that he let on, even to himself, that the bone and muscle and sinew of man might be vanquished, even if the spirit were not. Still, he would not flinch in front of his comrades. And for a brief spell the next morning, they made excellent time and it looked as if there were still a chance. But it did not last. 'Hopes raised high by spell of good surface but again on came soft stuff,' wrote Marshall. And, combined with the ill-effects of an altitude above 11,000 feet, that was that.

On the night of 3 January the four men held another council of war in a wind-rocked, frozen little tent at 87°28′S, 152 geographic miles from the Pole. One might assume that logic, or the threat of impending disaster, would have left them only one avenue to follow. Yet, despite the acknowledgement that the Pole was beyond their grasp, they agreed to one last throw of the dice – or was it simply a final postponement of the decision to turn back? It is not known if the determination was unanimous. Certainly Shackleton wanted to continue until the last possible moment, and Wild had by now unreservedly thrown in his lot with The Boss. Adams, too, seems to have been willing to follow Shackleton as far as he would lead. Yet Marshall, according to Adams, was doubtful about Shackleton's physical ability to continue. It is likely, therefore, that there was a split vote. Regardless of the dynamics of the decision, they would continue. 'We have now come to the conclusion that we cannot get to the Pole, so we are making a depot of sufficient food and oil to take us back to our last depot at the head of the glacier at 1/2 rations,' Wild wrote that night, 'and taking on only one tent and lightening our sledge as much as possible, do our best with the 10 days food we have left; five days out and five back.' Shackleton, he added in his cipher, 'is very disappointed.'

On the morning of 4 January 1909 Shackleton and his three companions set off on their riskiest gamble – and the one with potentially the lowest return. It was clear they could not reach the Pole, and equally obvious it would be a touch-and-go struggle to reach Cape Royds. Never the less, they kept their faces towards the south, hoping to get within 100 geographic miles of the southernmost place on Earth. It was irrelevant that for virtually the entire journey they had been thinking, planning and worrying in statute miles, and that in those terms their new goal would actually leave them 115 miles shy of the Pole. Now their entire beings revolved around degrees and minutes of latitude.

It was brutal progress. At an altitude of 11,200 feet, and with the temperature dropping to −20°, they struggled against drift driven straight in their faces. At noon Marshall took their temperatures, and three of them did not register on his clinical thermometer, which went down to 94°. It was accepted at the time that no lower temperature was required on a medical thermometer, because anyone lower than that had already died. And so the walking dead continued, their core temperatures slowly dropping and with no way of getting warm even at night. 'We had depoted our extra underclothing to save weight over 3 weeks ago and are now in the same clothes night and day,' Shackleton wrote, 'one suit of underclothing and a thin gabardine Burbury now all patched. No trousers and 2 guernseys. Our heads get iced up with moisture on the march.'

In these conditions they battled for twelve and a half miles. 'Found we could do no better with our 70 lbs than we did a fortnight ago with 200,' wrote Wild, 'which shows how we have all weakened.' In fact, they were so overcome with the effort that they agreed to increase their food consumption and continue only three more days.

But it was not only the road south that occupied their thoughts. They had left their remaining food and oil depoted on the greatest ice surface in the world, a featureless plain with no mountains or other landmarks to help fix its location. They were now too weak to build cairns to point the way for their return, and they had gone south 'trusting to our tracks to find our return depot'. They could only hope that the ferocious winds would not erase their footprints.

The next day was more of the same. They sank eight inches with each step, their feet coming to rest on sharp ice furrows. The wind increased and the temperature dropped. Never the less they achieved thirteen miles. But the worst had been saved for last. On 6 January the temperature fell to fifty-seven degrees of frost and the wind reached blizzard proportions, making them all gasp for breath in the swirling drift. 'I think today has been the worst we have yet experienced,' Wild wrote, echoing his colleagues. 'We have found it utterly impossible to keep ourselves warm, and we have all been frost-bitten . . . we had to camp at 4:30, or I really believe we should have collapsed.'

They had reached 88° 05'S according to each of their diaries – although their later figures were revised to 88° 07'S – and even Shackleton realised this would be their southernmost camp. Their goal of reaching a hundred miles from the Pole would be determined by one more march. 'Tomorrow,' wrote Marshall, 'we make our last dash without the sledge.'

Tomorrow, however, Nature had another laugh at their expense. Vicious winds roaring at ninety miles an hour kept them pinned in their tent all day. Shackleton and Wild tried to keep all their minds off their troubles by reading *The Merchant of Venice* aloud, but the inner thoughts were undoubtedly reflected by Marshall. 'In bags all day,' he wrote. 'Feel worse rather than better for it . . . Hope it will not obliterate our tracks for return to depot as this is almost our only hope of finding it.'

The following day it blew as hard again, the temperature dropped to −40°, and the four men lay shivering in their bags. The snow pushed on the outside of the tent, making the inner area even smaller, while the lining had become so thin that fine drift spread everywhere inside. Through it all, Shackleton had one thought. 'Suffering considerably physically from cold hands and feet and from hunger but more mentally . . . we simply lie here shivering', he wrote. 'We must do something more to the South even though food is going . . . must get within the 100 miles of the Pole.'

At 1.00 a.m. on 9 January, after howling for more than fifty hours, the wind began to ease. Sixty minutes later the party was up, and at 4.00 a.m. they left camp for their final dash. With them, they took only some biscuits and chocolate in their pockets, Queen Alexandra's flag on a bamboo pole, a camera, and a brass cylinder holding a number of the special stamps issued by the New Zealand government to help raise funds for the expedition.

They went as hard and as fast as they could, and that was very quick indeed, as the cold and the blizzard had made the surface solid, firm and good for marching. For five hours they pounded south, at times virtually running. At 9.00 a.m. they halted, and Shackleton, 'with a few well chosen words', planted the Union Jack and took possession of the region for Britain, naming it the King Edward VII Plateau. They then took two photographs to commemorate their farthest south and buried the cylinder of stamps. There was no reason to stay – indeed, every reason not to – and within a short period they had turned for the first time in months and were walking as fast as they could towards the north. It was none too soon – Adams would later state with total certainty, 'If we'd gone on one more hour, we shouldn't have got back.'

That night Shackleton succinctly recorded their achievement: 'We have shot our bolt and the tale is 88.23 S. 162 E.' They had passed the magic hundred-mile mark, and had been only ninety-seven geographic miles from the Pole. Ninety-seven miles. It was a figure that would later be disputed by people who did not believe that men so close to the end of their tether could walk sixteen miles – or was it eighteen? – in five hours. It was, in actuality, a figure that from the start was conjecture. To save weight, they had left the theodolite in camp, and their final estimation was just that: an estimation. But it was one upon which all four men agreed, and from which they would never waiver. It was an estimation that would go down in history as a fact.

Now, however, the most important facts related to the journey ahead. They were more than 700 statute miles from Cape Royds (and now that they had turned, they once again started thinking in statute miles). Moreover, they had a limited amount of time to reach base before *Nimrod* left. Finally, they were not only already starving, but were running out of the food they did have. It would all be a desperate gamble as to whether they could do it.

By way of a positive start, they made as good time on the return to their last camp as they had out. They reached it at 2.30 p.m., brewed a cup of tea while Marshall took a photograph, and raced on again after hurriedly packing. 'Rush we must now,' Wild recorded that night after they had travelled a remarkable total of forty miles. 'We have only 14 days short food to take us to our depot at the top of the glacier . . . a great part of it over pressure and crevasses. Tonight we celebrated our record by having an extra drop of pemmican, and a taste of sloe gin.'

Shackleton was more philosophical. 'Homeward Bound,' he wrote. 'Whatever regrets may be we have done our best. Beaten the South Record by 366 miles the North by 77 miles. Amen.'

It was truly a phenomenal record, the greatest advance toward either Pole that had ever been made. Against conditions worse than anyone could have predicted – the Barrier, the largest glacier that had ever been seen by man, and the frozen, rising, endless Plateau – they had pioneered the way to the heart of the Antarctic. They had not reached the Pole, but they had time and again accomplished the seemingly impossible. Yet, as Shackleton had written a week earlier, 'all this is not the Pole'.

What Shackleton most likely did *not* dwell on that night was his greatest achievement of all. Surely there had been the temptation to continue, to actually be the first to reach either end of the Earth. He could almost certainly have struggled to the Pole and gained immortality and martyrdom at the same time. It was a death that would have been applauded by many still imbued with Victorian notions of heroism. But Shackleton had turned with the Pole in his grasp, and that had taken a mettle, a fortitude, a strength of mind, character and spirit that set him apart from other heroes of his time. It was, in fact, one of the most courageous acts ever performed by an explorer.

Other explorers had died – or would die – while incautiously pursuing a goal, at the same time dragging their followers to the grave with them. But to Shackleton, the safety and well-being of those who had entrusted their lives to his care was first and foremost. He made light of this in England, responding to Emily's question of why he turned back by commenting, 'I thought you'd rather have a live donkey than a dead lion.' But on the Plateau it was a grimly serious issue, and the lives of his three comrades were ultimately his greatest concern. In hindsight, it was his success in protecting those dependent upon him that can be regarded as his crowning glory and that elevated him to a higher pantheon of heroes than other polar explorers.

In early January of 1909, however, it still remained to see if the party had turned in time. They had one advantage: the wind that had been so debilitating now became an ally. On the first full day of the return, they improvised a sail out of the floor cloth and poles of a tent, and the wind and a slight downward slope contributed to an advance of eighteen and a half miles. Equally as important, they picked up their sledge tracks, although not in the form they had expected. The snow that had been tightly compressed beneath the weight of the runners had remained when the high winds had swept away the surface drift, and the tracks comprised small raised formations creating lines running directly along their route. The next afternoon they reached the small depot in the midst of a march just short of seventeen miles. 'Thank God we picked up our depot,' Marshall wrote that night. 'Had we missed it our chances wd have been nil.'

It was not exactly time to rejoice. They had only twelve days' half rations to get back to Depot E high on the Great Glacier, a trip that had taken them seventeen days on the way out. And they were still plagued by altitude, cold, a difficult surface, dehydration and lack of food. 'We were incredibly hungry, all our thoughts dreams & conversation seemed to be of food,' Wild wrote. 'One night I dreamt I was dining with the King of Sweden . . . I had a most delicious steak in front of me & how I longed to get at it. Etiquette forbade me commence before the King, and I woke up.' It was typical of their dreams and thoughts, sleeping *and* waking.

'All day long we cannot help thinking about food, and at night we dream about it,' Wild wrote at another point. 'I jolly well mean to make up for all of this.'

19

THE WANDERING POLE

More than three-quarters of a century after James Clark Ross grudgingly abandoned his quest to reach the South Magnetic Pole, three men inching northward on a slowly melting iceway discussed following his example and giving up on the attainment of that same location. 'Yesterday I strongly pressed the impossibility of Magnetic Pole and urged what I had understood was to be the work of the expedition provided the Mag Pole were not reasonably obtainable,' Douglas Mawson wrote: 'the coast geographic and magnetic survey with detailed geological reconnaissances at picked spots, the whole allowing us to return to Dry Valley by January 1st 1909.'

Ross would have been horrified. In the summer of 1831, while serving under his uncle Sir John Ross on an expedition to discover the Northwest Passage, he led a sledge party along the rocky coast of Boothia Peninsula in the high Arctic of British North America. The journey was difficult and tedious, but he became the first person ever to reach one of the two places where a freely pivoted compass needle points vertically downward: the North Magnetic Pole. 'I believe I must leave it to others to imagine the elation of mind with which we found ourselves now at length arrived at this great object of our ambition,' he wrote. 'It almost seemed as if . . . our voyage and all its labours were at an end, and that nothing now remained for us but to return home and be happy for the rest of our lives.'

But the ensuing years proved Ross was not so easily contented, and his overriding ambition became notching up the other Magnetic Pole. When, as commander of the Royal Navy's Antarctic expedition of 1839–43, his discoveries opened not only vast new lands but the road to the geographic Pole, he remained unmoved. It was the South Magnetic Pole that beckoned him. Unfortunately, according to Ross' calculations, it lay 160 miles inland from the coast of Victoria Land. Would that he could plant the same Union Jack there as he had in the Arctic! He had brought that one along, but miles of fast ice prevented him from finding a place to land. He was forced to retreat believing his personal grail was just beyond reach, only a friendly harbour and a quick trek away.

In the spring of 1908, such notions soon made the Northern Party of Mawson, David and Mackay contemptuous of Ross' naïveté. Day upon day of relaying their sledges over slowly decaying sea ice while the sound gradually broke up to the one side and the mountains hovered over them on the other had exhausted and disheartened them. They lived with the constant fear that the fast ice might break off and sweep them out to sea. But a combination of steep mountain face and broken, pitted glacier had prevented them from advancing on real land. So they edged with agonising slowness along ice covered with a layer of snow made sticky by salt from the sea, the sledge runners gliding with the same ease as they would have through foot-deep molasses.

On 23 October 1908, within a week of leaving Cape Bernacchi, and less than three weeks out of Cape Royds, Mawson urged the change of plans, abandoning the Magnetic Pole and concentrating on pure science. 'There was great opposition,' he recorded, 'and this morning culminated in Prof offering up no alternative but Magnetic Pole, which must, he says, be done on ½ rations.' For the time being, they continued their march, the decision postponed.

Mawson had undoubtedly felt more pressure since they left Cape Bernacchi. David, serving as navigator from the lead pulling position, had suffered from snow blindness due to not wearing his goggles. He asked Mawson to take the lead, and the result was so encouraging that the younger man remained there throughout the journey. Several days later Mawson made his first discovery when they reached what had been charted as a small promontory halfway between New Harbour and the next major coastal indentation to the north, Granite Harbour. In reality, what they named Dunlop Island was separated from the mainland by a strait through which they sledged.

Man-hauling inch by inch through heavy snow that covered pointed brash ice and only grudgingly allowed them to pass, snagging their finnesko and carving out bits from the sledge, was both physically draining and frustrating. In addition, David's Victorian politeness – one might say passive-aggressive behaviour today – nearly drove the younger men round the bend. 'Yesterday morning put the cap on the chronometer question,' Mawson wrote with great irritation in late October.

> The chronometer which the Commander had specially given me to look after, regulate and be responsible for, has exercised the Prof ever since I got it. He was originally sulky about it; since then adopting the celestials' tactics, he has tried diplomacy to wrest it from me. On all occasions he has asked for the time, especially 3 or 4 times in the early hours of the morning, by saying till I am sick of it 'Would you mind kindly letting me know the time from your watch presently, there is no hurry, if it would not be troubling you too much, please.' He made it so obvious every time that he wanted the watch that, much annoyed at his roundabout tactics, I gave it him to look after yesterday on condition he took full responsibility and handed it over to me at completion of journey.

After the watch came an interaction about Mawson's headwear. 'Have just found out he thinks I have lost my burberry helmet,' Mawson groused to his diary.

> 2 hours ago he remarked: 'Do you find that helmet warm enough today without your burberry helmet?' I answered in the affirmative, saying had had it almost as cold in Adelaide. Long silence for 2 hours. Now he says: 'I suppose you have your burberry in the bag.' I said: 'Yes, evidently you think I have lost it.' He said: 'Well, I have lately been wondering whether you had lost it or not.' That is the way of the Prof. He will take all day putting roundabout questions to one in order to get a simple Yes or No answer. This worries one almost to distraction.

David's measured, methodical *actions* were just as annoying and worrying, but potentially more serious. 'He is full of great words and deadly slow action,' Mawson wrote. 'The more we bustle to get a move on the more he dawdles, especially tying strings to one another and all over the sledges, which all have to come off again in unpacking . . . I cannot see how it is at all possible for us to reach the Magnetic Pole in one season under such conditions.'

The situation came to a head at the end of the month, when it had become obvious that they would not be able to reach the Magnetic Pole *and* return to Butter Point. In fact, it was proving apparent that any kind of return down the coast might not be possible due to the break up of the sea ice. David and Mackay agreed, however, that all else should be given up in order to reach the Magnetic Pole. So Mawson outlined a plan to preserve a full ration of sledging food for the more than 400-mile journey inland; to go on half rations while next to the coast, supplemented by seal meat that they could take on the way; and upon their return to the coast to await *Nimrod* while again living on seal. The ideas, he recorded with no false modesty, 'were carried unanimously'.

The next day they arrived at a small granite island, where they paused for several days to repack and to develop a cooker that could burn blubber. They were soon successful, permitting them to conserve their paraffin for use on the inland passage. Mackay and David then built a cairn on the seaward end of a sheer cliff, where they left the geological samples and letters carefully stashed in a dried-milk tin tied to a flagstaff. One letter, addressed to the commander of *Nimrod*, indicated that they hoped by 15 December to reach the 'low sloping shore' marked on the Admiralty chart north of the Drygalski Ice Barrier (now the Drygalski Ice Tongue). There they would construct a depot and march inland to the Magnetic Pole. They would return to the depot at the 'low sloping shore' around 25 January.

As the three men would discover, there was only one problem with the plan. No area of 'low sloping shore' actually existed.

On 2 November the Northern Party started from the newly named Depot Island, but a rise in temperature and, therefore, the slushiness of the snow, limited them to two miles. In response, they decided to travel in the early hours of the morning, when the ice and snow were firmest. The following days saw slow, dull progress, creating a constant tension among them. Things not normally important took on major significance. One day Mackay was 'playing the skua' after lunch with tiny bits of food caught in the blubber lamp, when he accidentally swallowed one of the lamp's salt wicks. That evening, having been plagued by thirst throughout the afternoon, he asked if he might have some of the water that was melted down for the hoosh before the ingredients were put into it. After long debate, David and Mawson decided that, due to the unusual circumstances, this was acceptable, although they insisted that no precedent was being set. Offended by what he considered their grudging attitude, Mackay forcefully refused the drink. In the hasty interjections and gesticulations that followed, the pot atop the cooker was accidentally knocked off, and the water lost.

About a week from Depot Island, a blizzard descended, but the high wind and blowing snow affected the light more than the temperature, which remained warm. For two days, despite not being able to see more than a few yards, they continued to relay, moving more than ten miles. When it cleared, the outline of the Nordenskjöld Ice Barrier could be seen. Named for the Swedish scientist who had led an expedition to the Weddell Sea in 1901–04, it was shown on the charts as projecting twenty miles into the sea and being twenty-four miles wide, thereby forming a serious obstacle.

It proved, however, to be not nearly so wide, and they passed over it in two days, despite having to lower their sledges down the forty-foot cliffs forming the north terminus. The pleasure of that success was somewhat offset by Mawson's calculations that the Magnetic Pole was forty miles farther inland than had been determined by Louis Bernacchi on Scott's expedition.

For the next two weeks they continued northward through their alien, aqueous world dominated by water of all forms and temperatures. They had by now significantly changed their diet, seal meat and blubber having become the staples. Although this made them feel that they were eating too high a proportion of meat, it meant there was not the slightest sign of scurvy. Concurrently, the loss of fibre due to biscuit consumption dropping from nine to three per day resulted in diarrhoea. This, in turn, added to their mutual dissatisfaction. 'The Prof is certainly a fine example of a man for his age,' Mawson wrote,

> but he . . . does not pull as much as a younger man . . . when he led we could see he pulled comparatively little; since then it is difficult to judge but seeing he travels with thumbs tucked in his braces . . . one concludes he lays his weight on harness rather than pulling. Several times when we have been struggling heavily with hauling he has continued to recite poetry or tell yarns.

Mawson's complaints were not idle banter. For much of late November their distances decreased, and the two younger men believed this was attributable to David's inadequacies. But their progress was to become slower yet. On 26 November, while Mackay slaughtered a seal, David and Mawson climbed a rocky headland 600 feet high. From there they could see, ten to fifteen miles ahead, the vast Drygalski Ice Barrier. 'We were not a little concerned to observe with our field-glasses that the surface of the Drygalski Glacier was wholly different to that of the Nordenskjöld Ice Barrier,' David wrote, adding:

> The surface of the Drygalski Glacier was formed of jagged surfaces of ice very heavily crevassed, and projecting in the form of immense séracs separated from one another by deep undulations or chasms. It at once suggested to my mind some scaly dragon-like monster and recalled the lines of Milton . . . The 'Scaly horror of his folded tail' did not seem enchanting even at this distance . . . We could see much of this glacier was absolutely impossible for sledging.

Presumed impossible or not, the Drygalski Ice Tongue extends more than thirty miles into the Ross Sea, meaning it would have to be trekked across rather than around. On 1 December they started over what David described as 'high sastrugi, hummocky ice ridges, steep undulations of bare blue ice with frequent chasms impassable for a sledge, unless it was unloaded and lowered by alpine rope.' Three hours' hard labour gained only half a mile, and that afternoon they retreated to the sea ice to find another way. After two days travelling east they spied 'a broad-bottomed snow valley'. It was not so inviting as it appeared, however, and it took them a week of cruel hauling and constant danger to pass through an area that eventually looked 'as though a stormy sea had suddenly been frozen solid'.

On 9 December Mackay finally spied the sea north of the ice tongue. 'He announced his discovery with shouts of θάλαττα, θάλαττα, which thrilled us now as of old they thrilled the Ten Thousand,' wrote David, lapsing into his classical education to quote Xenophon's more than two-millennium-old rendering of 'The sea! The sea!' But although the coast was only four miles away, it took them another two days to reach it. Shortly before they did, Mackay went ahead to reconnoitre. Taking advantage of the break, Mawson disappeared into the tent to change the photographic plates, and David started to go make sketches. 'I had scarcely gone more than six yards from the tent, when the lid of a crevasse suddenly collapsed under me,' David later wrote. 'I only saved myself from going right down by throwing my arms out and staying myself on the snow lid on either side.'

Mawson was the Prof's only chance. But he did not immediately go to his mentor's aid, as he later explained to *The Sydney Morning Herald*:

I was busy changing photographic plates in the only place where it could be done – inside the sleeping bag . . . Soon after I had done up the bag, having got safely inside, I heard a voice from outside – a gentle voice – calling: 'Mawson, Mawson.'

'Hallo!' said I.

'Oh, you're in the bag changing plates, are you?' said the Professor.

'Yes, Professor.'

There was silence for some time. Then I heard the Professor calling in a louder tone: 'Mawson!'

'I answered again. Well, the Professor heard by the sound I was still in the bag. So he said: – 'Oh, still changing plates are you?'

'Yes.'

More silence for some time. After a minute, in a rather loud and anxious tone: 'Mawson!'

I thought there was something up, but could not tell what he was after. I was getting rather tired, and called out: 'Hallo. What is it? What can I do?'

'Well, Mawson, I am in a rather dangerous position. I am really hanging on by my fingers to the edge of a crevasse, and I don't think I can hold on much longer. I shall have to trouble you to come and assist me.'

I came our rather quicker than I can say. There was the Professor, just his head showing, and hanging on to the edge of a dangerous crevasse.

Mawson soon had David out of the crevasse, and the older man calmly began his sketching.

The next day David took another disaster just as stoically. When it became obvious that there was no 'low, sloping shore', he dispassionately suggested that they build a depot at a giant ice mound. It was far from the coast, but was 'a conspicuous object to any one approaching . . . by sea from the north'. Here they left the Christmas Tree sledge, geological specimens, spare clothing and a letter outlining their plans.

Those, in a nutshell, were to gain the Plateau via a large glacier that ran between two high, imposing peaks to the northwest, Mount Nansen and Mount Larsen, and thence to continue to the Magnetic Pole. Little did they know it, but even as they cooked seal meat in preparation for their ascent, Shackleton and his companions were slowly making their own way up an even larger glacier.

What a delight it must have been when they finally left the depot on 16 December, after two days kept in their tent by a blizzard. They were pulling approximately 670 pounds, but so comparatively rested were they that it moved almost with ease. More importantly, for the first time in more than two months they were not relaying, and for the first couple of days their mileage took an impressive jump.

The going did not remain easy, however. Heading for what later was named the Reeves Glacier, they encountered an exceedingly treacherous area, and on their third day they were brought up short by a barranca – a shallow, icy, heavily crevassed ravine, more than 120 yards wide. They camped until that night, when the temperatures were at their lowest, and then raced over it on an unstable ice bridge. Later that day, however, another snow bridge did not prove so strong. While crossing, Mawson fell clear through and was only stopped when the rope connecting him to the sledge pulled him up eight feet below the surface. Mackay and David hastily hauled him out, but not before he 'secured some ice crystals from the side of the crevasse, and threw them up for examination'.

By 20 December they found themselves in a labyrinth of pressure ridges and crevasses and realised they could not safely continue. Rather than retreating over their earlier tracks, they slowly made their way southwest on a small branch glacier. In the next several days they turned northwest, to a feature they named the Larsen Glacier, since it flowed past Mount Larsen. Here, at 2,000 feet above sea level, they spent a Christmas more or less unmarked except by a present from David and Mawson to Mackay. The Scot had long since run out of tobacco, and to substitute for its use in his pipe they presented him with a small supply of sennegrass, the valuable insulator for finnesko.

On 27 December, at a height of 2,800 feet, having reached a hard snow that made them think they were leaving the glacier ice, they depoted their ice axes, ropes, ski boots, geological specimens and a bit of food. As they moved on, Mackay, who had been observing the clouds, wrote that 'one large one straight in front of us seemed as it if were leading us to the promised land'.

Straight ahead it was indeed, and straightforward as well. For the next week the trio moved quickly across hard névé with no need to dodge and weave around natural barriers. The better surface allowed them to gain more than ten miles each day despite a continual ascent that brought them to 6,500 feet above sea level. However, a decision taken at the depot to hold back one-eighth of their food as an emergency ration meant correspondingly smaller meals, and this quickly affected them. 'The scarcity of food had been telling on us – we are now really weak,' Mawson wrote. 'The Professor seems most affected by the altitude, and is quite prostrated between hauls – so done does he seem that can scarcely give a hand in setting up tent and packing sledge. Also his memory seems fainter. He is certainly however doing his best.'

After a week of reduced rations – broken only by New Year's Day dinner – they realised that their pulling power was waning, so they returned to regular portions. Even this did not stop the thoughts of foods that had begun constantly to enter their minds. 'We are now almost mad on discussing foods,' Mawson wrote, 'all varieties having a great attraction for us. We dote on what sprees we shall have on return – mostly run to sweet foods and farinaceous compounds.' On 12 January, during their halts, they planned two dinners to be arranged by David in Sydney, one a Scots meal for Mackay, the other the 'Yorkshire Empire Dinner'. That night, each carefully listed the entire meals, the nine-course Scots dinner including such items as 'Grouse baked on toast with toasted crumbs and bread sauce, chipped potatoes' and 'Sheep's head and trotters garnished with carrots, turnips, kale, onions, potatoes.' After his wine list, Mackay noted that 'It is wonderful what a lot we think and talk about our bellies. I could almost eat my Finnskoe.'

In the week prior to this, they had continued their impressive progress, hauling ten to eleven miles each day despite slowly continuing their ascent even when they had unmistakably passed on to the Plateau. But on 13 January their excitement was dashed when Mawson's measurements showed the Magnetic Pole to be farther still – they would need another four days to reach it. Mackay became depressed about the extra time, which he thought would prevent them from returning safely, but never the less the threesome moved ahead over an area never before seen by man.

'The surface of the snow over which we were sledging was sparkling with large reconstructed ice crystals, about half an inch in width and one-sixteenth of an inch in thickness,' David wrote,

> crystals form on this plateau during warm days . . . We observe that after every still sunny day a crop of these crystals develops on the surface of the névé, and remains there until the next wind blows them off. In the bright sunlight the névé, covered with these sheets of bright reflecting ice crystals, glittered like a sea of diamonds. The heavy runners of our sledge rustled gently as they crushed the crystals by the thousand. It seemed a sacrilege.

At noon on 15 January, Mawson again took magnetic observations, which showed them to be near their goal, although precise measurement was difficult because 'the polar centre executes a daily round of wanderings about its mean position'. He determined that if they waited where they were for twenty-four hours, the Pole would likely come to them, but rather than do this, they decided to push on thirteen miles the next day to where he calculated the mean position to lie.

On the morning of 16 January, after travelling two miles, they depoted all their non-essential kit and continued six miles to where they lunched. Like Shackleton and his companions a week earlier, they left their gear other than a camera and flag and walked the final five miles to Mawson's 'mean position'. There, at 72°15′S, 155°16′E, and a height of 7,260 feet, David and Mackay hoisted the Union Jack while Mawson set up the camera so that it could be triggered by a string.

The men bared their heads, and as David pulled the string he declared, 'I hereby take possession of this area now containing the Magnetic Pole for the British Empire.' They gave three cheers for the King, but, despite having fulfilled Ross' wish that the British flag be planted at the South Magnetic Pole, 'we were too utterly weary to be capable of any great amount of exultation.'

They had achieved their goal, but now they had one even more important – to return alive. As with Shackleton, Wild, Marshall and Adams, who had been 1,112 miles farther south, there was no reason to linger. 'With a fervent "Thank God" we all did a right-about turn,' wrote David, 'and as quick a march as tired limbs would allow back in the direction of our little green tent in the wilderness of snow.'

*   *   *

The three were now racing against time. The next morning they calculated their position to be approximately 250 miles from their depot, and they had only fifteen days to reach it to meet *Nimrod*. They had to average better than sixteen miles a day, a vast total compared to what they had previously done, although they would be helped by having a lighter sledge and travelling downhill. Things were still not easy. Day after day it was about $-20°$ in the morning, and sometimes did not rise above $-6°$ even in the heat of the day. Moreover, Mawson soon injured his leg and could not pull at full strength, while the Professor was showing his age.

Never the less, they forced themselves to cover the required sixteen miles, and each day they did so, even if it meant pulling longer hours than their bodies could easily manage. As always, the more tired they were, the more argumentative, and soon tempers flared over the most trivial of matters. One morning, just for a change, Mawson put a lump of sugar in the hoosh. David's response was to describe him as 'a bold culinary experimenter', but Mackay's was more robust. Detecting an unusual flavour, he launched into a severe interrogation of the mess-man, who admitted to the sugar. Mackay became indignant and offensive, ultimately blaring out that Mawson was selfish and this 'awful state of affairs' had developed as the result of having to sledge with 'two foreigners'.

Shortly thereafter their epicurean woes continued, as a miscalculation meant they were short of tea for a week. However, like Shackleton's party, they were following their sledge tracks, so they stopped at successive outward camps and retrieved the used tea leaves, which they boiled again.

For eight of the next nine days they made their required mileage, only once stopping a mile short of the goal. Late in the month, the mountains, which they had lost sight of on their way out, hove up, each in turn giving additional encouragement. On 26 January, they reached an area of marble-like névé, broken into successive steep slopes, and, slipping and tumbling without crampons, they gained only fourteen and a half miles, although they did make a significant descent, dropping to an area that was considerably warmer.

Two days later, on David's fifty-first birthday, they made up for any shortfalls. They woke to a twenty-five-mile-per-hour wind, so they hoisted their floorcloth as a sail and raced twenty miles. 'Occasionally, in an extra strong puff of wind, the sledge took charge,' David wrote.

'On one of these occasions it suddenly charged into me from behind, knocked my legs from under me, and nearly juggernauted me. I was quickly rescued from this undignified position under the sledge runners.' That afternoon, 'with a faint hope of softening the stern heart of our messman for the week', David reminded Mackay that it was his birthday. The Scotsman took the hint and increased their food ration that evening.

The next day another twenty-mile performance took them to their depot and their much-missed ski boots, ice axes and ropes. But on 30 January they made a critical error. Mackay advocated retracing their steps of a month earlier, but Mawson and David overruled him, deciding to go straight down the Larsen Glacier to where it reached the Drygalski Ice Barrier. It proved to be one of the most difficult sections of ice they ever crossed, at points dropping forty-five degrees, and each of them went into crevasses. Mawson's leg gave him excruciating pain throughout the descent, leading him to complain: 'hardly ever had a worse time in my life. Agony all day.'

Near the bottom of the glacier was a chaotic nightmare of hidden 'hell holes' and serac ice. Here they tried a route that would take them away from the Drygalski and to the smooth sea ice, from where they could head for their depot. But on 31 January, despite taking only half a sledge-load, they met nothing but despair, disappointment and agonisingly slow progress. One after another, they fell into crevasses, and at one point they were confronted by such an enormous pressure ridge that they had to unload the sledge and manhandle each individual item over it. They could not find a place to camp until 7.00 the next morning. They were, according to their figures, sixteen miles from the depot, but they only had short rations for two days. More importantly, the ship might even then be passing and sailing away.

When the three men awoke on the afternoon of 1 February, a heavy snow was coming down. They tried to travel in it, but could only struggle a mile and a half, so they turned in again without eating. They had now been man-hauling for almost four months, and the physical beating they had taken is almost unimaginable. But on the Larsen Glacier and in the following days, it was their mental stamina, not their physical endurance, that finally snapped.

For some time Mawson had noted that the Professor had been

troubled. 'Something has gone very wrong with him of late as he almost morose,' he wrote, 'never refers to our work, shirks all questions regarding it, never offers a suggestion.' The terrible conditions had almost broken the older man. They proved even worse for Mackay. Both had started to come apart at the seams, as Mawson recorded:

> Prof's burberry pants are now so much torn as to be falling off. He is apparently half demented [judging] by his actions – the strain has been too great. He says himself that had we known the magnitude he would not have undertaken it . . . Mac, it seems, got on to the Prof properly at one halt during afternoon whilst I was reconnoitring. He told the Prof also that he would have to give me written authority as commander or he would, as medical man, pronounce him insane.

On the morning of 2 February the sun was shining, but Mackay's humanity was not as much in evidence. The three set off in desperate hope of reaching their depot, and after four miles they left behind their scientific equipment and all but their essentials. With the lighter load, they moved more quickly, but evidently not fast enough for Mackay, who several times during the day viciously kicked David in the ankles, as if to encourage him to pull harder. That evening, during a stop for a snack, Mawson spied the depot flag, and they changed course. At midnight, when the temperature had fallen to zero, David asked for a halt. His boots were frozen on, and when Mawson pulled them off, he found the Professor's feet were frostbitten. While Mawson helped restore their circulation, Mackay disinterestedly pronounced them more or less gangrenous. 'During most of the day the Prof has been walking on his ankles,' Mawson recorded, noting that when Mackay kicked him, 'He was no doubt doing his best.'

Bad feet or not, the three were desperate to reach their depot, and within the hour they continued, marching until they were halted by a barranca about 200 yards wide and forty feet deep. With their arms on the verge of giving out, they lowered the sledge to the floor, where, to their joy and relief, they saw numerous Emperor penguins. While Mackay killed and cut up several, Mawson and David walked to the far side to survey a way to the top. The Professor was, according to Mawson, 'now certainly partially demented'. Mackay had again threatened to certify him insane, and David pleadingly asked Mawson to assume leadership of the party. 'He said he would draw it up in writing and get me to sign it,' Mawson wrote. 'I said I did not like it and would think on it . . . he drew out his pocket book and began writing out my authority . . . and asked me to sign it. I again said I did not like the business and stated he had better leave matters as they were until the ship failed to turn up.'

Despite his own frustrations, Mawson had throughout the journey outwardly supported the man whose scholarship, personality and morale had been such a shining example to so many. Although he had put significant complaints in his diary, he was not about to change his conduct now. Whereas Mackay demonstrated that the brutal conditions of the journey had brought out the savage in him and caused him to lose his compassion – proudly writing in his diary, 'I have deposed the Professor' – this was not the case with Mawson. David's former student would continue to rally behind the man who had 'ever been a driving force behind my labours'.

Therefore Mawson abandoned the discussion, and continued his search for a way up the overhanging cliff face. But none existed, and the three were ultimately forced, with heart-breaking effort, to haul the sledge back up the high face that they had descended. It was now 7.00 a.m., and they had been on the move for twenty-three hours. Despite still having to make the final push to the depot, they were unquestionably relieved to have obtained fresh food, ending the threat of starvation. And since they were so near the coast, they felt that they could not help but be seen if *Nimrod* passed. With these self-assurances, they set up their tent right there and turned in.

As they got into their sleeping bag, each had the same set of questions. Should they wait for the ship or head south to Butter Point, a journey that would force them to leave the coast in places? Since they were several days late in arriving at the depot, would *Nimrod* try to find them or would she have left them for lost? In fact, as they had not followed Shackleton's instructions, or indeed their own plan left at Depot Island, would anyone even know where they were? Mackay was for heading south, but Mawson and David both knew that the schedule for picking them up was too tight for the ship to come this way more than once. Whatever they did, they told themselves as they dropped off to sleep, they had to keep to the shore so that they didn't miss the ship in her only pass.

They had not been asleep long before an increasing wind picked up the drift from the Drygalski Ice Barrier and blew it toward the north. As the wet snow swirled aimlessly, all sight of their tent and of the flag at the depot disappeared. In the heart of this squall, with nothing but whiteness to the west, *Nimrod* made her way slowly past their ice cliff and continued her voyage.

20

FORCED MARCH

Perhaps Columbus, 400 and more years earlier, would have truly understood the joy that a vision in the distance brought four men struggling north on 16 January 1909. Never in all their voyages across the oceans of the world had any of them been happier to see land than early that afternoon, when, still on the midst of the frozen watery waste that was the Polar Plateau, the Transantarctic Mountains slowly came into view. 'Saw the land again today after being out of sight for 3 weeks nearly,' Shackleton recorded in a diary entry that, like his others since they had turned about-face, was shorter than previously.

The reality was that they no longer had the energy to make extensive entries. They were physical wrecks – Shackleton's frostbitten heels had cracked open and were suppurating. They had not had enough to eat for months – and two days before had yet again cut back – and the altitude was playing havoc with their systems. Moreover, the temperature seldom rose above −20° any time of the day and dropped so low at night that the intense cold disturbed their sleep.

Yet they continued to cut into the more than 700 miles separating them from Cape Royds. Two mornings before, a stiff blizzard from the south had greeted them upon waking, but they had simply hitched up the floor cloth as a sail to take advantage of the wind. 'Had we been bound S. instead of N. we should have called this an awful day, and most likely would not have been able to leave our tents,' Wild wrote. 'As it is we have done the best days pulling of the journey.' They had made more than twenty miles, although the wind had caused the sledge to buck and kick like an unbroken pony. The four men had had to run along to keep up with it, using valuable energy braking it so that they did not lose control, and negotiating it around the hard sastrugi that dotted the landscape.

The following days produced more of the same, and although they were pleased with their distances, the exhausting rush was compounded by the loss of their sledgemeter, which snapped off unnoticed. 'This is a serious loss to us for all our Barrier distances are calculated between depots on it,' Shackleton wrote. 'We must now judge distance.'

The seventeenth January was the first of three successive record-setting days, as they dropped more than 500 feet of altitude while gaining twenty-two-and-a-half miles. The next morning saw them at the transition area to the Great Glacier, but, trusting to Providence, they stormed across crevasses large and small, completing twenty-six miles before camping near a large ice fall. 'I have been very unlucky today falling into many crevasses and hurting my shoulder badly,' Shackleton wrote that night. He was too sore and fragile to note that they had all had many close calls, and that one of the runners on the sledge had broken. Never the less, they did have thanks to give, as their lower altitude meant it was not so bitingly cold, and nearing the depot allowed them an increase in food. 'Thicker hoosh & an extra biscuit tonight,' Marshall noted, adding with a rare note of empathy, 'Never will I refuse a hungry man a feed & feed the hungry whenever possible!'

The next day topped them all, as, after about an hour of slogging out of the ice falls, they 'got the sail up and fairly romped along until noon, over névé and hard sastrugi'. Throughout the afternoon their biggest problem was the runaway sledge constantly overtaking them, despite them reefing sail to hold it back. They raced across crevasses at all angles, two men roped ahead of the sledge and two unroped steering at its sides, and they often broke through the covering, the side men carried across only by the sheer momentum of the sledge. When they finally camped only eight miles from the Mount Buckley depot, they had achieved twenty-nine miles. 'I don't know how S. stands it,' wrote Wild admiringly. 'Both his heels are split in four or five places, his legs are bruised and chafed, and today he has had a violent headache through falls, and yet he gets along as well as anyone.'

There is little doubt that Shackleton, leading by example, was overexerting and taxing his reserves more than was wise. 'The worse he felt, the harder he pulled,' said Adams, who, like Marshall, had concerns about the Boss working so hard he collapsed. His determination continued on the final struggle to the depot. After two hours of descending a snow field, they struck an area of crevassed blue ice, where their finnesko could not purchase a grip. They each had numerous falls,

Shackleton two particularly nasty ones. By the time they reached a steep gradient where they had hauled their sledges up by rope on the way south, a gale had picked up. With the constant threat of being blown down the face, they lowered the sledge by a rope, using an ice axe as a bollard. They finally reached the depot at midday, with Shackleton's earlier prediction – 'I expect there will be little in the locker by the time we strike our glacier head depot' – having proved correct: they had but one day's food remaining.

Night brought on a series of squalls, and, while making meteorological observations, Adams was blown over by a gust and threw his logbook towards Shackleton. It was carried away by the wind down a slope. 'You must go after it, Bill,' Shackleton calmly advised, 'no good going home without the records.' So Adams and Marshall scooted down the glacier to the edge of a crevasse to recover the little book. Shackleton shortly thereafter turned in, according to Wild, 'completely knocked up'. He did not go to sleep, however, before recording 'bad as the day has been, we have said farewell to that awful Plateau.'

That night, in their relief to be off the Plateau, the seriousness of their situation might not have struck them. It certainly did the next morning. The fine line they had trod with their provisions so far was nothing compared to what faced them going down the Great Glacier. They had taken twelve days to ascend the hundred miles from the lower glacier depot to Mount Buckley. They now had only five days' food at half rations.

Worse yet, early in the day Shackleton was so weak that he was forced to take himself out of harness. 'Pulse on march thin & thready,' Marshall recorded clinically, 'irregular about 170.' Wild, as usual, saw the matter differently:

Poor S. has been very ill today, the heavy falls he had yesterday have shaken him up badly, and he has had to walk by the sledge. It is not surprising, as for a good six weeks he has been doing far more than his share of work. His stomach is out of order and he has very little appetite and cannot eat his pemmican, which is a serious matter here. M's trace as slack as ever, though only three of us were in harness.

That the surface was relatively hard and they continued to drop in elevation helped, however, and they made more than seventeen miles.

Shackleton slowly improved during the next several days and was able to help guide the sledge over the badly broken ice, when respectable distances were attained.

It was just as well that Shackleton was back to normal by 24 January, because the first half of the day was 'a perfect nightmare', travelling over 'huge cracks and crevasses, hills and hollows, ridges and mounds of sharp-edged ice which was all the time playing hell with our sledge.' Coming down an ice fall, the back two feet of the starboard runner was ripped away, and by the end of the day, the once eleven-foot-long sledge was down to seven feet on one side. They went sixteen miles, but it took from 6.45 a.m. until after 9.00 p.m. Despite camping in sight of Mount Hope, they were still more than forty miles from their depot, with food for only two days and biscuits for one. 'Two or three days bad weather now would send us all to the Happy Land,' Wild jotted, 'as one cannot hold out long in this country without food.' But, he added hopefully, Marshall 'has been pulling almost his share today, so I think he must be getting scared about the food.'

They must all have, because the next day was a blue-ribbon pull if ever there were one. With their luck in the form of good weather continuing, they blasted down the glacier twenty-six miles to an altitude of only 2,600 feet, consuming almost all their food on the way. The final crumbs from their food bag served as breakfast on 26 January, although that did not seem a disaster, as they calculated they would reach the depot that afternoon. They calculated wrong, however – and it almost proved their undoing.

Immediately upon leaving camp at 7.00 a.m., they were faced with a series of pressure ridges, between which were undulating waves of soft snow that made pulling the damaged sledge incredibly difficult. Before noon this turned to a maze of crevasses thickly covered with soft snow that had fallen since their outward journey, leading them to lose their bearings, as no features were recognisable. When both lead men on the sledge went into a crevasse at the same time, it forced them to lengthen the harness of one of them, so they would be pulling at different distances from the sledge. The lunch break provided only a cup of tea with the last spoonful of sugar.

By mid-afternoon they were stumbling with hunger and exhaustion through a white plain of snow twelve to eighteen inches deep. Their progress had fallen to less than a mile an hour. A stop for another cup of tea reinforced with the last of the plasmon gave no help, so at 5.30 p.m.

Marshall produced a set of 'Forced March' tablets, a cocaine preparation that he had reserved against such a contingency. Designed to
'sustain strength' according to the manufacturers, these tablets helped
keep the men moving – albeit slowly. They could hardly drag their feet
above the snow. 'Several times I fell into crevasses, as everyone did,'
Wild wrote. 'Whilst hanging in the harness I prayed that the rope would
break so that I should have a nice long rest.'

Each hour Marshall dosed his party with the 'Forced March' tablets,
and each hour they were slightly revived and able to crawl on. At 10.00
p.m. they added a cup of cocoa to their tablet. 'Struggled on,' wrote
Marshall, the pain showing even in his scrawls. 'All played out, depot
always seeming within reach yet unable to make it. Pace funereal.' By
2.00 a.m., Marshall's wonder-drugs had been finished, and the men
were falling asleep on their feet. Then, with all of them sinking up to
their knees with every step, Wild collapsed, and they were forced to
camp three miles from the depot.

They were on their way again by 9.00 a.m., but at noon Adams
collapsed. He was able to continue a short while later, but by 1.00 p.m.
the entire party was utterly exhausted and had to stop. They had not
had solid food for thirty hours, and their strength and will were
virtually broken. 'I cannot describe adequately the mental and physical
strain,' Shackleton wrote about what he called 'the hardest and most
tiring days we have ever spent in our lives.'

Now an unexpected man stood forward for the role of hero. While
Shackleton watched over Adams and Wild, Marshall set off to bring
back food. Within twenty-five minutes he had reached the depot, after
escaping three falls into crevasses by hurling himself forward and
grasping for the edge as he felt his feet go through. There he collected
four pounds of pony meat, cheese, pemmican, biscuits and tobacco. 'By
arrangement with Shacks, I took 2 lumps of sugar from depot to help
me back,' he wrote. 'Very stimulating effect . . . and if I was asked to
choose between the relative merits of "Forced March" or sugar, under
similar conditions, I should choose sugar.'

Within the hour Marshall was back at camp, and they were digging
into a real meal. 'Good God, how we did enjoy it, and what resolutions
we made over it,' Wild wrote. Yet they were still so dreadfully weak
that they were forced to put up their tent for a sleep before proceeding
the final mile.

Early the next morning they advanced without incident to the depot, where they consumed another large meal, dumped their ski boots, took several photographs and collected geological specimens before heading towards The Gateway. Whilst making their way before a strong breeze, Shackleton was given a last farewell by the cracked blue ice of the glacier. 'I was plunged into a hidden crevasse and hauled out by Wild,' he wrote. 'My harness jerked up under my heart and gave me rather a shake up.' Never the less they reached the Barrier by 3.00 p.m. By the time they camped at the outer edge of a bergschrund (a crevasse formed at the head or end of a glacier), they had made fourteen miles and were only fifty to sixty miles from Grisi Depot. Shackleton's performance had impressed even Marshall, who noted with admiration, 'Sh. has stood it wonderfully. Wild & Adams rather played out.'

Shackleton, meanwhile, having left behind first the Plateau and now the Great Glacier, was already looking ahead to the final stage. 'It is with a feeling of relief that we left the glacier today for the strain has been great,' he wrote. 'We know that except for blizzards and thick weather, which two things can alone prevent us from finding our depots in time, we will be all right.'

As if to put an exclamation point on Shackleton's foresight, the next morning a thick, warm snow began to fall soon after they started. The temperature soared to 32°, and the snow melted on the men and their sledge immediately upon landing, making everything miserably damp. Little more than an hour later, with the air so full of snow they could hardly see, a cold wind sprang up, almost instantly dropping the temperature by twenty degrees and freezing solid everything that had been wet. They had no choice but to stop and try to warm up. When conditions did not improve, they were forced to wait out the blizzard, much to the chagrin of Wild, who noted: 'I hope this will not last long, or we shall soon have empty tummies again; we cut our lunch down as it was.'

Indeed, lack of food was a potentially fatal affair. Although they had been in desperate need of feeding up when they reached Depot D, given the amount of supplies there they had considerably overeaten. Now they were short again. To make matters worse, by the time the blizzard ended on 30 January, Wild had developed dysentery, and it was all he could do to stagger along. The others had to pull over a fine snow that made traction difficult and their advance painfully slow. Shortly after they started the wind whipped up again, blowing about the snow and blotting out their vision as they passed through a heavily crevassed area where the Great Glacier met the Barrier. But they could wait no longer, and trusting in Providence again became the order of the moment. Remarkably, by the end of a day on which they man-hauled for ten hours to net thirteen miles, they had not met a single crevasse.

On the final day of the month Wild again could only just continue plodding to keep up. The medicine Marshall gave him made him so drowsy that several times he fell asleep on the move. Worse yet, he could eat neither pemmican nor horse meat, and there were not enough biscuits for him to have extra. He was beginning to grow weaker. But that day an event occurred of such significance that Wild underlined every word he wrote about it:

> S. privately forced upon me his one breakfast biscuit, and would have given me another tonight had I allowed him. I do not suppose that anyone else in the world can thoroughly realise how much generosity and sympathy was shown by this; I DO, and BY GOD I shall never forget. Thousands of pounds would not have bought that one biscuit.

The gesture absolutely and utterly sealed their bond. Wild would irrevocably be Shackleton's man for the rest of his life.

Two days later, they were well off course when Shackleton spotted one of the mounds they had built. They changed direction immediately. It was extremely lucky because when the party reached Grisi Depot, at 82°39′S, they were again virtually without food. They feasted that night on pemmican and meat hoosh, and had a special celebration for the birthday of Shackleton's son Raymond.

The next day was a different matter, however. All four were hit with 'Grisi's Revenge', which Marshall attributed to a combination of the meat being bad because the pony had been killed in such an exhausted state, and the inability to cook it long enough due to a lack of paraffin. 'The horse flesh probably had a Vitamin C value,' he later wrote, 'countered no doubt by the severe enteritis which resulted, and 13 motions in 24 hours was recorded for one of the party.' Despite abandoning their creaky, damaged sledge for the one they had used to mark the depot, they were not able to make effective progress, covering only five miles before camping.

The morning of 4 February was beautiful, calm and sunny, yet not so warm that it affected the snow. Under normal conditions it would have been perfect for pulling. Instead, the men lay moaning in a camp that Marshall described as looking like a battlefield, all four down with acute diarrhoea. 'My pyjama trousers and shirt tail sacrificed,' Marshall noted, but Wild had greater concerns:

> It would not be so serious if we had plenty of food, but as it is we have not sufficient to take us to the next depot . . . and there we have only a small supply, so we shall be hungry all the way to the Bluff . . . and if this illness does not prove short, we shall *never* get there.

Wild's comment said it all. The next morning, despite Marshall and Adams still being unwell, they stumbled ahead, knowing that to stop would mean their lives. For the next two days fine weather helped them make a slow but sure advance, and they reached the latitude from which Shackleton had turned back with Scott. Then on 7 February a strong wind from the south filled the sails on their sledge and propelled them north at a rate they had thought impossible in their weakened condition. They made better than twelve miles, a figure equalled the following day when Marshall was slightly better. 'Chewed meat tonight,' he wrote, clearly pleased, 'but did not swallow.'

It was now a question of Nature's temperament. Any advance was a struggle, and a blizzard from any direction other than the south would have left them marooned in their tent. That would mean the end. But although the wind howled and the drift swirled past them, it continued to come from behind, and with their sail at full mast, day after day they pushed across the Barrier. 'God is good,' Wild wrote after the four skeletons somehow accounted for more than twenty miles. But the rugged explorer's total exhaustion was shown by his addition of: 'My greatest desire now seems to be to sit on the hearth-rug at Mother's feet and be petted, I feel *so* tired and hungry.'

At lunch the next day their supplies were so short that when Marshall spilled his cocoa, he carefully spooned it up from the floor cloth before returning that to its position as sail. Two days after that, they pulled into their depot at 81° 04′S, once again having run out of food. 'Lunched making splendid gravy with frozen blood dug up from slaughter house,' Marshall noted. Chinaman had made another notable contribution to their endeavour, and that night they thanked him by eating the whole of his liver 'boiled in fat. Gravy added. Very tender & tasty.'

But once again an adequate meal was to be followed by virtual starvation rations. And again no allowance had been made for dire weather or losing direction. They could only keep moving and praying for fine, clear weather. Remarkably, they got it. Two days after they left the depot, on Shackleton's birthday, they had a miserably hard pull with no wind but a good surface. They were totally spent that night but realised how fortunate they had been. 'We have a great deal to be thankful to the Almighty for,' Wild wrote, 'had the surface been the same as it was when we came down, we should all now be dead without a doubt.' With little that they could give The Boss on his birthday, the three others each found enough shreds of tobacco to make a thin cigarette for him.

At some point that week, Wild expressed what was perhaps the ultimate trust in and regard for his leader. One night Shackleton asked him if he would join him on another attempt at the Pole. It was only little more than a week before, on 5 February, the day after they were all kept in camp with dysentery, that Wild had given notice of his unwillingness ever to return to the frozen regions. 'This trip has completely cured me of any desire for more Polar exploration,' he had written, 'a good fire and a full tummy for me in the future.' But with Shackleton actually asking the question, his decision changed. 'So great was my regard for the "Boss" that without any hesitation I replied "Yes!" We then went on to discuss details.' Considering their lives were in the balance, the conversation was bizarre in the extreme. But at least it gave some variation from all of their other thoughts and discussions: it was not about food.

On 20 February the haggard party kept its record perfect by arriving at Depot A, at 79°36'S, without enough food left for a full meal. They were greatly appreciative of the new supplies – feasting on pemmican, biscuit, cocoa and a blackcurrant pudding made with a pound of Hartley's jam – but it says a great deal that although obsessed with their stomachs they no longer stressed in their diaries the lack of supplies for the future. It had now simply become a reality of life.

During the past days their spirits had risen as they had begun to see familiar landmarks. On 18 February Mount Discovery had reared her head, and the next day Mount Erebus. Then, the day after they left Depot A, the Bluff came into view. Somewhere out there, to the east of it, was the final depot. It was, they calculated, four days away, and they had picked up four days' food, 'not full, but much more than we have been having'.

Shortly after beginning their march, the temperature crashed to $-35°$. 'We are so thin that our bones ache as we lie on the hard snow in our sleeping-bags,' Shackleton wrote. But it was not just at night – a blizzard that under normal conditions would have kept them in their tents froze them during the day as well, although it also contributed to achieving a splendid advance. 'Distance speaks for itself,' Marshall laconically wrote after the first of two twenty-mile days. Their progress was so good that, believing they would easily find Joyce's depot, they increased their food. Somewhere, on the fringes of their minds, undoubtedly lurked the knowledge that it was a distinct possibility the depot had never in fact been laid. But if so, their stomachs must have responded, they were doomed anyway.

But in a moment such worries were set aside. On 22 February they suddenly came across the tracks of a party of four men, with dogs. It must be Joyce! All they had to do was follow the tracks to the depot. Later in the day there was even better news, as at the remains of a camp left by this other party there were tins different than those of the original stores – the ship must have arrived! They found three small bits of chocolate and a scrap of dog biscuit and drew lots for them. 'I was unlucky enough to get the bit of biscuit,' wrote Shackleton, 'and a curious unreasoning anger took possession of me for a moment at my bad luck. It shows how primitive we have become.'

That night they camped only twelve miles from where they assumed the depot must be, and the next morning, in anticipation, they wolfed down virtually all their remaining food. Then they headed for the depot – but it did not appear. The day drew on, and after more than four hours they began to worry. Had they without due consideration cheerfully finished off the rest of their food, just to be abandoned by Providence? They could only continue to follow the tracks, which were, in fact, not leading them to their stores. Then, around midday, as Marshall was taking a bearing, Wild caught sight of the depot flag, far off 'and only raised into view above the horizon by the accident of a mirage'.

The lesson still not learned, they immediately devoured their few remaining biscuits and headed for the depot. It was not as near as they had thought, and it was not until 4.00 p.m. that they finally arrived at the black flag flapping in the breeze. 'Good old Joyce,' wrote Wild, expressing the thoughts of all.

Their worries about starvation had ended. Joyce had left not only crates of essentials, but delectable titbits that the men had not seen for months. 'Carlsbad plums, eggs, cakes, plum pudding, gingerbread and crystallised fruit,' Shackleton listed in delight. After more than a thousand miles of want and hunger, they had all they could eat and more – but they gave it their best effort not to let it be more. They were eventually sated, but each took back to his sleeping bag a selection of sausages, chocolates, jams and other dainties.

But as their dreams of food ended, another nightmare began. It was now the night of 23 February, and Shackleton had left instructions with Murray saying that if they did not return by 1 March the ship could leave. Yes, three men and supplies were to remain at Cape Royds, but neither Shackleton nor his comrades wished to spend another year in the Antarctic under those conditions – the added time and the necessity of an extra relief expedition would take the lustre off their accomplishments. There were only six days left – five if the ship left first thing in the morning – days that could still mark the entire expedition with the stamp of failure.

Four men buoyed, rather than weighed down, by unusually heavy stomachs marched north from Bluff Depot the next day. On the way out, it had taken them more than a week from Hut Point to reach where they now were, and they planned to take a longer route, going farther east to avoid the crevasses near White Island. They had no time to waste. Although they were dragging a heavier load than previously, they now did not notice it as much, and that day they advanced fifteen miles.

At 4.00 the following morning, they awoke to begin a long day. But it was not to be the sort of day for which Shackleton hoped. On going into the other tent for breakfast, he found Marshall prostrate with cramps and dysentery. After all of the bad pony meat and the changes of diet for four months, the doctor had been knocked for six by a 'generous dose of a well-known brand of birthday cake deposited at Bluff Depot'. As if Marshall's reaction to the Fortnum & Mason cake purchased in honour of Brocklehurst's twenty-first were not enough, any thoughts of trying to travel anyway were laid to rest by a blizzard that rumbled in from the west and settled near Minna Bluff. For the whole day they were tent-bound.

Shackleton now contented himself with thoughts that he had occasionally mentioned to his colleagues. He had a solution for everything, even for what to do if they missed the ship. There was a whaleboat at Cape Royds, one of the first items landed the previous summer. In that, he said, they would sail to New Zealand. It would only take a month or two, and such a marvellous journey in an open boat would give them tales to tell for years. It was an idea he would not forget.

Meanwhile, soon after midnight the blizzard blew itself out, and the party was up and away. They pounded ahead relentlessly, not camping until almost 11.00 p.m., having made twenty-four miles. 'Marshall suffered greatly, but stuck to the march,' Shackleton recorded with admiration. 'He never complains.' Virtually before they were asleep, they were up again – it was 4.00 a.m. – and then off, continuing their dash. They made good progress until 4.00 p.m. when Marshall suddenly collapsed.

With the best will in the world, Shackleton could wait no longer. It was late on 27 February, *Nimrod* might sail within thirty-six hours, and they were still thirty-three miles from Hut Point. They pitched camp and, leaving Marshall in the care of Adams, he and Wild stormed off north, taking nothing except a compass, sleeping bags and food. Years later, Wild remembered what happened next:

> After we had covered a mile, Shackleton stopped & grasping my hand said 'Frank old man, it's the old dog for the hard road every time.' He & I were then 35 years of age & the two we had left behind were under thirty.
>
> In all my experience I have found the man of 30 to 40 a better stayer than the younger man. In a short strenuous spurt, as in a football or boxing match the young man wins, but when it comes to days, weeks, & months of solid toil & hardships the older man invariably beats the youngster.

Now it was time for them to prove it. With only a brief dinner stop, they ploughed ahead over a hard surface until 2.00 a.m. Near the northeast corner of White Island they tried to get some rest but could not sleep, so they hit the road again an hour and a half later. By late morning they were still on the go, having long since finished the carelessly inadequate amount of food that Adams had packed for them. At least, they told themselves, they would finish their journey as it had been spent – starving.

The final stages of their march now became a reprise of their entire journey – the gruelling placing of foot before foot, the insatiable hunger, the battling through the endless blanket of snow and the unimaginable mental strain. Throughout the day Shackleton kept flashing a heliograph hoping to catch the attention of anyone at Observation Hill, but he received no response. What did it mean? At 2.30 in the afternoon – after spending most of thirty-six hours on the move, they saw open water in the distance: the ice had broken out four miles south of Cape Armitage.

The two men continued on, dreading their alternatives, and then suddenly, at 4.00, Nature threw her last mean-spirited twist at them: the sky was blotted out, a ferocious wind picked up, and a blizzard blew heavy drift every which-way, slicing their vision to a matter of feet. With little warning, they arrived at the ice edge. Their road was cut off.

Shackleton now had a choice: a shorter way to the hut over the ice via Pram Point, or a longer but more secure detour around Castle Rock. It was late on 28 February and even a small loss of time could mean missing the ship, but despite this and concern about Wild's freezing feet, Shackleton's judgement in a crisis did not falter. As he felt the uninviting swaying of the ice edge, he turned towards the longer route. They abandoned the sledge and headed for an area normally avoided: one of pressure ridges and deep crevasses to the east of Castle Rock.

At 8.00 p.m. Shackleton and Wild stumbled and floundered through the labyrinthine tangle of scree and loose snow around Castle Rock towards the 'lowlands' of Hut Point. The last several hundred yards were the worst, as they realised *Nimrod* was not there, nor were there any inhabitants of the hut. Where was everyone? Could they be at Cape Royds? Could they find help for Adams and Marshall, and, indeed, themselves?

The answers came in the form of a letter nailed to a window of the hut. The ship, it declared, would shelter under Glacier Tongue until 26 February; there was no more about her plans. Shackleton scanned the letter again, and then again, only to confirm that, despite other information, there was no further mention of her, suggesting that after 26 February she would sail. It was now the night of 28 February. As Shackleton and Wild stood in front of the hut, they were hit with the realisation that, despite all of their efforts, *Nimrod* had gone.

21

RESCUE

All polar explorers were not blessed with Shackleton's understanding of the dangers of crossing sea ice, and on 3 January – while two sets of men struggled towards their respective poles – Æneas Mackintosh and three companions dropped over the side of *Nimrod* to take the post to Cape Royds. It was a journey that was 'only' twenty-five miles across the ice.

That the ship was anywhere in the vicinity might have been surprising to some. Joseph Kinsey, Shackleton's New Zealand agent, and Herbert Dorman, Emily's brother and the expedition solicitor, had found it no easy task to raise money for repairs and supplies necessary for *Nimrod* to return south. However, despite the carping of the press, there remained goodwill in abundance for Shackleton in New Zealand. The shipyard of M.J. Miller eventually took on the repairs, with a certain amount of credit being key to the agreement. In the ensuing months, the hull was caulked; the rudder, propeller and tail shaft overhauled; and the living quarters extended into the aft hold.

The other major change was in command, and here Sir James Mills of the Union Steam Ship Company again produced the goods – as before in the form of Frederick Pryce Evans, a tall, exacting Welsh-born New Zealander who had commanded *Koonya* when she towed *Nimrod* to the ice. Formidable, self-reliant, and accustomed to having his own way, Evans was now master of the expedition ship, and his officers were the same as when *Nimrod* previously went south, including Mackintosh, complete with glass eye.

When *Nimrod* departed Lyttelton on 1 December 1908, the farewell saw hundreds of well-wishers, bands and cheering crews of naval ships, a repeat in miniature of what had occurred when Shackleton had left eleven months before. Shortly after passing HMS *Powerful*, a twelve-year-old stowaway was discovered under one of the bunks. Evans was having no such nonsense, and a signal was sent to a launch trailing behind. The boy was transferred, and the relief expedition steamed on.

Two days later, the wind being favourable, the propeller was disconnected and the ship proceeded under sail in order to preserve coal. When, on 20 December, the ice pack was seen, the propeller was reconnected and the ship returned to steam. Slow progress through the pack was followed by an effort to reach King Edward VII Land, but, as before, heavy ice prevented a close approach. On 30 December they turned west toward Ross Island to collect the shore party.

It was, however, much earlier in the season than when *Nimrod* had previously visited McMurdo Sound, and ice extended all the way to Beaufort Island, some ten miles north of Ross Island. For two days Evans worked slowly through tightly packed pieces of screwed and hummocky ice before being stopped by an extensive, solid field twenty-five miles north of Cape Royds.

Then began one of the most ill-considered parts of the entire expedition. On the morning of 3 January Mackintosh and three sailors left the ship for Cape Royds. By lunchtime, pulling a heavy sledge – complete with tent, sleeping bags, cooking kit, food and large postbag – leading seaman James Paton was 'done up'. Mackintosh sent him back to the ship with AB Sidney Riches, while he and Thomas McGillion, a twenty-three-year-old ship's trimmer, depoted fifty pounds of supplies and continued. They were slowed by bad ice and camped shortly after 7.00 p.m. The next morning, they came to a wide lead of water separating them from the island. A return to the ship was soon stopped, however, when the appearance of killer whales in an area over which they had walked showed it had broken open. As a vast section of ice began to float out to sea, it was only with the greatest luck and hours of back-breaking efforts that the pair managed to pull the sledge from floe to floe and through huge patches of slushy decaying ice to where a small piece of glacier ice formed a bridge to the land. 'We were on terra firma!' wrote Mackintosh. 'None too soon, for fifteen minutes later there was open water where we had gained the land!'

The men stayed in their new camp for several days, suffering from snow blindness. When their sight returned, to their horror the ship had gone. They could, however, clearly see Cape Royds. 'The sight of it made me wonder how it would be to walk around there,' Mackintosh wrote on 7 January. 'Except for the mails, I thought it could be done.' Two days later Mackintosh and McGillion had a long walk to Cape

Bird (at the northern end of the island) and back, but still could not see the ship, so early on the morning of 11 January they left for the hut. Considering the terrain that they would be forced to cover and their lack of experience and equipment, it was a ludicrous decision. In fact, second officer Arthur Harbord recorded his hope that they would *not* attempt such a crossing 'as this means almost certain death, as the glaciated slopes that intervene are absolutely impassable to so slender a party'.

This Mackintosh and McGillion soon came close to finding out. After ascending several thousand feet, they were making their way unroped through what they thought to be a snowfield when, according to Mackintosh, 'I happened to look round to speak to my companion, when I was astonished to find that he had disappeared.' McGillion had fallen into a crevasse, saved from death only by a protruding boulder of ice. 'I took off my straps from the pack and then to them I tied my waist lashing, and lowered them down to him,' Mackintosh wrote. 'This just reached his hand, and with much pulling on my part and much knee-climbing on his, we managed to get him safe on the glacier again.' The accident had, however, cost them their primus stove and food.

For the rest of the day and into the evening they continued through a region of crevasses, some small and snow-covered, others with yawning maws that led to depths slowly turning from beautiful azure or aqua to deep, dark royal blue to a pitch-black 'hell hole'. At one point, while attempting to descend a long snow slope, their route was simply cut off, so they had to retrace their steps. Finally, reaching an area where on the slope above and in front were huge crevasses but below them was a steep snow field of 3,000 feet in height, they threw the dice. They sat down, dug their knives in to act as brakes on their glissade down, stuck their heels into the snow, and pushed themselves over. Down they raced, knives quickly torn from their hands, crevasses thirty feet wide flashing past on both sides, occasionally being thrust into the air as they shot over a hidden rock or piece of ice. But soon, at a terrifying rate of movement, they had reached the bottom. Remarkably, they were uninjured.

It was too cold to stay in one place for long, so they kept moving despite their fatigue. All through the night they travelled, until at 4.00 a.m. on 12 January they spied Cape Royds in the distance. They made directly for it, but before long a blizzard suddenly descended, the drift blowing so hard that it stung their faces and made them virtually the walking blind. By mid-morning, after they had been on the move without food for well over twenty-four hours, McGillion began to wear out. They tried to halt behind a large boulder, but found it too cold to remain motionless. McGillion 'then suggested that we should lie down, embrace each other, and cover ourselves with snow', Mackintosh wrote. 'I felt this would have been fatal.' So they kept on moving.

In the early afternoon, the snow ceased and to their horror they saw Cape Royds to the north – they had passed it miles back. They turned but were soon lost again in a fog. They wandered aimlessly. Suddenly, at 7.00 p.m., after more than thirty-six hours on the move, with virtually no food, water or rest, a figure appeared out of the mist. It was Day, who later reported that they had been in a state of complete exhaustion and were just managing to stagger along because they knew that to stop meant death. Within a few minutes he had them in the warmth of the hut.

Ironically, as Mackintosh and McGillion sat before the stove, Murray, who had been in charge of the base, was waiting aboard *Nimrod*. Even as Mackintosh had desperately attempted to get to shore, the break-up of the ice had allowed Evans to move down the sound. 'We were having tea on the afternoon of January 5,' wrote Murray, 'and Marston happening to open the door, there was the *Nimrod* already moored to the edge of the fast ice, not more than a mile away. The shore party quickly learned that the two men had disappeared, and the next day Joyce, Day and Riches attempted to search north of Cape Royds with a dog team, but were halted by the myriad of crevasses. After a day and a half, Evans took Murray and began a hunt, north along the dangerous, icy shore. Within hours, the rapidly moving pack jammed into the ship's propeller and then, embracing her in a great mass of ice, carried her helplessly north. It was to be more than a week before they were freed from the giant ice cube.

Upon the ship's return on 16 January, they discovered Mackintosh's campsite, including the postbag and a letter outlining his intention to cross the island to Cape Royds. 'Nothing more than madness!' Harbord wrote dejectedly. They did not expect to see either man again. Yet hours later, upon reaching Cape Royds, there was McGillion, accompanying Roberts out to meet them. They were the sole occupants of the hut; the others – Joyce, Marston, Day and Mackintosh – had gone south with the dogs to lay a depot for Shackleton.

For much of the next week, with Evans carefully conserving the limited supply of coal, *Nimrod* remained moored to a grounded iceberg at Cape Royds. By 23 January, however, the ice along the west coast of the sound had broken up enough to allow a search for the Western Party near Butter Point. Evans left promptly the next morning, but the delay meant he was almost too late.

'I have never spent a day that seemed as much a fortnight,' Priestley wrote at 3.00 a.m. on 24 January 1909. 'May I never have such an experience again.' Four hours before he had been lying in a tent on an ice floe heading out to sea, with killer whales hopefully waiting to add him to their diet. Then around midnight, Armytage went to check their position. Suddenly he screeched to Priestley and Brocklehurst that the floe was nearing a patch of fast ice. Within moments the tent had been collapsed, everything thrown on the sledge and the two youngsters were pulling for all they were worth towards him. Just as they reached him, the floe bumped into something solid.

'The snout of the glacier was some six feet above us,' Brocklehurst wrote. 'As it touched we scrambled up dragging what we could with us, some kit fell off as the sledge was perpendicular and hurriedly packed, so Raymond & Armytage held me by the heels as I collected the odds & ends.' Brocklehurst's use of 'collected' was generous according to Priestley: 'the sledge tipped over enough to tilt a couple of oil cans, boots, finnesko and some cakes of chocolate out, and Brocklehurst hurled these up indiscriminately, one passing within an inch of my nose and another hitting Armytage.'

Never the less, they had escaped, and from the only place possible. 'Not more than six feet of the edge touched, but we were just at that spot,' Armytage wrote. 'We had only just got over when the floe moved away again, and this time it went north to the open sea.' They stared at the disappearing floe that had been so close to being their final home, and they felt they were in turn being watched. 'The killers were all around the foot of the glacier,' Brocklehurst wrote, 'great ugly brutes deprived of their unusual breakfast.'

Feeling uncomfortable where they stood, the three men trekked back down the coast to Butter Point, where they raised their tent – on the shore. They had a meal of sardines, biscuits, chocolate and tea before turning in. But the experience was clearly implanted in their minds. 'I shall dream of killer whales for weeks', Priestley noted before closing his journal.

The next morning there was open water where they had previously camped, but beyond it, ten miles out, was *Nimrod*. They flashed her with the heliograph, and that afternoon they were picked up with their equipment and specimens. They all returned to Cape Royds, where the next week was spent freeing supplies that had never been chipped out of the ice, moving scientific and personal equipment to the ship, and adding as many samples to the scientific collections as possible. They also tried to make additional photographic records of the expedition. Murray took one intriguing picture of Priestley and his favourite dog, Cis. 'The photograph is especially interesting in that it shows my beard in all its grandeur and simplicity,' Priestley wrote. 'Everybody has been advising me to keep it on as it hides my face, but . . . I shaved a couple of days ago. I looked just like a Russian revolutionary with the beard on, and would have got six months hard from any magistrate on sight.'

While life thus seemed lighthearted, underneath the surface negative currents were beginning to cause dissension, as they impatiently awaited news of their missing colleagues. Evans had arrived bearing orders from Kinsey, putting him in command should Shackleton not be there. This he presumed to include all aspects of the expedition, and with his dominating presence he soon began to override the plans of the gentle Murray, including those made on clear instructions from Shackleton.

To compound matters, not all of Shackleton's directives were clear. Although he had left orders that if the Northern Party had not returned by 1 February a search was to be initiated, no one knew where David, Mawson and Mackay were supposed to be. Shackleton's vague instructions were simply that, should they not appear at Butter Point, the ship was to search for them along the western shores of Victoria Land. This meant a detailed examination of a shoreline more than 200 miles long, parts of which had never been charted.

Another significant aspect Shackleton had not considered was his nemesis from the earlier voyage: coal. A slow trip up the coast not only was exceedingly dangerous, as the ship needed to be kept as close to shore as the ice would permit, it also would burn a large amount of coal. Some of that which did remain might have to be left behind for those chosen to winter again, should Shackleton not appear. Evans was no keener than England to be left without adequate coal to get through the pack ice and home. Therefore he decided that the search would go only as far as Cape Washington, fifty miles north of the Drygalski Ice

Barrier. If the members of the Northern Party had not been found by that point, *Nimrod* would return directly to Cape Royds, leaving them to their fate.

On 1 February they crossed McMurdo Sound to Butter Point and headed north. The search turned out to be every bit as difficult as anticipated. They were prevented from getting close to the shoreline due to fast ice and jumbled pack, although the officers kept constant watch, using telescopes to view the territory they passed. For a hundred miles they were confident that they had missed nothing – although they did not notice the cairn at Depot Island. Then heavier ice forced the ship out to sea, and near the Nordenskjöld Ice Barrier they were so far out they could not even see the coast.

As the ship approached where it seemed most likely to find David's party, all eyes strained for the shore. They steamed as close as possible along the southern and northern fringes of the Drygalski Ice Barrier, discovering that the area had not been accurately charted, but seeing no sign of their colleagues. In the early hours of 3 February, while *Nimrod* neared the coast north of the Drygalski, a sudden squall with blowing snow made it impossible for John King Davis, the first officer, to see clearly, even from the look-out barrel on the main topmast. He was disturbed by the lack of clarity, but, as all he could make out were a group of tabular icebergs, the ship continued on her way. Later that day they reached Cape Washington. It was time to abandon the search.

When David, Mawson and Mackay left their tent after the blizzard of 3 February, it was nearing noon. A meal of boiled penguin made life seem better than it had in many days, and they were soon tramping along the edge of the long snow valley that had prevented them reaching the depot the night before. Progress was slow, but by evening they had at last found a way. Around 10.00 p.m., reaching a small bay where Mackay 'had dragged his sledge full of meat out of inlet on our earlier stay', they decided to camp, have a meal, and turn in, taking four-hour watches for the ship.

The next afternoon, Mawson woke his colleagues after allowing them several extra hours' sleep. They dined on penguin livers with a thin pemmican as a drink and then retired to the tent to discuss plans. They unanimously approved a move to the depot, which, being higher on the point, would allow a better view. There was less agreement on Mackay's plan to leave immediately for Cape Royds, hundreds of perilous miles away. Before the topic could get heated, however, a loud boom reverberated through the air. 'In a second,' Mawson wrote, 'I had overturned the cooker and was through the door where the bow of the *Nimrod* was just appearing round a corner in the inlet.'

'At the sight of the three of us running frantically,' recalled David, who was the last out of the tent, 'hearty ringing cheers burst forth from all on board. How those cheers stirred every fibre of one's being . . . In a moment, as dramatic as it was heavenly, we seemed to have passed from death into life.'

Within an instant, they were back at death's door, as Mawson suddenly dropped down a crevasse. Aghast, David and Mackay raced over to find him eighteen feet down, having landed flat on his back on a small, thin, ledge. They lowered a sledge harness to him, but were unable to pull him up. As *Nimrod* berthed along the ice edge 200 yards away, Mackay raced towards her, his voice carrying shrilly in the wind: 'Mawson has fallen down a crevasse, and we got to the Magnetic Pole.'

Davis led a party hurriedly scrambling from the ship. They quickly reached the crevasse, which they bridged with a piece of timber. Davis was lowered to the ledge, where he took off the rope and tied it to Mawson, who was pulled up; the first officer was then brought out as well. It was not the only part of the rescue for which he was responsible. Before *Nimrod* had turned south again, he had admitted to an annoyed Evans that he was concerned about a group of icebergs he had seen during a snowstorm, which might have masked an inlet in the ice barrier. Evans obviously did not want to expend the coal, and, according to Davis, 'Fixing me with his cool and disconcerting gaze, he said: "Are you sufficiently uncertain of what you saw to make it worth my while to return to those bergs?"' Davis answered in the affirmative, and the disgusted Evans ordered an about-face. When they reached the Drygalski, the air was clear and crisp. Behind the icebergs, but no longer hidden, was a small inlet, and above it Harbord spied the depot.

It was only after their reunion that those aboard *Nimrod* learned that the Professor and his companions had not reached what became known as Relief Inlet until *after* the ship had first passed. When Davis had gone aloft in the squall and seen the outline of the icebergs, they had still been camped several miles away, on the other side of the barranca. Even so, Davis later wrote:

had the weather been clear we might perhaps have sighted the flag they were flying above their tent. But had we missed it, under those circumstances, we should certainly have steamed straight for Cape Royds. Therefore, in some strange and providential way, my mistake in not taking the ship closer inshore to examine the tabular bergs . . . had made their rescue certain and assured!

The three men who Evans described as 'abnormally lean . . . the colour of mahogany with hands that resembled the talons of a bird of prey' now came aboard for what can only be described as a feeding frenzy. Offered a snack, they were still putting away huge quantities an hour and a half later when they were told that dinner would be served shortly. They were still clad in the clothes they had donned four months before, and their aroma was overpowering. 'We pressed them to adjourn to the engine-room for ablution and fresh raiment,' Evans wrote. 'They displayed no enthusiasm for such exercises and would willingly have dined without those preliminaries, but we were adamant.'

In the next three days sledge parties gathered the materials at the main depot and where the instruments had been left eight miles inland. Then, after failed attempts to collect the contents of two coastal depots, they hurried to Cape Royds. All that was left was to pick up Shackleton's party – if they had returned.

'The southern party are now overdue, and we are beginning to feel anxious about them,' Mackay wrote on 15 February, four days after *Nimrod* had reached Cape Royds and then promptly continued to Glacier Tongue. There had been no word of either Shackleton's party or Joyce's, and the tension among those waiting was palpable. It did not help that Evans had usurped Murray's power, and refused to discuss his plans with the members of the shore party, who were split between the ship and the base. It is significant that during this period David was not mentioned. Although he remained aboard ship, his condition, which had so deteriorated on the return from the Magnetic Pole, appears to have kept him from his previous role of mediator.

For two weeks, as the weather began to deteriorate – with frequent blizzards, colder temperatures and an increase in ice – Evans kept the ship out of danger, usually harbouring near Glacier Tongue but occasionally loading up scientific or personal supplies from Cape Royds and checking for arrivals from the south. On 20 February, everyone was cheered when Joyce, Day, Marston and Mackintosh were picked up at Hut Point, but subsequently deflated to find they had seen nothing of Shackleton.

By 25 February – when, according to Shackleton's orders, coal and supplies should be deposited at Cape Royds and the three men who would winter should be sent in search of the Southern Party – discontent had become widespread among the shore party. Evans having achieved a 'practical supersession [sic] of Mr Murray as commander of the land party' meant that none of these actions had been taken, and, moreover, the captain had not revealed what *would* happen. 'We are beginning to dislike his attitude,' Brocklehurst wrote. 'He considers himself too important and it looks as if he is going to make himself the head of the Expedition.'

Mackay, who was most outwardly disturbed by this 'hole-and-corner business', wrote a formal letter of protest because of his 'fear that a strong effort will be made to make this finishing up of the expedition a colonial business, to the discredit and dishonour of the British members of the land party.' In fact, Mawson – at Shackleton's wish – had already been selected to head a wintering party of six, the initial makeup of which does appear to have been non-British, and therefore to have included several of the crew. Mackay's protest led to two of these being replaced by Priestley and Mackintosh, and later, 'as a sop to Shackleton, Joyce was added . . . as a seventh man to look after the dogs'. Despite his protests, however, Mackay was not to remain, being supplanted by Dr Rupert Michell, *Nimrod*'s Canadian surgeon. This probably was in part Mawson's decision, as Mackay was told that 'several members of the party in the hut at Cape Royds had declared that they believed I was mad'. Mackay's treatment of David late in the journey had come back to haunt him.

While this infighting was going on, however, nothing was done to help the Southern Party. A search party was not sent south, a watch was not kept at Observation Hill and the *Discovery* hut was not manned, all of which Shackleton had ordered. Rather, the ship remained in 'absolute inactivity' near Glacier Tongue.

Thus, when Shackleton and Wild arrived at Hut Point on the night of 28 February 1909, they appeared to be on their own. But they would not give up. Hoping against hope that someone aboard *Nimrod* would see, they tried to burn the magnetic hut, but could not get it lit. They then ran up the hill to Vince's Cross – commemorating George Vince, the sailor who died on Scott's expedition – and tried to tie the Union Jack on to it. But their fingers were so cold they could not manage the knots. Overwhelmed by cold and hunger, the two men retired to the hut, where they improvised a cooking pot and made a dinner from the supplies stored there. They were utterly exhausted and had no sleeping bags, so they found a piece of roofing felt, wrapped it about themselves, and spent a miserable night 'almost paralysed with cold'.

Morning on 1 March brought with it warmth and hope at Hut Point. At 9.00 a.m. Shackleton and Wild were finally able to set the magnetic hut afire and they put up the flag. At Glacier Tongue, there was no such faith, and *Nimrod* sailed south to land the wintering party, in order, according to Evans, to find the bodies. They had, however, Harbord wrote, 'almost overlooked the fact that we were in the Land of Surprises, but we were reminded of it very forcibly when we saw two men on Hut Point waving a flag.'

Mackay and several others were in the wardroom when they heard a yell and a clatter of feet above. 'We all tumbled out, and rushed for'ard to the foc'sl head,' he wrote. 'There was a crowd there, some saying that they had seen a flash signal, and some a figure beside Vince's Cross. Soon we could make out two figures plainly, and the excitement was tremendous. We all danced about and cheered and waved our arms, and then fell to punching each other.'

The men on the land were equally delighted. 'No happier sight,' Wild wrote later, 'ever met the eyes of man.'

They had been saved, but not quite. There were still two men out on the Barrier, and Shackleton meant to rescue them – himself. As he and Wild boarded the ship, he immediately took charge, all questions of authority having ended. He ordered that a party be formed to collect Adams and Marshall, and while this was being done, he and Wild dined on bacon and fried bread, at the same time telling the crew the essence of the Southern Party's achievements.

Shackleton had been on the move for most of two days, with no proper sleep for fifty-five hours. But he had no intention of letting others do his job. He had hoped to take the dogs back for Adams and Marshall, but they had been transferred to Cape Royds. So, leaving Wild behind because he thought one of them had to stay in case of accident, he took Mawson, Mackay and McGillion – whom he did not know, because the man had not been on the first voyage south – and headed back across the Barrier. They marched for seven-and-a-half hours before halting for a dinner that Shackleton prepared while the others rested. After a short sleep, they were up again at 2.00 a.m., going full speed until they reached Adams and Marshall in the early after-noon.

Marshall was now well enough to help pull the sledge, and after lunch the party moved north. By mid-afternoon on 3 March, they had reached the ice edge, where Shackleton had told Evans to wait. But Evans had not followed orders, meaning once again the men had been left stranded.

One might have understood the ship not being there if it had been engaged in other important duties. But at the moment, it was sitting calmly at Glacier Tongue, leaving, according to Harbord, 'the party who had made a forced march from the South to get to the Hut as well as they might'.

In fact, after Shackleton left, Evans steamed to Cape Royds to load as much on to the ship as possible. For twelve hours, starting at 8.00 p.m., the shore party and the dogs pulled stores on sledges from the hut to a low ice cliff at Backdoor Bay, where the materials were lowered by ropes to boats. But with large quantities remaining, the sea became too rough, and Evans ordered that only men and dogs be brought back. One boat was able to return, but the next – holding Harbord, Murray, Mackintosh, Brocklehurst and a load of sailors and dogs – was unable to escape from where the cliff was deeply undercut. One of the oars broke, and, according to Brocklehurst, 'the waves were dashing over us & we were constantly dashed under the ice, as we were getting weaker every minute we were in a very dangerous & hopeless situation.' The sea pounded the boat broadside and the wet, freezing men would not have survived had they not been able to make fast to a line from an anchor that had been left near the cliff. A rope was then thrown down by the remaining men on shore – Priestley, Marston, Day and Joyce – who hoisted up first the dogs and then the men.

For the next twenty-four hours they were all trapped ashore. Most of the bedding had been transferred to the ship, and Priestley only 'managed to get a little sleep by using a couple of dogs as stomach and back warmers'. On the morning of 3 March, boats were put in the water, and the men and dogs taken off, although the remaining stores and personal equipment were left behind. The ship then returned to Glacier Tongue.

That afternoon Shackleton abandoned a sledge and tent at the ice edge and led his party towards Pram Point and around Crater Hill to the hut. They arrived shortly before 10.00 p.m. without any cooking supplies. 'Here Shackleton's resourcefulness came out,' Mackay wrote, 'for he soon had an excellent hoosh cooked for us in an old butter-tin.' Shortly thereafter, as the rest of the party turned in, Shackleton and Mackay went up to Vince's Cross with the making of a carbide flare, although they did not take any water with them, which needs to be applied to generate the gas for a flame. 'We burnt a flare,' Mackay wrote, 'by simply bursting open a tin of carbide, pump-shipping [urinating] on it, and setting a light to it. It went off with a slight explosion.'

Nine miles away, Mackintosh spotted the flare, and it was not long before Shackleton and Mackay could see Nimrod. The Boss collected Adams and they were the first to be taken to the ship, although not without a final incident. Adams, who had just donned new finnesko, stumbled at the ice edge, and just caught himself part way over. He was forced to hang on to the edge until rescued by the boat. 'Never was there such a return as when we climbed on Nimrod again,' he wrote. 'We had been given up for 10 days past & killed in a hundred different ways.'

Most remarkable had been the last five of those days, when Shackleton had been on the go virtually non-stop and had covered unimaginable distances, in the process walking into the ground such doughty figures as Mawson, Mackay and Wild. Back on the glacier, five weeks before, he had collapsed, but with a safe return in sight he seemed a man possessed, showing a capacity for sheer will to overcome physical limitations that is unmatched in the history of polar exploration.

By 1.00 a.m. the rest of the party was aboard. Shackleton was now as worried about ice conditions as Evans, and wanted to head north as quickly as possible. Never the less, later that morning they steamed past Cape Armitage towards Pram Point in order to pick up the abandoned sledges, which held the geological samples from the southern journey. As they went, they could see young ice forming over the calm water, so after they brought the sledges aboard Shackleton ordered all steam towards the north. They had hoped to pick up the anchor and small boat from Backdoor Bay, as well as the remaining personal items, but the wind prevented Nimrod from coming close in. Later, heavy ice stopped them reaching the geological samples at Depot Island. At neither location did they challenge the elements. None the less, according to Shackleton, they were more than a bit wistful as they passed Cape Royds:

> We all turned out to give three cheers and to take a last look at the place where we had spent so many happy days. The hut was not exactly a palatial residence . . . [but] it had been our home for a year that would always live in our memories. We had been a very happy little party within its walls, and often when we were far away . . . it had been the Mecca of all our hopes and dreams. We watched the little hut fade away in the distance with feelings almost of sadness, and there were few men aboard who did not cherish a hope that some day they would once more live strenuous days under the shadow of mighty Erebus.

But for now, after months of hardship, the members of the Southern Party could rest. 'I have just been back a week from the journey & have already put back on 12 lbs of the 24 I lost,' Adams wrote to a friend shortly thereafter. 'JBA weighing $8\frac{1}{2}$ stone was a poor sight but I'm truly grateful to Providence at being able to get back at all . . . It still seems too wonderful to be true.'

There was, however, one final effort still to make. No ship had ever succeeded in penetrating far in the heavy pack west of Cape North, so when they passed Borchgrevink's old camp at Cape Adare, they steamed west along the pack ice bordering north Victoria Land. Shackleton had hoped to link this unexplored part of the continent to Adélie Land far to the west, but heavy ice quickly showed such dreams to be unrealistic, although *Nimrod* did push farther west than any previous expedition.

But that was it. On 9 March 1909, with ice closing in, they headed north. It was almost too late. Within hours their progress had been halted by a seemingly impassable pack. That afternoon, however, a lead was discovered and *Nimrod* scooted through it. They were in the open sea and on the way back home.

22

HEROES RETURN

It was almost as if the members of the shore party had suddenly reverted to childhood. Their screeches and laughter could be heard all the way to the ship as they kicked water at each other, rolled half-naked on a deserted stretch of beach and floundered in the shallows trying to flip the colourful fish out of the water. As the sun heated their little haven, men slowly made their way into the luxuriant hardwood forests filled with tree ferns and a carpet of orchids. In a small cave near a patch of impenetrable bushes, Mawson found a little axe of green stone.

They could not have wished for a more delightful location for their first landfall since they had retrieved the sledge near Pram Point. It was 22 March and *Nimrod* was anchored in Lord's River on the nearly deserted south side of Stewart Island, just off the South Island of New Zealand. The men were having a glorious reunion with trees, flowers, colourful birds and water in which they could comfortably stroll. Although the next day they would be scratching where they had been mercilessly bitten by sandflies, for the moment they were in heaven.

There was one man notably missing from the celebrations ashore. Shackleton sat in a cabin carefully composing a detailed 2,500-word account. When he had made an agreement to send an exclusive report to the *Daily Mail*, it had been determined that he do so from Oban, the small village on Half Moon Bay, north Stewart Island, at a pre-arranged time. Ten days earlier the New Zealand government had sent down a special Morse operator to await his return and dispatch the message. The day *Nimrod* reached Stewart Island, it was too late for the message to be sent, so Shackleton kept the ship in seclusion.

At 10.00 a.m. on 23 March, Adams, Joyce, Marshall, Wild and Brocklehurst rowed Shackleton ashore in Half Moon Bay. While his companions waited silently in the boat, The Boss sent a coded message to the *Daily Mail*, followed by the longer account; he then sent several other messages. They returned to the ship to find it surrounded by launches, although all locals had steadfastly been refused permission to board. With him, Shackleton brought the thing his colleagues wanted most: news.

'We got the news of the result of the Burns–Johnson fight,' Brockle-hurst wrote excitedly, 'the first thing we asked for!' It had been Boxing Day – appropriately – in Sydney, after *Nimrod* had sailed south, that American Jack Johnson had toyed with world champion Tommy Burns of Canada – knocking him down twice in the first two rounds – before being awarded a victory in the fourteenth. It would forever change the sport that Brocklehurst and Shackleton loved: a black man had become heavyweight boxing champion of the world. To those on board, according to Brocklehurst, it was the most exciting news imaginable, but two days later when they entered Lyttelton, they found that everyone else had other ideas, and the greatest thrills were coming from a ship named *Nimrod*.

Shackleton's efforts at secrecy could not have been more successful, and the *Daily Mail* had an enormous scoop, a double scoop actually, as next to Shackleton's report was a message of congratulation from Queen Alexandra, who had also been notified because of her gift of the Union Jack. Within hours of its release, the story had gone round the world, and by the time the party reached Lyttelton, they had become inter-national celebrities. 'Steamers came out to us crowded with people, guns firing and flags waving,' Brocklehurst recorded. 'A boat came along side us & people crowded onto the Nimrod. We were flooded with questions from News reporters.'

It was just the beginning. When Shackleton walked off *Nimrod*, he stepped directly into a role of imperial hero, and immediately became the centre of a storm of patriotic fervour and public adoration. His striking looks, effervescent, charismatic personality, powerful speaking voice and honest, direct nature made him a favourite with men and women alike. He also came equipped with a tale of endurance, determination, grit and dash, and raw courage, all leading to achieve-ment against the odds. It was exactly what the public wanted – and Shackleton was just the showman to give it them.

But more than anything else, he was the elixir that the Empire needed for self-doubts brought about by the debacle of the South African War, for concerns about the thunderclouds slowly forming over Europe, and for the loss of economic and physical supremacy that happy breed of men had so long maintained. Throughout the Empire he was praised in the same fashion as in *The Sketch*, the day following his arrival in Lyttelton:

> It is one of the symptoms of this age of nerves and hysteria that we magnify everything, that our boasts are frantic and our scares pitiable, that we call a man who plays well in a football match a hero, and that all successes are triumphs . . . but Lieutenant Shackleton is in that rank of heroes whose names go down to posterity . . . when we are all feeling a little downhearted at seeing our supremacy in sport and in more serious matters slipping away from us, it is a moral tonic to find that in exploration we are still the kings of the world.

And king Shackleton was for the next three weeks in New Zealand. A thanksgiving service was given at Canterbury Cathedral for the expedition's safe return. The Lyttelton Harbour Board donated free of charge any services that might be needed for *Nimrod*. Shackleton was swamped with invitations to gala affairs and speaking engagements. Finally, on 14 April, Prime Minister Sir Joseph Ward and his Cabinet gave a farewell luncheon in Wellington before Shackleton sailed for Sydney. Overall, it could not have been more glowing if they had reached the Pole. 'So long as Englishmen are prepared to do this kind of thing,' it was proclaimed in *The Sphere*, 'I do not think we need lie awake all night every night dreading the hostile advance of "the boys of the dachshund breed".' It was virtually forgotten that the four men actually had turned back short of their destination.

Although the public cared little that Shackleton had not claimed the Pole itself, there were those who thought he might have claimed too much. Chief among them was that inveterate lover of intrigue, whispering and malicious intervention: Sir Clements Markham. 'He was a scurrilous old man,' the famed scientist Frank Debenham later stated. 'I had two hours with him once in which he told me more scandal than I'd heard before from anyone . . . if he took a fancy to anyone he could do no wrong, and if he took a dislike to a person he could do no right.'

Markham now took a dislike to Shackleton. Why is uncertain, although he had proven both friend (to his face) and foe (behind his back) previously. Despite Shackleton's troubles with Scott, he and Markham seemed to have been on excellent terms when he had left England. At that point, in October 1907, Markham had written: 'We have been such good and intimate friends for so long, that I am sure you will know that I am really sincere . . . when I wish you God speed . . . not only my most cordial wishes for your success will accompany you, but also a well founded hope.' Then, upon Shackleton's arrival in New Zealand in March 1909, Markham dashed a letter to Keltie, directing his former subordinate to 'put me down at once as his proposer for the Patron's Medal . . . My proposal is for reaching 88 degrees 23 minutes South and securing exceptionally valuable geographical results.'

But by April Markham had reconsidered. 'As I am responsible for having started all this Antarctic business,' he self-importantly and inaccurately wrote Major Leonard Darwin, the new president of the RGS, 'I think it right I should send you a note of what I think of recent developments.' He then launched a frontal assault:

> Shackleton's failure to reach the South Pole when it could have been done by another, and is really a matter of calculation, rather aggravates me. They will rouse ignorant admiration if the trumpets are blown loud enough, which they are sure to be. But I cannot quite accept the latitudes. For 88.20 they must have gone, dragging a sledge and on half rations, at the rate of 14 miles a day in a straight line, up a steep incline 9000 feet above the sea, for 20 days. I do not believe it.

Why had he suddenly rejected Shackleton's claim? Was he unhappy that a man tied to neither the Royal Navy nor the RGS had shattered the mark established on 'his' *Discovery* Expedition? Was he influenced by Scott, who dined with him near the time of that letter? According to Markham, Scott did not believe in the latitudes, and four days after his letter to Keltie, Markham had written to Scott, 'This is magnificent Daily Mail geography, and I am trying hard to swallow it, but I have not yet quite succeeded.' There is no certain answer. Nor is there evidence that Markham ever confronted Shackleton with his suspicions – *that* would have been too open, too candid, for Markham's temperament. After all, according to Debenham, 'He was fond of implying things.'

And it was perhaps Markham's letter – full of such implication – that led Keltie to make a cautious enquiry to Shackleton:

I suppose you made pretty sure what latitude you reached . . . I do not know you said anything about the instruments you had with you, and of course the difficulty of taking any observations under the conditions must have been fearfully trying, but still, I have no doubt you established your latitude to your complete satisfaction.

It was intended to be gently phrased, but Shackleton was nobody's fool. 'K. is tumbling over himself at the present time as regards the expedition,' he wrote to Mill. 'His first wire was a very guarded one, the second was the opposite. Even now he asks me if I can be sure of my latitude, as if I had not taken all possible means in my power to ascertain the exact position . . . in many things we have underestimated the results.'

By the time he wrote that letter, Shackleton was completing his triumphant tour across Australia. He had left New Zealand on a gesture that typified his generosity as much as his impetuosity, and had endeared him to the people of Wellington. A public lecture at the city hall had garnered £300, which was much needed for the expedition funds. Within a moment of receiving the payment, it was gone again, Shackleton having donated it to local charities. He did the same thing several times in Australia. These were not calculated plans, but honest gestures of goodwill to people who had enthusiastically taken him to their hearts, and for whom Shackleton felt equal affection. They were made for the best possible of reasons, but would never the less come back to haunt him.

As in New Zealand, Shackleton received an emotional welcome in Australia, although more tempered because the Australians – members of a new nation longing for their own heroes – had given their hearts to David and Mawson. In fact, David had been one of the first members of the expedition to leave Christchurch, returning on 30 March to Sydney, where he had been feted at numerous events, students turning up in their hundreds each time to honour their beloved 'Prof'.

Many of the others scattered soon thereafter. Wild caught a ship for England to help run the expedition office and give full details to Emily. Brocklehurst began a leisurely travel programme. Mawson returned to Adelaide via Sydney, where he received acclaim second only to David, who commented: 'Just as Shackleton was the general leader . . . Mawson was the real leader and was the soul of our expedition to the magnetic pole. We really have in him an Australian Nansen, of

infinite resource, splendid physique, astonishing indifference to frost.'
And *Nimrod* herself sailed first to Sydney for more repairs and then left
on the long passage home. Not surprisingly, it was planned as a voyage
of discovery.

John King Davis had only been employed as first officer because
England's initial choice had not panned out. But when Evans signed
off in Lyttelton, Davis found himself, at the age of only twenty-five,
promoted to master and assigned to take the suddenly famous ship
home. He was not to follow an ordinary passenger route, but a
remarkable itinerary of more than 5,000 miles in high southern
latitudes in midwinter, when most ships gave the area a wide berth.

At the time, the Admiralty charts showed a number of islands or sets
of islands in the sub-Antarctic area of the South Pacific as being of
doubtful existence. Four of these – the Royal Company Islands,
Emerald Island, the Nimrod Islands and Dougherty Island – had been
reported by early navigators but never seen since. Davis' instructions
were to locate and land on these islands if they existed, determine their
exact positions and describe their main features. If the islands did not
exist, deep-sea soundings were to be taken where they had been
reported. In addition, meteorological observations were to be taken
every two hours throughout the voyage.

It would not be easy. The short hours of daylight combined with
regularly cloudy skies made it not uncommon for forty-eight hours to
pass between instances of the sun showing her face. The heavy seas and
hurricane-force winds of the far south made soundings extremely
difficult. And bergy bits and growlers – fragments of glacier ice smaller
than icebergs and often almost hidden beneath the waves – were a
constant source of danger, particularly as lack of light made them
difficult to spot at a safe distance.

On 8 May, *Nimrod* sailed south from Sydney, with much of its
Antarctic crew still aboard, including Arthur Harbord, now promoted
to chief officer, Alf Cheetham as third officer, and Harry Dunlop as
chief engineer. Ten days later, some 450 miles south of Tasmania, the
ship passed directly over the position where the Royal Company Islands
had been reported to lie by a Spanish ship in 1776. Despite the poor
visibility, it was clear that there were no islands in the vicinity.

Davis now headed toward Macquarie Island, where he had been
instructed to collect local flora and fauna. He found it had not been

properly positioned on the Admiralty chart. More surprising was meeting a solitary man who the previous summer had established a hut there. A fifty-one-year-old Irishman named William McKibben, he had been left to collect the oil of elephant seals. He had a small, scrupulously clean hut with two rooms, each with a stove, and was so well stocked that he pulled out a fresh loaf of brown bread and a recently baked pie when Davis visited. Despite offers of a free trip home, McKibben stayed on with his dogs. Two years later, when Davis returned as part of another expedition, he was told by new residents that McKibben had been taken home but had never forgotten the young captain of *Nimrod*, whom he insisted was named Captain Jaeger, because that name had appeared in the Jaeger socks Davis had given him.

Nimrod sailed south from Macquarie, on 31 May passing over the supposed position of Emerald Island, which had first been reported in 1821. A little more than a week later, to their disappointment, they proved the Nimrod Islands, named in 1828, did not exist either. And a week after that the existence of Dougherty Island was disproved, taking the name of the captain who in 1841 had designated it after himself off the map. By the end of the month they were approaching Cape Horn, and the remainder of the voyage was little more than what most of the men had experienced at one time or another. On 24 August they sighted the Bishop's Rock Light, and by the next afternoon they were in Falmouth, the entire journey now consigned to memory, like some slowly fading dream.

Conversely, Shackleton's dream had been played out to its full during his waking moments, as he moved from one honour to another. He had left Australia on *India*, the same ship that had brought him out a year and a half before. With him were Adams, Armytage and Mackintosh, each, according to a fellow passenger, 'full of fun and high spirits . . . quite unspoiled, entering into the usual ship's amusements, playing with the children, yarning with the ship's company.'

All was not totally high jinks aboard, however. Hoping that his book about the expedition would produce a large payout, Shackleton worked regularly on it with Edward Saunders, a former reporter for the *Lyttelton Times*. At the recommendation of New Zealand's Prime Minister, Shackleton had hired Saunders as his secretary in order to complete the book hastily while there was still widespread excitement.

At Port Said, they transferred to the mail packet *Isis*, commanded, in a remarkable twist of fate, by Albert Armitage, his old colleague from *Discovery*. 'I heard all about his travels at first hand,' Armitage wrote. 'I also noticed a great change in him. He was no longer so dreamy; he was full of a restless, nervous energy and ideas for another journey.'

Disembarking at Brindisi, Italy, Shackleton took the fast train toward England, and arrived quietly in Dover on 12 June. It was a Saturday, and his official return was to be in two days. In the interim, he spent the weekend with Emily, after having been apart for almost two years. It was, she hoped, the final homecoming he had promised so often. 'I just want to tell you now darling Heart how much I love you how much I have missed you all this time and how I long to see you and our little ones again,' he had written from Sydney. 'Never again my beloved will there be such a separation as there has been never again will you and I have this long parting that takes so much out of our lives.'

Shackleton honestly meant what he said, but his later actions and her continuing dubiety (although accompanied by her support throughout) were proof that he did not know himself as well as Emily did. In a sense, it was only two days later, on 14 June, that she again lost him – this time to the rapacious British public.

The vast crowd that awaited Shackleton at Charing Cross Station when his train arrived at 5.00 p.m. that Monday was overwhelming even by the excessive standards of Victorian hero-worship. Not even an appearance by Livingstone or Gordon could have transcended the spirit of the multitude who pushed in for a view of their hero or attracted a greater showing of prominent figures from the geographical world. Major Darwin (president of the RGS), Keltie and Sir George Goldie were there, accompanied by Markham, for whom the glow of such a powerful limelight was too great to miss, despite his not-so-private misgivings. Even the man who wished to attend as little as any in the kingdom could not help but be there. 'I called at 1 Saville Row, on the day of his return, and met Scott there, gloomily discussing with Keltie whether he ought to go,' Mill wrote. 'He did not wish to go, but Scott was always a slave to duty, and we persuaded him that it was his duty to greet his former subordinate.'

It was not a day to miss. The crowd was so massive that after a speech, Shackleton and Emily were unable to reach their carriage for a considerable period. When they did, the calls of the crowd forced him to stand to show himself. After they started what virtually amounted to a royal procession, the carriage, according to legend, was stopped and the horses taken away. Local men formed into teams to pull it into the city. This is almost certainly not true, as no newspaper accounts of the day mention it. But could it simply have been because the press was so filled with its own idolatry for the new Caesar? As *The Daily Telegraph* expounded:

> We cannot make too much of him. In the strict sense of a strong word, he is one of the heroes . . . Let us remember at this moment that in our age, filled with vain babbling about the decadence of the race, he has upheld the old fame of our breed; he has renewed its reputation for physical and mental and moral energy; he has shown that where it exerts itself under fit leadership it is still second to none . . . and at a critical time in the fortunes of all the Britains he has helped to breathe new inspiration and resolve into the British stock throughout the world.

In the weeks before his homecoming Shackleton had already received unstinting praise from the international exploring community, some of the warmest and most heartfelt accolades coming from Nansen and Amundsen. Now, although the RGS maintained a guarded attitude, he overnight became the darling of the London social set. Throughout the summer he was feted and honoured, requested to speak, invited to luncheons, dinners and receptions, in short, entertained – and asked to entertain – in every possible manner. That he never lost his appeal to an audience speaks to a high degree of his wittiness, honesty, lack of sentimentality and a modesty best shown by his constant efforts to introduce the members of his expedition. 'I notice it is "Mr Ernest Shackleton" on the toast list,' he remarked at the Royal Societies Club luncheon the day after his return to London. 'That should be Ernest Shackleton and his comrades – because there are here in this room at the present moment the men who have gone with me through thick and thin, through the stress and difficulty and the joys and sorrows of the last expedition.'

Such statements made him only more appealing to the public, and Shackleton soon found himself a property claimed by any number of individuals and groups wishing to create of him a spokesman for their interests. He was an imperialist, said one, a believer in trade unions, another, a friend to impoverished sailors, a third claimed, and an Irishman, according to Sir Arthur Conan Doyle at the Royal Societies luncheon. It has been pointed out that at this time Shackleton did not dispute his Irishness. But nor did he deny virtually any other categorisation. He was attempting to be all things to all men, and there was no one he would refuse. But his real association with Ireland was shown by the fact that when he went to Dublin on a lecture tour the following December, it was the first time he had been there in a quarter of a century. After additional lectures in Cork and Belfast, he did not return. His real feelings were perhaps clarified by the polar explorer Sir Hubert Wilkins, who joined The Boss on a later expedition. Shackleton's 'blarney', Wilkins wrote, 'at times was purposely designed and accented because Shackleton, more than any other man I know, realised the influence and depended upon the influence of the spoken word, no matter the integrity.'

In the meantime, Shackleton found himself in a situation where 'it seemed as though nothing but happiness could ever enter life again'. He was the guest of honour at a dinner given by William Heinemann, who was publishing his book. He was the centrepiece of a reception in Park Lane at which the famed Italian operatic soprano Luisa Tetrazzini performed. And shortly after his return he was asked if he would consent to becoming a Younger Brother of the Corporation of Trinity House, the powerful guild controlling lighthouses and licensing maritime pilots. It was reputed to be only the second time in the history of the ancient Corporation that this honour had been extended in such a way, and it had required special approval of the Master of the Corporation, the Prince of Wales.

Shackleton's first week on British soil was highlighted on Friday evening by a dinner at the Savage Club in his honour. Although it was Shackleton who proudly signed his name on the wall in the manner of Nansen and other famous figures so exalted, the focus at one point turned to Brocklehurst. From the presiding chair, Scott stated that Mackintosh had perhaps suffered more than the others because he had lost an eye. Brocklehurst, he noted, was minus a toe, but to have left it in the Antarctic was a great honour. Shackleton leaned over to Scott, who then laughingly told the audience, 'I hear he has brought the toe back in a bottle.' The toe, which was preserved in a jar of spirits, Brocklehurst admitted, was in the process of making the rounds of London hospitals, being examined closely by doctors interested in frostbite. 'I wish I had it,' he told the Daily Dispatch. 'I can't regain possession of my toe. The doctors want it.'

Ironically, in this hullabaloo the one body that only grudgingly acknowledged the returning conquerors was the Royal Geographical Society. This was undoubtedly in part due to the influence of Markham, who wrote with glee, 'The King is not coming' when he found out that the sovereign would not attend the official RGS tribute to Shackleton and the expedition. But the Society's reluctance also reflected the ungenerous attitude of Keltie and other conservative and self-important Fellows. Shackleton was not the first: they had ostracised other of the world's greatest explorers – including Stanley and Richard Francis Burton – because they were viewed as rough-hewn men without the same accent, manners, or social upbringing (despite Burton having attended Oxford). Shackleton, who challenged their own Captain Scott, fell in the same category, as shown by a small-minded letter to the maker of the gold medal that the Society felt obliged to award him. 'We do not propose to make the Medal so large,' it stated, 'as that which was awarded to Capt. Scott.'

But once again the chance to bask in the glow of Shackleton's aura proved too attractive to miss, and on 28 June 1909 the RGS sponsored a grand event at the Albert Hall. A packed crowd was alternately thrilled, entranced and delighted by Shackleton's lecture, following which the Prince of Wales announced that, 'as a brother sailor, I am proud to hand him this medal'. He thereupon presented Shackleton with the Society's gold medal, emblazoned with the explorer's portrait, and then gave smaller silver replicas to the dozen members of the expedition who had been able to attend.

Two weeks later, Shackleton one-upped even himself, when he and Emily were commanded to come to Buckingham Palace. There they were received by King Edward and Queen Alexandra, and, following Shackleton's story of the expedition, the King bestowed upon him the rank of Commander of the Royal Victorian Order, as he had done to Scott previously.

But honours paid no bills, and of these Shackleton had even more than fine meals. He had hoped to pay off his expedition – and far more – from several sources, but these each now disappointed. From the *Daily Mail* he had received £2,000, but his book was not yet out – he diligently continued working on it with Saunders – and the planned series of lectures had not yet begun. Moreover, the wild hopes of gaining large sums from the stamps issued by the New Zealand government evaporated when dealers showed little interest. A cynic might have thought the greatest advantage of Shackleton's remarkable social agenda was that he was not home when debt collectors called.

In one fell swoop, however, hobnobbing with the rich and powerful suddenly paid off. In early August Shackleton again found himself at Cowes. But this year he was there at the invitation of Sir Donald Currie, chairman of the Union-Castle Mail Steamship Company, who was only too pleased to invite his former employee to the gala affair. On board Currie's new *Armadale Castle*, Shackleton met Sir Henry Lucy, the famed political journalist.

Lucy was immediately won over by Shackleton, but even more importantly Emily one evening confided to Lady Lucy about her husband's economic woes. When this information was passed on, Sir Henry was horrified that a man bringing such honour to the country could be left in the lurch financially for it, and he promptly wrote a signed article to the *Daily Express* about Shackleton's predicament. This was not just any journalistic hack spouting off; when Lucy put his name to an essay it meant something. He had initially become an enormously respected figure through his political articles for *The Daily News* and the innovative 'London Letters' that were widely reprinted in the provincial press. Then his huge success during a quarter of a century as the parliamentary correspondent for both *The Observer* and *Punch* – from where much of what he wrote was picked up by newspapers throughout the country – led to his knighthood. Thus, astonishingly quickly, an outcry on behalf of Shackleton rang out from not only the large London dailies but a vast array of regional newspapers. It rapidly became a situation that the government could not ignore.

On the evening of 5 August, the very day Lucy's article appeared in the *Daily Express*, Prime Minister Herbert Asquith sent for Shackleton. The man visiting the Prime Minister had stood against his party at the previous election, but Asquith had not reached his position by mis-understanding the public, and the issue of assisting the explorer moved quickly through Cabinet and into the Commons. On 19 August Asquith wrote to Shackleton:

> With reference to the interviews which we have had on the subject of the liabilities incurred in connection with the British Antarctic Expedition commanded by yourself, I am pleased to be able to inform you that the Government have decided to recommend Parliament to make a grant of £20,000 to meet a portion of the expenditure.

The grant did not solve all of Shackleton's financial worries, but it allowed him to redeem the bank guarantees and to pay off a good number of bills. It also added immeasurably to his respectability, as at one stroke he was recognised by Parliament and saved from his creditors. 'Isn't it splendid!' he wrote to Emily. 'Just think of your Boy getting £20,000 from the Country: What Oh!!'

Shackleton was now on top of the world, the recipient of popular, governmental and royal praise. He was a wildly fancied speaker, his appeal extending through every social class, financial strata and age group. Among the most dedicated of his partisans were wide swathes of children, to whom he seemed not only heroic, but, in his conspicuously laddish way, one of their own. When asked to participate in an honours day at a boys' school, he horrified the headmaster but delighted the pupils by commenting, as he presented one of the awards, 'This is the nearest I've ever got to handling a prize.' His sense of humour, which had easily won over men of different backgrounds on expeditions, vast crowds when standing for election, and mixed audiences at talks about his exploits, extended to teasing youngsters, with whom he was able to communicate throughout his life.

'My father knew we wore gym dresses and we had this elastic round our bloomers underneath,' Cecily later recalled about school uniforms that otherwise had no place for handkerchiefs. When a group of her friends came to meet her famous father, he was at his most mischievous.

> We were all sitting with very good behaviour facing him, and he'd been a little shocking, and he made some remark which I thought was very dubious, and then he suddenly gave a very loud false sneeze, and said 'Anybody got a handkerchief?' and of course everybody's skirts immediately came up . . . well, I had to send him out of the room and apologise for him. He really was very, very naughty.

Despite Shackleton's obvious charm, however, there were those who still refused to be won over. Beardmore was one. The loan of £1,000 that Shackleton had not reimbursed had been the breaking point for the Scottish entrepreneur. Business was business, and to him Shackleton had gone beyond the pale. The repayment in August of both that loan and the £7,000 guarantee would not bring forgiveness, nor would the eventual naming of the Great Glacier the 'Beardmore'. It was a relationship that had been broken forever.

Another breach was with Edward Wilson, who had set himself firmly in Scott's corner before Shackleton went south. Following Shackleton's return to England the two met. What was said went unrecorded, but shortly thereafter Wilson wrote to Shackleton criticising his decision to go to McMurdo Sound and insisting that he clear the way for Scott's planned expedition. 'I allow that you were in a very difficult position,' Wilson acknowledged,

> But I wish to God you had done any mortal thing in the whole world rather than break the promise you had made . . . My opinion as you know was that you ought to have thrown up the whole show, that, you said was out of the question. But why in the name of fortune did you promise to do the second best thing, & then do the very worst!

Wilson obviously believed that Shackleton's promise to Scott should have outweighed all his other commitments and undertakings and promises to the dozens of individuals who had contributed to the expedition funds, were taking part in it, or were supporting it in some other way, including the Queen. It was, by almost any standard, a thoroughly unreasonable position. But it did not stop there.

'You took Scott's job practically out of his hands against his wish & knowing that he was hoping to finish it,' Wilson wrote. 'Frankly admit that you have had your turn . . . No one but you can at the present moment clear the way for Scott. *But you can*, & what's more to the point, *you should*. Play the game now by him as he has played the game by you.' Again, it was a demand so one-sided as to be laughable. Certainly Scott had the right to return to McMurdo Sound – as Shackleton had had the right – but Wilson wanted Shackleton publicly to grant Scott everything he had been so vehemently denied by the Scott–Wilson coterie two years earlier. Yet remarkably, such was his feeling for his old *Discovery* comrade, that Shackleton again wrote to Scott renouncing his claim to McMurdo. Whether it was coincidence or reward, within a week of Shackleton writing the letter, Scott met with Wilson about assuming the position as Head of Scientific Staff for Scott's expedition.

What transpired personally between Shackleton and Wilson thereafter is again uncertain, but as with Beardmore, no efforts by Shackleton were to bring forgiveness. 'As for Shackleton I feel the less said the better,' Wilson wrote to a friend in August, adding:

I am afraid that he has become a regular wrong'un . . . In fact I have broken with him completely and for good, having told him in a some-what detailed letter exactly what I thought of him and his whole business. I consider he has dragged Polar Exploration generally in the mud of his own limited and rather low down ambitions.

Wilson was not the only one of Scott's associates unhappy with Shackleton. Markham's behaviour had already been duplicitous. After disputing Shackleton's claims, he had invited the explorer to dinner with the hypocritical words, 'receive my very cordial welcome as coming from one who has watched your career with the interest of a very sincere friend.' But his *final* verdict seems to have been reached during the summer, as in early September he wrote to Darwin that 'I felt very strongly that Shackleton's observations ought to have been closely scrutinised and examined, both for lat:, and courses and dists:, before the Society was committed to them. We ought not at once to have taken him at his own valuation and that of the Daily Mail.' He then stated the bold untruth that Shackleton's Master's Certificate had been awarded without exam for his participation on *Discovery*, before trying to damn the explorer by stating he had taken no observations on the southern journey.

Today one can see these comments for the bitter, twisted misrepre-sentations of what Debenham called 'a dangerous old man'. This is even more obvious when one realises that at this time Markham petulantly crossed out or amended all favourable entries about Shackleton in his extensive personal account of the *Discovery* Expedition. The reality was that Shackleton had earned his Master's Certificate by examination long before joining that expedition. And although Marshall had been in charge of determining their position and mapping the lands through which they travelled, the observations were checked not only by the members of the Southern Party but by A.E. Reeves, the Royal Geo-graphical Society's map curator and navigational expert. Reeves re-computed the latitudes using the most up-to-date refraction tables and found that none of the results differed from those obtained by Shack-leton's party by more than a minute, and that the farthest south observation was within a few seconds. In fact, Marshall's map would be validated on Scott's trip to the Pole.

The major issue behind Markham's attack, of course, was whether the Southern Party had truly reached 88° 23'S, or had fiddled the figures to break the hundred-mile barrier. Following Reeves' report, there could be little argument about Marshall's sun-sight of 3 January, which gave a noon latitude of 87° 22'S. During the remainder of that day and the next three, the whole numbers of the sledgemeter daily totals (5, 12, 13 and 13) had added up to forty-three geographical miles, putting them at 88° 05'S. When the fractions of each day were added to the total (including more than three-quarters of a mile on 3 January), the distance was recalculated as 88° 07'S. So the key questions were: unencumbered by the sledge provisions they normally pulled, could the four fatigued men actually march sixteen – or for those dubious of the re-assessed starting figure, eighteen – geographical miles directly south in five hours, and, if so, had they done it?

Adams later recalled proceeding at a 'jog-trot' throughout the day, indicating such a distance could be covered. Marshall recorded they 'marched hard'. The firm surface would have allowed swift progress. Certainly the men were worn from weeks of sledging, but they were giving their final push for the last goal they had decided was attainable. They would prove on their way back that unyielding determination and the human spirit can lead to miraculous achievements – there is no reason to think that such results could not have been reached at this time as well.

So did they reach 88° 23'S? Different historians have arrived at different conclusions (undoubtedly for different purposes), but to a balanced observer the key factor should surely be that all four men agreed throughout their lives that they had done so. In the accepted cases of false claims, such as those by Frederick Cook, Robert E. Peary and Richard E. Byrd to have attained the North Pole, there was only one man present who had the instrumental ability or information to determine location. As the size of parties with knowledge increased, the ability to fabricate results decreased. In this case, all four men were capable of making a judgement, and they all agreed upon the result, including recording it immediately in their journals. None of these men ever gave the slightest reason why one should doubt his word, so to doubt all four would seem to be a remarkable endorsement of negative faith. This is particularly true of Marshall, whose entire nature bespoke contempt for an abhorrence of insincerity, cant or dishonesty.

Suffice it to say that all four men honestly believed that they reached a point ninety-seven miles from the Pole. Equally important, so did the British public.

                    *   *   *

The weeks following the awarding of the government grant saw a further intensification of the public's exposure to the polar regions. On 1 September, *Nimrod* reached the East India Dock, where, under the direction of Joyce, she was prepared for an exhibition. Later in the month, she was opened to the public at Temple Pier, and thousands paid to traipse through her and see sledges, tents, cooking equipment, polar clothes, stuffed seals and penguins, and a vast array of other materials, including photographs. Near the beginning of November she proceeded on tour, although the financial success in the other cities – Liverpool, Manchester and Newcastle – did not equal that in the capital. As he had in New Zealand and Australia, Shackleton donated much of this money to local charities.

Meanwhile, on 2 September public interest in the other end of the planet was reinforced when *The New York Herald* announced that Frederick Cook had reached the North Pole. Five days later, Robert E. Peary's cable from Labrador claimed *he* had attained the Pole. The geographical societies, the popular press, and even the Congress of the United States were thrown into a long, ugly debate about who had been the first to what Peary pompously and erroneously called 'the last great geographical prize'.

The very next week, on 12 September, Scott made the official announcement of his next expedition. It might have been painful for Shackleton to realise that Scott – of all people – could eclipse his record, but he must have had some satisfaction in knowing beyond doubt that his former commander would simply be following in the path he had pioneered. Some of the distress was also likely taken away when he received a command to give a second lecture to the King, this time at Balmoral on 27 September, only days before his lecture tour was to begin on the Continent. 'The King enjoys a joke very much,' he wrote to Emily with great admiration. 'He asked me a lot about Cook and Peary and Scott: he seems to know everything that is going on.'

The admiration was mutual, and early in November it was proven publicly. On 9 November, the Honours List for the King's birthday announced that Ernest Shackleton would receive a knighthood. 'It is safe to say,' the *Daily Mirror* recorded with impressive accuracy, 'that none of the honours will be more popular with the general public.' This was also true of the book that became available that same week, Shackleton and Saunders having finished it in record time. The appearance of *The Heart of the Antarctic*, which was timed to coincide with

Shackleton's British lecture tour, came on 4 November; it was quickly proclaimed by *The Manchester Guardian* as 'The best book of Polar travel which has ever been written.' Positive reviews poured in from around the world, the two-volume work having been published simultaneously not only in Britain and the United States, but in French, German, Italian, Hungarian, Finnish and Swedish editions.

A month later, on 14 December 1909, Shackleton paused in the midst of a grinding series of what would eventually mount up to at least 123 public lectures on two continents, the price he had to pay for leading his expedition. That day, at Buckingham Palace, he was knighted by King Edward VII, the two swashbuckling figures meeting for the final time. After the investiture, Shackleton presented the members of his expedition to the King, who awarded each the Polar Medal, silver for the members of the shore party, and bronze for the officers and some of the crew of *Nimrod*.

Through the pomp and glitter of the glorious days of summer, Shackleton had always been surrounded by his comrades, Brocklehurst, Armytage, Adams, Wild, Joyce, Priestley, Day and Mackintosh being the most conspicuous. By the time Shackleton's lecture circuit was under way, however, they had long since scattered to different parts of the country or Empire. When, having reunited so briefly, the men of the British Antarctic Expedition left the palace that afternoon, no such gathering among them would ever occur again.

EPILOGUE

On 16 July 1910 Scott sailed on RMS *Saxon* for Cape Town, to join his expedition ship *Terra Nova*. The crowd bidding him farewell at the platform for the boat train from Waterloo Station to Southampton included not only Scott's close associates, but Sir Ernest Shackleton. As Shackleton called for three cheers for his former commander, neither knew it was to be the final time they would see each other.

There was certainly no love lost between these two men with ambitions so similar and personalities so disparate, but each knew the role he had to play for the public. Thus, just as Scott forced himself to spout words of praise for his nemesis, Shackleton felt obliged to return the gesture. The reality was that regardless of what he said for mass consumption, Scott seems to have continued to think of Shackleton as 'a professed liar', a man who had stolen a march on his own plans by under-handed play. Shackleton, in return, likely thought Scott to be disingenuous, as proven at the Savage Club the week Shackleton returned to Britain. In an after-dinner speech that was supposed to praise the achievements of the British Antarctic Expedition, Scott urged that an Englishman be the first to the South Pole, and stated that he was willing 'to go forth in search of that object'. He then said, with a subtle twist of the knife, 'All I have to do now is to thank Mr Shackleton for so nobly showing the way.'

Coincidentally, that same day Admiral Sir Lewis Beaumont, vice-president of the RGS, wrote a letter indicating his opinion that the Society should stay out of any impending clash between the two explorers. The RGS, he felt, should encourage Scott to lead a scientific expedition without an emphasis on the Pole. 'All of this long story is to incline you to put Scott off from making what I think will be a great mistake,' Beaumont wrote to Major Darwin, 'that is, competing with

Shackleton and organizing an expedition to go over the old route merely to do that 97 miles.'

The ninety-seven miles, however, were central to Scott's agenda, and he continued planning an expedition that included just such an attempt. He also wanted to keep Shackleton out of the area he still believed was rightfully his, and therefore he wanted the interloper to clarify his intentions. Not unreasonably – having been home for only a brief period of time – Shackleton had no concrete plans. Never the less, still feeling guilty about breaking his earlier promise, and with Wilson again taking a leading role in badgering him for an answer, Shackleton wrote Scott that 'I understand you have already your expedition in preparation, and it will not interfere with any plans of mine.'

Scott had leave to use McMurdo, as well as King Edward VII Land, and that should have been enough, particularly as Darwin soon made clear *his* view: 'Every explorer should in future be at liberty to go exactly where he likes, without, at all events, any liability to an accusation of breach of faith.' But it was *not* enough. In February 1910, Shackleton informed Scott, the Royal Society and the RGS of his tentative plans, which were for

> a purely Scientific Expedition to operate along the coast of Antarctica commencing in 1911. The Easterly base is Cape Adare and the farthest west Gaussberg . . . I am particularly anxious not to clash with your Expedition, nor in any way to hinder your pecuniary activities. With this object in view I have decided not to appeal for public funds, either Government help or for donations from Societies . . . The Expedition is purely *Scientific*, and . . . I shall be very glad to co-operate with your Expedition.

Remarkably, despite Shackleton's efforts to avoid overlapping with Scott's goals and even to eschew potential contributors, Scott showed that, to him, the Antarctic was not big enough for the both of them. 'I have always wished to retreat round Cape North for a second season,' he wrote to Darwin, about just the area Shackleton had mentioned, 'and possibly to establish meteorological stations on that coast.'

But the honesty of Scott's statement was questionable because he had already rejected the chance to do exactly that. Shackleton's proposed expedition had actually been worked out by Mawson, who in January 1910 had tried to convince Scott to incorporate it in his overall scheme.

Scott, according to Mawson, 'said that he had decided that he could not include a landing party on the N. coast', although he had suggested Mawson join his expedition, promising that he would be one of the final polar party. Mawson in turn had refused, in part because he believed there to be little of scientific value in a dash to the Pole, and in part, as he wrote without elaborating, 'I did not like Dr Wilson'.

Mawson thereafter decided to lead his own expedition, and he turned for guidance to Shackleton, who was 'warmly enthusiastic when the scheme was laid before him, and planned to lead the undertaking himself.' Mawson was most generous in phrasing it this way, as in reality he was rather taken aback when Shackleton appropriated his ideas and offered Mawson the position of chief scientist. Never the less, faced with the problems of funding, the younger man 'decided to fall in with him'.

By now, however, Scott's feud with Shackleton had reached a thoroughly inconsistent point. 'I don't want any objection from him to my going there,' Scott wrote to Darwin about the area he had already rejected. 'I want it settled before I leave that I am free to go where I please without the reproach that I am trespassing on his ground.' Scott had thus dismissed any notion of being bound by the rules that he had tried so vigorously to force upon Shackleton and that had been the basis of his proprietorial argument three years previously.

It undoubtedly reinforced Shackleton's contradictory feelings for his former commander. Although he avoided saying anything negative in public, those who knew him intimately were treated to occasional glimpses of his true feelings. 'I knew there was no love lost between him and Scott,' Shackleton's nephew Geoffrey – the son of Herbert Dorman – later said. 'For when Scott's last expedition was overdue, Uncle E said one evening at dinner at our house at Sydenham that he had been approached to lead a relief expedition, and if he had any trouble with Scott he'd "put him in irons".'

Meanwhile, for a variety of reasons, Shackleton gave up the idea of leading the coastal expedition. He was, however, invaluable in helping raise funds for what became Mawson's Australasian Antarctic Expedition (1911–14), which not only provided exceptionally valuable scientific and geographical results but gave the public another story of heroism and endurance. Mawson completed an epic journey by himself after one of his two companions died in a crevasse 310 miles from base, their tent and the majority of their food going down with him. The other died on the return journey, and Mawson spent a lonely month, weak and ill, struggling back to base, to find that the ship had left only hours before and that he had to remain in the Antarctic for another year.

Meanwhile, Scott's 1910–13 expedition did not reach the area over which so much disagreeable spleen had been vented. The main base was set up at Cape Evans, between Cape Royds and Hut Point. Then the members of the Eastern Party, after being unable to reach King Edward VII Land, stopped any effort to establish quarters on the Barrier when they found Roald Amundsen ensconced at the Bay of Whales, where Shackleton had once declined to land. That party of Scott's men, which included Raymond Priestley, wintered instead at Cape Adare, before spending a second winter in perhaps the most primitive conditions in the history of Antarctic exploration.

The story of Scott's journey to the Pole and of the tragic deaths of the polar party on their return is well known. Throughout the journey south, the effort smacked of imitating Shackleton, from the transport – following his unfortunate selection of Manchurian ponies – to the route itself. Shackleton was seemingly never far from Scott's mind: he took *The Heart of the Antarctic* to Cape Evans, and he had a copy of Wild's diary records of Shackleton's progress on his southern journey. Scott's diaries are littered with references to Shackleton and comparisons of their distances and times. He finally defeated the spectre that so obviously dogged his every step on 9 January 1912, three years to the day after Shackleton's farthest south. 'We made a very steady afternoon march,' he wrote, adding condescendingly, 'This should place us . . . beyond the record of Shackleton's walk.'

It was a far different response from that of Amundsen, who a month before had passed the same latitude. He, for one, had never changed the opinion that he formed immediately after the news broke of the Southern Party's record in 1909. 'What Nansen is in the North Shackleton is in the South,' he had written to Keltie. Bursting with enthusiasm, the normally restrained Norwegian had unhesitatingly declared: 'The English nation has by the deed of Shackleton won a victory in the Antarctic exploration which never can be surpassed.'

The death of Scott in 1912 did not end the bitterness that had accompanied his relationship with Shackleton. Markham continued his small-minded campaign for the rest of his life. At the Dundee meeting of the British Association in late 1912, he read a paper in which he praised Scott for both his expeditions while virtually ignoring Shackleton. In the following discussion, Marshall defended the British Antarctic Expedition and its achievements. Such arguments had little influence on Markham, however, and his later history of Antarctic exploration, *The Lands of Silence*, showed even more disregard for the feats of Shackleton's men. Markham himself died on 30 January 1916, after his bedclothes were accidentally set alight by the candle by which he read in bed. His room was supplied with electricity, but he had stubbornly followed this practice since his days as a midshipman.

Markham was not the only one who could hold a grudge. In July 1909 Shackleton showed a measure of vindictiveness of his own in a letter about the awarding of medals by the RGS. 'I do not see that I could recommend England,' he wrote to Darwin. 'I do not think that he should be entitled to it after viewing all the points of the case . . . it would at once put him on an equality with the members of the Expedition who were satisfactory and did their work throughout.'

Remarkably, Shackleton felt differently about Evans, who, according to virtually all of the shore party, had hampered all rescue efforts. Shackleton seems to have accepted Evans' version of events for the final days before his return, because when he saw the shore party he 'tore them off a hell of a strip for not sticking around'. This caused great offence to Murray, who believed that the account in *The Heart of the Antarctic* indicated he was responsible for the failure of relief to be sent. 'You left me in charge because you trusted me, and I believe that I deserved your trust,' Murray wrote to Shackleton, requesting changes to the second edition. 'How I carried it out you have been told (though I am not sure that you believe it) . . . I was prevented from sending a relief party, with Joyce and the dogs as arranged, by Evans's point-blank refusal to allow me the use of the ship to convey them to Hut Point.' It is unknown if Murray ever received a response, and the passages were not changed.

Murray was not the only member of the expedition who felt aggrieved. Others complained about their wages, and it did not help that Shackleton was turning hundreds of pounds over to charities. All were not paid off even after the government grant. It contributed to a growing distance between members of the expedition. 'We didn't see a lot of each other, because the whole party, I think they thought they were a bit hardly treated on the money side of the business,' Adams recalled later. 'I kept calling his attention to the fact that he did owe something to those chaps who had been with him, and that his promises should be kept . . . Of course money meant nothing to him, you see; he didn't know the meaning of the word money except spending it.'

Brocklehurst also encouraged The Boss to pay his men, although Shackleton's reticence did not trouble him deeply. In fact, in 1913 Shackleton was the best man at his wedding. That showed the extremes of feeling to which Shackleton drove those around him. He was equally capable of making men mistrusting, critical or antagonistic – as in the case of Marshall – or enthusiastic, forgiving, even devoted, as were Brocklehurst and Wild.

One reason Wild remained close to Shackleton was that, after brief unsuccessful excursions in everyday life, they both always refocused their dreams on the Antarctic. Like migrating birds, they returned to the far south again and again, seemingly unable to stop the forces driving them. After trying his hand at a variety of businesses, in late 1913 Shackleton reverted to form with the announcement of a new plan. The project was named the Imperial Trans-Antarctic Expedition, and the goal was to cross the Antarctic continent from the Weddell Sea to Ross Island via the South Pole. Remarkably, the long-suffering Emily once again showed the patience of a saint, blessing his effort with the simple words, 'How could you keep an eagle tied in a back-yard?'

Even the start of the First World War could not keep Shackleton and his contingent from the Antarctic, where they headed in August 1914 with Admiralty blessing. However, his plans evaporated when both his ships, *Endurance* in the Weddell Sea and *Aurora* in the Ross Sea, were caught in the ice. The saga of his travails after *Endurance* was crushed and sank – including keeping his men alive on the ice, getting them to Elephant Island, making an open-boat journey to South Georgia, crossing the mountains of that island, and finally rescuing his men – has been the subject of many studies. Four years after his return in September 1921, he headed south again, in command of the Shackleton–Rowett Antarctic Expedition in *Quest*. It was to have no happy conclusion, however, as early in the morning of 5 January 1922 Shackleton died of heart disease. At Emily's wish he was buried at Grytviken in South Georgia. Emily outlived her husband by fourteen years, the last seven residing in a grace-and-favour apartment at Hampton Court Palace, which had been granted her by Royal Warrant in 1929.

Wild, meanwhile, became the most experienced Antarctic explorer of his time. After turning down a place on Scott's expedition, he was named leader of the Western Party of Mawson's Australasian Antarctic Expedition. He was then appointed the second-in-command of the Imperial Trans-Antarctic Expedition and was left in charge of the men on Elephant Island, keeping them together through an incredibly difficult period. After Shackleton's death, Wild took command of *Quest*, but the expedition lacked the fire provided by its departed leader and accomplished little. In 1923 Wild moved to Natal to take up cotton farming, but within several years this failed, costing him his savings. The last decade of his life saw a sad run of poor-paying jobs that forced him to stay in South Africa long after he hoped to return to England. In August 1939 he died of pneumonia in the Transvaal.

Two other of Shackleton's men also participated in the Imperial Trans-Antarctic Expedition. Marston joined *Endurance* as expedition artist and remained with Wild on Elephant Island. Upon his return to England he taught for several years before joining the Rural Industries Bureau, of which he eventually became director. He died in 1940 of coronary thrombosis, at the age of fifty-eight. Joyce selected the dogs for Mawson's expedition, but after joining the party in Hobart was dismissed shortly before it left Australia. He remained in that country until he was invited to join the Ross Sea Party – which was sent to lay depots out to the Beardmore Glacier to provide for Shackleton's crossing. He disappeared from public view after that expedition, although he did publish a book entitled *The South Polar Trail* in 1929. Like Marston, he died in 1940, being found dead in his sleeping bag in a hotel room.

Many of the other men were not, in the long run, as close to The Boss. The first to part ways were Day and Priestley, who left the fold by joining Scott's expedition. Priestley had hoped to serve on Shackleton's proposed venture in 1911, and in the interim he worked with David in Sydney on the expedition's geological results. But David recommended him to Scott, and when Priestley realised it might be his only chance to go south again, he accepted, despite it meaning, as he later reflected, 'giving up my connection with Shackleton'. Following the First World War, Priestley turned to academic administration at the University of Cambridge, where he and Frank Debenham, a fellow geologist on Scott's expedition and one of David's former students, were the primary forces in the founding of the Scott Polar Research Institute. Priestley later served as vice-chancellor of Melbourne University and then of

Birmingham University, a post he held for fifteen years, during which he was knighted. From 1955 to 1958 he was acting director of the Falkland Islands Dependencies Survey (now the British Antarctic Survey), while its director, Vivian Fuchs, led the Commonwealth Trans-Antarctic Expedition, which fulfilled Shackleton's dream of crossing the continent. Priestley's last major office was as president of the RGS (1961–63). He died in 1974 shortly before his eighty-eighth birthday.

Day's career was as low-key as Priestley's was significant. After being in charge of the motor transport on Scott's expedition and serving in the First World War, he moved to Sydney, where he continued to work as an engineer. He died in the aftermath of a street accident in 1934.

Australia was also the scene of the first death amongst *Nimrod*'s shore party. After returning to Britain, Armytage tried to obtain a job at the War Office in London, but was turned down as being too old. In January 1910 he went back to Melbourne without his wife and daughter, because, according to a local newspaper, 'He seems to have longed for something definite to do.' However, a complete lack of success drove his depression to a critical stage, which reached a climax on 12 March 1910. After writing about his intentions to a friend, Armytage went to his room at the Melbourne Club, put on his full dinner dress and several silver medals he had been awarded, and, according to reports, set his other medals for his service in Africa and the Antarctic where he could see them. He then spread the counterpane from the bed on the floor, lay carefully down on it with two pillows under his head, and shot himself in the forehead. It was an act that devastated his old companions.

'We were awfully upset here about poor old Armytage's sad death,' Priestley wrote to Brocklehurst, continuing

> He came over to Sydney to see the Prof & myself but we were up in Queensland & just missed him. We can neither of us get rid of the feeling that if we had seen him we could probably have saved him . . . I have little or no doubt that if any of us had seen him & had pointed him out some way in which he could do useful exploring even in a small way it would have made all the difference to him. He was plainly much oppressed by the idea that he was no use in the world. He was a peculiar chap, very introspective but one of the best.

In the next decade three more of Shackleton's key men died – all of them in the polar regions. In 1913 Murray and Mackay joined Vilhjalmur Stefansson's Canadian Arctic Expedition. In the autumn their ship *Karluk* was beset in the ice, and in January 1914 she was crushed and sank in the Chukchi Sea north of Siberia, leaving the men stranded on the ice. On 5 February, with the party wracked by dissension, Murray, Mackay and two others attempted to reach the mainland. They disappeared without trace.

Two years later, Æneas Mackintosh showed that the deaths of his friends and his own experiences off the coast of Ross Island had not taught him about the dangers of crossing sea ice. In 1914 he had been appointed the leader of the Ross Sea Party, with the task of laying depots to the Beardmore Glacier. They were plagued by bad luck from the start, including the expedition ship *Aurora* being blown out to sea, leaving the men without full provisions. Never the less, depots were laid as far as Mount Hope. On 8 May 1916 Mackintosh and a colleague ignored the advice of their comrades and left to cross the sea ice to their main base at Cape Evans. Soon thereafter the weather turned ugly, and, unlike in 1909, Mackintosh was not able to effect a marvellous escape. The two men disappeared, and their bodies were never found.

The other members of *Nimrod*'s shore party lived to ripe old ages (except possibly for Roberts, who simply fell out of sight after 1909, and about whom little is known). David spent years writing up the scientific results of the expedition – working closely with Priestley – and wrote much of the second volume of *The Heart of the Antarctic*, covering both the journey to the Magnetic Pole and the geological findings. With typical foresight, he had also left a message at Cape Royds to tell future explorers what the expedition had accomplished. 'The door of the porch had carried away, but the inner door was standing,' Griffith Taylor, one of Scott's geologists, later wrote of the first visit to the hut since Shackleton's party left. 'A foot of ice sealed it at the bottom, but hanging to the door was an envelope addressed in Professor David's hand, "To anyone who may visit Cape Royds." It did not enter his mind that an old student of his would be the first to see this.' Taylor was yet another of the many exceptional scholars trained by David, and it was the success of his students as well as his own research, teaching and administrative contributions that led to David eventually being called the 'father of Australian geological science'. He was knighted in 1920, and when he died in 1934, he received a state funeral. Perhaps no tribute was more succinct than that by John King Davis, who wrote: 'He had that rare gift of ennobling all he touched.'

Twenty-four years later, David's greatest student also received a state funeral. Mawson had been knighted on his return from the Australasian Antarctic Expedition, and he later became professor of geology at the University of Adelaide. In 1929–31 he led the British, Australian, New Zealand Antarctic Research Expedition (BANZARE), which served as part of the basis for Australia's eventual claim to vast areas of Antarctica. Mawson remained a key figure in Antarctic and Australian science for decades and was so esteemed that the government granted him arguably the highest of all honours: placing his image on the national currency, the $100 note.

Most closely associated with Mawson throughout his career was Davis. After showing his ability as captain on the return voyage of *Nimrod*, he served as master of *Aurora* and second-in-command of Mawson's expedition. Several years later he turned down Shackleton's offer to command *Endurance*, but he ultimately became involved with the Imperial Trans-Antarctic Expedition as master of that same *Aurora* on the relief of the Ross Sea Party. In 1920 Davis was appointed the Commonwealth Director of Navigation, a position he held for twenty-nine years, during which time he also served as second-in-command of Mawson's BANZARE and captain of its expedition ship, *Discovery*. He died in 1967 having long since established himself as perhaps the greatest of the ship captains in the history of Antarctic exploration.

Neither of Davis' immediate predecessors as master of *Nimrod* remained at sea as long as their first mate. Not long after his return from the Antarctic, Rupert England married and founded his own business on land. He returned to maritime duty during the First World War, but then retired again. He died in 1942. Frederick Evans commanded troop ships during the First World War, then left the sea after qualifying as a lawyer. He lived in Sydney for many years, specialising in maritime law until his retirement in 1950. He died in 1959.

The ship that these three men captained had an even shorter career following the expedition. After serving as a travelling exhibition, *Nimrod* was sold and began a dreary existence shipping coal. Early on the morning of 30 January 1919, under the command of a Captain Doran and with a crew of twelve, she was en route from Blyth to Calais when a gale blew her on to the Barber Sands off the Norfolk coast. Her distress signals were seen, but tugs from Yarmouth and lifeboats from

Caister could not reach her in the winter darkness and an ever-increasing snowstorm. All efforts to get her refloated were prevented by the easterly squalls, and soon, with heavy seas breaking over the top of her, the engine-room was flooded to the tops of the cylinders and the fires in the boilers were doused. One lifeboat was destroyed, but the crew gathered at the other, waiting for a safe opportunity to launch it. But it did not come.

Unable to move to quieter waters, *Nimrod* continued to be battered and pounded by the heavy seas and violent winds until her back broke and she began to disintegrate. With waves bursting over the decks, the men were unable to launch the boat, and suddenly it was swept off the ship with most of the crew. For the next six hours the mate and boatswain hung on to the keel of the capsized lifeboat before being washed ashore as dawn was breaking, the only two to survive. The rising sun revealed that the noble little hunter of the seas had finally gone to her watery grave.

Other ships carrying men who had served on *Nimrod* also went to the deep. After the British Antarctic Expedition, Alf Cheetham served as boatswain on *Terra Nova* and then third mate on the doomed *Endurance*. He returned to England in time to serve in the First World War, and he drowned after his mine-sweeper was torpedoed several weeks before the Armistice. Seaman James Paton also served in *Terra Nova*, as did Thomas McGillion. Paton then sailed in *Aurora* during the Imperial Trans-Antarctic Expedition and Davis' relief of the Ross Sea Party. He was again serving in *Aurora* when she was lost at sea in 1917 on a voyage to Iquique, Chile. Arthur Harbord was more fortunate. He was later employed by both the White Star Line and the Booth Line and participated in an expedition to find the source of the Amazon. Despite sailing on three ships that were torpedoed during the Great War, he lived until 1962, dying at the age of eighty-eight.

That same year, Sir Jameson Adams died after a long career in the Ministry of Labour, broken by service with distinction in both world wars. Adams had been invited, he said, to go south again with Scott, but declined because 'I'd done my best; you can't do your best twice.' During the Second World War, while Adams was in Aden, a German bomber hit the Army and Navy Stores where he had placed all of his belongings. A massive fire destroyed everything within, including his diaries from *Nimrod* and the southern journey.

On 26 February 1963, just a day short of fifty-four years after he had collapsed on the final stage of the southern journey, Marshall died. One of Shackleton's severest critics, Marshall had early on distanced himself from the celebrations following the expedition's return. Before 1909 was out, he had joined the British Ornithologists' Union Expedition into the unknown interior of Dutch New Guinea. There, in the midst of a jungle cut off from the outside world by a series of 'razor-backed ridges', his companions started dying. By the time he reached civilisation in 1911 he was the sole survivor, twenty-three convict labourers and the other members having died of malaria and beri-beri. Combined with his previous efforts against scurvy, this caused Marshall to maintain a life-long interest in nutrition and deficiency diseases. As a medical officer in northern Russia at the close of the First World War he successfully battled scurvy in a Russian penal settlement near the White Sea. He thereafter lived a quiet life, his last years spent on the Isle of Wight. He remained, however, a prickly character to the end, and after donating his diaries of the British Antarctic Expedition to his old school, Monkton Combe, he later demanded them back and presented them elsewhere.

The last link to the British Antarctic Expedition was Sir Philip Brocklehurst, who served in the First World War with the Life Guards, following which he spent two years in the Egyptian Army. During the Second World War he commanded a brigade of the Arab Legion. Brocklehurst continued to live at his vast Staffordshire estate of Swythamley Park, and when he died in January 1975 his funeral at Macclesfield was almost a state affair. Around that time a story developed about his amputated toe, which he had finally retrieved from a London hospital and preserved in a jar. When Swythamley Park was later cleared, the toe had disappeared. However, the tale arose that it had been left in a place of honour on a mantelpiece, and, at Brocklehurst's wake, thinking it a cocktail nibble, one of the guests swallowed it. The story was apocryphal, but one cannot doubt that it would have been roundly applauded by those rough men who sailed on *Nimrod*.

Campbell Mackellar, Brocklehurst's friend who became one of Shackleton's most avid supporters, once commented to The Boss that there were tremendous hurdles to be surmounted in one of his plans. 'There would be nothing in it,' was the reply, 'if there were not great obstacles to be overcome.' This was the essence of Shackleton: the struggle, the fight, the attainment of goals others might think unachievable. It was also the spirit of the men of the British Antarctic Expedition. Under-equipped, inexperienced, ill-fed, they attained success by sheer will, drive and determination. Few expeditions in the history of exploration accomplished more: the farthest south, the ascent of Mount Erebus, the attainment of the Magnetic Pole and the fulfilment of a diverse scientific programme.

Yet, despite those achievements, a myth has flourished that the British Antarctic Expedition was single-mindedly devoted to reaching the South Pole at the expense of all else, particularly serious scientific investigation. Like Amundsen's attainment of the Pole, so the argument goes, Shackleton's expedition made great geographical strides, but did not balance them with the nobility of science, as did Scott's efforts. This myth has perhaps been perpetuated by Shackleton's personal lack of interest in science, and his swashbuckling image. It is a regrettable assessment; it is also inaccurate.

The science of the 'Heroic Age' of Antarctic exploration was decid-edly different from that today. Significant advances tended not to be made in theory or practice, but rather a general body of knowledge about the continent and its surrounding seas was built. This became the foundation for the remarkable scientific research that has since been conducted. Perhaps the most important contribution to Antarctic science of Shackleton's expedition was the introduction of three key figures. What Mawson learned in his 'new kind of laboratory' led him to plan and carry out the most in-depth and thorough scientific expedition that had ever been launched in the far south – the Aus-tralasian Antarctic Expedition. This, his later BANZARE, and his influence over subsequent Antarctic research made him unquestionably one of the greatest scientists of the region. Similarly, Priestley returned to carry out valuable geological investigations, and thereafter, as an academic and an administrator, became a major figure promoting and guiding Antarctic research. Although David died before Antarctic science attained a prominent role, he helped guide it to its modern form. He was at one time not only the most powerful proponent of Antarctic research in Australia, but possibly in the English-speaking world. He also gave invaluable moral encouragement to Shirase's Japanese expedition, praised Amundsen's achievements when they were not popular in the Empire, and emphasised the closeness of all scientists – including Germans – at the outbreak of the First World War.

He can truly be seen as the harbinger of international scientific co-operation in the Antarctic.

As were the scientists who sailed on *Nimrod*, the science itself was hugely significant. Large quantities of data were obtained by David and Mawson on the ascent of Mount Erebus, the journey to the Magnetic Pole, and the time at Cape Royds. Concurrently, Priestley considerably extended and corrected the work done by H.T. Ferrar in the western mountains on the *Discovery* Expedition. Although there was not a geologist on the southern journey, Shackleton brought back valuable specimens, some from Mount Buckley, where Scott's party would follow his example and gather samples that they would haul back with them to their deaths. As noted by Professor G.E. Fogg in *A History of Antarctic Science*:

> The Beacon Sandstone formation was found to extend to the Beardmore Glacier and fossils of *Archaeocytha* found in erratics from that area suggested that somewhere there were sedimentary rocks of Cambrian age between the basement and the Beacon Sandstone. Outcrops of coal-bearing strata were found near the head of the glacier. The monograph by David & Priestley (1914) on the geology of southern Victoria Land remained for many years the authoritative account.

David, Priestley and Mawson also contributed to glaciology, and Mawson engaged in the first serious study of the physical structure of Antarctic ice. As on Scott's last expedition, their work was 'naturally more descriptive than quantitative or theoretical although it covered details of crystal structure as well as grosser features'. Mawson and Murray were also at the forefront of work in physical limnology. And Murray's biological investigations included not only the first significant scientific examination of freshwater lakes in the Antarctic, but oceanic studies on the way to New Zealand. Despite Murray's interests being more experimental than taxonomic, he described numerous new species of rotifers and tardigrades, and extended his reputation as a pioneer of freshwater biology.

That such an impressive amount of scientific research could be carried out on an expedition so poorly funded – and in which most of the resources were dedicated to reaching the Pole – speaks highly of the scientists whom Shackleton recruited. Their results were published in a wide variety of scholarly fora, and that the science did not receive more external credit is perhaps down to Shackleton, who made little effort to advertise those successes. As Shackleton later told Sir Hubert Wilkins:

> Don't saddle yourself with too much scientific work. I . . . was intensely interested in the scientific aspect but I soon found out that to be a leader of an expedition and a popular hero was more than enough for a man to do. You must decide whether you want to be a scientist, or a successful leader of expeditions, it is not possible to do both.

However, the scientific studies – indeed, all of the accomplishments of the expedition – were overshadowed three years later by the attainment of the Pole by Amundsen and Scott and then the deaths of Scott's polar party, which refocused attention on that expedition. Later still came the story of endurance, survival and seamanship on Shackleton's Imperial Trans-Antarctic Expedition. Then the overwhelming horror and grief of the First World War forced the formidable deeds of the expedition to disappear into the haze forming the public consciousness.

Almost a century later, in retrospect and without prejudice or cant, the achievements of the British Antarctic Expedition – geographical and scientific – are obvious and impressive. It could be noted that Shackleton and his companions did not attain their goal of reaching the South Pole. They did, however, record the greatest advance towards either Pole ever made. Moreover, by pioneering the way to the central Polar Plateau, they proved beyond doubt the continental nature of Antarctica. Opening up that perilous path was a remarkable achievement, and having the courage to follow the Great Glacier to they knew not where showed inspiration and bravery of unimaginable proportion.

Three years later, when he first saw the approaches to the Beardmore, Captain Oates gave abundant praise to his predecessors: 'saw several enormous glaciers coming down between the mountains, and some of the chasms which stopped Shackleton. And now one is here one can realise what a wonderful journey his was and the daring which prompted him to strike up the glacier instead of following the coastline.' But it was the very act of *not* reaching the South Pole, of turning about only ninety-seven geographical miles short of their goal, for which Shackleton, Wild, Marshall and Adams deserve the greatest praise. Any or all of them could have continued and perhaps reached the Pole, although they certainly would have died on the return. With luck, they would have attained a kind of immortality. But although a Victorian by upbringing and basic mentality, here Shackleton diverged from the popular worship of the hero who died for his cause, such as Havelock or Gordon. Shackleton wanted fame and fortune, but he wanted to be alive to appreciate them. More importantly, as he would show again on *Endurance*, he was driven by the duty to protect his men. 'Shackleton paid more attention to the well-being, mental and physical, of his men than Scott did,' Debenham stated. 'With Scott the object was to get there, with Shackleton to get there with all alive.'

Thus, by Debenham's way of thinking, the British Antarctic Expedition can be considered a wonder of success. Not only did Shackleton and his companions attain a phenomenal farthest south, members of the expedition also made the first ascent of Mount Erebus, reached the South Magnetic Pole, carried out an extensive scientific programme, and brought back glory to the Empire, *all with no loss of life*. Such a combination of success and safety was never surpassed in the exploration of the polar regions.

If it is by these achievements that Shackleton and his companions are assessed, it is safe to say that their positions in the pantheon of polar explorers are secure. Indeed, they were thus positively judged by the man who was himself the first to reach the South Pole. In writing of passing that farthest south, attained three years earlier with such toil, determination, faith and resolve, Roald Amundsen remembered:

We did not pass that spot without according our highest tribute of admiration to the man, who – together with his gallant companions – had planted his country's flag so infinitely nearer to the goal than any of his precursors. Sir Ernest Shackleton's name will always be written in the annals of Antarctic exploration in letters of fire.

GLOSSARY

AB: able-bodied seaman

arête: a sharp ascending mountain ridge or spur

barranca: a shallow, icy, heavily crevassed ravine

bathymetrical: relating to the measurement of the depth of large bodies of water

bergschrund: crevasse at the head or end of glacier, usually between a containing rock wall and the main body of ice

bergy bit: a large fragment of ice (usually glacier ice) up to the size of a small house; although usually free-floating, they can also be frozen into sea ice or grounded

blue ice: hard glacier ice of a variety of bluish tones; when snow-free it can be glassy-smooth and exceptionally difficult to walk on

brash ice: small, floating fragments of ice, the debris from the wreck of larger pieces, typically bordering tracts of pack-ice

calved, calving: the breaking off of an iceberg from a glacier or of smaller pieces of ice from a parent iceberg

feldspar: any of a group of abundant rock-forming minerals occurring in igneous, sedimentary and metamorphic rocks and consisting of silicates of aluminium with potassium, sodium and calcium

finnesko: fur boots worn by Laplanders. They were made from reindeer skin, worn with the fur outside, and, as they were designed for walking through soft snow, had no hard sole. The interiors were lined with sennegrass.

growler: a piece of iceberg or other ice smaller than a bergy bit, almost submerged beneath the water's surface and therefore dangerous to ships

heliograph: an instrument for sending Morse code messages by reflecting light

hoosh: a thick, soup-like concoction made by mixing pemmican with water, and adding hard biscuit. For flavouring, hoosh could contain bacon, cheese, pea flour, sugar, or oatmeal

hummocky ice: broken, irregular ice forced by pressure into rough mounds

hypsometer: An instrument using atmospheric pressure to determine land elevations, by measuring the temperature at which distilled water boils

Maujee ration: a compressed feed for Shackleton's ponies consisting of dried beef, carrots, milk, currants and sugar

man-haul(ing): a human pulling by walking while wearing a harness roped or attached to the object being towed (usually a sledge).

moraine: an accumulation of boulders, stones, or other debris carried and deposited by a glacier

névé: the compacted snow that is in a stage of transition between soft, loose snow and glacier ice

nunatak: an island-like outcrop of rock projecting through a sheet of enveloping land ice

pannikin: a small bowl or mug

parasitic cone: a subsidiary cone of a volcano

pemmican: a concentrated mixture of dried meat and fat or lard made into cakes or canned for use at base or on sledging trips. Although originally prepared by the Cree Indians, it was then adopted by French voyageurs and British traders in North America and later became the main sledging ration for the Royal Navy's polar expeditions.

plasmon: a soluble milk protein added as a supplement to polar sledging rations, notably cocoa and sledging biscuits; it was a trade name of the Plasmon Manufacturing Company

Plimsoll line: a line or set of lines on the hull of a ship that indicate the depth to which it may be legally loaded under specified conditions

rotifer: any of various minute, multi-cellular aquatic organisms of the phylum Rotifera, having at the anterior end a wheel-like ring of cilia

sastrugi: wind-blown ridges in snow

screwed ice: sea ice ground together under pressure as one floe pushes against another, and heaped in piles as a result

sennegrass: the sedge *Carex vesicaria* from Scandinavia, which when dried was used in finnesko to keep the feet warm. Moisture absorbed by the fibres could be shaken out when frozen and the fibres used again.

seracs: sharp, irregular ridges or pinnacles of ice that appear on the surface of a glacier where it rides over an unusually rough or inclined bottom. A field of such pinnacles, jammed together in broken confusion, is called serac ice.

skua: a large, predatory bird of the genus *Catharacta*. In the Antarctic, it is one of the primary predators of penguin chicks

sledgemeter: a wheel hooked to a sledge that measures the distance travelled

snow bridge: an arch of snow spanning a crevasse or a stream; frequently highly unstable and subject to collapse

tardigrade: any of various slow-moving microscopic invertebrates of the phylum Tardigrada, related to the arthropods and living in water or damp moss

trace: a rope or strap harness by which men or sledge dogs are connected to a sledge

yard: a long, tapering spar slung to a mast to support and spread the head of a sail

NOTES

The following abbreviations have been used in the notes:

ÆM   Æneas Mackintosh
BAE   British Antarctic Expedition (1907–09)
BNAE   British National Antarctic Expedition (1901–04)
DM   Douglas Mawson
EAW   Edward Wilson
EHS   Ernest Shackleton
EmS   Emily Shackleton
ESM   Eric Marshall
FW   Frank Wild
PLB   Philip Brocklehurst
REP   Raymond Priestley
RFS   Robert Falcon Scott
SPRI   Scott Polar Research Institute
TWED   Edgeworth David

Preface

Page

xii 'A short': Cecily Shackleton, interview with James Fisher, 1 July 1955; SPRI MS 1581/3/2/1

1 A Race for Life

Page

5 'although a trifle': ÆM, letter to EmS, 22 March 1908; SPRI MS 1537/2/17/1
7 'decidedly angry': RFS, *The Voyage of the 'Discovery'*, vol. 2: 56
7 'suspicious looking': EAW, journal of BNAE, 24 December 1902; SPRI MS 232/2
7 'Got his': EHS, diary of BNAE, 26 December 1902; SPRI MS 1537/3/4/2
8 'What we': EAW, journal of BNAE, 1 January 1903; SPRI MS 232/2

8 'Did march': EHS, diary of BNAE, 7 January 1903; SPRI MS 1537/3/4/2

8 'I suppose': RFS, *Voyage*, vol. 2: 90–91

9 'Wilson and I': RFS, *Voyage*, vol. 2: 95

9 'Tennyson's Ulysses': EHS, diary of BNAE, 11 January 1903; SPRI MS 1537/3/4/2

9 '. . . that which': Alfred Tennyson, 'Ulysses', in *Poems*

9 'The food bag': RFS, *Voyage*, vol. 2: 99

10 'of no small': EAW, journal of BNAE, 14 January 1903; SPRI MS 232/2

11 'utterly useless': EAW, journal of BNAE, 14 January 1903; SPRI MS 232/2

11 'Am much': EHS, diary of BNAE, 17 January 1903; SPRI MS 1537/3/4/2

11 'splendid day': EHS, diary of BNAE, 21 January 1903; SPRI MS 1537/3/4/2

12 'having a cruel': RFS, *Voyage*, vol. 2: 114

12 'had it out': George Seaver, *Edward Wilson of the Antarctic*: 114

12 'home truths': George Seaver, *Edward Wilson*: 114

12 'the least': EAW, journal of BNAE, 26 January 1903; SPRI MS 232/2

12 'the cold': EAW, journal of BNAE, 27 January 1903; SPRI MS 232/2

13 'chock a block': EAW, journal of BNAE, 29 January 1903; SPRI MS 232/2

13 'His breathing': RFS, *Voyage*, vol. 2: 120

14 'our invalid': RFS, *Voyage*, vol. 2: 122

14 'They appeared': Louis Bernacchi, journals of BNAE, 3 February 1903; SPRI MS 353/3/3

14 'I turned': EHS, diary of BNAE, 3 February 1903; SPRI MS 1537/3/5

2 A Product of Empire

Page

15 'I contend': Cecil Rhodes, quoted in J.G. Lockhart and C.M. Woodhouse, *Rhodes*: 68

15 'superior race': David Livingstone, quoted in J.P.R. Wallis, *The Zambesi Expedition of David Livingstone*, vol. 2: 416

16 'In the first': Joseph Chamberlain, quoted in Jeffrey Richards, *Visions of Yesterday*: 11

16 'the idea': John Morley, 'The Liberal programme': 364

17 'a great country': Benjamin Disraeli, quoted in W.F. Monypenny and G.E. Buckle, *The Life of Benjamin Disraeli*, vol. 2: 536

18 'the people': Beatrice and Sidney Webb, letter to Graham Wallas, 29 July 1892; quoted in L.P. Curtis, *Anglo-Saxons and Celts*: 63

18 'unmixed congratulation': Lord Salisbury, quoted in Andrew Roberts, *Salisbury*: 53

18 'wild, reckless': Benjamin Disraeli, quoted in J. Morris, *Heaven's Command*: 157

20 'a gravedigger': quoted in H.R. Mill, *The Life of Ernest Shackleton*: 21

20 'He loved': Eleanor Shackleton, letter to Margery Fisher, 22 January 1956; SPRI MS 1456/81

20 'This was': Kathleen Shackleton, letter to James Fisher, 27 November 1955; SPRI MS 1456/83

20 'Good morning': Kathleen Shackleton, letter to James Fisher, 27 November 1955; SPRI MS 1456/83

21 'He found': Frank Hurley, letter to Margery Fisher, 26 April 1956; SPRI MS 1456/78

21 'Lord Kitchener': Augustine Birrell, *Things Past Redress*: 218

22 'Upon entering': Lord Wolseley, *The Story of a Soldier's Life*, vol. 1: 272
22 'the very model': W.S. Gilbert, 'The Pirates of Penzance' or 'The Slave of Duty', in *The Savay Operas*: 120
24 'Shackleton was': J.G. Dunlop, letter to Margery Fisher, 1 May 1959; SPRI MS 1456/99
25 'adored him': Eleanor Shackleton, letter to Margery Fisher, 22 January 1956; SPRI MS 1456/81
25 'I read': A.B. Cooper, 'How I Began': 43
25 'from what': Owen T. Burne, letter to H.R. Mill, 10 May 1922; SPRI MS 100/17
26 'Dr Jim': Lord Attlee, *Empire into Commonwealth*: 5–6
26 'I was more': A.B. Cooper, 'How I Began': 43
27 'He had no': Eleanor Shackleton, letter to Margery Fisher, 22 January 1956; SPRI MS 1456/81
27 'He suddenly': Nicetas Petrides, letter to *The Daily Telegraph*, 3 April 1923; SPRI MS 100/91/1
28 'care tuppence': Mrs J.Q. Rowett, interview with James Fisher, 29 November 1955; SPRI MS 1456/75
28 'I never learned': A.B. Cooper, 'How I Began': 42
28 'My father': A.B. Cooper, 'How I Began': 42

3 Life at Sea, Love on Land

Page

29 'When he': T. Peers, interview with James Fisher, 19 May 1957; SPRI MS 1456/74
29 'taught me': A.B. Cooper, 'How I Began': 42–43
30 'I can tell': EHS, letter to Nicetas Petrides, 7 January 1892; SPRI MS 100/91/2
30 'It was one': A.B. Cooper, 'How I Began': 42
30 'he is the': quoted in H.R. Mill, *Life*: 33
31 'but the first': EHS, letter to 'dearest Father, Mother, Grandmother, Brother and Sisters', 1890; quoted in H.R. Mill, *Life*: 31
31 'making': EHS, letter to Nicetas Petrides, 7 January 1892; SPRI MS 100/91/2
32 'I used to': Kathleen Shackleton, interview with James Fisher, 27 November 1955; SPRI MS 1581/3/4
33 'In the Empire': George Curzon, quoted in J. Morris, *Pax Britannica*: 122
33 'a whirlwind': T. Peers, interview with James Fisher, 19 May 1957; SPRI MS 1456/74
33 'We were loaded': T. Peers, interview with James Fisher, 19 May 1957; SPRI MS 1456/74
35 'I cannot': *The Times, The Daily Telegraph, The Evening News and Post*, 11 July 1894
35 'That's a rum': Owen T. Burne, letter to H.R. Mill, 10 May 1922; SPRI MS 100/17
36 'I dreamt': A.B. Cooper, 'How I Began': 44
37 'Ernest had': Kathleen Shackleton, letter to James Fisher, 27 November 1955; SPRI MS 1456/83
38 'I greatly': A.B. Cooper, 'How I Began': 43
38 'a marked': J. Dunsmore, 'Shackleton of the SS "Flintshire"': 213
39 'Well, Shacky': J. Dunsmore, 'Shackleton of the SS "Flintshire"': 213
39 'He told me': EmS, letter to H.R. Mill, 28 June 1922; SPRI MS 100/104/29

4 War or an Unknown Place?

Page

41 'Wednesday, Thursday': Henry Rawlinson, diary, 19 September 1899; Sir Anthony Rawlinson

42 'to avoid': Joseph Chamberlain, letter to Lord Lansdowne, 5 October 1899; quoted in Thomas Pakenham, *The Boer War*: 93

42 'bluff up': Joseph Chamberlain, letter to Lord Lansdowne, 5 October 1899; quoted in Thomas Pakenham, *The Boer War*: 93

42 'with the aid': Henry Rawlinson, diary, 19 September 1899; Sir Anthony Rawlinson

42 'less interesting': Henry Rawlinson, diary, 19 September 1899; Sir Anthony Rawlinson

43 'The voyage': Henry Rawlinson, diary; Sir Anthony Rawlinson

43 'He at once': J.A. Hussey, letter to H.R. Mill, 18 June 1922; SPRI MS 100/49/1–5

43 'I saw': EmS, letter to H.R. Mill, 25 May 1922; SPRI MS 100/104/20

44 'What are you': L.D.A. Hussey, interview with James Fisher, 12 November 1955; SPRI MS 1581/3/1

44 'The Boers': Henry Rawlinson, diary, 7–11 October 1899; Sir Anthony Rawlinson

45 'Our days': Bertha Synge, letter to Alfred Milner, 3 November 1899; quoted in C. Headlam, *The Milner Papers*: 44

46 'An unexpected': W.W.L. McLean and E.H. Shackleton, *O.H.M.S.*

47 'It is good': F.D. Baillie, *Mafeking: A Diary of the Siege*: 270

48 'the nearest': John Greenleaf Whittier, quoted in A.E. Keeling, *General Gordon: Hero and Saint*: 9

49 'An irresistible': Jules Ferry, quoted in H. Brunschwig, *French Colonialism Myths and Realities*: 82

49 'it is perhaps': Charles E. Callwell, *Small Wars: Their Principles and Practice*: 44

50 'Beyond the geographical': Anthony Fiala, *Fighting the Polar Ice*: 4

50 'I am doomed': Joseph Thomson, letter to J.B. Thomson, 1895; quoted in Alan Moorehead, *The White Nile*: 121

51 'All this': John Morley, quoted in J. Morris, *Pax Britannica*: 102

51 'he was attracted': J.A. Hussey, letter to H.R. Mill, 27 July 1922; SPRI MS 100/49/1–5

52 'he was going': Cecily Shackleton, interview with James Fisher, 1 July 1955; SPRI MS 1581/3/2/1

5 The Making of the British National Antarctic Expedition

Page

55 'the exploration': J. Scott Keltie and H.R. Mill, *Report of the Sixth International Geographical Congress*: 780

55 'a school': C.R. Markham, *The Lands of Silence*: 174

58 'has had no': 'The National Antarctic Expedition', *Nature*, 64 (16):103

58 'These mud': C.R. Markham, letter to J. Scott Keltie, 24 July 1899; quoted in Roland Huntford, *Shackleton*: 37

58 'quite exhausted': C.R. Markham, *Antarctic Obsession*: 142

58 'would turn': C.R. Markham, *Antarctic Obsession*: 142

59 'Scott said': Albert Armitage, Memo on Sir E.H. Shackleton to H.R. Mill, 24 May 1922; SPRI MS 367/1

60 'I thought': Albert Armitage, Memo on Sir E.H. Shackleton to H.R. Mill, 24 May 1922; SPRI MS 367/1
60 'Scott was': C.R. Markham, *Antarctic Obsession*: 15
61 'Shackleton had': C.R. Markham, *Antarctic Obsession*: 32
61 'We were armed': Kathleen Shackleton, letter to James Fisher, 27 November 1955; SPRI MS 1456/83
62 'As for me': EHS, letter to Charles Dorman, 3 August 1901; SPRI MS 1537/2/5/3

6 The Great White South

Page
63 'We set': EHS, diary aboard *Discovery*, 16 August 1901; Mitchell Library, State Library of New South Wales ML ref B 1456: CY Reel 1047; Mrs Anne M. Fright
63 'poo poohed': Charles Royds, diary of BNAE, 23 August 1901; Sir Richard Eyre
63 'Shackleton went': Charles Royds, diary of BNAE, 23 August 1901; Sir Richard Eyre
63 'soaking': EAW, journal of BNAE, 23 August 1901; SPRI MS 232/1
64 'I see wide': EHS, diary aboard *Discovery*, 25 August 1901; Mitchell Library, State Library of New South Wales ML ref B 1456: CY Reel 1047; Mrs Anne M. Fright
64 'found the minute': H.R. Mill, *The Life of Sir Ernest Shackleton*: 61
64 'To Shackleton': H.R. Mill, *Life*: 57
65 'has quite taken': EAW, journal of BNAE, 19 August 1901; SPRI MS 232/1
65 'There was always': J.W. Dell, interview with James Fisher, 10 October 1955; SPRI MS 1456/66
66 'There was the Navy': J.W. Dell, interview with James Fisher, 10 October 1955; SPRI MS 1456/66
66 'absolutely Navy': J.W. Dell, interview with James Fisher, 10 October 1955; SPRI MS 1456/66
66 'a grand shipmate': Michael Barne, interview with James Fisher, 16 October 1955; SPRI MS 1456/64
66 'he was rather': J.W. Dell, interview with James Fisher, 10 October 1955; SPRI MS 1456/66
67 'although Shackleton': Louis Bernacchi, *Saga of the 'Discovery'*: 218
67 'object was': William Edward Parry, *Journal of a Voyage for the Discovery of a North–West Passage*: 125
68 'There were literally': EAW, journal of BNAE, 8 January 1902; SPRI MS 232/1
68 'It is a unique': EHS, diary of BNAE, 1 February 1902; SPRI MS 1537/3/4/1
68 'skiing did': RFS, *Voyage*, vol. 1: 195
68 'the first': RFS, *Voyage*, vol. 1: 147
68 'perfect madness': EAW, journal of BNAE, 4 February 1902; SPRI MS 232/1
68 'be of little': RFS, diaries of BNAE, 14 February 1902; SPRI MS 352/1/2
69 'Simply done': EAW, journal of BNAE, 19 February 1902; SPRI MS 232/1
69 'They dressed': EAW, journal of BNAE, 19 February 1902; SPRI MS 232/1
70 'As far south': EAW, journal of BNAE, 20 February 1902; SPRI MS 232/1
70 'we slept': EAW, journal of BNAE, 22 February 1902; SPRI MS 232/1
70 'full of talk': Charles Royds, diary of BNAE, 22 February 1902; Sir Richard Eyre
70 'immediately started': Reginald Skelton, journals of BNAE, 22 February 1902; SPRI MS 342/1/2
71 'There were over': FW, Article notes; SPRI MS 944/3

71 'Apart from': FW, Memoirs: 15–16; Mitchell Library, State Library of New South Wales ML MSS 2198/1: CY Reel 15; Mrs Anne M. Fright

71 'It was certainly': C.H. Hare, letter to Margery Fisher, 30 December 1955; SPRI MS 1456/104

72 'something like': Albert Armitage, *Two Years in the Antarctic*

72 'aptitude for': Louis Bernacchi, *Saga*: 218

72 'the sun': EHS, diary of BNAE, 23 April 1902; SPRI MS 1537/3/4/1

72 'is still my': EAW, letter to O. Wilson; quoted in George Seaver, *Edward Wilson*: 104

73 'My surprise': EAW, journal of BNAE, 12 June 1902; SPRI MS 232/1

73 'he need hardly': EAW, journal of BNAE, 12 June 1902; SPRI MS 232/1

73 'I feel more': EAW, letter to O. Wilson; quoted in George Seaver, *Edward Wilson*: 106

73 'is to get': EAW, journal of BNAE, 12 June 1902; SPRI MS 232/1

7 The Southern Journey

Page

75 'A calm': EAW, journal of BNAE, 22 August 1902; SPRI MS 232/2

76 'I was under': Edgar Evans, quoted in Margery Fisher and James Fisher, *Shackleton*: 37

76 'competitions': Louis Bernacchi, *Saga of the 'Discovery'*: 63

77 'Scoffed unmercifully': RFS, *The Voyage of the 'Discovery'*, vol 1: 390

77 'While they': Reginald Skelton, journals of BNAE, 10 September 1902; SPRI MS 342/1/5

78 'The benefit': Reginald Koettlitz, 'The British Antarctic Expedition': 342–43

80 'Several times': Albert Armitage, Memo on Sir E.H. Shackleton to H.R. Mill, 24 May 1922; SPRI MS 367/1

81 'Beloved': EHS, letter to Emily Dorman, 1 November 1902; SPRI MS 1537/2/4/5

81 'Only once': EAW, letter to O. Wilson, quoted in George Seaver, *Edward Wilson*: 104–05

82 'three polar knights': Louis Bernacchi, journals of BNAE, 2 November 1902; SPRI MS 353/3

82 'most persistent': EAW, journal of BNAE, 6 November 1902; SPRI MS 232/2

83 'after a few': RFS, *Voyage*, Vol. 2: 24

83 'losing all': RFS, *Voyage*, Vol. 2: 24

83 'steadily melting': RFS, diaries of BNAE, 21 November 1902; SPRI MS 1464/3

84 'The common': Martin Conway, *With Ski and Sledge over Arctic Glaciers*: 194, 90

84 'Having taken': Charles Royds, diary of BNAE, 12 March 1902; Sir Richard Eyre

85 'What a little': EHS, diary of BNAE, 20 November 1902; SPRI MS 1537/3/4/2

85 'at his best': H.R. Mill, *An Autobiography*: 151

86 'he permitted': Louis Bernacchi, *Saga*: 219

86 'Come here': Albert Armitage, Memo on Sir E.H. Shackleton to H.R. Mill, 24 May 1922; SPRI MS 367/1

86 'I fancy': Frank Debenham, letter to James Fisher, 18 October 1956; SPRI MS 1456/97

87 'A beautiful': EHS, diary of BNAE, 1 March 1903; SPRI MS 1537/3/4/2

88 'he was very': EAW, journal of BNAE, 4 –24 February 1903; SPRI MS 232/2

88 'He was in great': Albert Armitage, Memo on Sir E.H. Shackleton to H.R. Mill, 24 May 1922; SPRI MS 367/1

88 'Shackleton came': C.R. Ford, letter to Margery Fisher, 12 January 1956; SPRI
    MS 1456/78
88 'Ah me': EHS, diary of BNAE, 2 March 1903; SPRI MS 1537/3/4/2
89 'and with songs': EHS, diary of BNAE, 2 March 1903; SPRI MS 1537/3/4/2

8 A Square Peg and a Round Hole

Page
91 'What a homecoming': Kathleen Shackleton, letter to James Fisher, 27 November
    1955; SPRI MS 1456/83
92 'I am quite': C.R. Markham, letter to EHS, 4 June 1903; SPRI MS 1537/2/5/8
94 'You may': *Pearson's Weekly*, 8 April 1909: 818
95 'we shall': EHS, letter to Emily Dorman, 10 February 1904; SPRI MS 1537/2/10/5
95 'I am missing': EHS, letter to Emily Dorman, 29 March 1904; SPRI MS 1537/2/
    10/9
96 'With all': Cecily Shackleton, interview with James Fisher, 1 July 1955; SPRI MS
    1581/3/2/1
96 'With life': EHS, letter to H.R. Mill, 22 November 1904; SPRI MS 100/106/8
97 'I went to': EHS, letter to EmS, 15 October 1905; SPRI MS 1537/2/9/2
97 'noted naval': *The Courier and Argus*, 16 November 1904
97 'Good fists': H.R. Mill, *Life*: 91
99 'not excluding': Henry Lucy, *Memories of Eight Parliaments*: 114
100 'I'll tell': *The Courier and Argus*, 12 January 1906
100 'As an Irishman': *The Courier and Argus*, 9 January 1906
100 'the lieutenant's': *The Courier and Argus*, 8 January 1906
101 'Come on our': H.R. Mill, *Life*: 95
101 'I got all': H.R. Mill, *Life*: 97
102 'He tells me': EHS, letter to EmS, April 1905; SPRI MS 1537/2/9/4
102 'It's one of': Cecily Shackleton, interview with James Fisher, 20 August 1955;
    SPRI MS 1581/3/2/2
102 'A fine fellow': A.B. Macduff, interview with James Fisher, 15 June 1956; SPRI
    MS 1456/72
103 'full of plans': C.R. Markham, quoted in Roland Huntford, *Shackleton*: 121
103 'I am quite': EHS, *Plan for an Antarctic Expedition*: SPRI MS 1456/13
103 'Ammundsen is': EHS, *Plan for an Antarctic Expedition*; SPRI MS 1456/13
104 'put a black': EHS, Letter to H.R. Mill, 4 February 1907; SPRI MS 100/106/10
104 'No you': Jameson Adams, interview with James Fisher, 5 October 1955; SPRI
    MS 1456/63
104 'went and called': Jameson Adams, interview with James Fisher, 5 October 1955;
    SPRI MS 1456/63
104 'I could see': A.B. Macduff, interview with James Fisher, 15 June 1956; SPRI MS
    1456/72

9 A Soul Whipped on by the Wanderfire

Page
105 'I see nothing': EHS, letter to H.R. Mill, 26 December 1906; SPRI MS 100/106/9
106 'He left': A.B. Macduff, interview with James Fisher, 15 June 1956; SPRI MS
    1456/72

106 'the first profits': Letter shown by A.B. Macduff to James Fisher, 15 June 1956; SPRI MS 1456/72
107 'You can imagine': EHS, letter to EmS, 12 February 1907; SPRI MS 1537/2/12/15
107 'She wasn't': Cecily Shackleton, interview with James Fisher, 20 August 1995; SPRI MS 1581/3/2/2
107 'I never': EmS, letter to H.R. Mill, 27 March 1922; SPRI MS 100/104/4
108 'It is held': *The Times*, 12 February 1907
109 'I am in': EAW, letter to EHS, 14 February 1907; SPRI MS 1537/2/14/1
109 'the country before': EHS, letter to EAW, 14 February 1907; quoted in George Seaver, *Edward Wilson*: 174
109 'I must refuse': EAW, letter to EHS, 15 February 1907; SPRI MS 1537/2/14/3
110 'I wish you': George Mulock, letter to EHS, 19 February 1907; SPRI MS 1537/2/14/10
110 'Oh! Mulock': EHS, letter to RFS, 27 February 1907; SPRI MS 1456/24
110 'I certainly': C.R. Markham, letter to EHS, 26 February 1907; SPRI MS 1537/2/14/14
110 'a horrid': RFS, letter to EHS, 18 February 1907; SPRI MS 1537/2/14/8
110 'I support': RFS, letter to EHS, 18 February 1907; SPRI MS 1537/2/14/9
110 '[I]t must be': RFS, letter to EHS, 18 February 1907; SPRI MS 1537/2/14/9
111 'Shackle': EAW, journal of BNAE, 21 January 1903; SPRI MS 232/2
111 'Our invalid': RFS, *Voyage*, vol 2: 121
111 'He has been': EAW, journal of BNAE, 30 January 1903; SPRI MS 232/2
112 'very earnest': EHS, letter to RFS, 28 February 1907; SPRI MS 25
112 'I am very': C.R. Markham, letter to EHS, 26 February 1907; SPRI MS 1537/2/14/14
112 'I feel very': C.R. Markham, letter to RFS, 6 March 1907; SPRI MS 10
113 'I don't want': Kathleen Shackleton, assessment for James Fisher; SPRI MS 1456/83
113 'I am representing': EHS, letter to EmS, 12 February 1907; SPRI MS 1537/2/12/15
113 'Don't go': Jean-Baptiste Marchand, letter to P. Bordarie, March 1898; quoted in J. Delebecque, *Vie du Général Marchand*: 113
113 'Now Shackles': EAW, letter to EHS, 28 February 1907; SPRI MS 1537/2/14/15
114 'Will meet': EHS, cable to RFS, 4 March 1907; SPRI MS 25
114 'what limits': EAW, letter to EHS, 8 March 1907; SPRI MS 1537/2/15/8
114 'I do not': EHS, letter to EAW, 11 March 1907; SPRI MS 1537/2/15/10
115 'I have been': EHS, letter to RFS, 23 March 1907; SPRI MS 1537/2/15/16
115 'I am leaving': EHS, letter to RFS, 17 May, 1907; SPRI MS 1537/2/15/21

10 *Nimrod*

Page
118 'the most eminent': *The Pall Mall Gazette*, 24 August 1896
119 'I raised': Fridtjof Nansen, *Farthest North*, vol. 2: 461–62
119 'Aren't you': Fridtjof Nansen, *Farthest North*, vol. 2: 462
119 'fell in love': Frederick Jackson, *A Thousand Days in the Arctic*, vol. 1: 3
120 'thoroughly satisfied': Frederick Jackson, *Thousand*, vol 1: 276
120 'I wish we': EHS, 'Life in the Antarctic': 313
122 'Designed to': 'By Motor Car to the South Pole', *The Sphere*, 13 July 1907
122 'the first': Genesis 10: 8–10

123 'I am going': EHS, letter to Elspeth Beardmore, 13 May 1907; National Maritime Museum Greenwich IVR/8

123 'at that particular': John King Davis, *High Latitude*: 59

123 'a young man': John King Davis, *High Latitude*: 59

125 'My experience': John King Davis, *High Latitude*: 60

126 'recompense me': Ernest Joyce, letter to Charles Royds, 7 April 1930; SPRI MS 641/14

126 'lent to British': Leif Mills, *Frank Wild*: 44

127 'I was just': J. Murray and G.E. Marston, *Antarctic Days*: xvii

128 'Take up': EHS, letter to PLB, n.d., Johnny Van Haeften, London

11 Underway at Last

Page

130 'That's my ship': Admiral Sir John Fisher, quoted in John King Davis, *High Latitude*: 65

130 'When Captain': *Daily Mail*, 5 August 1907

130 'May this Union': John King Davis, *High Latitude*: 65

131 'the dash': Henry Rawlinson, letter to General Lord Kitchener, 19 December 1899; Sir Anthony Rawlinson

132 'Shackleton sat': John King Davis, *High Latitude*: 66–67

132 'we formed': REP, Prelude to Antarctic Adventure; SPRI MS 1097/20/1: 6

133 'a permanent': Jameson Adams, interview with James Fisher, 5 October 1955; SPRI MS 1456/63

133 'Will you come': Jameson Adams, interview with James Fisher, 5 October 1955; SPRI MS 1456/63

134 'had great intuition': Jameson Adams, interview with James Fisher, 5 October 1955; SPRI MS 1456/63

134 'refused with': REP, Prelude to Antarctic Adventure; SPRI MS 1097/20/1: 1–2

134 'I was not': REP, Prelude to Antarctic Adventure; SPRI MS 1097/20/1: 3

134 'Would you': REP, Prelude to Antarctic Adventure; SPRI MS 1097/20/1: 1–2

134 'I was not bothered': REP, Prelude to the Antarctic Adventure; SPRI MS 1097/20/1: 3

135 'the frame': REP, Prelude to Antarctic Adventure; SPRI MS 1097/20/1: 6

135 'You simply': Helen Shackleton, letter to George Marston, 4 August 1907; SPRI MS 1547/2

135 'They were all': Paula Gow, interview with James Fisher, 1 April 1957; SPRI MS 1456/69

136 'not least from': REP, Prelude to Antarctic adventure; SPRI MS 1097/20/1: 6

136 'was the only': PLB, interview with James Fisher, 16 December 1955; SPRI MS 1456/64

137 'I have already': EHS, letter to EmS, August 1907; SPRI MS 1537/2/12

137 'the opinion': C.D. Mackellar, letter to James Fisher; SPRI MS 1456/83

137 'Your dear': EHS, letter to EmS, 31 October 1907; SPRI MS 1537/2/13/6

138 'It seems years': EHS, letter to EmS, 16 November 1907; SPRI MS 1581/1/2

138 'was glad': EHS, letter to EmS, 9 November 1907; SPRI MS 1537/2/13/7

139 'As a lecturer': quoted in M.E. David, *Professor David*: 52

139 'His heart': J.W. Dell, interview with James Fisher, 10 October 1955; SPRI MS 1456/66

140 'In view of': TWED, letter to Alfred Deakin, Prime Minister of Australia, 10

December 1907; printed by Government Order on 13 December 1907 as 1907 (Second Session) The Parliament of the Commonwealth of Australia, Code No. 140-F 15964

140 'If Professor': quoted in M.E. David, *Professor David*: 118

140 'My idea': DM, letter to Margery Fisher, 18 August 1956; The Mawson Collection MS 48DM

140 'the possible': TWED, Preliminary notes for meeting with Shackleton, December 1907; SPRI MS 1408/1

12 A Promise Broken

Page

144 'In getting': *The Daily Telegraph* (Sydney), 23 March 1908

145 'I have never': Arthur Harbord, diary of BAE, 8 January 1909; Alister Harbord

146 'a place that': REP, diaries of BAE, 1–8 January 1908; SPRI MS 298/1/1

146 'It is not': REP, diaries of BAE, 1–8 January 1908; SPRI MS 298/1/1

147 'They have not': ÆM, diary of BAE, 7 January 1908; Mrs G.E. Dowler

147 'Always wet': ESM, diary of BAE, 8 January 1908; SPRI MS 1456/8

147 'blowing a living': Sidney Riches, diary of BAE, 9 January 1908; SPRI MS 1611

147 'was the worst': J.G. Rutherford, diary of voyage of *Koonya*, 9 January 1908; MS 354, J.G. Rutherford papers, Item 1 Log 'On Board SS Koonya, during her towing of SY Nimrod from Lyttelton to the Antarctic Ice Jan 1908' ca 1 22 January 1908. Antarctic Manuscripts Collection, Canterbury Museum, Christchurch

147 'was catapulted': PLB, diary of BAE, 9 January 1908; Neil Silverman

148 'Not more than': ESM, diary of BAE, 9 January 1908; SPRI MS 1456/8

148 'I felt in': Archdeacon David, letter to Caroline David, quoted in M.E. David, *Professor David*: 124

148 'the great scientific': TWED, letter to Senate of Sydney University, February 1908; quoted in M.E. David, *Professor David*: 124

149 'charm a bird': EHS, letter to EmS, 22 January 1908; SPRI MS 1581/1/3

149 'Had a short': ESM, diary of BAE, 11 January 1908; SPRI MS 1456/8

149 'Mawson is': ESM, diary of BAE, 9 January 1908; SPRI MS 1456/8

149 'Prof. David': REP, diaries of BAE, 1–8 January 1908; SPRI MS 298/1/1

149 'One rumour': REP, diaries of BAE, 11 January 1908; SPRI MS 298/1/1

150 'Mere words': *The Daily Telegraph* (Sydney), 25 March 1908

150 'where we are': EHS, letter to EmS, 14 January 1908; SPRI 1537/2/21/1

151 'bad news': REP, diaries of BAE, 17 January 1908; SPRI MS 298/1/1

152 'undulating': REP, diaries of BAE, 24 January 1908; SPRI MS 298/1/1

152 'that under no': EHS, *The Heart of the Antarctic*, vol. 1: 76

153 'the success': ESM, diary of BAE, 24 January 1908; SPRI MS 1456/8

153 'was dictated': Arthur Harbord, interview with James Fisher, 9 June 1956; SPRI MS 1456/70

153 'at any rate': ESM, diary of BAE, 25 January 1908; SPRI MS 1456/8

154 'Shackleton's': ESM, letter to John Kendall, 17 August 1952; SPRI MS 656/1/16

154 'after a long': EHS, letter to EmS, 26 January 1908; SPRI MS 1537/2/16/3

155 'my private': EHS, letter to EmS, 26 January 1908; SPRI MS 1537/2/16/3

155 'My conscience': EHS, letter to EmS, 26 January 1908; SPRI MS 1537/2/16/3

13 Cape Royds

Page

157 'We are all': ÆM, diary of BAE, 20 January 1908; Mrs G.E. Dowler

158 'He was one': Sidney Riches, diary of BAE, 30 January 1908; SPRI MS 1611

159 'Day is quite': REP, diaries of BAE, 29 January 1908; SPRI MS 298/1/1

159 'alas! It': ÆM, diary of BAE, 1 February 1908; Mrs G.E. Dowler

159 'what appeared': ESM, diary of BAE, 31 January 1908; SPRI MS 1456/8

159 'Who is going': ESM, diary of BAE, 31 January 1908; SPRI MS 1456/8

160 'saw that he': Harry Dunlop, letter to J.D. Morrison, 3 June 1908; SPRI MS 1537/2/17/13

161 'cut and run': Arthur Harbord, diary of BAE, 4 February 1908; Alister Harbord

161 'It got on': Harry Dunlop, letter to J.D. Morrison, 3 June 1908; SPRI MS 1537/2/17/13

161 'terrible waste': ESM, diary of BAE, 6 February 1908; SPRI MS 1456/8

161 'the Captain': ÆM, diary of BAE, 6 February 1908; Mrs G.E. Dowler

161 'We thought': EHS, *The Heart of the Antarctic*, vol. 1: 102

162 'All hands': Harry Dunlop, letter to J.D. Morrison, 3 June 1908; SPRI MS 1537/2/17/13

162 'entirely lost': FW, letter to 'Dear Fred', 27 January 1908; SPRI MS 1413

162 'being at this': ÆM, letter to EmS, 22 March 1908; SPRI MS 1537/2/17/3

163 'all hands': Alf Cheetham, diary of BAE, 9 February 1908; SPRI MS 1609

164 'At 8 a.m.': Alf Cheetham, diary of BAE, 11 February 1908; SPRI MS 1609

165 'Every man jack': Arthur Harbord, diary of BAE, 12 February 1908; Alister Harbord

165 'with twenty-four': John King Davis, *High Latitude*: 82

165 'First about 20': *The Daily Telegraph* (Sydney), 3 April 1908: 7

166 'Shacks had a': PLB, diary of BAE, 17 February 1908; Neil Silverman

166 'Byron's description': *The Daily Telegraph* (Sydney), 3 April 1908: 7

167 'lost about': Harry Dunlop, letter to J.D. Morrison, 3 June 1908; SPRI MS 1537/2/17/13

167 'Amidst cheers': ÆM, diary of BAE, 22 February 1908; Mrs G.E. Dowler

14 New Worlds to Conquer

Page

169 'I cannot': EHS, letter to EmS, 15 February 1908; SPRI MS 1537/2/17/2

170 'to consult': ÆM, quoted in Stanley Newman, *Shackleton's Lieutenant*: 69

170 'He has not': EHS, letter to EmS, 22 February 1908; SPRI MS 1537/2/17/1

170 'He is the most': Harry Dunlop, letter to J.D. Morrison, 3 June 1908; SPRI MS 1537/2/17/13

171 'since the question': Rupert England, letter to J.J. Kinsey, 20 March 1908; SPRI MS 1456/67

171 'my resignation': Rupert England, letter to EmS, 23 April 1908; SPRI MS 1537/2/17/7

171 'England got': ESM, diary of BAE, 22 February 1908; SPRI MS 1456/8

171 'Looks as if': ESM, diary of BAE, 23 February 1908; SPRI MS 1456/8

172 'What a different': ESM, diary of BAE, 27 February 1908; SPRI MS 1456/8

172 'Keen on': EHS, letter to EmS, 22 January 1908; SPRI MS 1581/1/3

172 'Brocklehurst took': EHS, *The Heart of the Antarctic*, vol. 1: 129

174 'Mac Mawson': PLB, diary of BAE, 7 March 1908; Neil Silverman
174 'Never forget': ESM, diary of BAE, 7 March 1908; SPRI MS 1456/8
175 'All the land': TWED, 'The Ascent of Mount Erebus'
175 'After a continuous': TWED, 'Ascent'
176 'We all': TWED, 'Ascent'
176 'Very steep': ESM, diary of BAE, 10 March 1908; SPRI MS 1456/8
176 'Fell 100ds': ESM, diary of BAE, 11 March 1908; SPRI MS 1456/8
177 'If we lose': REP, diaries of BAE, 11 March 1908; SPRI MS 298/1/3
177 'Explorers Fight': Daily Mail, 11 March 1908
178 'I have been': RFS, letter to Hannah Scott, 26 March 1908; SPRI MS 1542/11/5
178 'It is certainly': J. Scott Keltie, letter to EmS, 19 May 1908; SPRI MS 1456/19
178 'Personally': J. Scott Keltie, letter to C.R. Markham, 31 March 1908; quoted in Roland Huntford, Shackleton: 226
178 'I strongly': C.R. Markham, letter to EmS, 26 May 1908; SPRI MS 1537/2/21/7
178 'It is in': H.R. Mill, letter to EmS, 22 June 1908; SPRI MS 1456/22

15 Waiting Out the Winter

Page
181 'Washed my': PLB, diary of BAE, 7 June 1908; Neil Silverman
183 'made a pile': EHS, The Heart of the Antarctic, vol. 1: 148
184 'put them in': PLB, diary of BAE, 16 February 1909; Neil Silverman
184 'The temperature': REP, diaries of BAE, June 1908; SPRI MS 298/1/3
185 'dressed up': REP, diaries of BAE, 23 March 1908; SPRI MS 298/1/3
185 'This amalgamation': Jameson Adams, letter to James Fisher, 17 June 1957; SPRI MS 1456/95
185 'Shackleton was': PLB, interview with James Fisher, 16 December 1955; SPRI MS 1456/64
186 'Dust from': J. Murray and G.E. Marston, Antarctic Days: 104–05
187 'To read': Bernard Day, letter to Caroline David; quoted in M.E. David, Professor David: 153
187 'Volunteers have': REP, 'A Messman'
188 'splendid man': EHS, letter to EmS, 22 January 1908; SPRI MS 1581/1/3
188 'Shackleton had': ESM, diary of BAE, 26 March 1908; SPRI MS 1456/8
188 'Armytage still': ESM, diary of BAE, 2 April 1908; SPRI MS 1456/8
188 'has certainly': ESM, diary of BAE, 10 July 1908; SPRI MS 1456/8
189 'He used to': REP, quoted in M. Fisher and J. Fisher, Shackleton: 186
189 'By Gd': ESM, diary of BAE, 16 March 1908; SPRI MS 1456/8
189 'Shall get': ESM, diary of BAE, 17 March 1908; SPRI MS 1456/8
189 'very down': ESM, diary of BAE, 17 April 1908; SPRI MS 1456/8
189 'Just seen': ESM, diary of BAE, 17 May 1908; SPRI MS 1456/8
189 'showed signs': ESM, diary of BAE, 23 June 1908; Royal Geographical Society (with the Institute of British Geographers)
189 'Sunday but': ESM, diary of BAE, 14 June 1908; SPRI MS 1456/8
190 'for breakfast': EAW, 'The Medical Aspects of the Discovery's Voyage to the Antarctic': 77
190 'the most important': K.J. Carpenter, The History of Scurvy & Vitamin C: 173
190 'could be produced': L.G. Wilson, 'The Clinical Definition of Scurvy and the Discovery of Vitamin C': 50–51

191 'a myocarditis': ESM, letter to John Kendall, 22 August 1950; SPRI MS 656/1/1

191 'ploughed him': ESM, letter to John Kendall, 22 August 1950; SPRI MS 656/1/1

191 'I saw much': ESM, diary of BAE, 24 June 1908; Royal Geographical Society (with the Institute of British Geographers)

191 'Pulm Systolic': ESM, diary of BAE, 12 July 1908; SPRI MS 1456/8

192 'Aroused by': ESM, diary of BAE, 3 August 1908; SPRI MS 1456/8

192 'received a good': EHS, *Heart*, vol. 1: 233

192 'A curious': REP, note of 22 February 1966, added across from entry in diaries of BAE, 10 September 1908; SPRI MS 1097/1

16 Across the Great Ice Barrier

Page

195 '(1) To take': EHS, letter to TWED, 19 September 1908, quoted in EHS, *Heart*: 73–75

196 'Prof finds': DM, diary of BAE, 8 October 1908; The Mawson Collection, 68DM

197 'You have never': EHS, letter to James Murray, 23 October 1908; SPRI MS 1537/2/21/10

197 'economic side': EHS, letter to TWED, 28 October 1908; SPRI MS 1537/2/21/14

198 'suggested that': EHS, letter to James Murray, 23 October 1908; SPRI MS 1537/2/21/12

198 'My own darling': EHS, letter to EmS, 29 October 1909; SPRI MS 1537/2/18/7

199 'He used to': L.D.A. Hussey, interview with James Fisher, 12 November 1955; SPRI MS 1581/3/1

199 'Last night': EHS, diary of southern journey, 29 October 1908; SPRI MS 1537/3/6

199 'We had tremendous': PLB, interview with James Fisher, 16 December 1955; SPRI MS 1456/64

199 'A glorious': EHS, diary of southern journey, 29 October 1908; SPRI MS 1537/3/6

200 'He was in': EHS, diary of southern journey, 29 October 1908; SPRI MS 1537/3/6

200 'The sledges': REP, diaries of BAE, 2 November 1908; SPRI MS 298/1/6

200 'Quan': EHS, diary of southern journey, 3 November 1908; SPRI MS 1537/3/6

200 'the ponies': EHS, diary of southern journey, 3 November 1908; SPRI MS 1537/3/6

201 'we must': EHS, diary of southern journey, 6 November 1908; SPRI MS 1537/3/6

201 'a dead white': EHS, diary of southern journey, 7 November 1908; SPRI MS 1537/3/6

201 'Examined': ESM, diary of BAE, 7 November 1908; SPRI MS 1456/8

202 'Poor little': ESM, diary of BAE, 8 November 1908; SPRI MS 1456/8

202 'There was nothing': EHS, diary of southern journey, 9 November 1908; SPRI MS 1537/3/6

202 'I spoke about': FW, diary of southern journey, 9 November 1908; SPRI MS 944/1

202 'I have been': FW, diary of southern journey, 10 November 1908; SPRI MS 944/1

203 'enjoyed it': FW, diary of southern journey, 15 November 1908; SPRI MS 944/1

203 'Surely there': ESM, diary of BAE, 18 November 1908; SPRI MS 1456/8

203 'It has been': EHS, diary of southern journey, 16 November 1908; SPRI MS 1537/3/6

203 'We seem to': EHS, diary of southern journey, 18 November 1908; SPRI MS 1537/3/6

204 'Lunched on': ESM, diary of BAE, 24 November 1908; SPRI MS 1456/8

204 'A day to': EHS, diary of southern journey, 26 November 1908; SPRI MS 1537/3/6

204 'a nice little': FW, diary of southern journey, 26 November 1908; SPRI MS 944/1

204 'This we have': EHS, diary of southern journey, 26 November 1908; SPRI MS 1537/3/6

204 'I am beginning': FW, diary of southern journey, 25 November 1908; SPRI MS 944/1

204 'so strange': EHS, diary of southern journey, 20 November 1908; SPRI MS 1537/3/6

204 'quite a brilliant': FW, diary of southern journey, 27 November 1908; SPRI MS 944/1

205 'Noble little': ESM, diary of BAE, 28 November 1908; SPRI MS 1456/8

205 'a long and': FW, diary of southern journey, 28 November 1908; SPRI MS 944/1

205 'the great part': EHS, diary of southern journey, 16 November 1908; SPRI MS 1537/3/6

205 'Got only': ESM, diary of BAE, 1 December 1908; SPRI MS 1456/8

205 'Last night': FW, diary of southern journey, 2 December 1908; SPRI MS 944/1

205 'It seems as': EHS, diary of southern journey, 1 December 1908; SPRI MS 1537/3/6

206 'We had got': EHS, diary of southern journey, 2 December 1908; SPRI MS 1537/3/6

206 'it was unanimously': ESM, diary of BAE, 2 December 1908; SPRI MS 1456/8

206 'a glacier': FW, diary of southern journey, 2 December 1908; SPRI MS 944/1

206 'leaving Socks': ESM, diary of BAE, 3 December 1908; SPRI MS 1456/8

206 'These got': FW, diary of southern journey, 3 December 1908; SPRI MS 944/1

206 'There burst': EHS, diary of southern journey, 4 December 1908; SPRI MS 1537/3/6

207 'as far as': ESM, 'An Antarctic Episode': 359

207 'must be the': FW, diary of southern journey, 3 December 1908; SPRI MS 944/1

207 'Tomorrow we': ESM, diary of BAE, 3 December 1908; SPRI MS 1456/8

208 'that taking two': FW, diary of southern journey, 4 December 1908; SPRI MS 944/1

208 'He behaved': FW, diary of southern journey, 5 December 1908; SPRI MS 944/1

208 'Two of us': FW, diary of southern journey, 6 December 1908; SPRI MS 944/1

208 'Just before camping': FW, diary of southern journey, 6 December 1908; SPRI MS 944/1

17 The Western Party

Page

212 'when we': REP, diaries of BAE, 23–28 November 1908; SPRI MS 298/1/6

212 'A few hours': REP, diaries of BAE, 23–28 November 1908; SPRI MS 298/1/6

212 'constant expectation': REP, diaries of BAE, 23–28 November 1908; SPRI MS 298/1/6

213 'we ate the dry': James Murray, quoted in EHS, *The Heart of the Antarctic*, vol. 2: 29–30

213 'but such fragments': REP, diaries of BAE, 23–28 November 1908; SPRI MS 298/1/6

213 'To an experienced': REP, diaries of BAE, 23–28 November 1908; SPRI MS 298/1/6

213 'Four men': REP, diaries of BAE, 23–28 November 1908; SPRI MS 298/1/6

213 'We left all': REP, diaries of BAE, 23–28 November 1908; SPRI MS 298/1/6

213 'was noticed': EHS, *Heart*, vol. 2: 35

214 'The going was': PLB, diary of BAE, 3 December 1908; Neil Silverman

214 'It was bad': PLB, diary of BAE, 14 December 1908; Neil Silverman

214 'I have seldom': REP, diaries of BAE, 21 December 1908; SPRI MS 298/1/7

215 'There are evidently': REP, diaries of BAE, 21 December 1908; SPRI MS 298/1/7

215 'One good': REP, diaries of BAE, 23 December 1908; SPRI MS 298/1/7

215 'One of the': PLB, diary of BAE, 16 December 1908; Neil Silverman

216 'Today the ship': PLB, diary of BAE, 15 January 1909; Neil Silverman

216 'that the ponies': REP, diaries of BAE, 26 December 1908; SPRI MS 298/1/7

217 'a cross': EHS, *Heart*, vol. 2: 55

217 'We expected': Ernest Joyce, quoted in EHS, *Heart*, vol. 2: 56

217 'One day I': Ernest Joyce, quoted in EHS, Heart, vol 2: 59–60

218 'We heard him': PLB, diary of BAE, 23 January 1909; Neil Silverman

218 'We began to': REP, diaries of BAE, 24 January 1909; SPRI MS 298/1/7

218 'No joke': PLB, diary of BAE, 24 January 1909; Neil Silverman

18 Nearest the Pole

Page

221 'The first few': FW, Memoirs: 82; Mitchell Library, State Library of New South Wales ML MSS 2198/1: CY Reel 15; Mrs Anne M. Fright

221 'Saw the pony': EHS, diary of southern journey, 7 December 1908; SPRI MS 1537/3/6

221 'Wild had': ESM, diary of BAE, 7 December 1908; SPRI MS 1456/8

221 'Fortunately for': EHS, diary of southern journey, 7 December 1908; SPRI MS 1537/3/6

222 'After shooting': ESM, quoted in Roland Huntford, *Shackleton*: 259

222 'Crossing crevasses': ESM, diary of BAE, 7 December 1908; SPRI MS 1456/8

222 'Provy' became': ESM, 'An Antarctic Episode': 360

223 'Hope there won't': ESM, diary of BAE, 10 December 1908; SPRI MS 1456/8

223 'expresses more': EHS, diary of southern journey, 12 December 1908; SPRI MS 1537/3/6

223 'Following Sh.': ESM, diary of BAE, 14 December 1908; SPRI MS 1456/8

223 'We were all': FW, diary of southern journey, 11 December 1908; SPRI MS 944/1

223 'Had a long': FW, diary of southern journey, 5 December 1908; SPRI MS 944/1

223 'Am waiting': FW, diary of southern journey, 8 December 1908; SPRI MS 944/1

223 'S. pulls like': FW, diary of southern journey, 11 December 1908; SPRI MS 944/1

223 'He was the': Jameson Adams, interview with James Fisher, 5 October 1955; SPRI MS 1456/63

224 'Plateau practically': ESM, diary of BAE, 15 December 1908; SPRI MS 1456/8

224 'We hope': FW, diary of southern journey, 15 December 1908; SPRI MS 944/1

224 'We have burnt': EHS, diary of southern journey, 17 December 1908; SPRI MS 1537/3/6

224 'Hope to gain': ESM, diary of BAE, 17 December 1908; SPRI MS 1456/8

225 'Another disappointment': FW, diary of southern journey, 19 December 1908; SPRI MS 944/1

225 'Sh. rather done': ESM, diary of BAE, 19 December 1908; SPRI MS 1456/8

225 'I can easily': EHS, diary of southern journey, 22 December 1908; SPRI MS 1537/3/6

226 'I sincerely': FW, diary of southern journey, 24 December 1908; SPRI MS 944/1

226 'May none but': FW, diary of southern journey, 25 December 1908; SPRI MS 944/1

226 'We are going': EHS, diary of southern journey, 25 December 1908; SPRI MS 1537/3/6

227 'As we have not': FW, diary of southern journey, 27 December 1908; SPRI MS 944/1

227 'Reverting': ESM, diary of BAE, 29 December 1908; SPRI MS 1456/8

227 'I cannot express': EHS, diary of southern journey, 30 December 1908; SPRI MS 1537/3/6

227 'We are so': EHS, diary of southern journey, 28 December 1908; SPRI MS 1537/3/6

227 'Neither A.': FW, diary of southern journey, 31 December 1908; SPRI MS 944/1

228 'every inch': ESM, diary of BAE, 2 January 1909; SPRI MS 1456/8

228 'God knows': EHS, diary of southern journey, 2 January 1909; SPRI MS 1537/3/6

228 'Hopes raised': ESM, diary of BAE, 3 January 1909; SPRI MS 1456/8

229 'We have now': FW, diary of southern journey, 3 January 1909; SPRI MS 944/1

229 'We had depoted': EHS, diary of southern journey, 4 January 1909; SPRI MS 1537/3/6

230 'Found we could': FW, diary of southern journey, 4 January 1909; SPRI MS 944/1

230 'trusting to our': ESM, diary of BAE, 4 January 1909; SPRI MS 1456/8

230 'I think today': FW, diary of southern journey, 6 January 1909; SPRI MS 944/1

230 'Tomorrow': ESM, diary of BAE, 6 January 1909; SPRI MS 1456/8

230 'In bags all': ESM, diary of BAE, 7 January 1909; SPRI MS 1456/8

231 'Suffering considerably': EHS, diary of southern journey, 8 January 1909; SPRI MS 1537/3/6

231 'with a few': FW, diary of southern journey, 9 January 1909; SPRI MS 944/1

231 'If we'd gone': Jameson Adams, interview with James Fisher, 5 October 1955; SPRI MS 1456/63

231 'We have shot': EHS, diary of southern journey, 9 January 1909; SPRI MS 1537/3/6

232 'Rush we must': FW, diary of southern journey, 9 January 1909; SPRI MS 944/1

232 'Homeward Bound': EHS, diary of southern journey, 9 January 1909; SPRI MS 1537/3/6

232 'all this is': EHS, diary of southern journey, 2 January 1909; SPRI MS 1537/3/6

233 'Thank God': ESM, diary of BAE, 11 January 1909; SPRI MS 1456/8

233 'We were': FW, Memoirs: 91; Mitchell Library, State Library of New South Wales ML MSS 2198/1: CY Reel 15; Mrs Anne M. Fright

233 'All day long': FW, diary of southern journey, 12 January 1909; SPRI MS 944/1

19 The Wandering Pole

Page

235 'Yesterday I': DM, diary of BAE, 23 October 1908; The Mawson Collection, 68DM

235 'I believe': James Clark Ross, in John Ross, *Narrative of a Second Voyage in Search of a North-West Passage*: 555

236 'There was great': DM, diary of BAE, 23 October 1908; The Mawson Collection, 68DM

237 'Yesterday morning': DM, diary of BAE, 29 October 1908; The Mawson Collection, 68DM

237 'Have just found': DM, diary of BAE, 29 October 1908; The Mawson Collection, 68DM

237 'He is full': DM, diary of BAE, 29 October 1908; The Mawson Collection, 68DM

238 'Were carried': DM, diary of BAE, 29 October 1908; The Mawson Collection, 68DM

238 'Low sloping': TWED, letter to commander of *Nimrod*, 2 November 1908; quoted in TWED, Professor David's narrative, in EHS, *The Heart of the Antarctic*, vol. 2: 110

239 'The Prof is': DM, diary of BAE, 23 November 1908; The Mawson Collection, 68DM

240 'We were not': TWED, Professor David's narrative, in EHS, *Heart*, vol. 2: 130

240 'high sastrugi': TWED, Narrative, in EHS, *Heart*, vol. 2: 135

240 'a broad-bottomed': TWED, Narrative, in EHS, *Heart*, vol. 2: 139

240 'as though a stormy': TWED, Narrative, in EHS, *Heart*, vol. 2: 142

240 'He announced': TWED, Narrative, in EHS, *Heart*, vol. 2: 143

240 'I had scarcely': TWED, Narrative, in EHS, *Heart*, vol. 2: 145

241 'I was busy': *The Sydney Morning Herald*, 17 April 1909: page 13

241 'a conspicuous object': TWED, Narrative, in EHS, *Heart*, vol. 2: 147

242 'secured some': TWED, Narrative, in EHS, *Heart*, vol. 2: 156

243 'one large one': A.F. Mackay, diary of northern journey, 27 December 1908; National Museums of Scotland

243 'The scarcity': DM, diary of BAE, 3 January 1909; The Mawson Collection, 68DM

243 'We are now': DM, diary of BAE, 6 January 1909; The Mawson Collection, 68DM

243 'Grouse': DM, diary of BAE, 12 January 1909; The Mawson Collection, 68DM

243 'It is wonderful': A.F. Mackay, diary of northern journey, 12 January 1909; National Museums of Scotland

244 'The surface': TWED, Narrative, in EHS, *Heart*, vol. 2: 178–179

244 'the polar': TWED, Narrative, in EHS, *Heart*, vol. 2: 179

244 'I hereby': TWED, Narrative, in EHS, *Heart*, vol. 2: 181

244 'With a fervent': TWED, Narrative, in EHS, *Heart*, vol. 2: 182

245 'bold culinary': TWED, Narrative, in EHS, *Heart*, vol. 2: 185

245 'awful state': A.F. Mackey, quoted in TWED, Narrative, in EHS, *Heart*, vol. 2: 185

245 'two foreigners': A.F. Mackay, quoted in TWED, Narrative, in EHS, *Heart*, vol. 2: 185

245 'Occasionally': TWED, Narrative, in EHS, *Heart*, vol. 2: 190

246 'with a faint': TWED, Narrative, in EHS, *Heart*, vol. 2: 190–191

246 'hardly ever': DM, diary of BAE, 30 January 1909; The Mawson Collection, 68DM

247 'Something has': DM, diary of BAE, 31 December 1908; The Mawson Collection, 68DM

247 'Prof's burberry': DM, diary of BAE, 31 January 1909; The Mawson Collection, 68DM

247 'During most': DM, diary of BAE, 2 February 1909; The Mawson Collection, 68DM

247 'certainly partially': DM, diary of BAE, 3 February 1909; The Mawson Collection, 68DM

248 'I have deposed': A.F. Mackay, diary of northern journey, 3 February 1909; National Museums of Scotland

248 'ever been a driving': DM, Award of the Bigsby Medal: xlvii

20 Forced March

Page

251 'Saw the land': EHS, diary of southern journey, 16 January 1909; SPRI MS 1537/3/6

251 'Had we been': FW, diary of southern journey, 14 January 1909; SPRI MS 944/1

252 'This is a serious': EHS, diary of southern journey, 15 January 1909; SPRI MS 1537/3/6

252 'I have been': EHS, diary of southern journey, 18 January 1909; SPRI MS 1537/3/6

252 'Thicker hoosh': ESM, diary of BAE, 18 January 1909; SPRI MS 1456/8

252 'got the sail': FW, diary of southern journey, 19 January 1909; SPRI MS 944/1

252 'I don't know': FW, diary of southern journey, 19 January 1909; SPRI MS 944/1

252 'the worse': Jameson Adams, interview with James Fisher, 5 October 1955; SPRI MS 1456/63

253 'I expect there': EHS, diary of southern journey, 13 January 1909; SPRI MS 1537/3/6

253 'You must go': Jameson Adams, interview with James Fisher, 5 October 1955; SPRI MS 1456/63

253 'completely knocked': FW, diary of southern journey, 20 January 1909; SPRI MS 944/1

253 'bad as': EHS, diary of southern journey, 20 January 1909; SPRI MS 1537/3/6

253 'Pulse on march': ESM, diary of BAE, 21 January 1909; SPRI MS 1456/8

253 'Poor S. has': FW, diary of southern journey, 19 January 1909; SPRI MS 944/1

254 'a perfect nightmare': FW, diary of southern journey, 24 January 1909; SPRI MS 944/1

254 'Two or three': FW, diary of southern journey, 24 January 1909; SPRI MS 944/1

255 'Several times': FW, Memoirs: 88; Mitchell Library, State Library of New South Wales ML MSS 2198/1: CY Reel 15; Mrs Anne M. Fright

255 'Struggled on': ESM, diary of BAE, 26–27 January 1909; SPRI MS 1456/8

255 'I cannot describe': EHS, diary of southern journey, 26 and 27 January 1909; SPRI MS 1537/3/6

255 'By arrangement': ESM, fragment of diary of BAE, 25–27 January 1909, included with letter to John Kendall, 1950; SPRI MS 656/1/9

255 'Good God': FW, diary of southern journey, 28 January 1909; SPRI MS 944/1

256 'I was plunged': EHS, diary of southern journey, 28 January 1909; SPRI MS 1537/3/6

256 'Sh. has stood': ESM, diary of BAE, 28 January 1909; SPRI MS 1456/8

256 'It is with': EHS, diary of southern journey, 28 January 1909; SPRI MS 1537/3/6

256 'I hope this': FW, diary of southern journey, 29 January 1909; SPRI MS 944/1

257 'S. privately': FW, diary of southern journey, 31 January 1909; SPRI MS 944/1

257 'The horse': ESM, letter to John Kendall, 24 August 1950; SPRI MS 656/1/2
258 'My pyjama': ESM, diary of BAE, 4 February 1909; SPRI MS 1456/8
258 'It would not': FW, diary of southern journey, 3 February 1909; SPRI MS 944/1
258 'Chewed meat': ESM, diary of BAE, 8 February 1909; SPRI MS 1456/8
258 'God is': FW, diary of southern journey, 10 February 1909; SPRI MS 944/1
258 'Lunched making': ESM, diary of BAE, 13 February 1909; SPRI MS 1456/8
259 'We have a great': FW, diary of southern journey, 15 February 1909; SPRI MS 944/1
259 'This trip has': FW, diary of southern journey, 5 February 1909; SPRI MS 944/1
259 'So great': FW, Memoirs: 101–02; Mitchell Library, State Library of New South Wales ML MSS 2198/1: CY Reel 15; Mrs Anne M. Fright
260 'not full': FW, diary of southern journey, 20 February 1909; SPRI MS 944/1
260 'We are so': EHS, *The Heart of the Antarctic*, vol. 1: 363
260 'Distance speaks': ESM, diary of BAE, 21 February 1909; SPRI MS 1456/8
260 'I was unlucky': EHS, *Heart*, vol. 1: 364
260 'and only': H.R. Mill, *The Life of Sir Ernest Shackleton*: 149
261 'Good old': FW, diary of southern journey, 23 February 1909; SPRI MS 944/1
261 'Carlsbad plums': EHS, *Heart*, vol. 1: 366
261 'generous dose': ESM, 'An Antarctic Episode': 361
262 'Marshall suffered': EHS, *Heart*, vol. 1: 367
262 'After we had': FW, Memoirs: 94; Mitchell Library, State Library of New South Wales ML MSS 2198/1: CY Reel 15; Mrs Anne M. Fright

21 Rescue

Page
266 'done up': ÆM, diary of BAE, 3 January 1909; Mrs G.E. Dowler
266 'We were on': ÆM, diary of BAE, 4 January 1909; Mrs G.E. Dowler
266 'The sight': AEM, diary of BAE, 7 January 1909; Mrs G.E. Dowler
267 'as this means': Arthur Harbord, diary of BAE, 8 January 1909; Alister Harbord
267 'I happened': ÆM, diary of BAE, 11 January 1909; Mrs G.E. Dowler
268 'then suggested': ÆM, diary of BAE, 12 January 1909; Mrs G.E. Dowler
268 'We were having': James Murray, report to EHS; quoted in EHS, *The Heart of the Antarctic*, vol. 2: 48
268 'Nothing more': Arthur Harbord, diary of BAE, 10 January 1909; Alister Harbord
269 'I have never': REP, diaries of BAE, 23 January 1909; SPRI MS 298/1/8
269 'The snout': PLB, diary of BAE, 24 January 1909; Neil Silverman
269 'the sledge tipped': REP, diaries of BAE, 23 January 1909; SPRI MS 298/1/8
269 'Not more than': Bertram Armytage, report to EHS, quoted in EHS; *Heart*, vol. 2: 69
269 'The killers': PLB, diary of BAE, 24 January 1909; Neil Silverman
269 'I shall dream': REP, diaries of BAE, 23 January 1909; SPRI MS 298/1/8
270 'The photograph': REP, diaries of BAE, 31 January 1909; SPRI MS 298/1/9
271 'had dragged': DM, diary of BAE, 3 February 1909; The Mawson Collection, 68DM
272 'In a second': DM, diary of BAE, 4 February 1909; The Mawson Collection, 68DM
272 'At the sight': TWED, Narrative, in EHS, *Heart*, vol. 2: 211
272 'Mawson has': TWED, Narrative, in EHS, *Heart*, vol. 2: 212

272 'Fixing me': John King Davis, *High Latitude*: 105
273 'had the weather': John King Davis, *High Latitude*: 107
273 'abnormally lean': F.P. Evans, Narrative of BAE: 8; SPRI MS 369
273 'The southern': A.F. Mackay, *Nimrod* diary, 15 February 1909; SPRI MS 1537/3/1
274 'practical supersession': A.F. Mackay, *Nimrod* diary, 25 February 1909; SPRI MS 1537/3/1
274 'We are beginning': PLB, diary of BAE, 24 February 1909; Neil Silverman
274 'hole-and-corner': A.F. Mackay, *Nimrod* diary, 25 February 1909; SPRI MS 1537/3/1
274 'as a sop': REP, diaries of BAE, 1 March 1909; SPRI MS 298/1/9
274 'several members': A.F. Mackay, *Nimrod* diary, 28 February 1909; SPRI MS 1537/3/1
275 'almost paralysed': FW, Memoirs; Mitchell Library, State Library of New South Wales ML MSS 2198/1: CY Reel 15; Mrs Anne M. Fright
275 'almost overlooked': Arthur Harbord, diary of BAE, 5 March 1909; Alister Harbord
275 'We all tumbled': A.F. Mackay, *Nimrod* diary, 5 March 1909; SPRI MS 1537/3/1
275 'No happier': FW, Memoirs: 54; Mitchell Library, State Library of New South Wales ML MSS 2198/1: CY Reel 15; Mrs Anne M. Fright
276 'the party': Arthur Harbord, diary of BAE, 5 March 1909; Alister Harbord
276 'the waves': PLB, diary of BAE, 2 March 1909; Neil Silverman
276 'managed to': REP, diaries of BAE, 2 March 1909; SPRI MS 298/1/9
277 'Here Shackleton's': A.F. Mackay, *Nimrod* diary, 5 March 1909; SPRI MS 1537/3/1
277 'Never was': Jameson Adams, letter to Mrs E. Phipps, 10 March 1909; SPRI MS 1456/16
278 'We all turned': EHS, *Heart*, vol. 2: 227
278 'I have just': Jameson Adams, letter to Mrs E. Phipps, 10 March 1909; SPRI MS 1456/16

22 Heroes Return

Page
280 'We got the': PLB, diary of BAE, 23 March 1909; Neil Silverman
280 'Steamers came': PLB, diary of BAE, 25 March 1909; Neil Silverman
281 'It is one of': *The Sketch*, 26 March 1909
281 'So long as': *The Sphere*, 3 April 1909: 14
281 'He was a scurrilous': Frank Debenham, interview with James Fisher, 5 October 1956; SPRI MS 1456/66
282 'We have been': C.R. Markham, letter to EHS, 26 October 1907; SPRI MS 1537/2/15/20
282 'put me down': C.R. Markham, letter to J. Scott Keltie, 27 March 1909; SPRI MS 1456/21
282 'As I am responsible': C.R. Markham, letter to Leonard Darwin, April 1909; SPRI MS 367/13/1
282 'This is magnificent': C.R. Markham, letter to RFS, 31 March 1909; SPRI MS 10
282 'He was fond': Frank Debenham, interview with James Fisher, 5 October 1956; SPRI MS 1456/66

283 'I suppose you': J. Scott Keltie, letter to EHS, 1 April 1909; SPRI MS 1456/19

283 'K. is tumbling': EHS, letter to H.R. Mill, 5 May 1909; SPRI MS 100/106/12

283 'Just as Shackleton': *The Sydney Morning Herald*, 31 March 1909: 8

285 'full of fun': Valerie Gould, memorandum to Margery Fisher, November 1955; SPRI MS 1456/83

286 'I heard all': Albert Armitage, Memo on Sir E.H. Shackleton to H.R. Mill, 24 May 1922; SPRI MS 367/1

286 'I just want': EHS, letter to EmS, 25 April 1909; SPRI MS 1537/2/24/3

286 'I called at': H.R. Mill, *An Autobiography*: 148

287 'We cannot': *The Daily Telegraph*, 15 June 1909: 10

287 'I notice it': *The Daily Telegraph*, 16 June 1909: 15

288 'Shackleton's blarney': Hubert Wilkins, letter to Margery Fisher, 27 June 1956; SPRI MS 1456/82

288 'it seemed as': EHS, *The Heart of the Antarctic*, vol. 2: 232

288 'I hear he': *The Observer*, 20 June 1909

288 'I wish I': *Daily Dispatch*, 20 June 1909

289 'The King': C.R. Markham, letter to RFS, 22 April 1909; SPRI MS 10

289 'We do not': J. Scott Keltie, letter to Cuthbert Bayes, 19 April 1909; quoted in M. Fisher and J. Fisher, *Shackleton*: 251

289 'as a brother': quoted in H.R. Mill, *The Life of Sir Ernest Shackleton*: 162

290 'With reference': Herbert Asquith, letter to EHS, 19 August 1909; SPRI MS 1537/2/24/6

291 'Isn't it splendid!': EHS, letter to EmS, 18 August 1909; SPRI MS 1537/2/24/12

291 'This is the nearest': Mrs J.Q. Rowett, interview with James Fisher, 29 November 1955; SPRI MS 1456/75

291 'My father': Cecily Shackleton, interview with James Fisher; SPRI MS 1581/3/2/1

292 'I allow': EAW, letter to EHS, 1909; SPRI MS 28

292 'You took Scott's': EAW, letter to EHS, 1909; SPRI MS 28

292 'As for Shackleton': EAW, letter to John Fraser, 19 August 1909; SPRI MS 1577/6/19

293 'receive my very': C.R. Markham, letter to EHS, 5 June 1909; SPRI MS 1537/2/21/19

293 'I felt very': C.R. Markham, letter to Leonard Darwin, 5 September 1909; SPRI MS 367/13/2

293 'a dangerous': Frank Debenham, interview with James Fisher, 5 October 1956; SPRI MS 1456/66

294 'jog-trot': M. Fisher and J. Fisher, *Shackleton*: 249

294 'marched hard': ESM, diary of BAE, 9 January 1909; SPRI MS 1456/8

295 'The King': EHS, letter to EmS, 25 September 1909; SPRI MS 1456/88

295 'It is safe': *Daily Mirror*, 8 November 1909

296 'The best': *The Manchester Guardian*, 17 November 1909

Epilogue

Page

297 'a professed liar': RFS, letter to J. Scott Keltie, 28 March 1908; quoted in Roland Huntford, *Shackleton*: 304

297 'to go forth': *The Observer*, 20 June 1909

297 'All of this': Admiral Lewis Beaumont, letter to Leonard Darwin, 19 June 1909; SPRI MS 367/11

298 'I understand': EHS, letter to RFS, 6 July 1909; SPRI MS 367/17/1

298 'Every explorer': Leonard Darwin, letter to EHS, 1909; SPRI MS 367/12

298 'a purely': EHS, letter to RFS, 21 February 1910; SPRI MS 367/17/2

298 'I have always': RFS, letter to Leonard Darwin, 29 March 1910; SPRI MS 367/14/7

299 'said that he': DM, Abbreviated Log: Australasian Antarctic Expedition, January 1910; The Mawson Collection, 54 AAE

299 'I did not like': DM, Abbreviated Log: Australasian Antarctic Expedition, January 1910; The Mawson Collection, 54 AAE

299 'warmly enthusiastic': DM, *The Home of the Blizzard*: xviii

299 'I don't want': RFS, letter to Leonard Darwin, 29 March 1910; SPRI MS 367/14/7

299 'I knew there': Geoffrey Dorman, letter to James Fisher, 30 December 1967; SPRI MS 1456/97

300 'We made a very': RFS, *Scott's Last Expedition*, vol. 1: 536

300 'What Nansen': Roald Amundsen, letter to J. Scott Keltie, 25 March 1909; SPRI MS 1456/16;

301 'I do not see': EHS, letter to Leonard Darwin, 23 July 1909; SPRI MS 367/16/1

301 'tore them': PLB, interview with James Fisher, 24 August 1955; SPRI MS 1456/64

301 'You left me': James Murray, letter to EHS, 15 September 1910; SPRI MS 1537/2/21/22

301 'We didn't see': Jameson Adams, interview with James Fisher, 5 October 1955; SPRI MS 1456/63

302 'How could you': Cecily Shackleton, interview with James Fisher; SPRI MS 1581/3/2/1

303 'giving up my': REP, letter to Frank Debenham, n.d.; SPRI MS 280/25

304 'He seems to': *The Argus* (Melbourne), 14 March 1910: 6

304 'We were awfully': REP, letter to PLB; Johnny Van Haeften, London

305 'The door of': Griffith Taylor, *With Scott: The Silver Lining*: 105

306 'He had that': John King Davis, *High Latitude*: 83

307 'I'd done my': Jameson Adams, interview with James Fisher, 5 October 1955; SPRI MS 1456/63

308 'There would be': C.D. Mackellar, correspondence with James Fisher, SPRI MS 1456/83

310 'The Beacon': G.E. Fogg, *A History of Antarctic Science*: 251

310 'naturally more': G.E. Fogg, *History*: 269

311 'Don't saddle': Hubert Wilkins, letter to Margery Fisher, 27 June 1956; SPRI MS 1456/82

311 'saw several': L.E.G. Oates, diary, 4 December 1911, quoted in Sue Limb and Patrick Cordingley, *Captain Oates*: 183

312 'Shackleton paid': Frank Debenham, interview with James Fisher, 5 October 1956; SPRI MS 1456/66

312 'We did not': Roald Amundsen, *The South Pole*, vol. 2: 114

BIBLIOGRAPHY

Published Sources

Books

Amundsen, R. 1908. *The North West Passage*. 2 vols. London: Archibald Constable & Company

Amundsen, R. 1912. *The South Pole*. 2 vols. London: John Murray

Armitage, A.B. 1905. *Two Years in the Antarctic*. London: Edward Arnold

Armitage, A.B. 1925. *Cadet to Commodore*. London: Cassell & Company

Attlee, Lord. 1961. *Empire into Commonwealth*. London: Oxford University Press

Ayres, P. 1999. *Mawson: A Life*. Melbourne: Melbourne University Press

Baillie, F.D. 1900. *Mafeking: A Diary of the Siege*. Westminster: Archibald Constable & Company

Bartlett, R., and R.T. Hale. 1916. *Northward Ho! The Last Voyage of the Karluk*. Boston: Small, Maynard & Company

Baughman, T.H. 1994. *Before the Heroes Came: Antarctica in the 1890s*. Lincoln, NE, and London: University of Nebraska Press

Baughman, T.H. 1999. *Pilgrims on the Ice: Robert Falcon Scott's First Antarctic Expedition*. Lincoln, NE, and London: University of Nebraska Press

Beckett, J.C. 1976. *The Anglo-Irish Tradition*. London: Faber & Faber

Begbie, H. 1922. *Shackleton: A Memory*. London: Mills & Boon

Bell, M., R. Butlin, and M. Heffernan (eds.). 1995. *Geography and Imperialism 1820–1940*. Manchester: Manchester University Press

Bernacchi, L.C. 1901. *To the South Polar Regions*. London: Hurst & Blackett

Bernacchi, L.C. 1938. *Saga of the 'Discovery'*. London: Blackie & Son

Birkenhead, Lord. 1978. *Rudyard Kipling*. London: Weidenfeld & Nicolson

Birrell, A. 1937. *Things Past Redress*. London: Faber & Faber

Borchgrevink, C.E. 1901. *First on the Antarctic Continent*. London: George Newnes

Brown, J.M., and W.R. Louis (eds.). 1999. *The Oxford History of the British Empire. Volume IV: The Twentieth Century*. Oxford: Oxford University Press

Brunschwig, H. 1966. *French Colonialism: Myths and Realities*. London: Pall Mall Press

Bryce, R.M. 1997. *Cook & Peary: The Polar Controversy, Resolved*. Mechanicsburg, PA: Stackpole Books

Bull, H.J. 1896. *The Cruise of the 'Antarctic'*. London: Edward Arnold

Cain, P.J., and A.G. Hopkins. 1993. *British Imperialism: Innovation and Expansion, 1688–1914*. London: Longman

Callwell, C.E. 1906. *Small Wars: Their Principles and Practice*. London: H.M. Stationery Office

Carpenter, K.J. 1986. *The History of Scurvy & Vitamin C*. Cambridge: Cambridge University Press

Cecil, R. 1969. *Life in Edwardian England*. London: B.T. Batsford

Chadwick, O. 1970. *The Victorian Church. Part II: 1860–1901*. London: A&C Black

Conway, W.M. 1897. *The First Crossing of Spitsbergen*. London: J.M. Dent & Company

Conway, W.M. 1898. *With Ski and Sledge over Arctic Glaciers*. London: J.M. Dent & Company

Curtis, L.P. 1968. *Anglo-Saxons and Celts: A Study of Anti-Irish Prejudice in Victorian England*. Bridgeport, CN: University of Bridgeport

David, M.E. 1937. *Professor David: The Life of Sir Edgeworth David*. London: Edward Arnold & Company

David, T.W.E., and R.E. Priestley. 1914. *British Antarctic Expedition 1907–09. Reports on the Scientific Investigations. Geology. Volume 1*. London: William Heinemann

Davis, J.K. 1962. *High Latitude*. Melbourne: Melbourne University Press

Deacon, M. 1971. *Scientists and the Sea 1650–1900: A Study of Marine Science*. London: Academic Press

Delebecque, J. 1936. *Vie du Général Marchand*. Paris: Hachette

Doorly, G.S. 1916. *The Voyages of the 'Morning'*. London: Smith, Elder & Company

Ensor, R. 1936. *England 1870–1914*. Oxford: Clarendon Press

Ferry, J. 1890. *Le Tonkin et la mère patrie*. Paris: Victor-Harvard

Fiala, A. 1907. *Fighting the Polar Ice*. London: Hodder & Stoughton

Fisher, M., and J. Fisher. 1957. *Shackleton*. London: James Barrie Books

Fogg, G.E. 1992. *A History of Antarctic Science*. Cambridge: Cambridge University Press

Friederichs, H. 1911. *The Life of Sir George Newnes, Bart*. London: Hodder & Stoughton

Garvin, J.L. 1932. *Life of Joseph Chamberlain*. 3 vols. London: Macmillan

Gernshiem, H., and A. Gernsheim. 1965. *A Concise History of Photography*. London: Thames and Hudson

Gilbert, W.S. 1930. *The Savoy Operas. London: Macmillan & Co.*

Hall, C.F. 1864. *Life with the Esquimaux*. 2 vols. London: Sampson Low, Son & Marston

Headlam, C. (ed.). 1933. *The Milner Papers. Volume 2: South Africa 1899–1905*. London: Cassell & Company

Herbert, W. 1989. *The Noose of Laurels*. London: Hodder & Stoughton

Hobsbawn, E.J., and T.O. Ranger (eds). 1983. *The Invention of Tradition*. Cambridge: Cambridge University Press

Hume, J.R., and M. Moss. 1979. *Beardmore*. London: William Heinemann

Huntford, R. 1979. *Scott and Amundsen*. London: Hodder & Stoughton

Huntford, R. 1985. *Shackleton*. London: Hodder & Stoughton

Huntford, R. 1997. *Nansen: The Explorer as Hero*. London: Gerald Duckworth & Company

Hynes, S. 1968. *The Edwardian Turn of Mind*. London: Oxford University Press

Jacka, F., and E. Jacka (eds.). 1988. *Mawson's Antarctic Diaries*. London: Unwin Hyman

Jackson, F.G. 1899. *A Thousand Days in the Arctic*. 2 vols. London: Harper & Brothers

Jackson, F.G. 1935. *The Lure of Unknown Lands*. London: G. Bell & Sons

Jeffery, K. (ed.). 1996. *An Irish Empire? Aspects of Ireland and the British Empire*. Manchester: Manchester University Press

Joyce, E.M. 1929. *The South Polar Trail*. London: Duckworth & Company

Keeling, A.E. 1927. *General Gordon: Hero and Saint*. London: Epworth Press

Keltie, J.S., and H.R. Mill (ed.). 1896. *Report of the Sixth International Geographical Congress*. London: John Murray

Kochanski, H. 1999. *Sir Garnet Wolseley: Victorian Hero*. London: The Hambledon Press

Limb, S., and P. Cordingley. 1982. *Captain Oates: Soldier and Explorer*. London: William Batsford

Lockhart, J.G., and C.M. Woodhouse. 1963. *Rhodes*. London: Hodder & Stoughton

Lowry, D. (ed.). 2000. *The South African War Reappraised*. Manchester: Manchester University Press

Lucy, H. 1908. *Memories of Eight Parliaments, 1868–1906*. London: William Heinemann

MacDonald, R.H. 1994. *The Language of Empire: Myths and Metaphors of Popular Imperialism, 1880–1918*. Manchester: Manchester University Press

MacKenzie, J.M. 1984. *Propaganda and Empire: The Manipulation of British Public Opinion 1880–1960*. Manchester: Manchester University Press

MacKenzie, J.M. (ed.). 1986. *Imperialism and Popular Culture*. Manchester: Manchester University Press

MacKenzie, J.M. (ed.). 1992. *Popular Imperialism and the Military, 1850–1950*. Manchester: Manchester University Press

Mangan, J.A. 1990. *Making Imperial Mentalities: Socialisation and British Imperialism*. Manchester: Manchester University Press

Marischal, M. 1953. *Union-Castle Chronicle, 1853–1953*. London: Longmans, Green

Markham, A.H. 1917. *The Life of Sir Clements Markham*. London: John Murray

Markham, C.R. 1921. *The Lands of Silence: A History of Arctic and Antarctic Exploration*. Cambridge: Cambridge University Press

Markham, C.R. 1986. *Antarctic Obsession: The British National Antarctic Expedition 1901–4*, C. Holland (ed.) Alburgh, Norfolk: Bluntisham Books and the Erskine Press

Marlowe, J. 1976. *Milner: Apostle of Empire*. London: Hamish Hamilton

Maurice, F. 1928. *The Life of General Lord Rawlinson of Trent*. London: Cassell & Company

Maurice, F., and G. Arthur. 1924. *The life of Lord Wolseley*. London: William Heinemann

Mawson, D. 1915. *The Home of the Blizzard*. 2 vols. London: William Heinemann

McDonald, J.G. 1927. *Rhodes: A Life*. London: P. Allen & Company

McLean, W.W.L., and E.H. Shackleton. 1900. *O.H.M.S.: An Illustrated Record of the Voyage of S.S. 'Tintagel Castle'*. London: Simpkin, Marshall, Hamilton, Kent & Co

McLynn, F. 1989. *Stanley: The Making of an African Explorer*. London: Constable & Company

McLynn, F. 1990. *Stanley: Sorcerer's Apprentice*. London: Constable & Company

McNicoll, R. 1988. *Number 36 Collins Street: Melbourne Club 1838–1988.* Sydney: Allen & Unwin

Mill, H.R. 1923. *The Life of Sir Ernest Shackleton.* London: William Heinemann

Mill, H.R. 1951. *An Autobiography.* London: Longmans, Green & Company

Mills, L. 1999. *Frank Wild.* Whitby: Caedmon of Whitby

Monypenny, W.F., and G.E. Buckle. 1929. *The Life of Benjamin Disraeli: Earl of Beaconsfield.* Revised edition. 2 vols. London: John Murray

Moorehead, A. 1960. *The White Nile.* London: Hamish Hamilton

Morley, J. 1903. *The Life of William Ewart Gladstone.* 3 vols. London: Macmillan & Company

Morris, J. 1968. *Pax Britannica: The Climax of an Empire.* London: Faber & Faber

Morris, J. 1973. *Heaven's Command: An Imperial Progress.* London: Faber & Faber

Muffett, D.J.M. 1978. *Empire Builder Extraordinary, Sir George Goldie.* Douglas, Isle of Man: Shearwater Press

Murray, J., and G.E. Marston. 1913. *Antarctic Days.* London: Andrew Melrose

Nansen, F. 1890. *The First Crossing of Greenland.* 2 vols. London: Longmans, Green & Company

Nansen, F. 1897. *Farthest North.* 2 vols. London: Archibald Constable & Company

Newman, S. (ed.). 1990. *Shackleton's Lieutenant: The Nimrod Diary of A.L.A. Mackintosh, British Antarctic Expedition 1907–09.* Auckland: Polar Publications

Pakenham, T. 1979. *The Boer War.* London: George Weidenfeld & Nicolson

Parry, W.E. 1821. *Journal of a Voyage for the Discovery of a North–West Passage from the Atlantic to the Pacific.* London: John Murray

Pearsall, R. 1973. *Edwardian Life and Leisure.* Newton Abbott: David & Charles

Peary, R.E. 1910. *The North Pole: Its Discovery in 1909 Under the Auspices of the Peary Arctic Club.* New York: Frederick A. Stokes Company

Porter, A. (ed.). 1999. *The Oxford History of the British Empire. Volume III: The Nineteenth Century.* Oxford: Oxford University Press

Pound, R., and G. Harmsworth. 1959. *Northcliffe.* London: Cassell & Company

Quartermain, L.B. 1981. *Antarctica's Forgotten Men.* Wellington: Millwood Press

Read, D. 1972. *Edwardian England: Society and Politics.* London: Historical Association

Read, D. (ed.). 1982. *Edwardian England.* London and Canberra: Croom Helm

Richards, J. 1973. *Visions of Yesterday.* London: Routledge & Kegan Paul

Richards, J. 1989. *Imperialism and Juvenile Literature.* Manchester: Manchester University Press

Richards, R.W. 1962. *The Ross Sea Shore Party 1914–17.* Cambridge: Scott Polar Research Institute

Riffenburgh, B. 1993. *The Myth of the Explorer.* London: Belhaven Press

Roberts, A. 1999. *Salisbury: Victorian Titan.* London: Weidenfeld & Nicolson

Ross, J.C. 1847. *A Voyage of Discovery and Research in the Southern and Antarctic regions.* 2 vols. London: John Murray

Ross, J. 1835. *Narrative of a Second Voyage in Search of a North-West Passage.* London: A.W. Webster

Scott, R.F. 1905. *The Voyage of the 'Discovery'.* 2 vols. London: John Murray

Scott, R.F. 1913. *Scott's Last Expedition.* 2 vols. London: Smith, Elder & Company

Seaver, G. 1933. *Edward Wilson of the Antarctic: Naturalist and Friend.* London: John Murray

Shackleton, E.H. (ed.). 1908. *Aurora Australis.* Privately printed

Shackleton, E.H. 1909. *The Heart of the Antarctic*. 2 vols. London: William Heinemann

Shackleton, E.H. 1919. *South*. London: William Heinemann

Shackleton, J., and J. MacKenna. 2002. *Shackleton: An Irishman in Antarctica*. Dublin: The Lilliput Press

Stafford, R.A. 1989. *Scientist of Empire: Sir Roderick Murchison, Scientific Exploration and Victorian Imperialism*. Cambridge: Cambridge University Press

Stanley, H.M. 1890. *In Darkest Africa, or the Quest, Rescue, and Retreat of Emin, Goveror of Equatoria*. 2 vols. London: Sampson Low, Marston, Searle, & Rivington

Sutherland, P.D. (ed.). 1985. *The Franklin Era in Canadian Arabic History 1845–1859*. Ottawa: National Museum of Man (Mercury Series, Archaeological Survey of Canada 131)

Sverdrup, O. 1904. *New Land: Four Years in the Arctic Regions*. 2 vols. London: Longmans, Green & Company

Taylor, G. 1916. *With Scott: The Silver Lining*. London: Smith, Elder & Company

Tennyson, A. 1845. *Poems*. Third edition. London: Moxon

Tidrick, K. 1990. *Empire and the English Character*. London: Tauris

Troup, J.R. 1890. *With Stanley's Rearguard*. London: Chapman & Hall

Tuchman, B.W. 1966. *The Proud Tower*. London: Hamish Hamilton

Verne, J. 1876. *Twenty Thousand Leagues Under the Sea*. London: Sampson & Low

Waller, J.H. 1988. *Gordon of Khartoum*. New York: Atheneum

Wallis, J.P.R. (ed.). 1956. *The Zambesi Expedition of David Livingstone 1858–1863*. 2 vols. London: Chatto & Windus

Wild, F. 1923. *Shackleton's Last Voyage*. London: Cassell & Company

Wolseley, Lord. 1903. *The Story of a Soldier's Life*. 2 vols. London: Archibald Constable & Company

Yelverton, D.E. 2000. *Antarctica Unveiled: Scott's First Expedition and the Quest for the Unknown Continent*. Boulder, CO: University Press of Colorado

Articles and Monographs

'About Lieutenant Shackleton'. *Royal Magazine*, June 1909: 192

Anderson, O. 1971. 'The Growth of Christian Militarism in Mid-Victorian Britain'. *English Historical Review*, 86: 46–72

Benyon, J. 2000. '"Intermediate" Imperialism and the Test of Empire: Milner's "Eccentric" High Commission in South Africa'. In: Lowry, D. (ed.). *The South African War Reappraised*: 84–103

'By Car to the South Pole'. *The Car*, 23 October 1907 (no. 283): 393, 397–98

'By Motor Car to the South Pole'. *The Sphere*, 13 July 1907

Condon, R.G. 1989. 'The History and Development of Arctic Photography'. *Arctic Anthropology*, 26 (1): 46–87

Cooper, A.B. 1910. 'How I began'. *The Captain*, April 1910: 42–45

David, T.W.E. 1908. 'The Ascent of Mount Erebus'. In: Shackleton, E.H. (ed.). *Aurora Australis*

Davis, J.K. 1910. 'Voyage of the S.Y. "Nimrod"'. *Geographical Journal*, 36 (6): 696–703

Dunsmore, J. 1922. 'Shackleton of the SS "Flintshire"'. *The United Methodist*, 4 May 1922: 213

'England's Latest Hero'. *Pearson's Weekly*, 8 April 1909: 818

Fitzpatrick, D. 1999. 'Ireland and the Empire'. In: Porter, A. (ed.). *The Oxford History of the British Empire. Volume III: The Nineteenth Century*: 495–521

Harcourt, F. 1980. 'Disraeli's Imperialism: A Question of Timing, 1866–68'. *Historical Journal*, 23 (1): 87–109

Holst, A., and T. Frölich. 1907. 'Experimental Studies Relating to Ship-beri-beri and Scurvy. II. On the Etiology of Scurvy'. *Journal of Hygiene*, 7: 634–71

Hyam, R. 1999. 'The British Empire in the Edwardian Era'. In: Brown, J.M., and W.R. Louis (eds.). *The Oxford History of the British Empire. Volume IV: The Twentieth Century*: 47–63

Irízar, J. 1904. 'Rescue of the Swedish Antarctic Expedition'. *Geographical Journal*, 23: 580–96

Johnson, D.H. 1982. 'The Death of Gordon: A Victorian Myth'. *Journal of Imperial and Commonwealth History*, 10: 285–310

Kendall, E.J.C. 1955. 'Scurvy During Some British Polar Expeditions, 1875–1917'. *Polar Record*, 7 (51): 467–85

Koettlitz, R. 1902. 'The British Antarctic Expedition: Precautions Against Scurvy in the Victualling of the "Discovery"'. *The British Medical Journal* I: 342–43

Locke, S. 2000. *George Marston: Shackleton's Antarctic Artist*. Winchester: Hampshire County Council (Hampshire Papers 19)

Lüdecke, C. 2003. 'Scientific Collaboration in Antarctica (1901–04): A Challenge in Times of Political Rivalry'. *Polar Record*, 39 (208): 35–48

Lynn, M. 1999. 'British Policy, Trade, and Informal Empire in the Mid-nineteenth Century'. In: Porter, A. (ed.). *The Oxford History of the British Empire. Volume III: The Nineteenth Century*: 101–21

MacKenzie, J.M. 1992. 'Heroic Myths of Empire'. In: MacKenzie, J.M. (ed.). *Popular Imperialism and the Military, 1850–1950*: 109–38

MacKenzie, J.M. 1995. 'The Provincial Geographical Societies in Britain, 1884–1914'. In: Bell, M., R. Butlin, and M. Heffernan (eds.). 1995. *Geography and Imperialism 1820–1940*: 93–124

MacKenzie, J.M. 1999. 'Empire and Metropolitan Cultures'. In: Porter, A. (ed.). *The Oxford History of the British Empire. Volume III: The Nineteenth Century*: 270–93

Mackinnon, C.S. 1985. 'The British Man-hauled Sledging Tradition'. In: Sutherland, P.D. (ed.) *The Franklin Era in Canadian Arctic History 1845–1859*: 129–40

Mangan, J.A. 1986. '"The Grit of Our Forefathers": Invented Traditions, Propaganda and Imperialism'. In: MacKenzie, J.M. (ed.). 1986. *Imperialism and Popular Culture*: 113–39

Markham, C.R. 1899. 'The Antarctic Expeditions'. *Geographical Journal*, 14 (5): 473–81

Marony, P.W. 1909. 'Antarctic Photography'. *The Australian Photographic Journal*, 22 November 1909: 322–25

Marshall, E.S. 1943. 'An Antarctic Episode'. *The Medical Press and Circular*, 8 December 1943: 359–62

Mawson, D. 1919. 'Award of the Bigsby Medal'. *Quarterly Journal of the Geological Society of London*, 75: xlvii

Mill, H.R. 1902. 'The Voyage Southward of the "Discovery"'. *Geographical Journal*, 19 (4): 417–23

Mill, H.R. 1909. 'Ernest Henry Shackleton, MVO'. *Travel and Exploration*, 2 (7): 1–10

Mill, H.R. 1922. 'Sir Ernest Shackleton, CVO'. *Scottish Geographical Magazine*, 38 (2): 118–21

Morley, J. 1867. 'The Liberal Programme'. *The Fortnightly Review* (New Series), 1: 364

Murray, J. 1894. 'The Renewal of Antarctic Exploration'. *Geographical Journal*, 3: 1–42

Pearson, M. 1992. 'Expedition Huts in Antarctica: 1899–1917'. *Polar Record*, 28 (167): 261–76

Priestley, R.E. 1908. 'A messman'. In: Shackleton, E.H. (ed.). *Aurora Australis*

Priestley, R.E. 1962. 'Commander Sir Jameson Boyd Adams'. *Geographical Journal*, 128 (3): 367

Richards, J. 1992. 'Popular Imperialism and the Image of the Army in Juvenile Literature'. In: MacKenzie, J.M. (ed.). *Popular Imperialism and the Military, 1850–1950*: 80–108

Sarolea, C. 1922. 'Sir Ernest Shackleton: A Study in Personality'. *The Contemporary Review*, 121: 321–28

Shackleton, E.H. n.d. *Plan for an Antarctic Expedition.* Privately published. (SPRI MS 1456/13)

Shackleton, E.H. 1903. 'Adventurous Voyage of the "Discovery" and the Sledge Journey to the Furthest Point South Ever Reached by Man'. *The Illustrated London News*, June/July, supplement

Shackleton, E.H. 1904. 'Life in the Antarctic'. *Pearson's Magazine*, 17 (21): 306–22

Shackleton, E.H. 1907. 'A New British Antarctic Expedition'. *Geographical Journal*, 29: 329–32

Shackleton, E.H. 1907. 'The New British Antarctic Expedition'. *Geographical Journal*, 30: 336–37

Shackleton, E.H. 1907. 'The British Antarctic Expedition, 1907'. *Scottish Geographical Magazine*, 23 (7): 372–74

Shackleton, E.H. 1909. 'Nearest the South Pole'. *Pearson's Magazine*, 28: 235–52, 346–67, 518–35

Shackleton, E.H. 1909. 'Some Results of the British Antarctic Expedition, 1907–09'. *Geographical Journal*, 34: 481–500

Shackleton, E.H. 1914. 'The Making of an Explorer'. *Pearson's Magazine*, 38 (224): 138–42

Shackleton, E.H. 1922. 'Adventure! A Message to Boys'. *Boy's Own Paper*, 44 (8): 493–94

Smith, I.R. 2000. 'A Century of Controversy Over Origins'. In: Lowry, D. (ed.). *The South African War Reappraised*: 23–49

Springhall, J.O. 1986. '"Up Guards and At Them!": British Imperialism and Popular Art, 1880–1914'. In: MacKenzie, J.M. (ed.). 1986. *Imperialism and Popular Culture*: 49–72

Summerfield, P. 1986. 'Patriotism and Empire: Music-hall Entertainment, 1870–1914'. In: MacKenzie, J.M. (ed.). 1986. *Imperialism and Popular Culture*: 17–48

'The National Antarctic Expedition.' *Nature*, 64 (1651): 102–03

Wallace, W. 1976. 'James Murray, FRSE, 1865–1914: A Belated Biography'. *Year Book of the Royal Society of Edinburgh*: 15–20

Waterston, A.R. 1976. 'James Murray, 1865–1914: Pioneer Freshwater Biologist, Polar Scientist and Taxonomist'. *Year Book of the Royal Society of Edinburgh*: 21–25

Wilson, E.A. 1905. 'The Medical Aspects of the *Discovery*'s Voyage to the Antarctic'. *The British Medical Journal*, 8 July 1905: 77–80

Wilson, L.G. 1975. 'The Clinical Definition of Scurvy and the Discovery of Vitamin C'. *Journal of the History of Medicine and Allied Sciences*, 30 (1): 40–60

Wright, A.E. 1900. 'On the Pathology and Therapeutics of Scurvy'. *The Lancet*, ii: 565–67

Newspapers and Periodicals

The Argus (Melbourne)
Boy's Own Paper (London)
The Cape Argus (Cape Town)
The Cape Times (Cape Town)
The Captain (London)
Christchurch Press
The Courier and Argus (Dundee)
Daily Dispatch (London)
Daily Express (London)
The Daily Graphic (London)
Daily Mail (London)
Daily Mirror (London)
The Daily News (London)
The Daily Telegraph (London)
The Daily Telegraph (Sydney)
Dundee Advertiser
The Evening News (London)
The Evening Star (Dunedin)
The Illustrated London News
Lyttelton Times
The Manchester Guardian
The Morning Post (London)
Nature (London)
The New York Herald
The New York Times
The Observer (London)
The Otago Daily Times (Dunedin)
The Pall Mall Gazette (London)
Pearson's Magazine (London)
Pearson's Weekly (London)
The Rand Daily Mail (Johannesburg)
The Register (Adelaide)
Royal Magazine (London)
The St. James's Gazette (London)
The Scotsman (Edinburgh)
Sea Breezes
The Spectator (London)
The Sphere (London)
The Standard (London)

The Star (Johannesburg)
The Sun (New York)
The Sunday Times (London)
The Sydney Morning Herald
The Times (London)
Westminster Gazette (London)
The World (New York)

Unpublished sources

The following abbreviations have been used:
BAE   British Antarctic Expedition, 1907–09
BNAE   British National Antarctic Expedition, 1901–04
SPRI   Scott Polar Research Institute

Diaries and journals

Adams, J.B. Meteorological observations, BAE southern journey (SPRI)
Bernacchi, L.C. Journals of *Southern Cross* expedition (SPRI)
—— Journals of BNAE (SPRI)
Brocklehurst, P.L. Diary of BAE (Mr Neil Silverman)
Cheetham, A. Diary of BAE (SPRI)
Harbord, A.E. Diary of BAE (Mr Alister Harbord)
—— Navigation workbook, *Nimrod* (SPRI)
Log of *Nimrod* (SPRI)
Mackay, A.F. Diary of BAE northern journey (National Museums of Scotland, Edinburgh)
—— *Nimrod* diary (SPRI)
Mackintosh, Æ.L.A. Diary of BAE (Mrs G.E. Dowler)
Marshall, E.S. Diary of BAE (SPRI; Royal Geographical Society)
Mawson, D. Diary of BAE (The Mawson Collection, South Australian Museum, Adelaide)
—— Abbreviated Log: Australasian Antarctic Expedition (The Mawson Collection, South Australian Museum, Adelaide)
Priestley, R.E. Diaries of BAE (SPRI)
Rawlinson, H. Diary 1899–1900 (National Army Museum, London; Sir Anthony Rawlinson)
Riches, S. Diary of BAE (SPRI)
Royds, C.W. Diary of BNAE (Sir Richard Eyre)
Rutherford, J.G. Diary of voyage of *Koonya* (Canterbury Museum, Christchurch)
Scott, R.F. Diaries of BNAE (SPRI)
Shackleton, E.H. Diary aboard *Discovery* (Mitchell Library, State Library of New South Wales, Sydney)
—— Diary of BNAE (SPRI)
—— Diary of BNAE southern journey (SPRI)
—— Diary of BAE (SPRI)
—— Diary of BAE southern journey (SPRI)
Skelton, R.W. Journals of BNAE (SPRI)

Wild, F. Diary of BAE southern journey (SPRI)
Wilson, E.A. Journal of BNAE (SPRI)
―――― Journal of BNAE southern journey (SPRI)

Correspondence and other manuscript sources

Adams, J.B. Correspondence (SPRI)
Armitage, A.B. Correspondence and papers (SPRI)
Beardmore, W. Correspondence (SPRI)
Beaumont, L.A. Correspondence (SPRI)
Bernacchi, L.C. Correspondence and papers (SPRI)
Brocklehurst, P.L. Correspondence and papers (Johnny Van Haeften, London)
Bruce, W.S. Correspondence (SPRI)
Darwin, L. Correspondence (SPRI)
David, T.W.E. Correspondence and papers (SPRI)
Dell, J.W. Correspondence (SPRI)
Dunlop, H.J.L. Correspondence (SPRI)
England, R. Correspondence (SPRI)
Evans, F.P. Narrative of BAE (SPRI)
Fisher, M., and J. Correspondence and papers (SPRI)
Goldie, G. Correspondence (SPRI)
Gregory, J.W. Correspondence and papers (SPRI)
Hare, C.H. Correspondence (SPRI)
Jackson, F.G. Correspondence and papers (SPRI)
Joyce, E.E.M. Correspondence (SPRI)
Keltie, J.S. Correspondence (SPRI)
Koettlitz, R. Correspondence and papers (SPRI)
Mackellar, C.D. Correspondence (SPRI)
Markham, C.R. Correspondence and papers (SPRI)
Marshall, E.S. Correspondence and papers (SPRI)
Marston, G. Correspondence and papers (SPRI; Hampshire Record Office, Winchester)
Mawson, D. Correspondence and papers (SPRI; The Mawson Collection, South
    Australian Museum, Adelaide)
Mill, H.R. Correspondence and papers (SPRI)
Murray, J. Correspondence (SPRI)
Petrides, N. Correspondence (SPRI)
Priestley, R.E. Correspondence and papers (SPRI)
Rawlinson, H. Correspondence (National Army Museum, London; Sir Anthony
    Rawlinson)
Rutherford, J.G. Papers (Canterbury Museum, Christchurch)
Saunders, E.C. Correspondence (SPRI)
Scott, R.F. Correspondence and papers (SPRI)
Shackleton, Aimée. Correspondence (SPRI)
Shackleton, Eleanor. Correspondence (SPRI)
Shackleton, Emily. Correspondence (SPRI)
Shackleton, Ernest Henry. Correspondence and papers (SPRI)
―――― Correspondence (National Maritime Museum Greenwich; Johnny Van Haef-
ten, Private Collection, London)

Shackleton, G. Alice. Correspondence (SPRI)

Shackleton, Kathleen. Correspondence (SPRI)

Skelton, R.W. Correspondence and papers (SPRI)

Thomson, K.G. Correspondence (SPRI)

Tripp, L.H. Correspondence (SPRI)

Wild, F. Correspondence and papers (SPRI)

—— Memoirs (Mrs Anne Fright; Mitchell Library, State Library of New South Wales, Sydney)

Wilson, E.A. Correspondence, papers and artwork (SPRI)

INDEX

A NOTE ON THE AUTHOR

Beau Riffenburgh is a historian specialising in exploration, particularly that of the Antarctic, Arctic, and Africa. Born in California, he earned his doctorate at the Scott Polar Research Institute, University of Cambridge, where he is currently the editor of *Polar Record*, the world's oldest journal of polar research. He is the author of the highly regarded *The Myth of the Explorer* and editor of the *Encyclopedia of the Antarctic*, intended to be the most comprehensive work of reference ever published about the Antarctic. He is currently working on a book about Douglas Mawson's Australasian Antarctic Expedition.

A NOTE ON THE TYPE

The text of this book is set in Linotype Sabon,
named after the type founder, Jacques Sabon. It was
designed by Jan Tschichold and jointly developed by
Linotype, Monotype and Stempel, in response to
a need for a typeface to be available in identical
form for mechanical hot metal composition and
hand composition using foundry type.

Tschichold based his design for Sabon roman on a
font engraved by Garamond, and Sabon italic on
a font by Granjon. It was first used in 1966 and
has proved an enduring modern classic.